The Future of Outer Space Law

This book identifies and discusses problems and opportunities for the future theory and practice of outer space law.

The corpus of outer space law, including the Outer Space Treaty 1967, has faced multiple challenges and critiques. In recent times, these have included advances in technology, the militarisation of outer space, space debris, and geopolitics. The prominent and emerging contributors to this collection draw on diverse research frameworks to discuss proposals for the future of outer space law and policy. These include addressing regulatory gaps and under-examined and emerging areas of the law, but also beyond, the Outer Space Treaty—especially related to potential extraterrestrial settlements, satellites technology, self-defence, self-determination, and the environment. The book discusses the tensions between universalism and localisation, as well as the regionalisation of outer space law and policy—and how these approaches might adapt to create a dynamic space industry for the future.

This book is both practical and theoretical in scope and will be of interest to academics, researchers, and students. It will also be of interest to international organisations, diplomats, and other government officials and policymakers.

Anna Marie Brennan is Senior Lecturer in the School of Law, Politics, and Philosophy at the University of Waikato, New Zealand. Her teaching and research interests address international criminal law, human rights law, international humanitarian law, and outer space law. She was previously a lecturer in law at the University of Liverpool in United Kingdom and at University College Cork in Ireland. In 2023, she was the Acting Dean of Te Piringa Faculty of Law and is currently the New Zealand Chair of the AI and Space Law Society.

Routledge Research in Air and Space Law

International Aviation Labour Law
Andrea Trimarchi

The Law and Regulation of Airspace Liberalisation in Brazil
What is the Way Forward?
Delphine Defossez

Aviation Law and Governance
Navigating Global Challenges and Conflicts
Jędrzej Górski and Yun Zhao

Safety Regulation in International Aviation Law
Normative Aspects of Safety
Grzegorz K. Zając

The Future of Outer Space Law
Edited by Anna Marie Brennan

For more information about this series, please visit: www.routledge.com/Routledge-Research-in-Air-and-Space-Law/book-series/SPACELAW

The Future of Outer Space Law

Edited by Anna Marie Brennan

Routledge
Taylor & Francis Group
LONDON AND NEW YORK

First published 2025
by Routledge
4 Park Square, Milton Park, Abingdon, Oxon OX14 4RN

and by Routledge
605 Third Avenue, New York, NY 10158

Routledge is an imprint of the Taylor & Francis Group, an informa business

British Library Cataloguing-in-Publication Data
A catalogue record for this book is available from the British Library

ISBN: 978-1-032-44108-5 (hbk)
ISBN: 978-1-032-44109-2 (pbk)
ISBN: 978-1-003-37049-9 (ebk)

DOI: 10.4324/9781003370499

Typeset in Times New Roman
by Apex CoVantage, LLC

Contents

Contributors

Lachlan Blake holds an LLB (Hons) and BA from the University of Adelaide. He was an associate in the Federal Court of Australia and currently practices as a lawyer in Sydney. He was a student editor of the *Adelaide Law Review* and has authored publications focusing on international public law, specifically regarding the development of norms surrounding deconfliction in outer space. He has also been a volunteer researcher for the Prisoners Legal Service of Queensland and a volunteer lawyer for the Refugee Legal Service in Victoria.

P.J. Blount is an assistant professor at Durham University. Previously, he was a lecturer in the School of Law and Politics at Cardiff University, an adjunct professor at the University of Mississippi School of Law, a postdoctoral researcher at the University of Luxembourg, and an adjunct professor at Montclair State University. He is an editor of the Proceedings of the International Institute of Space Law where he also serves as Executive Secretary and was formerly the Editor-in-Chief of the *Journal of Space Law*. He is a licensed attorney with the State Bar of Georgia (USA).

Ioana Bratu is an assistant professor in Space Law at Vrije Universiteit Amsterdam. She is the Co-Director of Amsterdam Law & Technology Institute, the Founder of AI ∞ Space Law Society and an affiliate of Université Paris Cité. Ioana's PhD examining non-contractual liabilities for damage caused by GNSS-enabled artificial intelligence represents the first research addressing the emerging intersection between the laws governing human activities in outer space and the opportunities and challenges posed by the adoption of artificial intelligence.

Anna Marie Brennan is currently the Borrin Foundation's Women Leaders in Law Fellow and a senior lecturer in law in the School of Law, Politics, and Philosophy at the University of Waikato in New Zealand where she served as Acting Dean in 2023. Prior to joining the University of Waikato, she held lectureships at University College Cork and the University of Liverpool. She holds a PhD from University College Cork which was externally funded by an Irish

Research Council Postgraduate Fellowship. Her book, *Transnational Terrorist Groups and International Criminal Law*, was published by Routledge in 2018.

Jennifer Brobst is an associate professor at Cecil C. Humphreys School of Law at the University of Memphis. Her practice experience has been solely devoted to the public interest as a deputy prosecuting attorney, a domestic violence clinic attorney, and a legal director at a large medical-mental health consortium in the United States. Her education includes a BA (with honors in archaeology and social anthropology) from University of Cape Town, a JD from the University of San Diego School of Law; and LLM from Victoria University at Wellington.

Melissa de Zwart is the Deputy Director and a chief investigator of the ARC Centre of Excellence in Plants 4 Space and Professor of Space Law and Governance at the University of Adelaide. She has worked closely with the Australian space industry, including serving as Deputy Director and Board Member of the Space Industry Association of Australia, as well as on the successful bid team for the 2025 International Astronautical Congress. Melissa was Dean of Law from 2017 to 2021. She holds a PhD from Monash University, as well as LLM, LLB (Hons), and BA (Hons) degrees from the University of Melbourne.

Danny Johansen recently completed his PhD at the Legal Institute of the University of Southern Denmark (SDU). During his PhD, he was part of the research group for international law and examines the issues of international law in the increasing privatisation of outer space.

William P. Schonberg is a professor of engineering at the Missouri University of Science and Technology. His research has been applied to a variety of engineering problems, including the development of orbital debris protection systems for spacecraft in low-Earth orbit and *in situ* resource utilization for lunar habitats. Schonberg has served on several national technical committees including NASA and the US Air Force. In 2019, he was awarded a Fulbright Distinguished Chair to visit the Defense Science and Technology Group in Melbourne and, in 2023, he visited the University of Aruba as a Fulbright Specialist.

Matthew Stubbs is a professor of law at the University of Adelaide, where he serves as Associate Dean (Research) of Adelaide Law School and Editor in Chief of the *Adelaide Law Review*. He has been awarded three national prizes for his teaching. He was inaugural Chair of the Space Law Committee of the Law Society of South Australia (of which he remains a member) and is also a member of the Law Council of Australia's National Human Rights Committee. Matthew was a core expert on the Woomera Manual on the International Law of Military Space Activities and Operations.

Fabio Tronchetti is an associate professor at Northumbria University. He was previously the Co-Director of the Institute of Space Law and Strategy and an associate professor at Beihang University. Currently, he holds the position of Adjunct Professor of Comparative National Space Law at the University of Mississippi. Fabio is the recipient of the 2019 International Institute of Space Law Young Achiever Award, the co-recipient of the 2015 International Academy of Astronautics Social Science Award for the book *Handbook on Space Law* (co-authored with Prof. von der Dunk), and Director of the International Institute of Space Law.

Acknowledgments

So many individuals have played a crucial role in helping this book to fruition and I am truly grateful to them all. I am immensely grateful for the scholars from which the contributors to this book have drawn their inspiration. Outer space law is a fantastic troupe of emerging intellect, innovative brainpower, strength, spirit, and determination.

I am very thankful to the people who have given me the space, time, and support to prepare and edit this book, especially my family and friends. And while appreciating the relative freedom of an extended period of research leave, I also wish to acknowledge the struggles and challenges. Like many women researchers, carving out research time continues to be difficult. This book was completed amid pregnancy during the Covid-19 pandemic, a stint in the neo-natal intensive care unit at Waikato Hospital, night feeds, daycare drop-offs and pick-ups, building a new home, half-hearted house cleaning and laundry, faculty meetings, teaching, and a busy nine-month stint as an acting dean. My partner, Fritz, reluctantly read drafts of my chapters before being sent for peer review and became more and more intrigued by the ambiguities and lacunae that persist within the realm of outer space law, which spurred me on.

I wish to acknowledge and thank a fantastic network of support at the University of Waikato without which this book would not have been possible, especially Nicola Win, Penny Xie, Simon Lovett, Nicola Starkey, Alpana Roy, Alison Kirkman, Suliana Mone, Leo Liao, Bryony James, Tracy Bowells, and Trevor Daya-Winterbottom. Many thanks to P.J. Blount, Fabio Tronchetti, Jennifer Brobst, Melissa de Zwart, Danny Johansen, William P. Schonberg, Lachlan Blake, Matthew Stubbs, and Ioana Bratu for contributing insightful chapters to this volume. Despite their great collaborative effort, all errors and omissions are, of course, my sole responsibility. I extend my deep thanks to the staff at the Peace Palace Law Library and our reviewers for their insightful comments on the contributor's draft chapters. Thank you to the editorial team at Routledge and to our supportive series editors. I wish to thank the participants and attendees of the Virtual Outer Space Law Conference 2021—a one-day event presented by Te Piringa Faculty of Law. The focus of the wider conference held on 3 September 2021 at the University of Waikato was the exploration and debate of the future of outer space law and its contemporary challenges.

The conference included two keynote speeches by University of Nebraska-Lincoln's Professor Frans von der Dunk and Western Sydney University's Professor Steven Freeland and sessions on the promise, politics, and future of the international law on outer space, as well as future challenges to regulatory gaps and challenges of future technology developments and futures for extraterrestrial settlement beyond Earth. I wish to thank our other speakers, Dr Cassandra Steer, Dr Maria Pozzi, Josselin Lavigne, and Dr Solène Guggisberg. During the time between the conference and finishing this book I was fortunate to liaise with Dr Duncan Blake and Dr Stacey Henderson who broadened my perspective and approach to outer space law. I really appreciate their advice, support, and mentorship.

This book, whose creation predates him, is for my son Zach with gratitude for always making me laugh and keeping me on my toes, and in the hope that his generation might be more captivated by outer space exploration than our generation.

1 Introduction

The Future of Outer Space Law

Anna Marie Brennan

1 Introduction

Debate surrounding the starting point for outer space law continues unabated. Some argue that it is 1903 with the publication of Konstantin Tsiolkovsky's paper foreseeing the expansion of human civilisation into outer space with liquid fuel rockets.[1] Others believe that it is 1910 when Belgian scholar, Emile Laude contended, '[u]n droit nouveau régira les relations juridiques nouvelles. Ce ne sera plus du droit aérien. . . . Mais à coup sûr il s'agira du Droit de l'Espace.'[2] Yet, it was not until 1932 that the first definitive study of space law was published by Vladimir Mandl.[3] Noting that humankind's exploration of outer space would raise a myriad of legal issues, Mandl asserted there would eventually be a need for a new body of law to regulate the area.[4] The United Nations Ad Hoc Committee on the Peaceful Uses of Outer Space raised similar concerns following its creation in 1959 that 'serious problems could arise if States claimed, on one ground or another, exclusive rights over all or part of a celestial body' and urged that 'some form of international administration over celestial bodies might be adopted.'[5] With the establishment of the UN Committee on the Peaceful Uses of Outer Space (UNCOPUOS) in 1960, unease about the need for legal principles governing the exploration and use of outer space increased.[6] The eventual adoption of the Outer Space Treaty in 1967 hastened the rapid development of outer space law as an area of study and practice

1 Boris Rauschenbach, *Thirty Years of the Space Age*, unpublished paper presented at the International Astronautical Federation Annual Congress (Brighton 1987). See also Stephen Doyle, *Origins of International Space Law and the International Institute for Space Law of the International Astronautical Federation* (Univelt 2002) 1–20.

2 Emile Laude, 'Comment s'Appellera le Droit qui Régira la Vie de l'Air' (2010) 1910 Revue Juridique de la Locomotion Aérienne 16.

3 Vladimir Kopal, 'Origins of Space Law and the Role of the United Nations' in Christian Brunner and Alexander Soucek (eds), *Outer Space in Society, Politics and Law* (Springer 2011) 221–33, 221.

4 Vladimir Mandl, *Das Weltraum-Recht: Ein Problem der Raumfahrt* (Bensheimer 1932) 48.

5 Report of the UN Ad Hoc Committee on the Peace Uses of Outer Space, UN. Doc. A 4141/25 (1959). See also Paul Dembling and Daniel Arons, 'The Evolution of the Outer Space Treaty' (1967) 33 Journal of Air Law and Commerce 419.

6 Nandasiri Jasentuliyana (ed), *Space Law: Development and Scope* (Bloomsbury Publishing 1992) 18–19.

DOI: 10.4324/9781003370499-1

that addresses the question of how 'outer space and activities in or with respect to that realm' are regulated.[7] Despite being studied for well over 80 years outer space law still occupies a niche place within the broader field of public international law and is certainly not at its apex.

In recent years, UNCOPUOS and its associated 'outer space law' project have garnered criticism and critique leading to a hastening identification and diagnoses of its missed opportunities, anxieties, and inequities. Some scholars point out that the initial development of outer space law missed or concealed post-colonial, gendered, economic, environmental, and political challenges as well as completely side-stepped the dilemma of non-state actors.[8] Given the lack of momentum to update the corpus of outer space law, perhaps it may seem that (alongside the privatisation of the space industry and a lack of an international enforcement mechanism) the project is all but over, even though, as an intellectual project outer space law, is quickly gaining momentum. Arguably, there is no clear point in time from which to distinguish a period of future challenges and opportunities from past challenges and opportunities with regards outer space law. Our views and perceptions of past development and how it relates to the present day shape our projections for the future of outer space law, even if they are fundamentally different.

This introductory chapter seeks to examine the issues of temporality, newness, and future in relation to outer space law. It considers what the 'future' of outer space law might mean and what approaches could be utilised towards considering its future. It contends that just as it is possible that outer space law has several definitions and starting points, there will also be potentially several futures for outer space law. These include its mechanism, subject matter, enforcement, crises, and opportunities. Those futures are relational as the perceptions, purpose, and operation of outer space law are shaped by international organisations, states, and non-state actors such as corporations and civil society. The contributors to this book present various visions and analyses of outer space law and its future. They examine how the historical development of outer space law reverberates now and in the time ahead in ways that may not be foreseeable nor fixed, linear or singular. Many challenges within outer space law have existed since its inception but as space technology rapidly develops there are new legal challenges for which the answers are unclear, or they give rise to questions for which outer space law has no significant jurisprudence.

Moreover, any consideration of challenges that may be of future concern are perhaps contingent on the perspective and the degree of abstraction. Outside the

7 Frans von der Dunk, 'International Space Law' in Frans von der Dunk with Fabio Tronchetti (eds), *Handbook of Space Law* (Edward Elgar Publishing 2017) 29, 29. See also Peter Malanczuk, 'Space Law as a Branch of International Law' (1994) 25 Netherlands Yearbook of International Law 143; Bin Cheng, *Studies in International Space Law* (Clarendon Press 1997) 70–87; Clarence Jenks, 'International Law and activities in Space' (1956) 5 International and Comparative Law Quarterly 99.

8 Sandeepa Bhat B, 'An Introduction to International Space Law' in Sandeepa Bhat B, Dilip Ukey and Adithya Variath (eds), *International Space Law in the New Space Era: Principles and Challenges* (OUP 2024) 1.

parameters of outer space law, is artificial intelligence such an innovation that law will long struggle with it? Was the exercise of the right to return during the Covid-19 pandemic really such a new challenge or simply a facet of a long-standing human rights and immigration law dilemma? Can UNCOPUOS be described as consummate and effective, and what will its implications be for outer space law in 10, 20, 50, or 100 years from now? A variety of methodological approaches might assist to answer these questions, but perhaps there is a danger that any new outer space law institutions in the future might become welded to existing formal and informal rules.[9] Undoubtedly, our understanding and preferred approach to certain issues will 'depend on the observer's changing and subjective context, which, in turn may be shaped by dynamic, social, political, cultural structures.'[10]

This book seeks to examine the future of outer space law not because the issues have never arisen before for critical examination but because the authors, reflecting upon their diverse backgrounds and contexts, believe that they are issues that will potentially emerge but remain relatively overlooked. Therefore, this book endeavours to incorporate interdisciplinary approaches and perspectives to outer space law—including through engagement with human rights, engineering, international relations, politics, colonialism studies, and sustainable development as well as other concepts and approaches. While outer space law is ripe for reform and development, contributors were advised not to adopt a critical, problem-solving, or reformist approach but to instead address their respective topics in an inquiring manner by utilising their preferred methodologies and frameworks. Accordingly, the list of topics addressed in this book is not comprehensive, but all are nevertheless novel and make proposals about the future of outer space law.

2 The Outer Space Realm: Norms and Governance

Martha Finnemore and Kathyrn Sikkink describe norms as standards 'of appropriate behaviour for actors with a given identity.'[11] With respect to the realm of outer space the contributors to this book regard norms as dynamic, evolving, and influenced by state and non-state actors as well as international institutions. Norms are intrinsically social and value-laden rules that are indicative of conduct that state and non-state actors 'ought' to obey.[12] Thus, compliance with norms is greatly influenced by the 'social and political expectations that they set, internationalization of

9 Fiona Mackay, 'Nested Newness, Institutional Innovation and the Gendered Limits of Change' (2014) 10 Politics and Gender 549.

10 Emma Palmer and Susan Harris Rimmer, 'Introduction: The Futures of International Criminal Justice' in Emma Palmer and others (eds), *Futures of International Criminal Justice* (Routledge 2022) 1, 4.

11 Martha Finnemore and Kathryn Sikkink, 'International Norm Dynamics and Political Change' (1998) 52 International Organization 887, 891. See also Joseph Raz, 'Legal Principles and the Limits of Law' (1972) 81 Yale Law Journal 823 and Hans Kelsen, *The Pure Theory of Law* (Lawbook Exchange 1934).

12 Jessica West and Almudena Ortega, *Norms for Outer Space: A Small Step or a Giant Leap for Policymaking?* (UN Institute for Disarmament Research 2022) 15.

the rules and values, a sense of social or moral duty, [and] fear of condemnation.'[13] While norms are often depicted as 'not really law' they have been adapted by various state, government, military, legal, and civil society actors as well as space commercial enterprises.[14] For example, the Outer Space Treaty 1967 codified universal norms with regards the free use and exploration of outer space. Thus, norms that are viewed as non-legally binding can often constitute the forerunners to both customary law and treaty law.[15] Norms constitute an 'expression of values, principles, and practices, law is often the basis for norms.'[16] In outer space, the legal principle that the 'exploration and use of outer space, including the Moon and other celestial bodies, shall be carried out for the benefit and in the interests of all countries . . . and shall be for the province of all [hu]mankind' inform remote sensing practices in disaster management. As West and Ortega posit, 'norms often inform and reflect how law is interpreted and applied in practice and can help to resolve conflicting legal rules.'[17]

We see open and equitable access as well as its peaceful use and exploration as outer space law's primary norms. However, these norms have not given rise to institutional forms of enforcement such as a dedicated international space court or tribunal even as a 'last resort.' This lack of development in outer space law arguably has consequences—such as the potential flouting of the rule of law and limitations on who can access and explore outer space. As discussed in the first section of this introduction, outer space law has gradually evolved from aviation law and post–World War II events, which propound some precedence towards the current institutional framework offered by organisations such as UNCOPUOS and others such as the International Telecommunication Union and the World Trade Organisation, in which the norm's peaceful use and exploration cascade outer space initiatives domestically. Not only that, but there is a need for a specific court at the international level to implement these norms to promote the progressive aims of outer space use and exploration.

The myriad troubles facing outer space law, especially the quandary of enforcement in relation to space debris and human rights, can be easily viewed as potential crises. While these crises are predictable and disappointing they are at least worthy of ongoing scholarly evaluation. Outer space law had a promising beginning, but its development has arguably stalled, and it now lags considerably behind rapid developments in business, science, and technology. Moreover, researchers have started to highlight the silenced, hidden, and largely excluded actors from outer space use and exploration, especially women, indigenous peoples, persons with disabilities, the LGBTQIA+ community, and citizens/residents of developing nations. Indeed,

13 West and Ortega (n 12) 15. See also Richard McAdams, 'The Origin, Development and Regulation of Norms' (1997) 96 Michigan Law Review 338, 340.

14 Michael Bothe, 'Legal and Non-Legal Norms—A Meaningful Distinction in International Relations' (2009) 11 Netherlands Yearbook of International Law 65.

15 West and Ortega (n 12) 15.

16 West and Ortega (n 12) 15.

17 West and Ortega (n 12) 15.

perhaps outer space law can be described as harmful to those whose right to the use and exploration of outer space it is most overtly tasked with safeguarding. In view of the state-centric nature of outer space law from its inception perhaps it was a given that this would ultimately transpire. The future of outer space law, however we choose to define it, seems to be unpredictable but also fragmented. Our conceptions about the discipline are also complicated by history, time, and the future.

This section considers how outer space norms and their institutionalisation indicate that outer space law has multiple possible trajectories. There is a clear normative facet to outer space law. Martti Koskenniemi has contended:

> the field in which we have made our professional careers is more than just another technical discipline. It possesses an inbuilt moral direction to make human rights, justice and peace universal. To 'do' international law is to operate with the teleology that points from humankind's separation to unity.[18]

Comparably, and directed towards outer space law, P.J. Blount in this volume aptly notes:

> [t]hrough the recognition of narrative structures in the context of the interpretation of international law we gain a finer-grain understanding of how states create normative content and then impart that content into the legal framework that contains them. These structures are intentionally constructed by states to serve their ends, but there seems to be clear intent to change the discourse and rhetoric around certain issues to support normative interpretation and change.[19]

Norms arguably propel behaviour, and despite several scholars claiming that outer space is a 'Wild West' the main outer space treaties and conventions adopted throughout the 1960s, 1970s, and 1980s have codified several norms that are still relevant to today's space sector, including those contained in a number of UN General Assembly resolutions relating to the free use and exploration of outer space for the benefit of all humankind.[20] As West and Ortega posit, it is 'not uncommon that norms eventually become binding laws through codification in legal agreements.'[21] Norms in the outer space realm can also gain customary status slowly over time if states conduct

18 Martti Koskenniemi, 'Law, Teleology and International Relations: An Essay in Counter-Disciplinarity' (2012) 26 International Relations 3, 4.

19 P.J. Blount (Chapter 3 at page 58).

20 For example, see Anja Pečujlić, *The Space Law Stalemate: Legal Mechanisms for Developing New Norms* (Routledge 2023). UN General Assembly Resolution 1962(XVIII) 18th Session, Declaration of Legal Principles Governing the Activities of States in the Exploration and Use of Outer Space (13 December 1963); UN General Assembly Resolution 1884 (XVIII), 18th Session (Question of General and Complete Disarmament (17 October 1963).

21 West and Ortega (n 12) 15.

themselves in a particular way because they believe the law requires them to do so.[22] For example, on 3 December 1986 the UN General Assembly adopted Resolution 41/65, Principles Relating to Remote Sensing of the Earth From Outer Space (UN Remote Sensing Principles). According to Ram Jakhu, Ray Harris, and Joanne Gabrynowicz the principles have gained customary law status since they amount to 'evidence of a general principle accepted as law' pursuant to Article 38(1)(b) of the Statute of the International Court of Justice.[23] On the other hand, as will be explored in Chapter 9, the issue of space debris is garnering increasing concern and this in turn has led to a process of normative creation with the adoption of the UN Space Debris Mitigation Guidelines by UNCOPUOS in 2007, which are largely based on the space debris mitigation guidelines adopted by the Inter-Agency Space Debris Coordination Committee (IADC) in 2002. Despite many spacefaring states now requiring launch operators to have orbital debris mitigation and prevention plans in place before launch licences can be secured, scholars continue to question whether the mitigation and prevention of space debris falls within the remit of customary international law.[24]

Thus, the development of norms in the outer space realm are clearly uneven and fragmented. While they have a crucial role to play in achieving safe and sustainable outer space exploration, the potential for the law to achieve this objective continues to remain elusive. On 7 December 2020, the UN General Assembly adopted Resolution 75/36 on 'Reducing Space Threats Through Norms, Rules and Principles of Responsible Behaviours' with a vote of 150 in favour, with eight against and seven abstentions.[25] The resolution introduced by the United Kingdom reaffirmed 'the applicability of international law, including the Charter of the United Nations, two activities in outer space.'[26] The resolution did not include a definition of the terms 'threat' or 'weapon' but it called upon the UN Secretary General 'to seek the views

22 Almudena Ortega and Hellmut Lagos Koller, 'The Open-Ended Working Group on Reducing Threats Through Norms, Rules and Principles of Responsible Behaviours: The Journey So Far, and the Road Ahead' (2023) 48 (Special Issue) Air and Space Law 19–40.

23 *Statute of the International Court of Justice*, 18th April 1946 (33 UNTS 993, UKTS 67 (1946) Cmd 7015, 3 Bevans 1179, 59 Stat 1055, 145 BSP 832, TS No 993), Article 38. Ram Jakhu, 'International Law Governing the Acquisition and dissemination of Satellite Imagery' in Robert Huebert (ed), *Commercial Satellite Imagery and United Nations Peacekeeping: A View from above* (Routledge 2004) 259 *et seq*; Ray Harris, 'Current Policy Issues in Remote Sensing: Report by the International Policy Advisory Committee of ISPRS' (2003) 19 Space Policy 293–96; Joanne Gabrynowicz, 'The Promise and Problems of the Land Remote Sensing Policy Act of 1992' (1993) 9 Space Policy 319–28.

24 For example, Poonugani believes that the prevention of space debris has gained customary status while Marc Carns does not. For further academic commentary please see Sraavya Poonugani, 'It's Raining Rockets: Heightening State Liability for Space Pollution' (2023) 23(2) Chicago Journal of International Law 490, 512; Marc Carns, *Orbital Debris Prevention and Mitigation Efforts among Major Space Actor* (Brill Nijhoff 2023) 297.

25 UN General Assembly Resolution 76/231, 76th Session on Reducing Space Threats Through Norms, Rules and Principles of Responsible Behaviours (24 December 2021) <https://undocs.org/A/RES/76/231> accessed 1 November 2024. For further information about the vote please see <https://www.un.org/en/ga/76/resolu tions.shtml> accessed 1 November 2024.

26 UN General Assembly Resolution 76/231 (n 25) para. 2.

of Member States' on 'existing and potential threats and security risks to space systems, including those arising from actions, activities or systems and outer space or on earth.'[27] Arguably, the resolution was a springboard for the development of norms on sustainable and secure outer space activities since it encouraged states to reach 'a common understanding of how best act to reduce threats to space systems in order to maintain outer space as a peaceful, safe, stable and sustainable environment' as a building block towards 'further development and implementation of norms, rules and principles of responsible behaviours and on the production of the risks of misunderstanding and miscalculations with respect to outer space.'[28]

Thirty states as well as the European Union, the International Committee of the Red Cross, the United Nations Institute for Disarmament Research, the Observer Research Foundation, and the Rand Corporation submitted replies to the UN Secretary General.[29] A rudimentary analysis of state responses indicates that they all had similar concerns. For example, New Zealand noted, a 'transparent, representative, and multilateral approach is critical to addressing issues of responsible behaviour in outer space.'[30] With regards a collective agreement on such norms and standards of conduct, New Zealand maintained, 'states must be able to identify and agree responsible and irresponsible behaviours in outer space . . . [and] considers it important that these discussions be conducted transparently and inclusively with all relevant stakeholders.'[31] Similarly, Luxembourg submitted, '[w]hile all space actors are claiming to behave responsibly in their operations, we see that transparency is lacking.'[32] Recognising the importance of non-binding norms to constructing a common space governance system, it was suggested that

> a legally binding instrument appears, at this stage, difficult given national positions in general mistrust, a common framework defining legally binding rules to govern a set of critical risky behaviours, respected by and apply to all actors and space, and should remain the ambition for the future and remain our desired end state.[33]

Following the conclusion of this consultation process stemming from UN General Assembly 76/231 an open-ended working group (OEWG) was established 'to make

27 UN General Assembly Resolution 76/231 (n 25) para. 1.

28 UN General Assembly Resolution 76/231 (n 25) page 3.

29 For further information please see <https://disarmament.unoda.org/topics/outerspace-sg-report-outer-space-2021/> accessed 1 November 2024.

30 New Zealand Ministry of Foreign Affairs and Trade, 'Norms, Rules and Principles of Responsible Behaviour in Space' para. 8 <https://front.un-arm.org/wp-content/uploads/2021/05/Space-responsible-behaviours-submission-to-UN-New-Zealand.pdf> accessed 1 November 2024.

31 Resolution 75/36 Reducing Space Threats Through Norms, Rules and Principles of Responsible Behaviours: Contribution of the Grand Duchy of Luxembourg to the UN Secretary General, 4 <https://front.un-arm.org/wp-content/uploads/2021/05/210430-Luxembourg-contibution-to-the-UN-SG-Res75-36-Reducing-space-threats.pdf> accessed 1 November 2024.

32 Contribution of the Grand Duchy Luxembourg to the UN Secretary General (n 31) 4.

33 Contribution of the Grand Duchy Luxembourg to the UN Secretary General (n 31) 4.

recommendations on possible norms, rules and principles of responsible behaviours relating to threats by states to space systems . . . [and] how they would contribute to the negotiation of legally binding instruments, including on the prevention of an arms race in outer space.'[34] While it is important to note that the Working Group has not been the only mechanism established to safeguard international peace and security in outer space, it 'present[ed] a new chance for the international community to build a common understanding to achieve this goal.'[35] Designed to be open and inclusive, it 'represent[ed] the possibility of convergence of different views and approaches, which have traditionally existed on opposite sides of the geopolitical spectrum and have commonly been understood as incompatible, to attain and maintain peace and security in space.'[36] Ortega and Koller opine that the OEWG was quite different to previous mechanisms created to tackle international peace and security concerns in outer space.[37] By implementing a 'bottom-up' approach the OEWG sought to provide all states and non-governmental organisations such as academia, civil society organisations, and corporations with the chance to contribute their views 'in an inclusive manner, which . . . [was] important for a domain such as space, from which all [s]tates and all humanity depend on and profit from.'[38] Moreover, it was thought that the OEWG would also enlighten 'the international community of the perceived incompatibility between non-legally binding mechanisms and legally binding measures.'[39] Form 30 January to 3 February 2023, the third substantive session of the OEWG took place in Geneva where 'recommendations on possible norms, rules and principles of responsible behaviours relating to threats by [s]tates to space systems, including, as appropriate, how they would contribute to the negotiation of legally binding instruments, including on the prevention of an arms race in outer space.'[40] Crucially, states confirmed that outer space is a realm for all humankind and emphasised the need to observe international law, especially the UN Charter which prohibits the use of force.[41] While some delegations suggested that certain principles contained in the five outer space treaties required clarification nevertheless, the significance of the treaties to continue maintaining international peace and security in outer space was recognised.[42] A number of state delegations 'indicated that non legally binding norms, rules and principles

34 UN General Assembly Resolution 76/231 (n 25) para. 5(c).

35 Ortega and Koller (n 22) 20.

36 Ortega and Koller (n 22) 20.

37 Ortega and Koller (n 22) 27.

38 Ortega and Koller (n 22) 27.

39 Ortega and Koller (n 22) 27.

40 UN General Assembly Resolution 76/231 (n 25) para. 5(c).

41 UN General Assembly, 'Chairperson's Summary: Open-Ended Working Group on Reducing Space Threats Through Norms, Rules and Principles of Responsible Behaviours' A/AC.294/2023/WP.22, Item 6 of the Agenda: Consideration of issues contained in paragraph 5 General Assembly Resolution A/RES/76/231 (1 September 2023) 10 <https://docs-library.unoda.org/Open-Ended_Working_Group_on_Reducing_Space_Threats_-_(2022)/A-AC.294-2023-WP.22_2023-09-01_14h00.pdf> accessed 1 November 2024.

42 UN General Assembly (n 41) para. 16.

would aid in creating the foundation of common understanding needed to build an effective legally binding agreement on space security.'[43] In addition to the increasing number of both state and non-state actors in outer space, especially commercial entities, building trust, transparency, and confidence among stakeholders is pivotal. In particular, a number of states pointed out 'the importance of not using norms, rules and principles as tools to limit access to space or the development of space systems for peaceful purposes for emerging [s]tates.'[44] While the third substantive session was widely regarded amongst academic commentators as a success several states noted that there was an urgent need to enhance the exchange of information on space security issues, in particular behaviours that could be deemed dangerous and threatening.[45] There was a frank exchange of views about the potential use of space situational awareness to track compliance with the outer space legal framework.[46] However, some states expressed the view that for this technology to track compliance there would need to be a process or mechanism to safeguard its impartiality.[47]

The fourth substantive session of the OEWG took place in Geneva from 28 August to 1 September 2023 and aimed to draft a final report and recommendations by consensus for the UN General Assembly on potential norms, rules, and principles of responsible conduct in outer space. In contrast to the three previous substantive sessions non-state representatives were excluded from the discussions, and despite cautious optimism the OEWG was 'unable to adopt either a substantive report or even the most basic procedure and description of the meetings.'[48] Instead, the Chair resorted to providing a mere summary of the discussions to the UN General Assembly.[49] Despite this failure, many states believed that the OEWG 'inspired open, substantive, interactive, and enlightening discussions pertaining to outer space security' and was 'a constructive platform for an inclusive dialogue among Member States with the participation of all relevant stakeholders on reducing space threats.'[50] This conclusion was also reiterated in the OEWG Chair's Summary to the United Nations General Assembly: '[s]tate[s] had the opportunity to express their concerns and to put forward their ideas and proposals.'[51] However,

43 Ortega and Koller (n 22) 35.
44 Ortega and Koller (n 22) 35.
45 Chairperson's Summary (n 41) 9 and 10.
46 Chairperson's Summary (n 41) 2.
47 Chairperson's Summary (n 41) 2.
48 Jessica West, 'The Open-Ended Working Group on Reducing Space Threats: Recap of the Fourth and Final Session' (*Ploughshares*, August 2023) 5 <https://cdn.prod.website-files.com/63e066081ef50cb16a3f4157/659d7d3f0629657a2e5b3f4e_OEWG2023FinalRecap.pdf> accessed 1 November 2024.
49 Chairperson's Summary (n 41).
50 Concluding Joint Statement of the Philippines, 'Final Session of The United Nations Open-Ended Working Group on Reducing Space Threats Through Norms, Rules, and Principles of Responsible Behaviour' 28 August–1 September 2023 <https://docs-library.unoda.org/Open-Ended_Working_Group_on_Reducing_Space_Threats_-_(2022)/PHL-_STATEMENT_-__Concluding_Joint_Statement.pdf> accessed 1 November 2024.
51 Chairperson's Summary (n 41) para. 6.

the adoption of a substantive report was not possible for two reasons. Firstly, the United States submitted that a final report was not possible because of 'redlines' imposed by some countries, and secondly, Russia took issue with the basic concept of 'responsible behaviour' which it regarded as fundamentally defective.[52] Several states have called for a renewal of discussions since it improved 'understanding of how states perceive threats; nurturing a convergence of views on numerous topics that reached unanimity on the applicability of international law to outer space; and also nurturing an unprecedented level of cross-regional cooperation.'[53] While it remains to be seen whether future discussion will in fact take place, it is reassuring that during the fourth substantive session states confirmed, 'possible solutions to outer space security can involve a combination of legally binding obligations and non-legally binding measures, and that work in both of these areas can be further pursued in a progressive, sustained and complementary manner, without undermining existing legal obligations.'[54] Moreover, it was recognised:

> non-legally binding measures applicable to outer space activities, while not a substitute for legally binding arms control instruments, could contribute to the consideration of concepts and proposals for such measures as well as verification provisions included in legally binding international instruments, including on the prevention of an arms race in outer space.[55]

Moving forward, there will be a need to rebuild trust and confidence considering the increasing number of both state and non-state actors in outer space. In these uncertain political times, perhaps it is promising that states discussed during the session how trust could be developed, especially with regards to ensuring respect for all states to take part in outer space security governance as well as sharing information, providing assistance and training, transferring technology, and distributing space situational awareness data.[56]

Koskenniemi posits, in relation to international law generally, that it 'offers a continuing self-interpretation to society in terms of what has taken place in the past and how society sees its own future.'[57] While it is difficult to determine how the norms of outer space law will develop many scholars remain optimistic for the future of outer space law—whatever that may represent to them. The lure and excitement surrounding outer space law is inevitable, but scholars still need to find ways to harness the law as an instrument. Law, according to Koskenniemi, has a 'never-ending character (as political decisionmakers sometimes despairingly notice). It makes it possible to constantly produce new interpretations of its rules and prior judgments, thus cultivating the gap between the institutional present and

52 West (n 48) 5.
53 West (n 48) 5.
54 Chairperson's Summary (n 41) para. 4.
55 Chairperson's Summary (n 41) para. 5.
56 Chairperson's Summary (n 41) paras. 8, 9, and 10.
57 Koskenniemi (n 18) 23.

the legal ideal.'[58] Applying Koskenniemi's reasoning to outer space law, we can certainly analyse the historical development of the field with an eye to imagine its future. Just as outer space law has several potential birth dates, it could also have multiple futures. As a result, I now consider what 'future innovativeness' might entail in relation to outer space law.

3 The Future Innovativeness of Outer Space Law

To delineate the theme of this book a comprehension of the concept of 'future' with respect to outer space law is needed. According to the *Oxford English Dictionary*, the future can be defined as 'the time that will come after the present or the events that will happen then.'[59] While both parts of the definition are pertinent to this book the contributors approach the concept from their own unique perspective. We regard the notion of 'future' to be comparable to concepts that are innovative and groundbreaking, as well as what is regarded as archaic and outmoded. For the origin of outer space law, it is inherently useful to draw upon Isabella Diederiks-Verschoor and Vladimir Kopal's historical account. According to them, the launch of Sputnik I by the former Soviet Union in 1957 heralded the hasty development of legal principles to regulate outer space.[60] Indeed, Bin Cheng discerned, 'the treaty was drawn up not only in some haste within the space of less than 12 months but also less than ten years after the launch of the earth's first artificial satellite.'[61] The negotiation and adoption of the Treaty on Principles Governing the Activities of States in the Exploration and Use of Outer Space, Including the Moon and Other Celestial Bodies (the Outer Space Treaty) in 1967 portended the foundation of a new branch of public international law.[62] While outer space law is original and innovative, any future rules, as evidenced in the previous section of this chapter, will likely be nestled within the existing legal framework. Consequently, the future of outer space law may be distinct and divergent but at the same time cushioned within the viscousness of existing structures.[63] While the enforcement of outer space law is vital, the norms and practices are often perhaps sidestepped and taken for granted by both state and non-state actors within the space sector. Fiona Mackay notes that by 'successfully intervening to insert new actors, new values, and new rules into new institutions, reformers may profoundly

58 Koskenniemi (n 18) 21.

59 Albert Hornby, Michael Ashby and Sally Wehmeier, *Oxford Advanced Learner's Dictionary of Current English* (OUP 2000).

60 Isabella Diederiks-Verschoor and Vladimir Kopal, *An Introduction to Space Law* (Wolters Kluwer 2008) 2.

61 Bin Cheng, *Space Objects and Their Various Connecting Factors, in Outlook on Space Law Over the Next 30 Years* (G Lafferranderie and D Crowther eds, Brill 1997) 203.

62 Peter Jankowitsch, 'The Background and History of Space Law' in Frans von der Dunk and Fabio Tronchetti (eds) *Handbook of Outer Space Law* (Edward Elgar Publishing 2015) 1, 5.

63 Fiona Mackay, 'Nested Newness, Institutional Innovation, and the Gendered Limits of Change' (2014) 10 Politics and Justice 549.

influence the future developments of an institution.'[64] Nevertheless, reform of outer space law must struggle with 'organizational and institutional legacies and path dependencies, with unintended consequences of design decisions, and with ongoing institutional dynamics with the wider environment.'[65] Therefore, '[n]ested newness is a metaphor used to capture the ways in which the new is embedded in time, sequence, and its institutional environment.'[66]

Crucially, unlike other branches of public international law, outer space law does not yet have a bespoke court to adjudicate and resolve disputes. Thus, the concept of 'institution' does not refer to a court as such but instead to the formal and informal institutions that have moulded outer space law more broadly so far. Of course, outer space law has been and continues to be influenced by several state and non-state actors. Thus, for the purposes of this book, we contemplate that the future of outer space law necessitates a consideration of the challenges of the past and the present to hypothesise the dynamics of the future. That said, the future of outer space law is not predictable and while the contributors to this book do present ideas about the future of the discipline, they do not offer predictions. Highlighting how the future of outer space law is linked to the past and present, we contemplate how outer space law has thus far not been able to future-proof against predicted advancements in science and technology. As such, can we really contend that current outer space law embraces the future? Instead, it reflects the old legal order—especially forms of sovereignty and domination despite attempts to introduce new guidelines that endeavour to promote the long-term sustainability of outer space activities.[67] As examined in the previous paragraph, the prevailing structures of outer space law provide viscousness but not a pathway to predict the future of the discipline.

Against the backdrop of the history of outer space law, can we view its future as haphazard? Certainly, the early days of spacefaring were dominated by two superpowers but outer space use and exploration since then has grown considerably with over 77 states now having space programs. While the development of outer space law has occurred in a fragmented way, nobody in 1967 could have predicted the rise of corporate actors and that the future of outer space law would be found in the Supreme Court of Mississippi or the Court of Justice of the European Union.[68] Some scholars had hoped for the establishment of an International Space Court but this has not occurred, perhaps partly because the domestic laws and practices of space-faring states are now so numerous and diverse. This is conceivably for the

64 Mackay (n 63) 549.

65 Mackay (n 63) 549.

66 Mackay (n 63) 552.

67 UN Guidelines for the Log-Term Sustainability of Outer Space Activities of the Committee on Peaceful Uses of Outer Space (Vienna, 2021) <https://www.unoosa.org/documents/pdf/PromotingSpaceSustainability/Publication_Final_English_June2021.pdf>

68 *Pigott v. Boeing Company, Supreme Court of Mississippi*, 240 So. 2d 63 (Miss.1970); *European Communities, Court of Justice, Judgment of 18 March 1980 (Procureur du Roi v. Marc I.V.C. Debauve and Others)*. (BB) (ESA).

best if the 'concrete realization' of such a court would entail 'some distribution of power, and with it, some privileging of preferences and values.'[69] Thus, this book does not offer direction on the possibility of a future court to adjudicate on outer space disputes. Instead, the contributors present proposals springing from their interests, perspectives, and scholarly experiences. They have not been asked to present proposals for the reform of outer space law or its 'future that would never arrive but for which the present would nevertheless be sacrificed.'[70] While most of the contributors to this volume believe that the development of outer space law is a crucial endeavour linked as it is to future global sustainability, we also believe that perhaps a variety of futures can be envisaged. As an alternative to inventorying the history of outer space law, the book seeks to consider a variety of challenges and opportunities for outer space law and its possible future.

4 Overview of the Book

Consistent with the thought that outer space law has multiple potential future directions, this book addresses a variety of topics that are not necessarily consistent with each other and may be more or less likely. The contributors make practical suggestions for outer space law which deal with the current economic and political climate, the array of other institutional and political structures and priorities (especially maintaining peace and security), and developments in the areas of the environment, migration, technology, and liability. By doing so, the chapters seek to draw attention to the ongoing tensions between 'domestic,' 'international,' and 'universal' notions of outer space use and exploration as these develop over time. The first section of the book addresses the promise of outer space law more generally. Brobst argues that while humanity has decided to set foot in outer space for multiple reasons perhaps it also showcases humanity's 'frontier mentality.' Highlighting that outer space law has not considered how social and family structures will adapt to the perils of the outer space environment, Brobst steps away from conventional space topics such as satellites, space traffic management, and remote sensing and advocates for supporting interdisciplinary research into human nature as well as our collective memory of past frontier isolation to amplify our understanding of how humanity will subsist and survive in outer space. She calls for an examination of modern human nature in tandem with concepts of natural law, rather than customary international law, to better foster sustainable human settlements on celestial bodies in the long term. Ultimately, she affirms that for *Homo sapiens* to be a resilient species in outer space, there needs to be an awareness of human nature, to inform the species' ability to adapt so that 'pioneering social structures are not aggressively competitive.'[71]

69 Martti Koskenniemi, 'The Subjective Dangers of Projects of World Community' in Antonio Cassese (ed), *Realizing Utopia: The Future of International Law* (OUP 2012) 12.

70 Koskenniemi (n 69).

71 Brobst (page 42 of Chapter 1).

Blount observes that outer space law can be regarded as a normative framework that is the result of interwoven narratives. Defining narrative as a 'fabric of interacting stories that bring meaning to things within society, including the law,' he contends that for international space law the main approach to normative growth is derived from using narratives to determine the substance of the law.[72] While acknowledging that this is not the only way that outer space law can evolve and develop, Blount asserts that narratives can offer a pragmatic means through which to consider states' normative engagement especially in the outer space domain since it does not yet have legal institutions with interpretive ability. Moreover, he asserts that much normative development occurs at the narrative level 'within the stories that states and others tell about normative frameworks.'[73] Stories provide a forum for interpreting and perhaps contesting norms and their content. Tronchetti steers the book from beyond the theoretical to analyse how outer space has become a central element of the debate on international security. With states' growing reliance on space assets and infrastructure, not only for services such as high-speed internet access but also national security purposes, questions are emerging about the exercise of the right to self-defence in the outer space realm. The need to protect high-value and strategic space infrastructure is palpable, and Tronchetti questions how the application of the right in outer space is likely to be controversial moving forward. He also considers how the scope of the right to self-defence remains unclear due to interpretive challenges. Many of these interpretive challenges are because the UN Charter was drafted before outer space use and exploration were envisaged. In addition, there is also very little, if any, state practice on how to respond to threats to space infrastructure. Finally, he calls for a clearer understanding of the events that could trigger the right of self-defence in outer space to sidestep confusion and misunderstanding which could lead to an escalation of political tension and possibly armed conflict.

Looking beyond outer space law *stricto sensu*, de Zwart hypothesises the rules that will regulate the return of humans to the Moon over the next decade. Without a clear framework concerns are growing that this may lead to political tension. Drawing upon the Artemis Accords, which provide that *in situ* resource utilisation will be essential to accomplish a permanent human base on the Moon, de Zwart argues that urgent clarification of the rules is needed to ensure that they are enunciated in a way that enhances the 'human experience' on the Moon instead of recreating Earth-based problems. Highlighting China's and Russia's plans to also establish a base on the Moon, which will entail 'experimental research facilities created on the surface or in the moon,' questions are emerging about whether this proposed activity will be in keeping with outer space law and whether locations of historical significance such as the landing of the first human on the moon on 21 July 1969 will be afforded protection.[74] De Zwart believes that rules need to be developed and

72 Blount (page 49 of Chapter 2).
73 Blount (page 51 of Chapter 2).
74 de Zwart (page 93 of Chapter 5).

agreed upon at the global level very shortly to keep pace with the speed at which the plans of China, Russia, and the United States are coming to fruition.

Building upon de Zwart's contribution, Johansen addresses the application of Article 8 of the Outer Space Treaty to facilities constructed on celestial bodies with raw materials extracted from the celestial body itself. In deciphering whether the extraction of resources from the Moon is appropriation, he discusses whether constructing a base utilising these raw materials and claiming quasi-territorial jurisdiction is potentially contrary to the non-appropriation principle enshrined in Article 2 of the Outer Space Treaty. Johansen determines that if a facility is built with raw materials originating from Earth, states will likely retain jurisdiction over these materials. Moreover, states will also potentially retain jurisdiction over 3D-printed space stations built from a mixture of both Earth-based materials and celestial-based materials. Building on the theme of human settlements in outer space, Brennan critiques the intersection between outer space law and immigration law. In particular, she analyses whether the right to liberty of movement will exist as a human right on extraterrestrial settlements in a similar way to how it exists on Earth. While foreseeing every practical human rights impact in outer space is not possible, she contends that the implications of restricting freedom of movement will be far reaching. In addition, whether the first wave of migrants to outer space and their descendants will retain a right to enter/return to Earth remains to be seen.

Both Schonberg and Brennan take on the persistent challenge of space debris. While legal scholars have seemingly reached consensus on the definition of this phenomenon, there continues to be ambiguities whether states and space companies are allowed to remove objects from outer space that do not belong to them if there are concerns that the object will cause damage not only to another space object but also to the environment of outer space and Earth. Since the UN Space Debris Mitigation Guidelines are not legally binding, there is growing consensus that a new legal framework is needed to regulate this challenge. Schonberg and Brennan begin by deciphering the relationship between outer space law and environmental law to suggest the path for the future scope, structure, and direction of legal research on space debris. The chapter offers suggestions about which topics will potentially engage legal researchers on space debris over the next decade and ascertains some of the most critical lines of inquiry that will potentially shape the law of space debris in the future. They focus in particular on the domestic implementation of the UN Space Debris Mitigation Guidelines and the need for a legal enforcement mechanism for this phenomenon at the international level.

Unfortunately, outer space law continues to insufficiently address space resource utilisation and safety zones. Therefore, Blake and Stubbs consider the legal principles at the core of the Outer Space Treaty which are pertinent to potential safety zones concerning space resource utilisation activities. Recent developments which could assist with determining the precise norms that may be deployed in the declaration of safety zones include the Building Blocks for the Development of an International Framework on Space Resources which was adopted by The Hague Space Resources Governance Working Group in 2019 and the Artemis Accords which were concluded in 2020. Blake and Stubbs assert that there is emerging state practice that affirms the Building Blocks and Artemis Accords and very few countries dispute the legality of proposed safety zones under the Outer Space Treaty. Criteria for the institution of a safety zone are examined at length, and the authors conclude that it is critical for a safety zone to have a defined physical scope that must also be proportionate and reasonable so that it does not interfere with the operation or facility contained within. Bratu's chapter swings the book back into low-Earth orbit by discussing how our global navigation satellite systems (GNSS) have developed to become central to civil infrastructure. Examining how GNSS do not have a sufficient legal framework despite conferring considerable benefits on society, she reflects upon the future parameters of the concept of 'GNSS liability' under European tort law. She makes recommendations to strengthen the future regulatory regime and advocates for the incorporation of the UN Sustainable Development Goals.

In the final chapter of the book, Brennan returns our attention to the multifaceted future of outer space law by analysing this theme against recent developments and emerging issues. While this chapter will predominantly consider how the past and present of outer space law are not separate and distinct but instead are interconnected, she will also examine what is potentially in store for the future of outer space law. Recognising the normativity enmeshed with this undertaking, she does not endorse linear conceptions of time or support a particular future for outer space law. Pinpointing potential challenges and finding solutions to those challenges, including establishing institutions and legal enforcement mechanisms, may lead to additional complexities, especially with Donald Trump's second term as the United States president on the horizon. Nevertheless, an analysis of the possible future of outer space law remains an important endeavour.

Bibliography

Sandeepa Bhat B, 'An Introduction to International Space Law' in Sandeepa Bhat B, Dilip Ukey and Adithya Variath (eds), *International Space Law in the New Space Era: Principles and Challenges* (OUP 2024) 1.

Michael Bothe, 'Legal and Non-Legal Norms—A Meaningful Distinction in International Relations' (2009) 11 Netherlands Yearbook of International Law 65.

Marc Carns, *Orbital Debris Prevention and Mitigation Efforts Among Major Space Actor* (Brill Nijhoff 2023) 297.

Bin Cheng, *Space Objects and Their Various Connecting Factors, in Outlook on Space Law over the Next 30 Years* (G. Lafferranderie and D. Crowther eds, Brill 1997).

Bin Cheng, *Studies in International Space Law* (Clarendon Press 1997).

Concluding Joint Statement of the Philippines, Final Session of the United Nations Open-Ended Working Group on Reducing Space Threats Through Norms, Rules, and Principles of Responsible Behaviour, 28 August–1 September 2023 <https://docs-library.unoda.org/Open-Ended_Working_Group_on_Reducing_Space_Threats_-_(2022)/PHL-_STATEMENT_-__Concluding_Joint_Statement.pdf> accessed 1 November 2024.

Isabella Diederiks-Verschoor and Vladimir Kopal, *An Introduction to Space Law* (Wolters Kluwer 2008).

Stephen Doyle, *Origins of International Space Law and the International Institute for Space Law of the International Astronautical Federation* (Univelt 2002).

Martha Finnemore and Kathryn Sikkink, 'International Norm Dynamics and Political Change' (1998) 52 International Organization 887.

Joanne Gabrynowicz, 'The Promise and Problems of the Land Remote Sensing Policy Act of 1992' (1993) 9 Space Policy 319.

Ray Harris, 'Current Policy Issues in Remote Sensing: Report by the International Policy Advisory Committee of ISPRS' (2003) 19 Space Policy 293.

Albert Hornby, Michael Ashby and Sally Wehmeier, *Oxford Advanced Learner's Dictionary of Current English* (OUP 2000).

Ram Jakhu, 'International Law Governing the Acquisition and Dissemination of Satellite Imagery' in Robert Huebert (ed), *Commercial Satellite Imagery and United Nations Peacekeeping: A View from above* (Routledge 2004) 259.

Peter Jankowitsch, 'The Background and History of Space Law' in Frans von der Dunk and Fabio Tronchetti (eds), *Handbook of Outer Space Law* (Edward Elgar Publishing 2015) 1.

Nandasiri Jasentuliyana (ed), *Space Law: Development and Scope* (Bloomsbury Publishing 1992).

Clarence Jenks, 'International Law and Activities in Space' (1956) 5 International and Comparative Law Quarterly 99.

Hans Kelsen, *The Pure Theory of Law* (Lawbook Exchange 1934).

Vladimir Kopal, 'Origins of Space Law and the Role of the United Nations' in Christian Brunner and Alexander Soucek (eds), *Outer Space in Society, Politics and Law* (Springer 2011) 221.

Martti Koskenniemi, 'Law, Teleology and International Relations: An Essay in Counter-Disciplinarity' (2012) 26 International Relations 3.

Martti Koskenniemi, 'The Subjective Dangers of Projects of World Community' in Antonio Cassese (ed), *Realizing Utopia: The Future of International Law* (OUP 2012) 12.

Emile Laude, 'Comment s'Appellera le Droit qui Régira la Vie de l'Air' (2010) 1910 Revue Juridique de la Locomotion Aérienne.

Fiona Mackay, 'Nested Newness, Institutional Innovation, and the Gendered Limits of Change' (2014) 10 Politics and Justice 549.

Peter Malanczuk, 'Space Law as a Branch of International Law' (1994) 25 Netherlands Yearbook of International Law 143.

Vladimir Mandl, *Das Weltraum-Recht: Ein Problem der Raumfahrt* (Bersheimer 1932) 48.

Richard McAdams, 'The Origin, Development and Regulation of Norms' (1997) 96 Michigan Law Review 338.

New Zealand Ministry of Foreign Affairs and Trade, 'Norms, Rules and Principles of Responsible Behaviour in Space' para. 8 <https://front.un-arm.org/wp-content/uploads/2021/05/Space-responsible-behaviours-submission-to-UN-New-Zealand.pdf> accessed 1 November 2024.

Almudena Ortega and Hellmut Lagos Koller, 'The Open-Ended Working Group on Reducing Threats Through Norms, Rules and Principles of Responsible Behaviours: The Journey So Far, and the Road Ahead' (2023) 48 (Special Issue) Air and Space Law 19.

Emma Palmer and Susan Harris Rimmer, 'Introduction: The Futures of International Criminal Justice' in Emma Palmer and others (eds), *Futures of International Criminal Justice* (Routledge 2022) 1.

Anja Pečujlić, *The Space Law Stalemate: Legal Mechanisms for Developing New Norms* (Routledge 2023).

Pigott v. Boeing Company, Supreme Court of Mississippi, 240 So. 2d 63 (Miss.1970); *European Communities, Court of Justice, Judgment of 18 March 1980 (Procureur du Roi v. Marc I.V.C. Debauve and Others)*. (BB) (ESA).

Sraavya Poonugani, 'It's Raining Rockets: Heightening State Liability for Space Pollution' (2023) 23(2) Chicago Journal of International Law 490.

Boris Rauschenbach, *Thirty Years of the Space Age*, unpublished paper presented at the International Astronautical Federation Annual Congress (Brighton 1987).

Joseph Raz, 'Legal Principles and the Limits of Law' (1972) 81 Yale Law Journal 823.
Report of the UN Ad Hoc Committee on the Peace Uses of Outer Space, UN. Doc. A 4141/25 (1959). See also Paul Dembling and Daniel Arons, 'The Evolution of the Outer Space Treaty' (1967) 33 Journal of Air Law and Commerce 419.
Resolution 75/36 Reducing Space Threats Through Norms, Rules and Principles of Responsible Behaviours: Contribution of the Grand Duchy of Luxembourg to the UN Secretary General, 4 <https://front.un-arm.org/wp-content/uploads/2021/05/210430-Luxembourg-contibution-to-the-UN-SG-Res75-36-Reducing-space-threats.pdf> accessed 1 November 2024.
Statute of the International Court of Justice, 18th April 1946 (33 UNTS 993, UKTS 67 (1946) Cmd 7015, 3 Bevans 1179, 59 Stat 1055, 145 BSP 832, TS No 993).
UNGeneral Assembly, Chairperson's Summary: Open-Ended Working Group on Reducing Space Threats Through Norms, Rules and Principles of Responsible Behaviours, A/AC.294/2023/WP.22, Item 6 of the Agenda: Consideration of issues contained in paragraph 5 General Assembly resolution A/RES/76/231 (1 September 2023) 10 <https://docs-library.unoda.org/Open-Ended_Working_Group_on_Reducing_Space_Threats_-_(2022)/A-AC.294-2023-WP.22_2023-09-01_14h00.pdf> accessed 1 November 2024.
UN General Assembly Resolution 1884 (XVIII), 18th Session (Question of General and Complete Disarmament (17 October 1963).
UN General Assembly Resolution 1962 (XVIII) 18th Session, Declaration of Legal Principles Governing the Activities of States in the Exploration and Use of Outer Space (13 December 1963).
UN General Assembly Resolution 76/231, 76th Session on Reducing Space Threats Through Norms, Rules and Principles of Responsible Behaviours (24 December 2021) <https://undocs.org/A/RES/76/231> accessed 1 November 2024.
UN Guidelines for the Log-Term Sustainability of Outer Space Activities of the Committee on Peaceful Uses of Outer Space (Vienna, 2021) <https://www.unoosa.org/documents/pdf/PromotingSpaceSustainability/Publication_Final_English_June2021.pdf>
Frans von der Dunk, 'International Space Law' in Frans von der Dunk with Fabio Tronchetti (eds), *Handbook of Space Law* (Edward Elgar Publishing 2017) 29, 29.
Jessica West, 'The Open-Ended Working Group on Reducing Space Threats: Recap of the Fourth and Final Session' (*Ploughshares*, August 2023) 5 <https://cdn.prod.website-files.com/63e066081ef50cb16a3f4157/659d7d3f0629657a2e5b3f4e_OEWG2023FinalRecap.pdf> accessed 1 November 2024.
Jessica West and Almudena Ortega, *Norms for Outer Space: A Small Step or a Giant Leap for Policymaking?* (UN Institute for Disarmament Research 2022).

Part I

The Promise of Outer Space Law

2 From Wagon Trains to Rocket Ships

Frontier Mentalities and Natural Law in Outer Space

Jennifer Brobst

1 Introduction

Our entry into outer space reveals humanity's frontier mentality for the first time in generations and the key question is what is necessary to ensure human society can thrive there. Space travel is often described as exploration[1] but eventually could include darker purposes such as banishment or escape from Earth. Thus, over time space settlers will likely approach their relationship to Earth with varied enthusiasm. Some may simply desire to create new societies in peace and isolation, while others may seek conquest. To argue that clearly delineated, comprehensive laws must precede space settlement assumes that human societies in space would accept the imposition of existing legal frameworks. The laws that we do have in place for the most remote, isolated places on Earth, those addressing Antarctica and the high seas as international commons beyond national jurisdiction,[2] offer little help in this matter, for settlement in these areas has also never been an option. Outer space is equally, if not more, inhospitable, but it is different.

Consideration of a modern understanding of human nature and more general concepts of natural law, rather than current customary international law, will aid in better promoting sustainable human communities in outer space in the long term. Unquestionably, however, during this period of nascent entry into near space where ties to Earth are critical to survival, international space law and customary international law are integral to a logical and desired framework to promote

1 In a Congressional hearing on a proposed Mars settlement, Chairman Babin stated, 'The exploration of space, particularly human exploration of Mars, has intrigued generations around the world. Our sister planet holds many mysteries, and quite possibly, the keys to our past and our future. The profound goal of putting humans on Mars and perhaps establishing a settlement there, fuels our desire to push the boundaries of what is possible and to reach far beyond our own planet. Space exploration is in our DNA.' Hearing Before the Subcommittee on Space, 'Next Steps to Mars: Deep Space Habitats,' 114th Congress, No 114–78 (18 May 2016) 4.

2 See generally Anja Nakarada Pečujlić, *The Space Law Stalemate: Legal Mechanisms for Developing New Norms* (Routledge 2023) 91.

DOI: 10.4324/9781003370499-3

cooperative and peaceful multilateral endeavours.[3] Unfortunately, cooperation works best when parties need each other but dissipates when they become more self-sufficient, as shown by China's development and launch of its own space station TIANGONG in 2021 after it was no longer permitted to use the International Space Station.[4] In a pragmatic rather than philosophical sense, long-term human survival in space will emerge from an understanding of our human nature in social, legal, medical, and scientific contexts, such as the source of limitation on trust and cooperation.

The current commercially driven space race may prove more cost effective and innovative, but a profit motive may be antithetical to satisfying essential human needs for survival in space.[5] As American philosopher and historian Thomas Kuhn noted, fearing the authoritarian power of government over scientific research, the ability of science 'to survive and grow may be indicated by the very tenuousness of humanity's hold on the scientific enterprise.'[6] Rather, the United Nations and other representative governmental bodies must consider constituent needs, rights, and duties, and even then it is a difficult task. For example, the jurisdictional nature of space settlements is a critical question. The United Nations Charter in 1945, following a long, divisive period of colonisation, annexation, and eventual independence, endorsed respect for self-determination among nations '[t]o develop friendly relations among nations based on respect for the principle of equal rights and self-determination of peoples, and to take other appropriate measures to strengthen universal peace.'[7] Yet separatist and independence movements inherently conflict with the United Nations' corresponding recognition of territorial integrity. Also, in the interests of international peace, self-determination may be honoured but offer little protection against oppression of minority populations within nations.[8] From Earth, legally circumscribing what constitutes a community or sovereign nation in outer space, even in the pursuit of peace, may ultimately be impracticable. Although it is outside the scope of this chapter to consider specific legal rights and structures, some have argued that the law of space colonies should divest itself

3 Frans G von der Dunk, *Advanced Introduction to Space Law* (Edward Elgar Publishing 2020) 41 (assuring that 'all key stakeholders agree' that the *lex specialis* of international space law should be supported by all current governments).

4 Pečujlić (n 2) 34 (discussing the 2011 Wolf Amendment in which the United States effectively prohibited working with China in space).

5 Originally scientific exploration was the most stated purpose for space travel, but even this was held wanting by some. Dr Alvin M Weinberg, Director of the Oak Ridge National Laboratory in the United States, cautioned scientists in space and generally against 'short-sighted seeking after fragile monuments of big science, [which is] to be diverted from our real purpose, which is the enriching and broadening of human life.' Leonard S Silk, 'Values and Goals of Space Exploration' in Howard J Taubenfeld (ed), *Space and Society* (Albert Press 1964) 43, 45–46.

6 Thomas Kuhn, *The Structure of Scientific Revolutions* (3rd edn, University of Chicago Press 1996, orig. pub. 1962) 167.

7 United Nations, Charter of the United Nations (24 October 1945) 1 UNTS XVI, TS No 993, Ch 1, Art I, pt 2.

8 See Vita Gudeleviciute, 'Does the Principle of Self-Determination Prevail Over the Principle of Territorial Integrity?' (April 2005) 2(2) International Journal of Baltic Law 48, 64.

from the colonial mindset with a view toward greater respect for self-determination of settlements from the outset.[9]

However, despite jurisdictional legal challenges and conflicts of interest among human populations, their intrinsic commonality on Earth and in space is their humanity.[10] Remote settlements, far removed in space and time from Earth, will do well to carefully maintain a record of human history with all its knowledge about what it means to be human. How to identify shared aspects of humanity, both helpful and hurtful, as it may inform the development of societies in space is the focus of this chapter. Perhaps the natural law foundations underpinning international customary law[11] and other cultural conceptions of what it means to thrive or to be good[12] could offer a useful perspective toward fostering new customary law for humanity far away from Earth.

2 The Utility of International Customary Law as the Initial Framework Governing Humans in Space

As rigid and bureaucratic as modern law may appear today, indigenous customary law and variable blends of law and culture, including natural law, have persisted through human migration, colonialism, industrialisation, and global market interdependence.[13] Natural law, a nebulous but widely adopted concept or theory, became the focus of deep criticism.[14] John Dewey, for example, wrote in 1922 that

9 See for example Josselin Lavigne, 'Political Sovereignty in Outer Space' (2022) 48 North Carolina Journal of International Law 147, 199; Humaid Alshamsi and others, 'Space Station Asgardia 2117: From Theoretical Science to a New Nation in Outer Space' (2018) 16 Santa Clara Journal of International Law 37 (imagining a new space station as a sovereign state).

10 This argument does not consider post-humanist positions, but that would of course change critical factors in the discussion. See Donna Haraway, *Manifestly Haraway* (University of Minnesota Press 2016) 33 (stating in 'A Cyborg Manifesto' that '[c]ommunications technologies and biotechnologies are crucial tools recrafting our bodies'). It also acknowledges, but does not address here, the growing debate regarding the legal and ethical comparable treatment of AI, robots, and humans in outer space, a region that already relies heavily on AI capacities for the operation of essential systems. See Ugo Pagallo and others, 'The Normative Challenges of AI in Outer Space: Law, Ethics, and the Realignment of Terrestrial Standards' (2023) 36 Philosophy & Technology 23.

11 See for example James Tully (ed), *Pufendorf: On the Duty of Man and Citizen* (CUP 2006) 34 (writing in the 17th century in Book I 'On natural law' that 'all the advantages that attend human life today derive from men's mutual assistance').

12 See for example Yi-Fu Tuan, *Human Goodness* (University of Wisconsin Press 2008) 209 (noting cross-cultural shared views within all cultures of notions of 'us' and 'them,' human consciousness, and the possibility of individual enlightenment).

13 See for example Susana Nuccetelli, 'Is 'Latin American Thought' Philosophy?' (2003) 34(4) Metaphilosophy 524 (addressing the intersections in Latin America of indigenous philosophical thinking, alongside interpretations of classical Western philosophy, and unique adoptions of European philosophy, such as Marxism); Kwasi Wiredu, *Philosophy and an African Culture* (CUP 1980) 28 (asserting that certain traditional African philosophies may conceive of 'man and society, their ideas of law and government, their doctrines of God and of the Good' without any concession to European philosophy).

14 Edwin W Patterson, 'A Pragmatist Looks at Natural Law and Natural Rights' in Arthur Leon Harding (ed), *Natural Law and Natural Rights* (Southern Methodist UP 1955) 48, 49 (explaining

sceptics 'thought to find in the doctrine of native instincts a scientific support for asserting the practical unalterability of human nature,' regardless of circumstances.[15] But as technology continues to rapidly change society and human experience, discussions of what makes humans flourish amidst this change have resurfaced.[16]

International human rights and outer space treaties have presumed the need for application of existing conceptions of natural law onto new frontiers, often dominated by Western rights ideals but not necessarily so.[17] The increase in the number of nation states as a result of postwar decolonisation has led gradually to a less Eurocentric approach to international law, but also 'great suspicion of the customary law process' and the practice of majority voting.[18] And yet Grotius, the father of international law in 1670, in a time of conquest and war, professed that nation states need to create a set of universal principles 'out of the chaos of lawless and unreasoning strife.'[19]

(a) The Limited Impact of International Space Law

Structurally, international treaties hint at applications of existing law into unknown worlds and associations, but they have yet to fully embrace whether concrete principles should apply in the universe. Examples include the United Nations 2019 Resolution on the International Cooperation in the Peaceful Uses of Outer Space[20] and the broad former provisions of the 1996 Declaration on International Cooperation in the Exploration and Use of Outer Space for the Benefit and in the Interest of All States.[21] The 2019 resolution 'emphasizes' that space exploration and the use of space science and technology are 'for the benefit of all humankind' with the aim

that the appeal of natural law was its recognition of a physical order in the universe and, since medieval times, for some that its principles were founded in 'divine reason' and were therefore unquestionable).

15 John Dewey, *Human Nature and Conduct* (Dover Publication 2002) 106–7.

16 E.g., Avigail Ferdman, 'Human Flourishing and Technology Affordances' (2024) 34 Philosophy & Technology 1, 2 (seeking to demonstrate how a perfectionist approach of the good life could help to evaluate the goodness or badness of technology, in order to be better placed to regulate existing technologies and design future ones).

17 James A Vedda, 'The Role of Space Development in Globalization' in Steve J Dick and Roger D Launius (eds), *Societal Impact of Spaceflight* (NASA 2007) 193, 205 (noting the emergence of China and India as space powers).

18 Vera Gowlland-Debbas, 'Introductory Remarks' in Vera Gowlland-Debbas (ed), *Multilateral Treat-Making: The Current Status of Challenges to and Reforms Needed in the International Legislative Process, papers presented as the Forum Geneva, 5/16/98* (Martinus Nijhoff Publishers 2000) 1, 3.

19 David J Hill, 'Introduction' in Hugo Grotius (ed), *The Rights of War and Peace, Including the Law of Nature and of Nations* (AC Campbell tr, first published as *De Jure Belli ac Pacis* in 1670, 1901) 1.

20 *International Cooperation in the Peaceful Uses of Outer Space*, Resolution adopted by the United Nations General Assembly (13 December 2019), A/RES/74/82.

21 Declaration on International Cooperation in the Exploration and Use of Outer Space for the Benefit and in the Interest of All States, Taking Into Particular Account the Needs of Developing Countries (1996) A/RES/51/122, par.

of 'the development of the international legal regime governing space activities.'[22] However, these texts only loosely connote what will form peaceful, beneficial human relations.

In outer space, absent substantial genetic innovation, humans will still be humans. For millennia, we have not biologically evolved in any significantly meaningful way, other than to survive longer as we are.[23] Yet the species has produced scientific and technological tools and domestic and political structures that would be wholly unrecognisable to past ancestors. Astronomer Carl Sagan aptly stated, 'we have become powerful without becoming commensurately wise.'[24] However, natural law and its manifestation in international law do reflect humanity's interest in order and some promise in an ability to thrive. Our focus on natural order is ancient. Ovid put forth in *Metamorphoses* that Nature or God created a universe or 'cosmic parts' of planets, stars, sun, land, water, and sky, and 'set them each in its own place, and bound them fast in harmony.'[25] Early commentary devising a natural law theory or concept expressed that natural law originally offers 'order in the universe and in man' because of the human capacity to notice a corresponding order and reason in the universe.[26] It is difficult to avoid framing human consciousness and experience against an extant universe,[27] but these are mere reminders, not based on a concerted attempt to address metaphysics and phenomenology.

A reframing of what humans need to thrive in the earliest stages of space exploration may not even require a fundamental re-examination of natural law. Initially, imposition of existing legal frameworks will apply to tentative exploration and small groups of humans still tethered to the interests of Earth. For example, the existing international human right to leave a nation and to return to it could apply to those who abandon Earth in self-made rockets but then opt to return.[28] However, eventually this approach will pass or fade. Frontier outposts in outer space will need social order and cooperation to ensure safety and survival, but formal legal

22 *International Cooperation in the Peaceful Uses of Outer Space*, Resolution adopted by the United Nations General Assembly (13 December 2019), A/RES/74/82, par 2.

23 Alan R Templeton, 'Has Human Evolution Stopped?' (2 July 2010) 1(1) Rambam Maimonides Med. J. <https://www.ncbi.nlm.nih.gov/pmc/articles/PMC3721656/> accessed 6 December 2022 (noting that many scholars have asserted that natural selection has ceased regarding human biological evolution, but positing that cultural adaptation continues to have an influence on human health, genetic drift, and natural selection).

24 Carl Sagan, *Pale Blue Dot: A Vision of the Human Future in Space* (Ballantine Books 1994) 316–17.

25 Ovid, *Metamorphoses* (Frank Justus Miller tr, 3rd edn, first published near 20 B.C.E., Harvard UP 1977) lines 27–28, at p. 5.

26 Paul E Sigmund, *Natural Law in Political Thought* (Winthrop Publishers, Inc. 1971) viii.

27 Korean poet Yoon Dong-ju (1917–1945) invoking transition and the passage of time wrote in 'Counting the Stars at Night': 'Up where the season pass|The sky is filled with autumn.|In this untroubled quietude|I could almost count these autumn-couched stars.|But why I cannot now enumerate|Those one or two stars in my breast|Is because the dawn is breaking soon,|And I have tomorrow night in store,|And because my youth is not yet done.' Yoon Dong-ju, *Counting the Stars at Night: The Complete Works in Verse and Prose* (Insoo Lee tr, Resource Publications 2022) 45.

28 Theodore Meron, *Human Rights and Humanitarian Norms as Customary Law* (Clarendon Press 1989) 97 (citing United Nations Document E/CN .4/sub. 2/ 1987/10, 7).

structures may not be necessary initially. Acceptance of new customary international law, prescriptive in nature, is not a swift process, where custom is defined as 'evidence of a general practice accepted as law.'[29] Treaty creation also requires extensive time to allow the parties 'to reflect accurately the balance of their conflicting interests, and to represent their considered interests.'[30]

Most international law scholars would agree that many, if not most, of the international laws and agreements relating to human activity in outer space have not yet crystallised into customary law but could be deemed general law.[31] For example, in the context of space resource extraction for commercial profit, NASA's Artemis Accords have created non-binding bilateral arrangements among 20% of the world's 195 nations, avowedly consistent with the Outer Space Treaty, but with the stated opposition of China, Russia, and other nations.[32] In this particularly tendentious realm of space law, some have argued that the Outer Space Treaty in Articles VI and VII, relating to state responsibility and liability for space activities, presents less potential for customary international law status related to mining in outer space than Articles I and II, which incorporated customary international law regarding freedom, common interest, and non-appropriation pre-dating the Outer Space Treaty itself.[33] That is, customary international law has not crystallised for space resource extraction, nor may it do so in the foreseeable future.[34] More broadly, the role of customary international law has come under scrutiny, particularly in space law, given that the majority of space actors work in the private sector, not the government sector. According to Professors Ram Jakhu and Steven Freeland, 'there is no longer uniform agreement among international law commentators that the two elements [of consistent state practice and *opinio juris*] are still 'necessary' to prove the existence of a rule of customary international law.'[35] If formal multilateral agreements occur more frequently as space activities increase, then perhaps the diminution of customary international law is not a grievous loss.

With the benefit of retained knowledge of human history, development of civilisations, and the promise of research and technology, perhaps new societies will

29 Meron (n 28) 3 (quoting the United Nations, Statute of the International Court of Justice, Art. 38(1)(b) (18 April 1946).

30 HWA Thirlway, *International Customary Law and Codification: An Examination of the Continuing Role of Custom in the Present Period of Codification of International Law* (AW Sijthoff 1972) 76.

31 Thirlway (n 30) 71.

32 See generally Melissa J Durkee, 'Space Law as Twenty-First Century International Law' (November 2023) 6(1) J of Law & Innovation 12, 23 (addressing The Artemis Accords: Principles for Cooperation in the Civil Exploration and Use of the Moon, Mars, Comets, and Asteroids for Peaceful Purposes, U.S. National Aeronautics and Space Agency (13 October 2020).

33 See Ram S Jakhu and Steven Freeland, 'The Relationship Between the Outer Space Treaty and Customary International Law' (2016) 59th IISL Colloquium on the Law of Outer Space, 67th International Astronautical Congress 7–8.

34 See Melissa de Zwart, Stacey Henderson, and Michelle Neumann, 'Space Resource Activities and the Evolution of International Space Law' (October 2023) 211 Acta Astronautica 155, 161 (concluding that a lack of clarity persists whether domestic space law and multilateral agreements will lead to new customary international space law, given the high threshold for crystallization).

35 Jakhu and Freeland (n 33) 2.

start not fresh, but fresher. Ideally, they will develop new customary law that enables human individuals to reside together and recognise their role as caretakers not merely for the 'benefit and interest of all countries' but for the benefit and interest of humanity in the universe. As new customary law evolves over centuries into more complex and tailored legal structures in outer space, legal structures defining an ordered society will need to better reflect a dedication to balance, such as balancing the natural human need for both privacy and social interaction and both self-interest and an interest in caring for others. This last component has been undervalued in the space law discourse, a short-sighted view when reflecting that long-term human survival is not a guarantee in the far reaches of space.

In our early Space Age, legal structures have been dominated by multinational corporate pressure on the power of individual governments, as well as military funding.[36] Some suggest that this is the norm for human exploration. That is, 500 years of history have shown that even if scientists act on benign intellectual curiosity, they set neither the agenda nor the use of their inventions funded by governmental and corporate interests, including military agendas.[37] That this is reflected in space law could have been foreseen, where, in the 20th and 21st centuries, the international treaties addressing as yet untouched regions share the interests of those who could financially and logistically afford to explore and develop the regions, including the high seas and deep sea beds, polar regions, cyber and electromagnetic space on Earth, and near-Earth and orbital regions in space.[38] It is doubtful that the space exploration community is any more collegial than any other human enterprise,[39] but it aspires to promote cooperation.

The United Nations Commission on the Peaceful Uses of Outer Space generally seeks to create order through five treaties and five principles, considering arms control, freedom of exploration, safety and rescue of humans, and the settlement of disputes.[40] Much seems aspirational, legal fictions of a concept of equality borne in the West but never fully attained in the West where social hierarchies permit human inequity to persist on a large scale. Yet the aspirations are worthy. Article I of the United Nations Charter, for example, states as its objective: 'To maintain international peace and security, and to that end . . . to bring about by peaceful means . . . adjustment or settlement of international disputes or situations which might lead to

36 von der Dunk (n 3) 21 (noting that the first cosmonauts and astronauts were military personnel).

37 Yuval Noah Harari, *Sapiens: A Brief History of Humankind* (Harper Collins 2015) 273–74 (describing a 'feedback loop' in the last 500 years between science, imperialism, and capitalism).

38 Delbert D Smith, *Space Stations: International Law and Policy* (Westview Press 1979) 20 (acknowledging that as the United States was initially the primary nation with a space shuttle program, its national priorities would govern its priorities, including addressing any challenges to its funding policies related to the use of outer space).

39 Pierre Lévy, 'The Invention of the Computer' in Michel Serres (ed), *A History of Scientific Thought: Elements of a History of Science* (Bordas tr, Blackwell 1995) 636, 663 (describing the invention of computers as a struggle of disparate ideas, attempts at misappropriation, and endless court cases regarding intellectual property rights).

40 United Nations, 'Office for Outer Space Affairs, Committee on the Peaceful Uses of Outer Space' <https://www.unoosa.org/oosa/en/ourwork/copuos/index.html> accessed 21 August 2021.

a breach of the peace.'[41] Surely this expressed agreement, although more contractual than legislative, will remain necessary in the near future as space exploration involves interactions among governments and multinational corporations. Many smaller island nations, as early as 1972, collaborated with 'launcher nations' for satellite telecommunication service, and 102 nations had already joined the International Telecommunications Satellite Organization (INTELSTAT).[42]

Aspirations may conflict with historical realities, of course. Imperialism and conquest throughout human history have wrought the destruction of extensive social structures across the globe. Today, we continue to see this, as shown by the discovery of the mistreatment and death of many young indigenous schoolchildren taken from their homes by Western colonial settlements for the purpose of forced acculturation.[43] Non-Western societies have also relied on hierarchy and social inequity to ensure cooperation and survival at the expense of individual well-being.[44] And yet, what was lost can be regained at times. In 2021, for example, 1.25 million acres of bison ranging land in Montana in the United States was returned to the indigenous peoples who had cared for the land for centuries.[45] Despite increasing evidence of an interconnected global society, the negotiations by individuals and between sovereign states over what constitutes expectations of justice and customary international law remain actively in flux.

International human rights treaties reflect an aspirational quality, where loose and sporadic enforcement and evidence of restraint are deliberate in order to bring state parties to the table without much fear of recourse. As a result, '[h]umanitarian conventions may have lesser prospects for actual compliance than other multilateral treaties, even though they enjoy stronger moral support.'[46] Legal nonconformance in the form of human rights violations such as human torture may be widespread; however, judicial reluctance to abandon expressed human rights or to concede an emergence of new, less humane customary law has been characterised as 'essential for the preservation of an international public order.'[47]

(b) The Incompatibility of Custom, Ideals, and Natural Law as Bases of International Law

A tribunal could see that evolving custom is 'an accumulation of acts contrary to existing law' and eventually 'establish new law' where it is *lex posterior derogat*

41 Article 1(1) of the UN Charter.

42 Smith (n 8) 64.

43 See for example, Susan Montoya Bryan, 'Legal Group Backs U.S. Review of Indigenous Boarding Schools' *PBS Newshour* (US, 10 August 2021, 4:49 PM EDT), at Legal group backs U.S. review of Indigenous boarding schools | PBS NewsHour (including a federal mandate to investigate the 'root causes of human rights abuses' at the school).

44 See for example, JW Jandora, 'Developments in Islamic Warfare: The Early Conquests' (1986) 64 Studia Islamica 101.

45 Robert McDonald, 'Coming Full Circle' *National Wildlife Magazine, The National Wildlife Federation* (August–September 2021) <Coming Full Circle (nwf.org)>

46 Meron (n 28) 44.

47 Meron (n 28) 57–58 (quoting Oscar Schachter, 'In Defense of International Rules on the Use of Force' (1986) 53 University of Chicago Law Review 113, 131).

priori.[48] Applying international customary law in new outer space frontiers will have its critics. On Earth, the proliferation of international human rights treaties has been described as the product of a narrow, Western, and insufficiently capacious view of the diversity of human societies and ways of life on Earth.[49] The relatively new 2007 United Nations Declaration on the Rights of Indigenous Peoples demonstrates an effort to respect greater diversity, providing cognisable rights and a forum to assert the rights of indigenous persons against a sovereign state.[50] Historically, customary international law has justified human slavery[51] and discrimination against women, for example.[52] In contrast, customary international law has been implemented as support by the High Court of Australia to prohibit racial discrimination,[53] and for the United States Supreme Court to prohibit the criminal execution of juvenile inmates.[54]

In other words, normative human rights are founded less in custom than in ideals and, perhaps, notions of natural law common to all humanity. Nevertheless, natural law as a foundation for customary international law has also been used to defend both 'slavery and freedom; hierarchy and equality; revolution and reaction.'[55] The postwar Geneva Conventions of 1949 for the Protection of Victims of War chose to bind parties that withdraw from the Conventions, on the basis of natural and customary law: 'by virtue of the principles of the law of nations, as they result from the usages established among civilized peoples, from the laws of humanity and the dictates of the public conscience.'[56] Also, treaties related to controversial human rights are not only binding between states, but will apply to each nation's treatment of its own citizens.[57]

Hierarchies based on appearance or the vagaries of birth resulting in enslavement or other discriminatory treatment have met eventually with modern universal declarations against slavery and racism, resulting in anti-discrimination laws, resolutions, and human rights treaties.[58] However, the practice of such discrimination in reality remains rife, such as discrimination based on gender identity or disability,

48 Thirlway (n 30) 131.

49 See Kristen A Carpenter and Angela R Riley, 'Indigenous Peoples and the Jurisgenerative Moment in Human Rights' (2014) 102 California Law Review 173; Arvind Sharma, *Are Human Rights Western? A Contribution to the Dialogue of Civilizations* (OUP 2006).

50 United Nations Declaration on the Rights of Indigenous Peoples (13 September 2007) A/RES/61/295.

51 See, for example, *The Antelope* [1825] 23 U.S. 64 (common usage of the slave trade is not contrary to the Law of Nations); but see *U.S. v. The La Jeune Eugenie* [1822] 2 Mason 409, 26 Fed. Cas. 832 (Mass.) (invoking the Law of Nations as reflecting the abolition of slavery).

52 Meron (n 28) 95 (citing *Restatement of the Law (Third), Foreign Relations Law of the United States* § 702).

53 *Koowarta v. Bjekle-Petersen & Others* [1985] 68 Int'l L. Rep. 181.

54 *Roper v. Simmons* [2005] 543 U.S. 551.

55 Sigmund (n 26) 206.

56 Meron (n 28) 6 (citing the Common Article 63/62/142/158).

57 Meron (n 28) 18 (noting the Inter-American Court of Human Rights Advisory Opinion (1982)).

58 See, e.g., Universal Declaration of Human Rights (10 December 1948) A/RES/217 A, Art. 4 ('No one shall be held in slavery or servitude; slavery and the slave trade shall be prohibited in all their forms.').

and cultural practices based on religious belief, marriage, childrearing, and political association. Inherent conflicts may arise with respect to nations within nations, such as the expansion of indigenous rights under international law where indigenous practices may violate human rights instruments.[59] International law, including international space law, will not alone effect positive change, particularly if the law does not reflect the interests of those subject to it.

International customary law has not unified the globe, where nations vociferously protect their sovereignty and national and regional interests and social structures. Thus, it is not the obvious framework or panacea for outer space settlements. Perhaps most impactful, the sovereignty of nations within a framework of the law of property ownership persists, as shown by Justice Story's opinion in his 1822 opinion in the United States circumscribing the nature of a civil society as a matter of international customary law, a decision entered more than a century before international human rights treaties:

> Principles no less fundamental, and asserted by all writers, and sanctioned by universal assent, are the sovereignty of each state within its own territories. And that *each nation may regulate every interior interest without giving offence, and without accountability to any other nation*. The form of government, and mode of administration; religion and mode of worship; what shall be deemed to be property, and what shall not be; the mode of acquisition, possession, and alienation; what acts shall be deemed crimes, and what forfeitures shall ensue, are all subjects which each nation reserves to itself.[60]

Usurping the land rights of indigenous peoples within a sovereign state, as a matter of conquest, has remained a point of contention, particularly considering that many natural law scholars and classical philosophers have supported a right of conquest, themselves citizens of colonial empires.[61] In Australia, for example, amendments related to indigenous land title were subject to challenge by indigenous groups 'on the grounds of constitutional invalidity and as contravening Australia's international legal obligations.'[62] International space law has sought to hold back the natural self-interest of nations and individuals with respect to property rights in space, but those efforts now face numerous challenges with respect to the proliferation of satellites and the interest in resources extraction on celestial bodies.

59 Rebecca Gross, 'The 'I' in Indigenous: Enforcing Individual Rights Guarantees in an Indigenous group Rights Context' (2010) 23 New York International Law Review 65 (focusing on indigenous women's rights in Mexico).

60 *U.S. v. The La Jeune Eugenie* [1822] 2 Mason 409, 26 Fed. Cas. 832 (Mass.) (emphasis added).

61 See Federico Lenzerini, 'Sovereignty Revisited: International Law and Parallel Sovereignty of Indigenous Peoples' (2006) 42 Texas Int'l L.J. 155.

62 See, e.g., Gary D Meyers and Sally Raine, 'Australian Aboriginal Land Rights in Transition (Part II): The Legislative Response to the High Court's Native Title Decisions in *Mabo v. Queensland* and *Wik v. Queensland* (2001) 9 Tulsa J. Contemp. & Int'l L. 95, 167.

Outer space, at present, is stateless to a degree. Article II of the Outer Space Treaty of 1967 declares that celestial bodies are 'not subject to national appropriation by claim of sovereignty.'[63] Individual nations have internally interpreted this restriction in their own way. For example, the United States Department of Defense asserts that with respect to the vertical boundary between airspace and outer space, outer space 'is not subject to the sovereignty of any State.'[64] However, this department has also noted, 'The upper limit of airspace subject to national jurisdiction has not been authoritatively defined by international law. International practice has established that airspace terminates at some point below the point at which artificial satellites can be placed in orbit without free-falling to earth.'[65] In addition, the Department holds the position that 'the space systems of all nations have rights of passage through space without interference.'[66] Lack of clarity in international law lends itself to the self-interest of nations. If international space treaties fail to curb human interest in acquiring property, the same may be argued with respect to war and self-defence:

> None of [the outer space treaties] has any specific provision that indicates whether the parties intended that the agreement apply in wartime. There appears to be a strong argument that the principle of noninterference established by these agreements is inconsistent with a state of hostilities, at least where the systems concerned are of such high military value that there is a strong military imperative for the adversary to be free to interfere with them, even to the extent of destroying the satellites in the system.[67]

In New Zealand, national outer space law considers national security and industry interests.[68] However, self-interest may coalesce with broader beneficial interests, such as New Zealand's orbital debris mitigation plan, including disposal 'in a way that minimizes risks to, or in, Earth's environment and in the space environment (including the risk of collisions).'[69]

–Military conduct in outer space represents some of our worst fears.[70] International law is ill-equipped to address it when it has arisen from a history of conquest

63 The Outer Space Treaty, Treaty on Principles Governing the Activities of States in the Exploration and Use of Outer Space, Including the Moon and Other Celestial Bodies [27 January1967] 610 UNTS 205, 18 UST 2410, TIAS No. 6347, A/RES/2222/XXI, Art. II.

64 United States Office of General Counsel, Department of Defense, *Department of Defense Law of War Manual* (June 2015, updated May 2016) § 14.2.2, at p. 896, note 40.

65 United States Office of General Counsel, Department of Defense (n 64) § 14.2.2, 896.

66 United States Office of General Counsel, Department of Defense (n 64) § 14.10.1, 914.

67 United States Office of General Counsel, Department of Defense (n 64) § 14.10.2.1, at p. 915, note 153.

68 New Zealand Outer Space and High-Altitude Activities 2017, s 3 (Purpose).

69 New Zealand Outer Space and High-Altitude Activities (Licenses and Permits) Regulation 2017, s 13(2)(c)(iv), 2017/250.

70 Stephen B Johnson, 'The Political Economy of Spaceflight' in Steve J Dick and Roger D Launius (eds), *Societal Impact of Spaceflight* (NASA 2007) 141, 142 (describing the reasoning for initial

and mutual suspicion. Should conflicts of interpretation arise, or domestic remedies prove inadequate, international bodies such as the United Nations Human Rights Commission have little to offer in the form of relief other than declarations.[71] According to Rebecca Gross, 'the problem is not a lack of *de jure* [domestic and international] laws protecting gender equality, or the equal right to political participation, but rather, a lack of clear mechanisms by which to enforce those laws.'[72] In The Hague, the International Court of Justice and the International Criminal Court, a court of last resort for the prosecution of genocide and crimes against humanity, emphasise mediation and conciliation, not an international system of enforceable punitive sanctions.[73]

Thus, to apply international space law to vulnerable, remote outer space communities would not offer much in the way of protection. International law is a framework that upholds state sovereignty[74] and those living in space frontiers may have views of political existence that do not involve statehood. Should the legitimacy of state sovereignty under international law require a government, 'representative of the people living in the territory upon which it extends its scope,'[75] that legitimacy may not be supported in fact by the will of a people who do not seek to be democratised. Legitimacy must rest on agreed upon principles and aims for humanity, which, if inherent and self-evident, necessitates a reflection on the possibilities of a modern understanding of natural law.[76]

3 The Ethereal Foundations of Natural Law in the Space Frontier

In the outposts of outer space, it is expected that the diversity of societal formation over millennia on Earth will produce a diversity of societal formation on other planets and space communities. This is already happening with respect to limiting cultural practices in space, such as the questionable funerary right to blast ashes into space as a matter of federal law in the United States.[77] Embracing a re-examination of natural law in our current Space Age, rather than an ossification of international space law, is a promising approach for a creative and flexible strategy for future survival.

---

satellite launches by the military as seeking to attain the 'high ground' for reconnaissance of the activities of 'adversaries').

71 Meron (n 28) 142.

72 Gross (n 59) 65, 106.

73 See generally Sandy Gandhi, 'Human Rights and the International Court of Justice, The *Ahmadi Sadio Diallo* Case' (2011) 11 Human Rights Law Review 527.

74 See, e.g., United Nations, International Criminal Court <https://www.icc-cpi.int/about/how-the-court-works> accessed 21 August 2021.

75 Lenzerini (n 61) 160.

76 See Jean-Jacques Rosseau, *A Discourse on Inequality* (Maurice Cranston tr, first published 1755, Penguin Books 1984) 70 ('for it to be a law, not only must the will of the being it obliges be able to obey it consciously, but also, for it to be natural, it must be spoken directly by the voice of nature').

77 William A. Drennan, 'Hire the Funeral Clowns, Blast My Ashes Into Orbit, and Deduct It All!' (March/April 2021) Probate & Property, American Bar Association 27.

Despite centuries of Western classical philosophy addressing human nature and its interest in order through reason, there is remarkably little agreement on any fundamental interest in natural law apart from a self-evident interest in survival. Justifiable hierarchies based on biological differences in gender and reproductive roles have proved elusive, refuted time and again with examples of a variety of gender roles in a variety of societal structures.[78] Hierarchies based on age have fared better, with universal recognition of the long developmental stage of humanity's infancy into adulthood and the need for adult humans to protect and carefully cultivate the lives of infants and children. Yet, space travel has thus far been devoid of youth and family, relegated to the realm of a handful of individual, mostly male, adults with no family relationship to each other. However, reflecting on human nature promotes preparation for societies in space built on more reasoned perceptions of healthy human relationships. Natural law also has the advantage of its role in the foundations of customary international space law and positive law generally. In essence, natural law theory purportedly provides a more useful framework to address how humans fundamentally and reasonably guide their own actions, wherever they live, historically applying a lens of practical rationality, political theory, or religious morality.[79]

Arguably, the theory of natural law has reflected the human more than nature. In the 17th century, Thomas Hobbes suggested that our ability to reason would elevate us from the violence of our natural state,[80] while John Locke trusted that the human capacity for reason showed inherent goodness from birth allowing us 'to order our affairs correctly.'[81] A century later, Rousseau put forth that the natural, unreasoned man was the better man, where reason and complex civilisation have a tendency to corrupt.[82] All of these men, writing in a time of active conquest and colonialism, would force freedom on some but forcibly deprive it to others, all while espousing the idealism of a common good.

We are all born into an existing societal order, and yet it is anything but static. Anthropologist Clifford Geertz asserted, 'it may be in the cultural particularities of people—in their oddities—that some of the most instructive revelations of what is to be generically human are to be found.'[83] Even those born in new, isolated space colonies will require a lengthy period of nurturing, which inevitably entails acculturation and the skill to socially adapt. Immanuel Kant asked, 'what is the real significance of freedom in a universe not of our own making?'[84] To that one could respond that it is the experience and perception of freedom that affects the quality

78 Kathryn Abrams, 'From Autonomy to Agency: Feminist Perspective on Self-Direction,' (1999) 40 William & Mary Law Review 805, 820 ('These complex, contingent, intersectional patterns create a vast mosaic of socially-engendered practices and responses that are difficult to generalize about or to predict in advance.').

79 Mark C Murphy, *Natural Law and Practical Rationality* (CUP 2001) 3–4.

80 Sigmund (n 26) 77.

81 Lloyd L Weinreb, *Natural Law and Justice* (Harvard UP 1987) 78.

82 Weinreb (n 81) 84; Sigmund (n 26) 123.

83 Clifford Geertz, *The Interpretation of Cultures* (Basic Books 1973) 43.

84 Weinreb (n 81) 94.

of life, as well as our devotion to others and the health of our social relationships. The human species will remain a social creature by choice and by necessity, which any legal structure must foster and protect.

If human civilisations represent a determinate natural order, classical Western philosophers have considered that positive laws enforcing such order are adhered to more easily, enabling the growth of larger societies through reason and shared morality or at least a shared goal of a good life. From Aristotelian logic regarding the common good to the medieval European Thomistic assertions of a divinely given self-determination within the natural order, laws are only effective if they are supported.[85] This is where international space law with its reticence to address humanity's potential for conflict and greed falls short. Laws perceived to be immoral may justify a right to equity or even revolution under natural law.[86] More recently, American jurist Oliver Wendell Holmes asserted, '[i]t is commonly known that the early forms of legal procedure were grounded in vengeance,' as a response to intentional wrongs.[87] He connects early resolution by the violence of feud to the structured hearings of grievances in court.[88] If Holmes is correct, he does not provide a reason why vengeance might be sought, such as instinctual reaction or a reasoned choice to set an example to avoid future conflict.[89] Holmes instead suggests that the reason is elusive:

> In the course of centuries the custom, belief, or necessity disappears, but the rule remains. The reason which gave rise to the rule has been forgotten, and ingenious minds set themselves to inquire how it is to be accounted for. Some ground of policy is thought of, which seems to explain it and to reconcile it with the present state of things; and then the rule adapts itself to the new reasons which have been found for it, and enters on a new career.[90]

Human individuals are not as conformist as Holmes would suggest, or at least they may not be content even if they are conformist. When promoting opportunities for legal development in future space law, disrespecting humanity's need to thrive as individuals in society will come at a cost. Already, the commercial and capitalist enterprises that currently supply the capital to fund space exploration often encourages speed in acquisition and assent—'rapid, massive diffusion of new

85 See Murphy (n 79) 46 (defining Aristotle's natural law theory as welfarist to achieve well-being beyond a limited hedonist interpretation); Weinreb (n 81) 31 (providing the example of Plato's *Laws* at 10.903, in which the individual works 'for the sake of the whole, directing his effort towards the common good').

86 Weinreb (n 81) 4. Sophocles' *Antigone*, written around 440 B.C.E., is often cited as one of the earliest popular justifications for civil resistance to tyranny—'Great words by men of pride/bring greater blows upon them.' *Id.* at 21–23 ('the first great heroine of civil resistance').

87 Oliver Wendell Holmes, Jr., *The Common Law* (first published 1881, Barnes & Noble, Inc. 2004) 2.

88 Holmes, Jr. (n 87) 2.

89 See, e.g., Harari (n 37) 107 (describing the use of force to ensure cooperation in food production, protection against enemies, and the expansion of territory as a means of the security and survival of a society of millions).

90 Holmes, Jr. (n 87) 4.

technology.'[91] Given the poor and unpredictable track record of imperialist conquest and commercialisation and its disruptive impact on the well-being of human societies, this grab for competition and avoidance of government regulation is ill advised. Natural law theorists acknowledge humanity's competitive nature along with other characteristics that provide balance and sustainable relationships.

Modern critics have debated whether the development of Western natural law should include an innate capacity for compassion and care and the desire to avoid the oppression of others. Repeated examples of this abound in both Western and non-Western conceptions of law. For example, the Code of Hammurabi, attributed to the king of the Babylonian Empire around 1,770 B.C.E., is a code of justice and retribution, expressing that its purpose is 'to make justice prevail in the land, to abolish the wicked and the evil, [and] to prevent the strong from oppressing the weak.'[92] At least 1,500 years ago, the Buddhist canon espoused the liberation of all beings from suffering, not merely humans, where 'life is suffering; the cause of suffering is greed; [and] suffering can be ceased by the elimination of greed.'[93] This is achieved through abstinence of certain harmful conduct, as well as the practice of kindness, compassion, and equanimity.[94] Around 1270, Thomas Aquinas in *The Summa Theologica* proposed, 'the rational creature is subject to divine providence in a most excellent way . . . by being provident both for itself and others.'[95] As a supporter of a modern democratic ideal that accommodates diversity, John Stuart Mill put forth in 1859 that full freedom of the individual should be granted as long as such freedom does not impinge upon the freedom of others.[96]

International space law treaties do invoke a common interest in helping others, such as the Rescue Agreement,[97] but not in a comprehensive manner that could easily be applied to human settlement in space. While the suppositions of natural law theorists have an ethereal quality that could arguably be as loosely interpreted as international customary law, what we now have is the benefit of more research and experience on the needs of humanity since the last century. Modern space pioneers should be better informed about the benefits and risks we pose to ourselves and to others, which should in turn enhance choices made with respect to future legal and societal structures.

4 Incorporating a Modern Understanding of Human Nature Into Natural Law Theory and Future Customary Space Law

If one considers natural law as the foundation of customary law, it could be argued that the suffering and inequality extant in complex modern societies on Earth

91 Smith (n 38) 76.

92 Harari (n 37) 106.

93 Sovan Tun, 'Relational Suffering: Causes and Liberation According to Buddhism' [Oct. 2015] 4 J. Dialogue & Culture 38, 39.

94 Tun (n 93) 41.

95 Sigmund (n 26) 52.

96 Weinreb (n 81) 135; Sigmund (n 26) 149.

97 Agreement on the Rescue of Astronauts, the Return of Astronauts and the Return of Objects Launched Into Outer Space (entered into force 3 December 1968), 672 UNTS 119, 19 UST7570.

reveals a perversion of our natural state. Another way to consider humanity's history of conflict is to recognise why we have survived despite those conflicts.

(a) Missing the Obvious

A right to self-defence and self-preservation are well-established elements of natural law, apparent in the focus on the need to control military actions in international space law. But life is much more than mere survival for the human species, which will be true in future Earth and outer space communities. In modern philosophy, John Finnis suggested a requirement of nine basic aspects for human well-being: 'life, knowledge, aesthetic experience, excellence in play and work, excellence in agency, inner peace, friendship and community, religion, and happiness.'[98] The aspect 'life' is the preservation or protection of one's own life,[99] but nowhere does he assert devotion to the preservation or protection of others. Several concepts that are integral to human nature but left out of much of the space law literature are discussed as follows.

(i) Joy and Compassion

Numerous conceptions of natural law have failed to consider that there is joy in selfless acts, considering the interests of others not merely as a consequentialist intelligent act, but as an act that contributes to individual and societal feelings of well-being. For example, philosopher Mark Murphy argues against discrimination, lying, and 'callousness,' because they are wasteful and inefficient,[100] not because they create suffering and misery. A desire for joy, contentment, and appreciation of others must be paramount in considering the quality of life of space pioneers and their ability to sustain life for future generations.

Historically, natural law has not fully contemplated that individual well-being should be promoted. In 1670, Grotius put forth that nature for humans and other animals seeks the preservation of life, including the right to use force in self-defence.[101] He then adds a much more specific universal right of human burial in war as a question of compassion and the dignity of man, but also because it is repugnant to the feelings of men to see 'our perishable nature.'[102] This suggests the need in future space colonies for human ritual with respect for the emergence of life and the inevitability of death. Nevertheless, he also asserted a natural right to plunder the enemy, even of 'sacred' items,[103] and a right to the conquest of land as payment of the debt of war,[104] both of which in modern times would meet with

98 Murphy (n 79) 96.
99 Murphy (n 79) 101.
100 Murphy (n 79) 239.
101 Hugo Grotius, *The Rights of War and Peace, Including the Law of Nature and of Nations* (AC Campbell tr, first published as *De Jure Belli ac Pacis* in 1670, 1901) 32.
102 Grotius (n 101) 215.
103 Grotius (n 101) 332–33.
104 Grotius (n 101) 335.

disapproval. A modern conception of natural law would expand not only upon the dignitary interests of humanity, but also upon the psychological and mental health needs for well-being in space travel and settlement.[105]

(ii) A Focus on Family

Many classical philosophers, including natural law theorists, happen to be men living in times of social discord and discontent who have been marginalised or exiled at some point. They tend to eschew a manifest appreciation for the core unit of society—the family.[106] Rousseau, for example, expressly wrote against the family unit, stating, '[h]is appetite satisfied, the man has no longer any need of the woman, nor the woman of one particular man.'[107] In contrast, long before Rousseau, the Roman writer and poet Ovid carefully set out stories of family devotion and willing sacrifice among husbands and wives, such as Pyrrha and Deucalian, the last humans on Earth.[108] He also wrote passionately of the bond between parent and child, such as the story of Daedalus suffering when his son Icarus flew too close to the sun.[109] 'His lips, calling to the last upon his father's name, were drowned in the dark blue sea.'[110] An instinct for care and affection should never have been disparaged as sentimental or weak in classical theory, nor should it be relegated as unnecessary to legal discourse on human exploration in space.

The health of the family structure and the freedom of the members within it should also be prioritised. While Jeremy Bentham in 19th-century England suggested that the family represents simplicity, common sense, and the value of unwritten law, his model was one of domestic hierarchy without valuing the gender equality cherished in a more reasoned society today. He wrote, 'But in the bosom of his family, the lawyer, by the force of good sense, returns to this simple method [of dictating the rule of law] from which he is led astray at the bar by the folly of learning.'[111] Gender equality is not only a component of human well-being but also one which biologically impacts the prospect of human survival in outer space. Much Western natural law theory has insisted on the subjugation of women by men

105 See Jennifer Brobst, 'Public Health Common Law in Space' in Sandeepa Bhat B and Shouvik Kumar Guha (eds), *Fundamentals of National Space Laws* (Thomson Reuters 2022) 285, 293–95.

106 See, for example, Rosseau (n 76) 34 (explaining in the Introduction that Rousseau was often ostracized). 'Family' is meant in its broadest sense here, thus, for example, Jeremy Bentham would not be included in this list of lonely philosophers where he had numerous academic disciples in his lifetime and died unmarried but surrounded by friends. *Jeremy Bentham, Stanford Encyclopedia of Philosophy* (8 December 2021) <https://plato.stanford.edu/entries/bentham/>.

107 See for example, Rosseau (n 76) 34.

108 Ovid (n 25) lines 263–356, at pp. 27–29, and lines 183–235, at pp. 27–28, respectively.

109 Ovid (n 25) lines 263–356, at pp. 27–29, and lines 183–235, at pp. 27–28, respectively.

110 Ovid (n 25) lines 229–30, at pp. 421–22.

111 Jeremy Bentham and J Dumont (eds), *Treatise on Judicial Evidence, Extracted From the Manuscripts of Jeremy Bentham, Esq.* (J.W. Paget 1825) 7.

due to women's reproductive roles in pregnancy and childrearing.[112] While international space law has not taken the opportunity to address equitable social relationships, it is imperative that this component be promoted in any modern concept of natural law and evolving customary international law.

Skills in the domestic sphere are integral to the healthy development of any human society. For example, parenting requires promotion of one's own survival as well as that of the child cared for, cultivating social relationships, communication skills, and the resulting brain development from birth and throughout adulthood.[113] That is, in an isolated community in space, childrearing will still be time-consuming and be, in essence, the way to create humans who know how to survive as humans. In this way, the parent ensures 'group cohesion' through generations and instils an ethic of care by enlisting other family members to assist in raising offspring.[114]

However, recent feminist theorists have suggested that there is little commonality of interest among women outside of their immediate family and social structure, particularly in postcolonial multiethnic societies that imposed brutal racist and sexist practices upon indigenous women. It must be understood in preparing for new societies off-planet that, here on Earth, 'while gender is a potential bond, women participate in the oppression of other women all over the world.'[115] Instead, we should be aware that we are loyal not to large identifiable groups but to smaller sets of people with whom we are familiar. This is how humanity supports the other natural law elements, such as self-preservation, freedom, and self-defence. However, the latter is a matter of last resort, whereas close social interaction is a daily investment in general human well-being.

According to anthropological research, individuals across the globe thrive through a smaller network of intimate relationships, which 'appear to be among the most stable, fundamental features of human nature.'[116] Images of space travel often conjure up extreme social isolation and quiet, but humanity cannot sustain itself in this manner. For example, from a medical perspective, touch and reassurance positively impacts human heart rates, sleep, and immune system responses,[117] as shown by both infant and elder studies related to neglect.[118] Thus, a simple, solitary

112 See for example *Bradwell v. Illinois* [1873] 83 U.S. 130 (justifying the denial of a right for a woman to a license to practice law because the Court perceived that it was the paramount destiny and mission of women to be a wife and mother).

113 Mary Ellen Morbeck, Allison Galloway and Adrienne L. Zihlman (eds), *The Evolving Female, A Life-History Perspective* (Princeton UP 1997) xiv.

114 Morbeck, Galloway and Zihlman (eds) (n 113) xiv.

115 Cheryl Johnson-Odim, 'Common Themes, Differing Contexts: Third World Women and Feminism' in Chandra Talpade Mohanty and others (eds), *Third World Women and the Politics of Feminism* (Indiana UP 1991) 314, 325.

116 Barbara B. Smuts, 'Social Relationships and Life Histories of Primates' in Mary Ellen Morbeck, Allison Galloway, and Adrienne L Zihlman (eds), *The Evolving Female, A Life-History Perspective* (Princeton UP 1997) 60, 60.

117 Smuts (n 116) 62.

118 See, e.g., Evan L Ardiel and Catharine Rankin, 'The Importance of Touch in Development' (2010) 15 Paediatric Child Health 153; E. Bush, 'The Use of Human Touch to Improve the Well-Being of Older Adults. A Holistic Nursing Intervention' (2001) 19 Journal of Holistic Nursing 256.

survival instinct as the basis of natural law is astonishingly meagre when considering the benefits humanity has to offer the universe should it utilise its capacity for order, reason, compassion, and care of others. That we can conceive of an order beyond mere survival and self-interest is evidence that it can be accomplished in exploration and life in outer space.

(iii) Pre-Empting Humanity's Flaws and Weaknesses

If a reasoned instinct for self-preservation, autonomy, social interaction, and a sense of care and compassion comprise essential components of natural law, there are certainly negative aspects of human nature which are also inherently present. Promotion of inequity and excessive competition increase a sense of futility and lack of agency, particularly when power structures are far removed from those subject to their control.[119] As inequity persists, human history has shown that the hypocrisy of governmental promises of liberty and equality or totalitarian protection undermines the stability of nations.[120]

Technology, science, and medicine promote the interests of the individual and care for others, not only for their beneficial impacts but for the creative act of innovation itself. While the freedom to innovate supports creative autonomy and self-determination, it clearly poses a danger if conducted without societal restraint, serving as a tool of aggression and conquest, for example. As a matter of natural law, that innovative spirit must be fostered in a measured way, which is demonstrated in the field of space law by the need to balance the spectacular benefits of satellite technology with the problems of orbital debris.[121] We should also promote the avoidance of cultural imperialism, constraining the rich diversity of the arts and cultural practice that is largely governed by unwritten law and social relationships. Wisely, one area of law that colonial powers more often left to the diversity of regional control was that of family law, where the need for codification and certainty was less than it was for commercial law and the risks of revolt much greater due to the importance of family to the individual.[122]

One of humanity's greatest frailties is that although our species has a strong capacity for memory, we are born with no knowledge at all. Thus, mechanisms, including legal mechanisms, need to be promoted for any future society to ensure retention of knowledge and training so that each generation can progress. Since at least 3,500 B.C.E., with Sumerian writing, the human invention of a system of storing and

119 Weinreb (n 81) 136.

120 Arvind Sharma, *Are Human Rights Western? A Contribution to the Dialogue of Civilizations* (OUP 2006) 149 (listing evidence of mass violations of human rights by the West, including apartheid, racial oppression in the United States, toxic waste dumping by multinational corporations, and the Union Carbide Bhopal plant disaster).

121 See Tomasz Balcerzak and Rongeet Poddar, 'Mitigating Space Debris Under the National Space Laws: An Appraisal' in Sandeepa Bhat B and Shouvik Kumar Guha (eds), *Fundamentals of National Space Laws* (Thomson Reuters 2022) 199.

122 David C Buxbaum, 'Introduction' in David C Buxbaum (ed), *Family Law and Customary Law in Asia: A Contemporary Legal Perspective* (Martinus Nijhoff, The Hague 1968) xxxviii.

processing information outside of our brains, preserved through time, has allowed the significant accumulation and cataloguing of knowledge in our species.[123] The accumulation of knowledge and experience will be all the more critical for frontier communities in outer space, if they are particularly isolated from each other.

(b) Forging Ahead

Natural law concepts are meant to provide the tools for a healthy order and structure in human society, concepts so inherent that most humans could come to social agreements on their basis. Such tools, including a desire for self-preservation, autonomy, and positive social relationships, obligate our species to exert its agency in a beneficial manner that allows any future society, on Earth or in space, to thrive. Our earliest ventures into space have shown that we have the capacity to achieve this. For example, multilateral agreements have generated international law and 'the principle of consensus' as guidance for the multinational crew of the International Space Station in making medical decisions and responding to public health emergencies.[124] Nonetheless, asserting here that a better understanding of our human nature will illuminate what constitutes a potentially unifying natural law does require the difficult determination of deciding which factors count.[125]

Although it is posited here that outer space human settlements should not be overly reliant on existing legal structures on Earth, particularly international space law and customary law, none of this analysis of human nature and the risks of complex society is meant to suggest that lawlessness is natural or advisable. Humans do, indeed, seek and create order in life.[126] Moreover, we are well aware of the human tendency toward excessive self-interest and the potential for oppression. However, in applying natural law concepts to life in outer space, our knowledge of frontier mentalities may offer some additional insights into human nature. Although the technological aids and social hierarchies were different in humanity's known years of conquest on Earth, the interactions among its people are still informative.

For example, in the westward exploratory period of the United States between 1775 and 1850, accounts by frontiersmen frequently related a desire for rich land they could work and 'make their own.'[127] Hence, the need for autonomy and the desire for property were in evidence. One pioneer wrote, 'it is literally true every Man sets under his own Vine and Fig tree and none to make them afraid.'[128] This perspective was imbued with self-interest and disregard for the resulting denigration of claims of indigenous peoples and the subjugation of enslaved men and women, but such hopes for a better future purportedly 'carried them through the

123 See Harari (n 37) 122.

124 Brobst (n 105) 285, 295.

125 George W Constable, 'Who Can Determine What Natural Law Is?' (1962) 7 Natural Law Forum 58.

126 Sigmund (n 26) viii.

127 Malcolm J Rohrbough, *The Trans-Appalachian Frontier, People, Societies, and the Institutions 1775–1850* (OUP 1978) 397.

128 Rohrbough (n 127) 404 (referencing the Christian Bible at Kings 4:25).

hard struggle.'[129] Not surprisingly, their hopes eventually receded into despair of a future 'filled with the monotony of repetitious hard work' in the new frontier.[130] Pioneers bent on survival and a better future will still desire creative autonomy, variety in life, and sufficient safety and comfort.

For most ordinary pioneers, it was reported, '[e]ven on the distant frontiers men and women remained social people,' traveling in groups, living near enough to provide support, and improvising new social institutions despite the relative chaos and anarchy of a first frontier society.[131] What they sought the most was apparently a means of communication given their extreme isolation and palpable loneliness, superstition, and fatalism.[132] After the first pioneers, new settlers arrived from a more elite, wealthy class, buying up vast tracts of land and offending those pioneers who arrived first with an attitude of noblesse oblige, returning the pioneers to the class divisions and extreme poverty they had hoped to leave behind.[133] Also, political corruption and profiteering were enabled by the relative lawlessness of the frontier landscape, where political leaders took advantage of useless and fraudulent land title, financially destroying pioneer and working class families 'root and branch.'[134] Space profiteering or piracy by individuals, corporations, and national governments is to be anticipated and pre-empted by legal foresight.

Looking forward to future space travel and settlement, humanity has an opportunity to fill in the interstices left by international space law through a modern understanding of human nature and natural law, whether through gradual development of customary law or non-legal shared customs. What we can offer to future settlers is a growing collective memory of humanity and a better understanding of our needs as humans, including concepts not traditionally included in natural law theory such as a need for joy and humour, care and compassion, close and trusted relationships, and creativity and innovation.

5 Conclusion

From wagon trains to rocket ships, absent a post-humanist revolution, the space pioneer's needs in a new frontier will undoubtedly remain much the same, particularly with respect to human social relationships and individual needs. Despite the debate over transposing existing legal frameworks onto the future, the determination of such frameworks do not require a template. Initially, as we tentatively explore outer space closest to Earth, in small groups still tied to Earth's national governments and multinational corporate interests, international space law and negotiation will be practicable and relatively familiar.

129 Rohrbough (n 127) 397.
130 Rohrbough (n 127) 398.
131 Rohrbough (n 127) 5.
132 Rohrbough (n 127) 18 and 401.
133 Rohrbough (n 127) 402 and 406.
134 Abraham Bishop, *Georgia Speculation Unveiled* (first published 14 October 1797, Readex Microprint Corp. 1966) 39.

Over time, new customary international law will develop slowly for orbital space projects, particularly those that are temporary in nature with a home base on Earth. However, settlement in outer space will develop a different legal approach, particularly as international space law has only addressed the efforts of adult astronauts and passengers and has never addressed societal structures in space. Infants and children, the youngest members of our species, will require significant time and effort, as will an eventual aging population. Regional cultural practices would be stifled with excessive rigidity of regulation from a home planet that will feel more and more remote and unfamiliar.

To ensure that our species is resilient in the great expanse of outer space requires self-awareness of human nature, an ability to adapt, and, perhaps most important, preservation of our collective memory. It will be a precarious adventure to settle in the cosmos.[135] While nature is not chaos, we must reluctantly accept that it also does not promise preservation of our species. This reality only portends a greater need to ensure pioneering social structures are not aggressively competitive and that they build on our better qualities of capacity for mutual support and affection, not only for survival but also for quality of life. As Sun Tzu stated over 2,500 years ago: 'The art of war teaches us to rely not on the likelihood of the enemy's not coming, but on our own readiness to receive him.'[136] In the 19th century, Charles Darwin would have agreed, where he defines the struggle for existence as a matter of natural selection, 'including dependence of one being on another, and including . . . not only the life of the individual, but success in leaving progeny.'[137] Hopefully, we can entrust future settlers in outer space with humanity's breadth of knowledge and self-awareness of its needs and gifts.

Bibliography

Kathryn Abrams, 'From Autonomy to Agency: Feminist Perspective on Self-Direction' (1999) 40 William & Mary Law Review 805.

Agreement on the Rescue of Astronauts, the Return of Astronauts and the Return of Objects Launched Into Outer Space (entered into force 3 December 1968), 672 UNTS 119, 19 UST7570.

Humaid Alshamsi and others, 'Space Station Asgardia 2117: From Theoretical Science to a New Nation in Outer Space' (2018) 16 Santa Clara Journal of International Law 37.

Evan L Ardiel and Catharine Rankin, 'The Importance of Touch in Development' (2010) 15 Paediatric Child Health 153.

Tomasz Balcerzak and Rongeet Poddar, 'Mitigating Space Debris Under the National Space Laws: An Appraisal' in Sandeepa Bhat B and Shouvik Kumar Guha (eds), *Fundamentals of National Space Laws* (Thomson Reuters 2022) 199.

Jeremy Bentham and J Dumont (eds), *Treatise on Judicial Evidence, Extracted From the Manuscripts of Jeremy Bentham, Esq.* (J.W. Paget 1825).

135 Yi-Fu Tuan, *Human Goodness* (University of Wisconsin Press 2008) 211 ('The universe is vast, pitch-black, cold, empty, and violent. On one speck of dust called Earth, life emerged to become successively plants, animals, and humans. . . . Conscious life brings 'light' into the universe.').

136 Sun Tzû, *The Art of War* (Fall River Press 2015) Ch. VIII(11), at p. 76.

137 Charles Darwin, *On the Origin of Species* (first published 1859, Harvard UP 1964) 62.

Abraham Bishop, *Georgia Speculation Unveiled* (first published 14 October 1797, Readex Microprint Corp. 1966).
Bradwell v. Illinois [1873] 83 U.S. 130.
Susan Montoya Bryan, 'Legal Group Backs U.S. Review of Indigenous Boarding Schools' *PBS Newshour* (US, 10 August 2021, 4:49 PM EDT).
E Bush, 'The Use of Human Touch to Improve the Well-Being of Older Adults. A Holistic Nursing Intervention' (2001) 19 Journal of Holistic Nursing 256.
David C Buxbaum, 'Introduction' in David C Buxbaum (ed), *Family Law and Customary Law in Asia: A Contemporary Legal Perspective* (Martinus Nijhoff 1968) xxxviii.
Kristen A Carpenter and Angela R. Riley, 'Indigenous Peoples and the Jurisgenerative Moment in Human Rights' (2014) 102 California Law Review 173.
George W Constable, 'Who Can Determine What Natural Law Is?' (1962) 7 Natural Law Forum 58.
Charles Darwin, *On the Origin of Species* (first published 1859, Harvard UP 1964) 62.
Melissa de Zwart, Stacey Henderson, and Michelle Neumann, 'Space Resource Activities and the Evolution of International Space Law' (October 2023) 211 Acta Astronautica 155.
Declaration on International Cooperation in the Exploration and Use of Outer Space for the Benefit and in the Interest of All States, Taking Into Particular Account the Needs of Developing Countries (1996), A/RES/51/122, par.
John Dewey, *Human Nature and Conduct* (Dover Publication 2002).
Yoon Dong-ju, *Counting the Stars at Night: The Complete Works in Verse and Prose* (Insoo Lee tr, Resource Publications 2022) 45.
William A Drennan, 'Hire the Funeral Clowns, Blast My Ashes into Orbit, and Deduct It All!' (March/April 2021) Probate & Property, American Bar Association 27.
Melissa J Durkee, 'Space Law as Twenty-First Century International Law' (November 2023) 6(1) Journal of Law & Innovation 12, 23.
Avigail Ferdman, 'Human Flourishing and Technology Affordances' (2024) 34 Philosophy & Technology 1.
Sandy Gandhi, 'Human Rights and the International Court of Justice, The *Ahmadi Sadio Diallo* Case' (2011) 11 Human Rights Law Review 527.
Clifford Geertz, *The Interpretation of Cultures* (Basic Books 1973).
Vera Gowlland-Debbas, 'Introductory Remarks' in Vera Gowlland-Debbas (ed), *Multilateral Treat-Making: The Current Status of Challenges to and Reforms Needed in the International Legislative Process, papers presented as the Forum Geneva, 5/16/98* (Martinus Nijhoff Publishers 2000) 1.
Rebecca Gross, 'The 'I' in Indigenous: Enforcing Individual Rights Guarantees in an Indigenous group Rights Context' (2010) 23 New York International Law Review 65.
Hugo Grotius, *The Rights of War and Peace, Including the Law of Nature and of Nations* (AC Campbell tr, first published as *De Jure Belli ac Pacis* in 1670, 1901).
Vita Gudeleviciute, 'Does the Principle of Self-Determination Prevail over the Principle of Territorial Integrity?' (April 2005) 2(2) International Journal of Baltic Law 48.
Yuval Noah Harari, *Sapiens: A Brief History of Humankind* (Harper Collins 2015).
Donna Haraway, *Manifestly Haraway* (University of Minnesota Press 2016).
Hearing before the Subcommittee on Space, 'Next Steps to Mars: Deep Space Habitats' 114th Congress, No 114–78 (18 May 2016).
David J Hill, 'Introduction' in Hugo Grotius (ed), *The Rights of War and Peace, Including the Law of Nature and of Nations* (AC Campbell tr, first published as *De Jure Belli ac Pacis* in 1670, 1901) 1.
Oliver Wendell Holmes, Jr., *The Common Law* (first published 1881, Barnes & Noble, Inc. 2004) 2.
International Cooperation in the Peaceful Uses of Outer Space, Resolution adopted by the United Nations General Assembly (13 December 2019), A/RES/74/82, par 2.

Ram S Jakhu and Steven Freeland, 'The Relationship Between the Outer Space Treaty and Customary International Law' (2016) 59th IISL Colloquium on the Law of Outer Space, 67th International Astronautical Congress 7–8.

JW Jandora, 'Developments in Islamic Warfare: The Early Conquests' (1986) 64 Studia Islamica 101.

Stephen B Johnson, 'The Political Economy of Spaceflight' in Steve J Dick and Roger D Launius (eds), *Societal Impact of Spaceflight* (NASA 2007) 141.

Cheryl Johnson-Odim, 'Common Themes, Differing Contexts: Third World Women and Feminism' in Chandra Talpade Mohanty and others (eds), *Third World Women and the Politics of Feminism* (Indiana UP 1991) 314.

Thomas Kuhn, *The Structure of Scientific Revolutions* (3rd edn, University of Chicago Press 1996, orig. pub. 1962) 167.

Josselin Lavigne, 'Political Sovereignty in Outer Space' (2022) 48 North Carolina Journal of International Law 147.

Federico Lenzerini, 'Sovereignty Revisited: International Law and Parallel Sovereignty of Indigenous Peoples' (2006) 42 Texas International Law Journal 155.

Pierre Lévy, 'The Invention of the Computer' in Michel Serres (ed), *A History of Scientific Thought: Elements of a History of Science* (Bordas tr, Blackwell 1995) 636.

Robert McDonald, 'Coming Full Circle' *National Wildlife Magazine, The National Wildlife Federation* (August–September 2021) <Coming Full Circle (nwf.org)>

Theodore Meron, *Human Rights and Humanitarian Norms as Customary Law* (Clarendon Press 1989) 97 (citing United Nations Document E/CN.4/sub. 2/ 1987/10, 7).

Gary D Meyers and Sally Raine, 'Australian Aboriginal Land Rights in Transition (Part II): The Legislative Response to the High Court's Native Title Decisions in *Mabo v. Queensland* and *Wik v. Queensland*' (2001) 9 Tulsa Journal of Comparative and International Law 95.

Mary Ellen Morbeck, Allison Galloway and Adrienne L Zihlman (eds), *The Evolving Female, A Life-History Perspective* (Princeton UP 1997).

Mark C Murphy, *Natural Law and Practical Rationality* (CUP 2001).

New Zealand Outer Space and High-altitude Activities 2017, s 3 (Purpose).

New Zealand Outer Space and High-altitude Activities (Licenses and Permits) Regulation 2017, s 13(2)(c)(iv), 2017/250.

Susana Nuccetelli, 'Is "Latin American Thought" Philosophy?' (2003) 34(4) Metaphilosophy.

Edwin W Patterson, 'A Pragmatist Looks at Natural Law and Natural Rights' in Arthur Leon Harding (ed), *Natural Law and Natural Rights* (Southern Methodist UP 1955) 48, 49.

Ugo Pagallo and others, 'The Normative Challenges of AI in Outer Space: Law, Ethics, and the Realignment of Terrestrial Standards' (2023) 36 Philosophy & Technology 23.

Anja Nakarada Pečujlić, *The Space Law Stalemate: Legal Mechanisms for Developing New Norms* (Routledge 2023).

Malcolm J Rohrbough, *The Trans-Appalachian Frontier, People, Societies, and the Institutions 1775–1850* (OUP 1978).

Roper v. Simmons [2005] 543 U.S. 551.

Jean-Jacques Rosseau, *A Discourse on Inequality* (Maurice Cranston tr, first published 1755, Penguin Books 1984) 70.

Carl Sagan, *Pale Blue Dot: A Vision of the Human Future in Space* (Ballantine Books 1994).

Arvind Sharma, *Are Human Rights Western? A Contribution to the Dialogue of Civilizations* (OUP 2006).

Paul E Sigmund, *Natural Law in Political Thought* (Winthrop Publishers, Inc. 1971).

Leonard S Silk, 'Values and Goals of Space Exploration' in Howard J Taubenfeld (ed), *Space and Society* (Albert Press 1964) 43, 45–46.

Delbert D Smith, *Space Stations: International Law and Policy* (Westview Press 1979).

Barbara B Smuts, 'Social Relationships and Life Histories of Primates' in Mary Ellen Morbeck, Allison Galloway and Adrienne L Zihlman (eds), *The Evolving Female, A Life-History Perspective* (Princeton UP 1997) 60.

Alan R Templeton, 'Has Human Evolution Stopped?' (2 July 2010) 1(1) Rambam Maimonides Medical Journal <https://www.ncbi.nlm.nih.gov/pmc/articles/PMC3721656/> accessed 6 December 2022.

The Outer Space Treaty, Treaty on Principles Governing the Activities of States in the Exploration and Use of Outer Space, Including the Moon and Other Celestial Bodies [27 January1967] 610 UNTS 205, 18 UST 2410, TIAS No. 6347, A/RES/2222/XXI, Art. II.

HWA Thirlway, *International Customary Law and Codification: An Examination of the Continuing Role of Custom in the Present Period of Codification of International Law* (AW Sijthoff 1972).

Yi-Fu Tuan, *Human Goodness* (University of Wisconsin Press 2008) 209.

James Tully (ed), *Pufendorf: On the Duty of Man and Citizen* (CUP 2006) 34.

Sovan Tun, 'Relational Suffering: Causes and Liberation According to Buddhism' (October 2015) 4 Journal of Dialogue & Culture 38.

Sun Tzû, *The Art of War* (Fall River Press 2015).

United Nations, Charter of the United Nations (24 October 1945) 1 UNTS XVI, TS No 993.

United Nations, Office for Outer Space Affairs, Committee on the Peaceful Uses of Outer Space <https://www.unoosa.org/oosa/en/ourwork/copuos/index.html> accessed 21 August 2021.

United Nations Declaration on the Rights of Indigenous Peoples (13 September 2007) A/RES/61/295. *The Antelope* [1825] 23 U.S. 64.

United States Office of General Counsel, Department of Defense, *Department of Defense Law of War Manual* (June 2015, updated May 2016).

U.S. v. the La Jeune Eugenie [1822] 2 Mason 409, 26 Fed. Cas. 832 (Mass.)

James A Vedda, 'The Role of Space Development in Globalization' in Steve J Dick and Roger D Launius (eds), *Societal Impact of Spaceflight* (NASA 2007) 193.

Frans G von der Dunk, *Advanced Introduction to Space Law* (Edward Elgar Publishing 2020).

Lloyd L Weinreb, *Natural Law and Justice* (Harvard UP 1987)

Kwasi Wiredu, *Philosophy and an African Culture* (CUP 1980).

3 A Narrative of Space Law

Extra-Textual Extra-Terrestrial Law Formation

P.J. Blount

1 Introduction

In Arthur C. Clarke's second published short story—1938's 'How We Went to Mars'—his narrator makes reference to fictional court cases and statutes that result from a rocket that 'descended in the Houses of Parliament.'[1] Though not central to the story, Clarke's inclusion of the law in this early story about human space travel was a prescient recognition that law is interwoven with all human activity and creates textual/narrative structures that construct the world around us.[2] Naturally, then, for Clarke—writing 20 years before the launch of Sputnik I—in a space age world, the narrative of law would be extended to these activities. Law regarding space becomes part of the narrative in Clarke's fictional England, because it is part of the narrative of everyday life. Indeed, the fact that these references are not critical parts of this story enhances this notion. Clarke's story is not about the law, but the law nevertheless functions to create the world in which the story unfolds. It is a meta-narrative to Clarke's narrative.

This chapter takes up the notion of narrative as a device for constructing the world around us. Its claim is that much of our understanding of the interpretive world of the law is through narrative processes that gloss the text of the law and shape its meaning. Specifically, this chapter takes this up in the context of international space law. In this context, this chapter argues that international space law in its contemporary form is a normative framework created by interwoven narratives that construct the law through interpretation. From this viewpoint, international space law is not static, and its loci of development are located around narratives that give the law its content. Due to the non-centralized nature of international space law, these narratives come from various places within the normative spectrum. This means that the substantive text that we can identify as law, for instance the Outer Space Treaty, can only be understood within the context of a wider fabric

1 Arthur C Clarke, 'How We Went to Mars,' in Arthur C Clarke (ed), *The Collected Stories* (Gollancz 2000).

2 See for instance Robert M Cover, 'Foreword: Nomos and Narrative' (1983) 97 Harvard Law Review 4–68.

DOI: 10.4324/9781003370499-4

of interpretive narratives that bring meaning to the text. Such construction is a function of epistemic legitimacy, and the narrators of the law vie for such legitimacy as they seek to frame normative rights and wrongs in the domain of space. In other words, 'stories' are told about the law with the goal of having interpretive impact on the law.

This chapter is somewhat experimental in scope, but it seeks to highlight that the making of international space law is a complex endeavour that requires a multifaceted approach to interpretative practices. It seeks to expose that the sharp dividing lines between law and not-law are quite fuzzy due to the way that normative content is structured and advanced by the narrators of the law. While space law literature often engages with the non-legal mechanisms within international governance, there is a lack of a theoretical structure to explain how these non-legal sources impact our legal understanding. Using the lens of narrative—of stories about the law to build the content of the law—this brief chapter seeks to engage with this problem and lay a foundation for analysing how non-legal mechanisms contribute to the law.

This chapter will first investigate the notion of narrative and how it can be understood in the context of the law. It will then turn to a discussion of narrative in international law and suggest that a narrative lens is appropriate for understanding how the overall system of international law can be understood through a narrative context. Section 4 of this chapter investigates narrative in two issue areas in international space law, namely space sustainability and space resource utilization. The final substantive section will reflect on why the narrative lens has advantages for developing our understanding of international space law.

2 Narrative

At the core of the claims made in this chapter is the notion of narrative itself, and this chapter will, admittedly, use this term in a somewhat loose fashion. There has been significant and rigorous research on the notion of narrative, which has generated the discipline of narratology.[3] Narratological theories focus on what constitutes a narrative within the rigid paradigm of the story. These theories seek to understand what the necessary elements are that create a plot across the narrative structure.[4]

Herein, the definition is not as rigid. Herein, narrative is still accepted as a type of storytelling, but rather than being aligned with an independent fictional story and a plot, narrative is considered to be part of the fabric through which humans develop meaning and understanding of the world that surrounds us.[5] We each

3 For a good overview see Genevieve Liveley, *Narratology* (OUP 2019).

4 See Wolfgang Kemp, 'Narrative' in Robert S Nelson (ed), *Critical Terms for Art History* (University of Chicago Press 1996) 58–69, and Seymour Chatman, 'Towards a Theory of Narrative' (1975) 6(2) *New Literary History* 295–318.

5 See generally Roland Barthes and Lionel Duisit, 'An Introduction to the Structural Analysis of Narrative' (1975): 6(2) *New Literary History* 237–72.

build our own narratives, but these are often based on larger societal narratives that create meaning that is then internalized and co-opted into the narratives at the individual level. Such societal narratives in turn interact with other narratives at different levels including legal narratives.[6] Law is often used to reify societal narratives or to shift or create narratives as 'part and parcel of a complex normative world.'[7] These interlocking structures create the world around us and frame our understanding of it. Indeed, one of the reasons that the power of mass media and social media have become contested areas is because of the power these outlets hold in constructing narratives with societal impact.

The notion of constitutionalism gives an excellent example. Constitutions serve as legal-political frames that structure a given society. They are foundational in scope and structure the ultimate metes and bounds of a society. However, constitutions are notoriously incomplete, vague, and ambiguous. In the domestic context of most liberal democracies the expectation is that the constitution serves as the foundation that other laws are built upon and the judiciary within a state has the ability to make determinations as to whether these new laws fit within the constitutional order. Courts have the epistemic legitimacy to tell stories about the law that become the definitive account of what the law means. Even this is fraught, as courts can overrule themselves and vary the narrative of the law. For instance, in the United States the Supreme Court can shift the interpretation of and narrative of what is constitutional. For instance, shifting societal narratives between a post–Civil War America comfortable with racial inequality and the emergence of the civil rights movement in post–World War II America led to a similar shift between *Plessy v. Ferguson* (1896),[8] which held racial segregation in schools to be constitutional, and *Brown v Board of Education* (1954),[9] which held racial segregation in schools to be unconstitutional. In this case, shifting societal narratives on racial inequality had a profound impact on how the law was interpreted by the Court, making clear that the theoretical objectivity of the court in interpreting a legal text is connected to narratives that run concurrently with the law. This is possible because the Constitution 'is a center about which many communities teach, learn, and tell stories,' and '[t]he objectification of the norms to which one is committed . . . entails a narrative—a story of how the law, now object, came to be.'[10] In such situations a meaning of a norm 'does not lie hidden in or behind the norm text but is a product of interpretation.'[11] Interpretation is

6 For instance, Iser, in discussing fictional narratives, argues for a communicative theory in which narratives consist of 'social and cultural norms' and 'incorporates elements and indeed whole traditions or past literature that are mixed together with these norms.' Wolfgang Iser, 'The Reality of Fiction: A Functionalist Approach to Literature' (1975) 7(1) *New Literary History* 29.

7 Robert M Cover, 'Foreword: Nomos and Narrative' (1983) 97 Harvard Law Review 9.

8 *Plessy v. Ferguson* 163 U.S. 537 (1896).

9 *Brown v. Board of Education* 347 U.S. 483 (1954).

10 Robert M Cover, 'Foreword: Nomos and Narrative' (1983) 97 Harvard Law Review 25, 45–46.

11 Ingo Venzke, *How Interpretation Makes International Law: On Semantic Change and Normative Twists* (OUP 2012) 4.

not linked to 'the word itself but in a sense to the totality of what surrounds the words, their *context*.'[12]

These concurrent narratives are important as they expose a second layer of constitutional narratives. Clearly, courts have not considered all constitutional questions, nor are they able to. As a result, narratives of constitutionality are rife within society.[13] Through the invocation of a constitutional basis for one's actions or preferences in society, we seek to generate legitimacy for our viewpoint by tapping into the root document that creates shared societal legitimacy. Thus, in contested areas, both sides of an issue will often seek to assert the legitimacy of their claims through notions of constitutionality. This does more than simply impact the understanding of a discrete issue; it creates a narrative of constitutional law that is taken up by individuals and constructs the normative world in which they live. Here it is not the court that creates the legal narrative but society, and as seen in the shift to the aforementioned *Brown v. Board of Education*. These societal narratives can have impact on official legitimated narratives as well.

Narrative then is a fabric of interacting stories that bring meaning to things within society, including the law. Within domestic systems, courts have a clear function as entities with legitimacy to interpret the law, but there is still interpretive space for other actors to engage in narrative construction of the law. The international system is less clear in these respects due to its horizontal nature and the limited nature of courts' and tribunals' binding powers. This leads to a more complex interaction of narratives that seek to construct the meaning of the law and frame the normative structure of the international community. The next section will take this notion up by investigating the phenomenon within the context of international law generally and international space law specifically.

3 Narrative and Law

A significant amount of literature on international law is concerned with its sources.[14] Almost every student of international has been introduced (usually on the first day of their international course) to the 'sources doctrine,' which turns to Article 38 of the Statute of the International Court of Justice (ICJ) to explain what constitutes international law:

1. The Court, whose function is to decide in accordance with international law such disputes as are submitted to it, shall apply:
   a. international conventions, whether general or particular, establishing rules expressly recognized by the contesting states;
   b. international custom, as evidence of a general practice accepted as law;

12 Venzke (n 11) 3 (emphasis in original).

13 Ngoc Son Bui, 'Discursive Constitutionalism' (2023) 23/2 Chicago Journal of International Law 342–90.

14 See Harlan Grant Cohen, 'Finding International Law: Rethinking the Doctrine of Sources' (2007) 93 Iowa Law Review 65.

c. the general principles of law recognized by civilized nations;
d. subject to the provisions of Article 59, judicial decisions and the teachings of the most highly qualified publicists of the various nations, as subsidiary means for the determination of rules of law.[15]

Students are thus taught that the sources of international law are treaties, custom, and general principles that are subject to interpretive sway by judgements and publicists. Despite the doctrinal position of the source's doctrine, it has numerous acknowledged shortcomings. It is, by its own terms, only a limitation on what the International Court of Justice will apply to the cases arising before it and not a statement of what constitutes international law more generally. As a salient example, the UN Charter enables the UN Security Council to make legally binding resolutions,[16] which clearly represent a form of international law, yet is not acknowledged as a source of international law in Article 38. This illustrates the gap between the 'sources doctrine' and a holistic understanding of the structure of international law.

More troubling, though, is that Article 38 excludes any notion of epistemic growth of the law. In a domestic system, such growth is enabled through judicial interpretation, legislative acts, and executive regulations. Article 38 treats the text of international law as mostly static and only subject to growth through clear action by states. Once a treaty enters into force it becomes a solidified body of meaning. Even the ICJ's own decisions do not substantiate a locus of interpretive growth of the law since they are only binding on the parties to the case. Even if such decisions had broader epistemic impact, ICJ decisions are relatively rare compared to other judicial systems. In this light, the ICJ looks less like an interpretive judiciary and more like a dispute settlement body.

Despite this, most international legal scholars would recognize that international law is not a static enterprise waiting for treaties to be negotiated.[17] While customary international law gives some room for normative growth, it too falls short of capturing where and how international law grows due to the rigid formalistic approach through which norms are only identifiable through state practice and *opinion juris*. This has led to numerous scholars engaging with attempts to locate the epistemic nodes of international law and how it is interpreted. For instance, Reisman argues that we find international law in the responses of states to international incidents that allow states to make judgements about the law.[18] Venzke looks to interpretive activities that occur within international organizations that have grasped legitimacy within their interpretations.[19] Guzman has sought out a

15 Statute of the international Court of Justice (18 April 1946).

16 UN Charter (1945) Art. 25.

17 See for instance Harlan Grant Cohen, 'Finding International Law: Rethinking the Doctrine of Sources' (2007) 93 Iowa Law Review 65, and Brian Israel, 'Treaty Stasis [Agora: The End of Treaties?]' (*AJIL Unbound* [blog], 8 May 2014) <https://www.asil.org/blogs/treaty-stasis-agora-end-treaties>.

18 W Michael Reisman, 'International Incidents: Introduction to a New Genre in the Study of International Law' (1984) 10 Yale Journal of International Law 1.

19 Venzke (n 11).

compliance-based approach to international law as a way to investigate the growth of normative structures through examination of their impact.[20] Each of these scholars (and numerous others) seek to account for normative growth in international law that is external to Article 38, but each takes a very different view of from whence such growth emerges.

These views and others have a similar line that seeks to identify the factors of legitimation that enable epistemic normative growth through interpretive nodes. The problem that these approaches all face is that the trends they identify are difficult to universalize across international law. For instance, the factors that give an international organization legitimacy in one legal context may be missing in another legal context. This situation is part and parcel of the increasingly acknowledged phenomenon of fragmentation in international law through which there has been acknowledgement that international law often functions differently within sub-disciplines of the field.[21] This phenomenon recognizes that international law is increasingly differentiated around subject areas as well as geographic regions.

One possible understanding of fragmentation is that it threatens to undermine the cohesiveness of the system. Such a viewpoint is short sighted and ignores that even in vertical municipal systems different areas are governed by different rules customized to those areas. Indeed, the field of international relations gives the notion of 'epistemic communities' as places where norms can grow out of groups of individuals with specialized knowledge.[22] The question becomes, if a fragmented system has resulted in uneven interpretive capacities in different areas of the law, can there be any unifying principle to help explain normative growth? If not, then there is potential that international law itself becomes difficult to understand as a system that has interior logic. This chapter suggests that this can be found in understanding international law as a discursive process constructed of competing narratives of norms.

To be more precise, the claim is that a substantial locus for normative growth happens at the narrative level within the stories that states and others tell about normative frameworks. These stories represent a place for interpretation of and contestation over norms and their content. This is not to say that, for instance, diplomatic statements are containers of law, but rather that in an international legal system structured without a hierarchy of legal interpretation, what states (and potentially others) say about the law can be a powerful indicator of the meaning and content of the law. International law is not static despite often being contained in unmoving texts and seemingly waiting for the stars to align on an international dispute over which the ICJ has jurisdiction for interpretation. International law is in a continuance state of interpretation through the discourse and interactions of states and their norm-building activities. Such interpretative acts come through statements,

20 Andrew T Guzman, 'A Compliance-Based Theory of International Law' (2002) 90 California Law Review 1823–88.

21 See Martti Koskenniemi and Päivi Leino, 'Fragmentation of International Law? Postmodern Anxieties' (2002) 15(3) Leiden Journal of International Law 553–79.

22 Peter M Haas, 'Introduction: Epistemic Communities and International Policy Coordination' (1992) 46(1) International Organization 1–35.

policies, political agreements, and myriad form of governance documents that are put forward by states as embodiments of normative content. The notion of narrative allows us to understand the structure of legal development and to comprehend the unevenness of interpretative process across different areas of the law.

This can clearly be seen in the domain of international space law, which generally lacks case law or a treaty body to provide interpretation. Scholars have noted the end of formal international space lawmaking that came with the negotiation and subsequent failure of the Moon Agreement in the late 1970s and early 1980s.[23] It is a common trope to suggest that the Outer Space Treaty is no longer fit for purpose because it was negotiated in the 1960s and not with current technology in mind.[24] These treaty texts are not frozen in time, however, and instead present sites of normative growth through an iterative process through which states use narrative and discourse to build meaning around ambiguous terms and adapt norms to current technology.[25]

4 Space Norms and Narratives

This section will engage directly with sites of narrative normative growth within space law. Specifically, it will address two areas where these processes can be observed. It will address the normative growth through narrative processes around the issues of space sustainability and space resources. These case studies will reveal different aspects of the role of narrative in the making of international space law.

(a) Space Sustainability

A common rhetorical flourish found in the domain of outer space governance is the notion of a 'secure, safe, and sustainable' space environment. Each of the three

23 See, for instance, Sergio Marchisio, 'The Evolutionary Stages of the Legal Subcommittee of the United Nations Committee on the Peaceful Uses of Outer Space (COPUOS)' (2005) 31 Journal of Space Law 219; Stephan Hobe, 'International Space Law in Its First Half Century' in *57th International Astronautical Congress* (American Institute of Aeronautics and Astronautics 2006); and Verda Neslihan Akün, 'Space Law Under International Conventions and International Documents' in *Proceedings for the First Symposium on Space Economy, Space Law and Space Sciences* (Istanbul UP 2022) 102. See also P.J. Blount, 'Innovating the Law: Fifty Years of the Outer Space Treaty' in Mahulena Hofmann and P.J. Blount (eds), *Innovation in Outer Space: International and African Legal Perspective* (Nomos Verlagsgesellschaft mbH & Co. KG 2018) 31–52.

24 As a media trope see, for example, John Hickman, 'Still Crazy After Four Decades: The Case for Withdrawing From the 1967 Outer Space Treaty' *The Space Review* (24 September 2006) <http://www.thespacereview.com/article/960/1> and Paul Forrester, 'Withdraw From the Outer Space Treaty' *The Chronicle* (14 December 2016) <http://www.dukechronicle.com/article/2016/12/withdraw-from-outer-space-treaty>; and Jill Stuart, 'The Outer Space Treaty Has Been Successful So Far, but Is It Fit for the Modern Age?' *The Wire* (31 January 2017) <https://thewire.in/space/outer-space-treaty-fit-for-modern-age>. For a more scholarly approach, see Jacob A Reed, 'Cold War Treaties in a New World: The Inevitable End of the Outer Space and Antarctic Treaty Systems' (2017) 42(4/5) Air and Space Law.

25 Brian Israel, 'Treaty Stasis [Agora: The End of Treaties?]' (*AJIL Unbound* [blog], 8 May 2014) <https://www.asil.org/blogs/treaty-stasis-agora-end-treaties>.

S's has its own pedigree, but this section will engage specifically with the notion of sustainability, and it will seek to present sustainability as a rhetorical shift in the discourse surrounding space that led to more concrete normative growth.

As global environmental concerns began to loom larger within the international community, the notion of sustainability became an important touchpoint for thinking about how to address such widespread issues. It entered into the rhetoric and narrative of international environmental law and politics through the 1987 Brundtland report.[26] This report defined sustainable development as that which 'meets the needs of the present without compromising the ability of future generations to meet their own needs.'[27] Sustainability effectively shifts discourse away from notions of protecting or preserving the environment and recasts environmental discourse towards questions of usage of the environment and its resources. The term is used to suggest that humanity must use the Earth in such a way that it supports current societal needs, but also preserves resources and environments for future generations. This framing embraces both use and preservation of the environment, meaning that onboarding stakeholders into the normative framework became less burdensome because it moved away from rhetoric that would deny usage of the environment. This term has become the prevalent narrative within environmental governance.

The sustainability narrative was later imported into the space domain to address the growing concern of the space environment resulting from the increase in debris brought on by the increasing numbers of global users. The notion of space sustainability was first used in academic literature in the early 2000s.[28] The notion of long-term sustainability of space activities is taken up as an agenda item by the Scientific and Technical Subcommittee (STSC) of the UN Committee on the Peaceful Uses of Outer Space (UNCOPUOS) in 2010 and a corresponding Working Group is established the same year.[29] Sustainability becomes part of the governance narrative for space through the Long-Term Sustainability Guidelines (LTSG) which were developed by the STSC Working Group and adopted by UNCOPUOS in 2019.[30] It is notable that the Guidelines emerge from the Scientific and Technical Subcommittee rather than the legal subcommittee as they represent an emerging form of technical governance rooted in a norms narrative of sustainability.[31] Sustainability is a narrative that has framed the adoption of a normative governance

26 Report of the World Commission on Environment and Development: Our Common Future. U.N. Doc. A/42/427 (1987).

27 Report of the World Commission on Environment and Development (n 26) 26.

28 Google Scholar indicates an early usage in 2000 in Robbie E Davis-Floyd, 'Commercializing Outer Space: The SATWG Stories' (2000) 7 Para-Sites: A Casebook Against Cynical Reason 433. Uptake of the term would not occur until later in the decade.

29 Report of the Scientific and Technical Subcommittee on its forty-seventh session, held in Vienna from 8 to 19 February 2010, U.N. Doc. A/AC.105/958 (2010) para. 181.

30 Report of the Committee on the Peaceful Uses of Outer Space, U.N. Doc. A/74/20 (2019) para. 163 and Annex II.

31 See P.J. Blount, 'Technically Speaking: UNCOPUOS and the Technical Governance of Space' (2023) 1 Indian Review of Air and Space Law 1–12.

document, but this document is considered to be technical rather than legal. Nevertheless, the LTSG have become an important part of the normative landscape for space activities and give texture to the legal provisions found in the treaty regime.

The narrative of sustainability served as a way to leverage the normative narrative of environmental governance to impart legitimacy in normative frameworks for the space domain. Not coincidently, this timeline of the transition of the sustainability narrative into the space domain tracks with a timeline of the emergence of the bloom of commercial actors connected to the so-called New Space economy. In this case the narrative itself was already accepted in the terrestrial arena with wide global uptake of the sustainability rhetoric. This meant that deployment in the space domain was relatively easy and gave states an accepted policy perspective to engage in multilateral discussions that resulted in the narrative being elevated to a higher level of normative cohesion. It also created space for commercial actors to engage in this normative development, because the sustainability narratives help to legitimate these actors as stakeholders in sustainability rather than the simple subjects of regulation. Though sustainability has not been adopted within a legal text in international space law, it is clearly part of the discourse surrounding the norms that guide actors in space, and as such clearly impacts interpretation of the law in context.

(b) Resources

The issue of space resource exploitation presents a good example for observing narrative change through narrative processes. The non-appropriation principle found in Article II of the Outer Space Treaty has been a traditional source of academic debate.[32] Specifically, its content and whether it allows for the private exploitation of resources have been a tension point in space law. However, in the 2010s the normative content of this treaty provision began to solidify on an interpretation that allows for the commercial exploitation of space resources. This can be attributed to a narrative deployment by the United States that was taken up and adopted by other states and stakeholders.

The establishment of two high-profile companies, Planetary Resources and Deep Space Industries, led to renewed interest in the idea that commercial companies might lead the charge in extracting resources from outer space. This also led to renewed questions about the legality of such activities, which became connected to the fundraising efforts of these companies.[33] Industry lobbied for the establishment of 'legal certainty' surrounding the issue so that they could assure potential investors. The passage of the Space Resource Utilization Act as part of the US Commercial Space Launch Competitiveness Act (CSLCA) in 2015 was a watershed moment as it was the first time that a state had adopted a law concerning

32 See generally Philip de Man, *Exclusive Use in an Inclusive Environment: The Meaning of the Non-Appropriation Principle for Space Resource Exploitation* (Springer 2016).

33 Spurring Private Aerospace Competitiveness and Entrepreneurship Act of 2015, 161 Cong. Rec.at H3514, H3515-H3516, H3519 (daily edition 21 May 2015).

resource exploitation.[34] The CSLCA makes it legal for US citizens and businesses to extract, own, and commercially dispose of space resources. The US did not, however, stop with this measure. In 2020 NASA released a procurement for the purchase of lunar soil to be extracted by a commercial company, but without the requirement that it be returned to the surface of the Earth.[35] This measure was intended to create state practice around the commercial disposition of space resources by making 'a small first step toward creating a lunar marketplace' and 'normalizing the concept of buying materials that are excavated from the Moon and other worlds in the Solar System.'[36]

The United States also made the principle of commercial exploitation a core part of the Artemis Accords, a nonbinding political agreement signed by the NASA administrator.[37] The Accords have now garnered the signatures of nearly 40 other state entities. Section 10(2) of the Accords states, '[t]he Signatories affirm that the extraction of space resources does not inherently constitute national appropriation under Article II of the Outer Space Treaty, and that contracts and other legal instruments relating to space resources should be consistent with that Treaty.' Clearly, there is an intent not to change the law, but to influence the normative content of the law through interpretation. As such the Accords create a narrative around this interpretation, and as more states join the Accords the narrative is shared and strengthened. It is important to note that this is not traditional legal interpretation as one might expect from a court, but rather is a political narrative with the intent of influencing the future development of the law. The engagement by NASA here is important as it is neither a regulator nor a holder of diplomatic authority and is instead functioning more like a norm entrepreneur attempting to create normative content.[38] NASA's activities are intended to bolster a US narrative that this activity fits within a proper interpretation of Article II with the goal of seeing widespread uptake of the normative content of the narrative and the potential for a norm cascade.[39]

The deployment of this narrative has had significant success and is likely already shaping the interpretation of Article II. In addition to the growing number of signatories to the Artemis Accords, three other states have followed suit and adopted national legislation that supports the exploitation of space resources: Luxembourg, Japan, and the United Arab Emirates.[40] Each of these states has important influence

34 U.S. Commercial Space Launch Competitiveness Act, Pub. L. No. 114–90 (2015).

35 Loren Grush, 'NASA Wants to Buy Moon Rocks From Private Companies' *The Verge* (10 September 2020) <https://www.theverge.com/2020/9/10/21429850/nasa-moon-rocks-sampling-commercial-space-transaction-lunar-marketplace>.

36 Grush (n 35).

37 The Artemis Accords: Principles for Cooperation in the Civil Exploration and Use of the Moon, Mars, Comets, and Asteroids for Peaceful Purposes (13 October 2020).

38 See Martha Finnemore and Kathryn Sikkink, 'International Norm Dynamics and Political Change' (1998) 52(04) International Organization 887–917.

39 Finnemore and Sikkink (n 38) 887–917.

40 Loi du 20 juillet 2017 sur l'exploration et l'utilisation des ressources de l'espace (Luxembourg); Federal Law No. (12) of 2019 on the Regulation of the Space Sector, Art. 18 (United Arab Emirates);

within their respective regions. Luxembourg is instructive. In conjunction with the passage of its law, Luxembourg started its spaceresources.lu initiative which seeks to support the nascent space resources industry. Luxembourg is currently the home of the European Space Resources Innovation Centre (ESRIC), which maintains cooperation with the European Space Agency (ESA). As a result, Luxembourg has become a proponent of the space resources narrative and has begun to influence other European States and ESA as well.[41]

The further success of this narrative can be seen in the establishment of the civil society Hague Space Resources Working Group with the support of the Dutch government. This group, with representation from stakeholders, drafted Building Blocks for the development of international governance of space resources. Key amongst these is BB 1.1, which states that any international framework 'should create an enabling environment for space resource activities that takes into account all interests and benefits all countries and humankind.'[42] These Building Blocks can be seen as an initial effort at structuring what a potential regime for the usage of space resources might look like, but as this was a civil society forum it is clear that the Building Blocks only serve to create narrative weight behind the notions of exploitability. Such narratives can also be seen in the establishment of the Space Resources Working Group as part of the Legal Subcommittee of UNCOPUOS. This group aims to '[p]repare a draft set of initial recommended principles for such activities.'[43] The results of this group will be driven by the viewpoints of states and the normative narratives that they have internalized regarding the issue. Within this context, efforts such as the Artemis Accords may prove significant in shaping the guidelines adopted by the Working Group. Indeed, China's recent statement to the Working Group displays the potential uptake of the normative interpretation. First the delegation emphasizes that any activities should be consistent with international law and specifically the non-appropriation principle.[44] At the same time, the delegation argues that non-governmental actors engaging in these activities should be subject to 'sufficient supervision' consistent with Article VI of the Outer Space Treaty.[45] While there will clearly be difficult negotiations within the Working Group, the Chinese statement is on its face consistent with the US position that

and Act on the Promotion of Business Activities for the Exploration and Development of Space Resources, Act No. 83 of 2021 (Japan).

41 See Luxembourg Space Agency, 'SpaceResources.Lu Initiative' <https://space-agency.public.lu/en/space-resources/the-initiative.html> accessed 23 July 2024.

42 Hague Space Resources Governance Working Group, *Draft Building Blocks for the Development of an International Framework on Space Resource Activity* (University of Leiden 2017).

43 UNOOSA, 'Working Group on the Legal Aspects of Space Resource Activities' (n.d.) <https://www.unoosa.org/oosa/en/ourwork/copuos/lsc/space-resources/index.html>.

44 Submission by the Delegation of China to the Working Group on Legal Aspects of Space Resource Activities of the Legal Subcommittee of the Committee on the Peaceful Uses of Outer Space, U.N. Doc. A/AC.105/C.2/2024/CRP.5 (2024) para. 9 <https://www.unoosa.org/documents/pdf/copuos/lsc/space-resources/LSC2024/English_Chinas_submission_to_the_working_group_on_space_resources.pdf>.

45 Submission by the Delegation of China (n 44) para. 12.

non-governmental space resource activities are legal and can be carried out consistent with the treaty. The normative narrative of space resources is filtering up into the international realm.

5 The Narrative Lens

It could reasonably be argued that these activities by states are simply manifestations of the traditional mechanisms of customary international law, namely *opinio juris* and state practice. Such a view would not be incorrect as these narratives form part of the evidence of customary international law. As seen earlier, NASA's plan to buy lunar soil was explicitly geared towards establishing state practice.[46] However, it is suggested here that the framing of these processes as narrative has theoretical advantages over framing it as the components of customary international law, which gives us a more nuanced understanding of normative construction.

First, by framing this activity as narrative it helps to expose the variance in norm-building strategies of states, gives a tool for understanding how norm formation happens across a range of issues, and provides a unique vantage point for the analysis and identification of Finnemore and Sikkink's notion of a norm cascade through which norms see rapid uptake.[47] If seen as components of customary international law only, then there is only a backwards-facing inquiry as to whether a norm has formed and ossified. Such an analysis gives no vantage point from which to judge how and why a norm is forming. This shifts the inquiry from being purely concerned with what the law is and gives us tools to investigate how the law forms.

A second advantage is that by viewing through a narrative lens, these activities can be analysed for their normative content rather than strictly legal content. The delineation between law and not law is too often employed as a borderline in legal studies. If something is not law, then it is considered to not be within the domain of the lawyer. This is increasingly an artificial dividing line both in theory and in practice, especially considering the debates around soft law and governance mechanisms that have taken a central stage in our understanding of space law. From a theoretical standpoint this ignores the interpretive practices of states, which obfuscates one of the core methods through which international law develops. Indeed, in the domain of international space law, there is minimal interpretation from more traditionally recognized sources such as courts, and is it suggested that narrative practice presents a more coherent way of understanding the normative framing of space activities. From a practical perspective, such a footing tends to ignore that the role of the lawyer often extends beyond shall and shall nots for operators and into the realm of what an operator should do and should not do. This means that in practice lawyers have become increasingly concerned with governance frameworks

46 Grush (n 35).
47 Finnemore and Sikkink (n 38) 887–917.

that help to construct what the realm of reasonable action is within the context of a given activity.

Through the recognition of narrative structures in the context of the interpretation of international law we gain a finer-grain understanding of how states create normative content and then impart that content into the legal framework that contains them. These structures are intentionally constructed by states to serve their ends, but there seems to be clear intent to change the discourse and rhetoric around certain issues to support normative interpretation and change. This has a follow-on impact on legal scholarship in that it forces the analyst away from the pure text of the law and requires engagement with the fabric of discourse. Arguably, this pushes legal scholarship into the realm of the political, but this should hardly be surprising when one considers the high political content of the international legal system. It is not a system mediated by a disinterested court, but rather a system in which the legislative, enforcement, and judicial functions have been compressed into a nation state. In such a system, the content of the law becomes more malleable than in other contexts. This does not remove power dynamics, as can clearly be seen in the United States' deployment of its interpretation of Article II, but it also does not discount narratives that emerge from other nodes, such as that surrounding sustainability.

6 Conclusion

This short experimental chapter has sought to understand international space law through the lens of narrative. It has suggested that the primary mode of interpretation and normative growth comes from the deployment of narratives that construct the content of the law. This is not to suggest that this is the only means through which the law develops, but rather to suggest that this is a useful lens through which to view the normative engagement of states. In a realm that is highly impacted through diplomacy and national activities, narrative gives a frame for understanding those actions as interpretive, law-building exercises by the state. Further, following these deployments and their uptake by other states allows for clear analysis of how the law is developing in real time.

While this methodology can be employed in most if not all areas of international law, it is particularly apt in the space domain due to a lack of formalized institutions with interpretive ability. This means that lawyers must be more aware of the frame of governance that impacts their clients' activities and become accustomed to interpretive practices that sit within the context of changing technology. It also means that lawyers in the field at the operator, state, and international level all have a role to play in helping to construct narratives that support both innovation and long-term access and use of space. The institutional gap in space law means that discourse and contestation are key aspects to norm building in the field, and the narratives that emerge and are accepted will be critical touchpoints for analysing the content of the law in context.

Bibliography

Verda Neslihan Akün, 'Space Law Under International Conventions and International Documents' in *Proceedings for the First Symposium on Space Economy, Space Law and Space Sciences* (Istanbul UP 2022).

Roland Barthes and Lionel Duisit, 'An Introduction to the Structural Analysis of Narrative' (1975) 6(2) New Literary History 237–72.

P.J. Blount, 'Innovating the Law: Fifty Years of the Outer Space Treaty' in Mahulena Hofmann and P.J. Blount (eds), *Innovation in Outer Space: International and African Legal Perspective* (Nomos Verlagsgesellschaft mbH & Co. KG 2018) 31–52.

P.J. Blount, 'Technically Speaking: UNCOPUOS and the Technical Governance of Space' (2023) 1 Indian Review of Air and Space Law 1–12.

Brown v. Board of Education 347 U.S. 483 (1954).

Ngoc Son Bui, 'Discursive Constitutionalism' (2023) 23/2 Chicago Journal of International Law 342–90.

Seymour Chatman, 'Towards a Theory of Narrative' (1975) 6(2) New Literary History 295–318.

Arthur C Clarke, 'How We Went to Mars' in Arthur C Clarke (ed), *The Collected Stories* (Gollancz 2000).

Harlan Grant Cohen, 'Finding International Law: Rethinking the Doctrine of Sources' (2007) 93 Iowa Law Review 65.

Robert M Cover, 'Foreword: Nomos and Narrative' (1983) 97 Harvard Law Review 4–68, 9, 25, 45–46.

Robbie E Davis-Floyd, 'Commercializing Outer Space: The SATWG Stories' (2000) 7 Para-Sites: A Casebook Against Cynical Reason 433.

Philip de Man, *Exclusive Use in an Inclusive Environment: The Meaning of the Non-Appropriation Principle for Space Resource Exploitation* (Springer 2016).

Martha Finnemore and Kathryn Sikkink, 'International Norm Dynamics and Political Change' (1998) 52(04) International Organization 887–917.

Loren Grush, 'NASA Wants to Buy Moon Rocks From Private Companies' (*The Verge*, 10 September 2020) <https://www.theverge.com/2020/9/10/21429850/nasa-moon-rocks-sampling-commercial-space-transaction-lunar-marketplace>

Andrew T Guzman, 'A Compliance-Based Theory of International Law' (2002) 90 California Law Review 1823–88.

Hague Space Resources Governance Working Group, *Draft Building Blocks for the Development of an International Framework on Space Resource Activity* (University of Leiden 2017).

Peter M Haas, 'Introduction: Epistemic Communities and International Policy Coordination' (1992) 46(1) International Organization 1–35.

Stephan Hobe, 'International Space Law in Its First Half Century' in *57th International Astronautical Congress* (American Institute of Aeronautics and Astronautics 2006).

Wolfgang Iser, 'The Reality of Fiction: A Functionalist Approach to Literature' (1975) 7(1) New Literary History 29.

Brian Israel, 'Treaty Stasis [Agora: The End of Treaties?]' (*AJIL Unbound* [blog], 8 May 2014) <https://www.asil.org/blogs/treaty-stasis-agora-end-treaties>.

Wolfgang Kemp, 'Narrative' in Robert S Nelson (ed), *Critical Terms for Art History* (University of Chicago Press 1996) 58–69.

Martti Koskenniemi and Päivi Leino, 'Fragmentation of International Law? Postmodern Anxieties' (2002) 15(3) Leiden Journal of International Law 553–79.

Genevieve Liveley, *Narratology* (OUP 2019).

Luxembourg Space Agency, 'SpaceResources.Lu Initiative' <https://space-agency.public.lu/en/space-resources/the-initiative.html> accessed 23 July 2024.

Sergio Marchisio, 'The Evolutionary Stages of the Legal Subcommittee of the United Nations Committee on the Peaceful Uses of Outer Space (COPUOS)' (2005) 31 Journal of Space Law 219.

Plessy v. Ferguson 163 U.S. 537 [1896].

Jacob A Reed, 'Cold War Treaties in a New World: The Inevitable End of the Outer Space and Antarctic Treaty Systems' (2017) 42(4/5) Air and Space Law (2017).

W Michael Reisman, 'International Incidents: Introduction to a New Genre in the Study of International Law' (1984) 10 Yale Journal of International Law 1.

Report of the Committee on the Peaceful Uses of Outer Space, U.N. Doc. A/74/20 (2019).

Report of the Scientific and Technical Subcommittee on its forty-seventh session, held in Vienna from 8 to 19 February 2010, U.N. Doc. A/AC.105/958 (2010).

Report of the World Commission on Environment and Development: Our Common Future. U.N. Doc. A/42/427 (1987).

Spurring Private Aerospace Competitiveness and Entrepreneurship Act of 2015, 161 Cong. Rec.at H3514, H3515-H3516, H3519 (daily edition 21 May 2015).

Statute of the International Court of Justice (18 April 1946).

Jill Stuart, 'The Outer Space Treaty Has Been Successful So Far, But Is It Fit for the Modern Age?' *The Wire* (31 January 2017) <https://thewire.in/space/outer-space-treaty-fit-for-modern-age>.

Submission by the Delegation of China to the Working Group on Legal Aspects of Space Resource Activities of the Legal Subcommittee of the Committee on the Peaceful Uses of Outer Space, U.N. Doc. A/AC.105/C.2/2024/CRP.5 (2024) para. 9 <https://www.unoosa.org/documents/pdf/copuos/lsc/space-resources/LSC2024/English_Chinas_submission_to_the_working_group_on_space_resources.pdf>

The Artemis Accords: Principles for Cooperation in the Civil Exploration and Use of the Moon, Mars, Comets, and Asteroids for Peaceful Purposes (13 October 2020).

UNOOSA, 'Working Group on the Legal Aspects of Space Resource Activities' (n.d.) <https://www.unoosa.org/oosa/en/ourwork/copuos/lsc/space-resources/index.html>

U.S. Commercial Space Launch Competitiveness Act, Pub. L. No. 114–90 (2015).

Ingo Venzke, *How Interpretation Makes International Law: On Semantic Change and Normative Twists* (OUP 2012).

4 The Right of Self-Defence in Outer Space

Legal Issues and Way Forward

Fabio Tronchetti

1 Introduction

Space has never been as important as it is today. Modern societies depend on satellites for the provision of vital services, such as telecommunication, navigation, internet access, and banking, among others.[1] Also, the military apparatus of the most advanced countries relies on space assets to perform national defence tasks as well as to enhance the effectiveness of military operations.[2] The increasing relevance of space, from both an economic and a military perspective, inevitably puts satellites at risk of being targeted in the event of conflict amongst nations. Unsurprisingly, recent years have witnessed numerous developments intended to protect valuable space assets and give states the means to respond to a threat to their space objects. For example, a few countries have established military branches specifically designed to operate in outer space, the so-called space forces, and have developed and tested various counterspace capabilities.[3]

In such a dynamic scenario, it seems logical to reflect upon the applicability of the right of self-defence in outer space, particularly on the circumstances triggering recourse to this right and the circumstances according to which such a right can be exercised. As this chapter will explain, the way in which the right of self-defence

1 World Economic Forum, 'The Space Economy Is Booking: What Benefits Can It Bring to Earth?' <https://www.weforum.org/agenda/2022/10/space-economy-industry-benefits/> accessed 8 July 2024; UK Space Agency, 'Why Space Matters?' <https://www.gov.uk/government/publications/infographic-why-space-matters/why-space-matters> accessed 8 July 2024.

2 LT Gen Steven L Basham, 'The Critical Role of Space in Modern Warfare and the Imperative of Joint Space Capabilities in Europe' (9 February 2024) <https://www.eucom.mil/article/42685/the-critical-role-of-space-in-modern-warfare-and-the-imperative-of-joint-spacecapabilitie#:~:text=In%20today's%20rapidly%20evolving%20security,fabric%20of%20modern%20military%20operations> accessed 8 July 2024; North Atlantic Treaty Organization, 'NATO's Approach to Space' <https://www.nato.int/cps/en/natohq/topics_175419.htm> accessed 8 July 2024; US Department of State, The Space Force's Critical Role in National Security, May 9, 2024 <https://www.state.gov/briefings-foreign-press-centers/the-space-forces-critical-role-in-national-security>; Joint Air Power Competence Centre, 'Space Support in Operations' <https://www.japcc.org/warfare-areas/space/> accessed 8 July 2024.

3 See Section 2 of this chapter.

DOI: 10.4324/9781003370499-5

applies to outer space remains largely controversial.[4] This is mostly due to two factors: (1) the international treaties governing activities in outer space contain no provisions on the exercise of the right of self-defence therein; (2) the existing public international law rules on self-defence were designed to be applied in relation to events occurring on Earth, either on the ground, sea, or air, not in outer space. Furthermore, due to the peculiar characteristics of the space environment and space objects, it is simply not possible to take those rules as they stand, as well as their interpretation, and apply them to events happening in outer space; instead, in the majority of cases, it is necessary to adapt those rules or to perform an effort of creative interpretation.[5]

Following a brief examination of the relevance of self-defence in outer space in today's geopolitical environment, this chapter will analyse the right of self-defence, first from an international law perspective and then in the specific context of outer space. The final section of this chapter will envisage a series of scenarios intended to demonstrate the challenges that one faces when attempting to exercise the right of self-defence in outer space. These examples will be instrumental to demonstrate the need for existing rules on self-defence to be adapted, and possibly modified, into the specific characteristics of outer space and space objects.

2 Why Analyse the Right of Self-Defence in Outer Space?

Several states and scholars view any discussion about self-defence as a threat to the peaceful nature of outer space which they regard as a sanctuary, the peaceful nature of which should be preserved at all costs. In their mind, reflecting on the applicability of the right of self-defence to outer space would encourage states to use force against space objects and would trigger an arms race in outer space. The present chapter disagrees with this view; indeed, due to the uncertainty surrounding the meaning of self-defence in space, it is not possible to predict how states would react to events that they view as a threat, or even as an attack, against their space objects. This unpredictability is extremely dangerous because it could lead to overreactions, fuel mistrust, and even result in an open confrontation among adversaries. On the contrary, reflecting on the way the right of self-defence applies to space would be beneficial from a double perspective: (1) it would generate a level of predictability of behaviours instrumental to prevent unnecessary escalations and (2) it would limit the consequences of hypothetical self-defence actions to an extent that they would not compromise the long-term sustainability of outer space.

Refusing to discuss the issue of self-defence in outer space would also seem to be inconsistent with the growing strategic relevance of space assets and the

4 Anne Sophie Martin, 'State's Right to Self-Defence in Outer Space' (2020) 30 The Journal of the JAPCC; Fabio Tronchetti, 'The Right of Self-Defence in Outer Space: An Appraisal' (2014) 63 Zeitschrift für Luft-und Weltraumrecht 92.

5 Ricky J Lee, 'The Jus Ad Bellum in Outer Space: The Interrelationship Between Article 103 of the Charter of the United Nations and Article IV of the Outer Space Treaty' (2002) 45 Proceedings of the International Institute of Space Law (2002) 139.

consequent increasing level of risks that they face. Interestingly, there are those who speak about the 'inevitability of conflict' in outer space,[6] even though this is not an opinion shared by all.[7] The fact remains that in 2019 the North Atlantic Treaty Organization (NATO) declared space as a new operational domain, alongside air, land, maritime, and cyberspace.[8] Reference to the possibility to act in self-defence in outer space occurs with greater frequency in national security documents. For example, the 2020 National Space Policy of the United States provides, 'the United States will continue to use space for national security activities, including for the exercise of the inherent right of self-defense.'[9] Furthermore, the US Defence Space Strategy indicates, 'DoD will be prepared to protect and defend U.S. and, as directed, allied, partner, and commercial space capabilities and to deter and defeat adversary hostile use of space.'[10] Also, the Russian Federation submitted a Working Paper to the United Nations Committee on the Peaceful Uses of Outer Space on Achieving a uniform interpretation on the right of self-defence in outer space.[11] While this initiative did not gain any traction, it should be viewed in a positive light because, in seeking a uniform interpretation of self-defence, it attempted to directly tackle the problems deriving from the absence of a consistent way to understand and apply the right of self-defence in outer space.

3 Counterspace Capabilities and Military Developments

To implement the goal of protecting space assets and deterring attacks, states have developed various counterspace capabilities and set up military branches dedicated

6 Statement by Michael Schmitt, quoted in Stuart Clark, 'It's Going to Happen: Is the World Ready for War in Space?' *The Guardian* (15 April 2018) <https://www.theguardian.com/science/2018/apr/15/its-going-to-happen-is-world-ready-for-war-in-space> accessed 6 August 2024.

7 US Deputy Defense Secretary Hicks said on 10 January 2024: 'I want to be clear: Conflict is not inevitable in space or anywhere else. And the United States of America is committed to preventing conflict through deterrence by making clear to our competitors that the costs of aggression would far outweigh any conceivable benefits' at <https://www.defense.gov/News/News-Stories/Article/Article/3641577/hicks-us-aims-to-prevent-conflict-in-space-other-domains-through-deterrence/>.

8 North Atlantic Treaty Organization, 'NATO's Approach to Space' (*NATO*, 21 March 2024) accessed 6 August 2024; North Atlantic Treaty Organization, 'NATO's Overarching Space Policy' (*NATO*, 30 May 2024) <https://www.nato.int/cps/en/natohq/official_texts_190862.htm>.

9 Office of Space Commerce, 'National Space Policy of the United States of America, Principles' (*White House*, 9 December 2020) <https://trumpwhitehouse.archives.gov/wp-content/uploads/2020/12/National-Space-Policy.pdf> accessed 6 August 2024.

10 Department of Defense, '2020 National Space Defense Strategy' <https://media.defense.gov/2020/Jun/17/2002317391/-1/-1/1/2020_DEFENSE_SPACE_STRATEGY_SUMMARY.PDF> (DoD, June 2022) accessed 11 July 2024.

11 Achievement of a uniform interpretation of the right of self-defence in conformity with the United Nations Charter as applied to outer space as a factor in maintaining outer space a safe and conflict-free environment and promoting the long-term sustainability of outer space activities, Working Paper submitted by the Russian Federation to the Legal Subcommittee of the United Nations Committee on the Peaceful Uses of Outer Space, A/AC.105/C.1/2015/CRP.22, 2 February 2015.

to fighting conflicts in space.[12] Satellites can be 'attacked' by using kinetic means and non-kinetic means. The former can physically destroy a satellite by directly colliding with it (for this reason, they are usually referred to as ASAT weapons), while the latter may only temporarily halt the functionality of the satellite without causing its physical destruction.[13]

(a) Kinetic ASAT Devices

Countries which have demonstrated the capability to destroy a satellite by using a direct-ascent kinetic ASAT device are China, the United States, India, and the Russian Federation.[14] The first country to test an ASAT weapon of this kind was China on 11 January 2007, which destroyed one of its weather satellites, the FY-1C polar orbit satellite, by using a kinetic kill vehicle.[15] The Chinese test prompted a response from the United States, which on 21 February 2008 destroyed its decaying satellite USA-193 by shooting a modified SM-3 missile from the warship USS *Lake Erie*.[16] While the US move was officially dictated by safety concerns, one cannot underestimate the fact that it also gave the United States the optimal opportunity to show China its ability to strike a satellite by means of a direct-ascent device. More recently, in 2019 and 2021, India[17] and the Russian Federation[18] successfully tested direct ascent kinetic kill weapons by destroying their own satellites in low-Earth orbit. Both tests received strong criticism from the international community due to the increase in the orbital debris population deriving from them.[19] Particularly, the Russian one was strongly condemned by several countries because

12 Brandon L Hart, 'Anti-Satellite Weapons: Threats, Laws and the Uncertain Future of Space' (2008) 33 Annals of Air & Space Law 358; Secure World Foundation, 'Global Counterspace Capabilities Report' (2024) <https://swfound.org/counterspace/> accessed 8 July 2024.

13 Secure World Foundation, 'Global Counterspace Capabilities Report' (Secure World Foundation, April 2024) <https://swfound.org/media/207826/swf_global_counterspace_capabilities_2024.pdf> accessed 6 August 2024.

14 Jeff Foust, 'More Countries Encouraged to Commit to Halt Destructive ASAT Tests' *SpaceNews* (15 June 2023) <https://spacenews.com/more-countries-encouraged-to-commit-to-halt-destructive-asat-tests/> accessed 6 August 2024.

15 Nader Elhefnawy, 'Making Sense of China's Weapons Test' *The Space Review* (2007) <https://www.thespacereview.com/article/801/1#:~:text=On%20Thursday%2C%20January%2011%2C%202007,its%20kind%20since%20the%201980s> accessed 11 July 2007.

16 Dwayne A Day, 'Burning Frost, the View From the Ground: Shooting Down a Spy Satellite in 2008' *The Space Review* (21 May 2021) <https://www.thespacereview.com/article/4198/1> accessed 11 July 2024.

17 Ajey Lele, 'Indian ASAT: Mission Shakti Should Be a Comma, Not a Full Stop' *The Space Review* (27 March 2023) <https://www.thespacereview.com/article/4556/1#:~:text=On%20March%2027%2C%202019%2C%20India,US%2C%20Russia%2C%20and%20China> accessed 11 July 2024.

18 Shanno Bugos, 'Russian ASAT Test Creates Massive Debris' (*Arms Control Today*, 1 December 2021) <https://www.armscontrol.org/act/2021-12/news/russian-asat-test-creates-massive-debris> accessed 11 July 2024.

19 Chelsea Gohd, 'Russia Anti-Satellite Missile Test Was the First of Its Kind' (*Space.com*, 10 August 2022) <https://www.space.com/russia-anti-satellite-missile-test-first-of-its-kind> accessed 7 August 2024.

it was conducted at a higher altitude than the Indian test and the resulting debris directly endangered the occupants of the International Space Station (ISS), who had to first take shelter in the spacecraft that had brought them on board and later perform a debris collision avoidance manoeuvre.[20]

Importantly, satellites can also be damaged, if not destroyed, through an intentional collision with another satellite, usually of a smaller size. Indeed, these microsatellites, while generally not designed to be used for anti-satellite purposes but rather to perform on-orbit servicing, might be manoeuvred to approach and collide with a satellite belonging to another country. No country has officially tested this kind of technology, in the sense of destroying a satellite via a microsatellite; however, there are several reports that both China and Russia have tested the technology by disguising the tests under the umbrella of a proximity operation for civil purposes.[21] These activities, even though they do not violate any specific international rule, have sparked concern because of their secretive nature and the fact that recourse to this technology may result in the voluntary or accidental increase of the debris orbital population.[22]

(b) Non-Kinetic (Non-Physical) Means of Attacking Satellites

Non-kinetic means of attacking a satellite include cyber-attacks, jamming, and interference. Each of these will be considered in turn.

- *Cyber-Attacks*

A cyber-attack is an attack on or through the 'cyberspace', namely the Global Information Infrastructure.[23] Cyber-attacks thus affect an adversary's information and information systems.[24] Cyber-attacks may constitute very effective anti-satellite weapons, as they can be directed not only against the computer on board a satellite, but also against the ground station that controls it.[25] In the latter case, a cyber-attack may steal information and data and insert fake components

20 Brett Tingley, 'International Space Station Dodges Space Debris From Russian Anti-Satellite Test' (*Space.com*, 26 October 2022) <https://www.space.com/international-space-station-dodges-russian-space-debris> accessed 7 August 2024.

21 Andrew Jones, 'China's Secretive Spaceplane Conducts Proximity Operations With Small Spacecraft' <https://spacenews.com/chinas-secretive-spaceplane-conducts-proximity-operations-with-small-spacecraft/>.

22 Theresa Hitchens, 'LeoLabs: Russia, China Time Suspicious Space Activity for Some US Holidays' (*Breaking Defense*, 12 December 2023) <https://breakingdefense.com/2023/12/leolabs-russia-china-time-suspicious-space-activity-for-some-us-holidays/> accessed 7 August 2024.

23 See National Defense Panel, Transforming Defense National Security in the 21st Century (1997).

24 Christopher M Petras, 'The Use of Force in Response to Cyber-Attack on Commercial Space Systems—Reexamining Self-Defense in Outer Space in Light of the Convergence of U.S. Military and Commercial Space Activities' (2002) 67 Journal of Air Law and Commerce 1213, 1249.

25 Jacob G Oakley, *Cybersecurity for Space: Protecting the Final Frontier* (Apress 2020); Charlotte Van Camp, Walter Peeters, 'A World Without Satellite Data as a Result of a Global Cyber-Attack' (2022) 59 Space Policy 1.

into the satellite system. However, cyber-attacks might also have more devastating physical consequences.[26] If the cyber-attacker is able to gain access to the system controlling the satellite, it might activate its manoeuvring engines in a way that would cause it to lose altitude and burn off upon reaching the atmosphere.[27] In other words, cyber-attacks have the potential to be used both as destructive and non-destructive ASATs.

- *Jamming*

Jamming enables the temporary interruption of the functionality of a satellite without having to destroy it. Jamming can be performed by 'overloading enemy receivers with strong signals'[28] or by 'sending deceptive signals.'[29] Jamming a satellite's signal does not necessitate expensive or high-tech technology. Several countries possess the capability for jamming satellite transmissions, and cases of 'jammed' transmissions have occurred over the years.[30] The jamming of navigation signals (such as GPS) and communication satellites during a conflict is generally regarded as a routine activity. Indeed, all major space-faring powers concur on the legality of satellite jamming in wartime and possess satellite jamming capabilities.[31] On the contrary, far more controversial is the question of satellite interference outside of a direct conflict, a practice that has occurred repeatedly in recent years.[32] While the United States considers satellite interference outside of a theatre of conflict to be an 'irresponsible' and potentially dangerous behaviour, it does not go as far as calling it an act of war. Instead, the head of the Russian Space Agency, Dimitry Rogozin, stated, '[o]fflining the satellites of any country is actually a *casus belli*, a cause for war.'[33] In fairness, however, Rogozin's view is not shared by many, as there is no

26 Mark Holmes, 'The Growing Risk of a Major Satellite Cyber-Attack' (*Via Satellite*, 2024) <https://interactive.satellitetoday.com/the-growing-risk-of-a-major-satellite-cyber-attack/> accessed 11 July 2024; See also P Shakarian, *An Introduction to Cyber-Warfare: A Multidisciplinary Approach* (Syngress 2013).

27 Walter Peeters, 'Cyber Attacks on Satellites: An Underestimated Political Threat' (*London School of Economics Ideas*, 10 November 2022) <https://www.lse.ac.uk/ideas/projects/space-policy/publications/Cyberattacks-on-Satellites> accessed 7 August 2024.

28 US, Office of Technology Assessment, Anti-Satellite Weapons, Countermeasures, and Arms Control (1985) at 9.

29 US, Office of Technology Assessment (n 28).

30 Pavel Veskovsky, Jnani Mohan and Maxwell Simon, 'Satellite Jamming' (*Issue Briefs*, 3 April 2019) <https://ontheradar.csis.org/issue-briefs/satellite-jamming/#:~:text=For%20example%2C%20interference%20with%20satellite,of%20the%20International%20Telecommunications%20Union> accessed 11 July 2024.

31 T Hitchens, 'Satellite Jamming Normal by Militaries During Conflict, Not Peacetime: State Dept. Official' (*Breaking Defense*, 21 March 2022) < Satellite jamming 'normal' by militaries during conflict, not peacetime: State Dept. official—Breaking Defense> accessed 7 August 2024.

32 Secure World Foundation (n 13).

33 Hitchens (n 31).

indication that countries view reversible satellite interference as an act of war calling for an armed response.

- *Interference*

Another way to affect the functionality of a satellite is to interfere with its transmissions, for example by reducing its ability to communicate and to receive instructions from the respective ground station. An action of this kind can be performed not only through a cyber-attack but also by a satellite positioned in the vicinity of the targeted satellite. While a similar interference would not directly cause the destruction of the latter satellite, it might lead to negative consequences on the ground, such as the interruption or alteration of services relying on the satellite signal.

(c) Space Forces

The United States, the Russian Federation, and China have all established forces specifically designed to protect not only their national interests in space but also to actively respond to threats to their space assets. These forces have been named the US Space Force,[34] the Russian Aerospace Forces,[35] and the People's Liberation Army Aerospace Force.[36] These forces share similar goals, namely to enable the implementation of their respective space policies and to ensure the ability to safely enter, exit, and operate in outer space. From an international law perspective, the establishment of these entities does not clash with any specific rule, as their purpose is primarily defensive and is intended to provide a country with the means to protect its national interests in outer space. However, considering the uncertainty surrounding the concept of the use of force, or threat of use of force, against space objects and the way to respond to it, reflecting upon how the right of self-defence applies to outer space emerges as an even more pressing need.

4 The Right of Self-Defence in Public International Law

The right of states to act in self-defence is a fundamental principle of international law. Every state enjoys the right to protect its territorial integrity, political independence, persons, and properties falling under its jurisdiction from foreign attacks and to react in self-defence when such attacks occur. As stated by the International

34 United States Space Force <https://www.spaceforce.mil/> accessed 11 July 2024.

35 Russia's Defense Industry, 'Russia Establishes Aerospace Forces as New Armed Service' <http://tass.com/russia/812184> accessed 11 July 2024.

36 Matt Bruzzese and Peter Senger, 'Farewell to China's Strategic Support Force. Let's Meet Its Replacements' (*Defense One*, 28 April 2024) <https://www.defenseone.com/ideas/2024/04/farewell-chinas-strategic-support-force-lets-meet-its-replacement/396143/> accessed 11 July 2024. National Space Intelligence Center/National Air and Space Intelligence Center, *Competing in Space* (2nd edn, 2023) <https://www.spoc.spaceforce.mil/Portals/4/Images/2_Space_Slicky_11x17_Web_View_reduced.pdf> accessed 11 July 2024.

Court of Justice (ICJ) in the *Oil Platforms* case, measures of self-defence are necessary to protect the essential security interests of a state.[37] This case concerned a series of naval disputes between the United States and Iran in the late 1980s. The Court reaffirmed that the right of individual self-defence is dependent on a state being the victim of an armed attack and also that the force used in self-defence must be necessary and proportionate. Significantly, the Court confirmed the high threshold test from the *Nicaragua* case to determine the existence of an 'armed attack', namely to limit it to 'the most grave forms of the use of force' (excluding, thus, minor use of force that does not reach such a threshold).[38] The *Oil Platforms* case also gave the Court the opportunity to develop the law on the use of force; in particular, the Court opened up the possibility for an armed attack to occur not only as a result of a single event but also through a series of events that combined together would reach the threshold of an armed attack (this is the so-called theory of accumulation of events).[39] The right of self-defence is formally enshrined in Article 51 of the United Nations Charter, which provides, '[n]othing in the present Charter shall impair the inherent right of individual or collective self-defense if an armed attack occurs against a Member of the United Nations, until the Security Council has taken measures necessary to maintain international peace and security.'[40] Notably, the right of states to act in self-defence represents one of the two exceptions to the prohibition on the use of force that the Charter lays down in Article 2(4),[41] the other one being the use of force authorized by the Security Council under Chapter VII of the Charter.[42] The meaning and scope of self-defence has been highly debated in international law circles.[43] Discussions have often centred on three elements: (a) the notion of an armed attack; (b) the timeframe for the exercise of the right of self-defence; and (c) the scope of self-defence. Each of these elements will now be considered in turn.

37 *Islamic Republic of Iran v. United States of America* [2003] ICJ Rep 161 (Oil Platforms case), at para. 51.

38 Nicaragua case [1986] ICJ Rep 14, 91. According to the ICJ in the Nicaragua case, the gravity of a particular use of force is judged according to its 'scale and effects': [1986] ICJ Rep 14, 103.

39 Oil Platforms case (Merits) [6 November 2003] ICJ [64] at 1 May 2004. The Court stated there that 'the question is whether that attack, either in itself or in combination with the rest of "the series . . . of attacks" cited by the United States can be categorized as an "armed attack"'

40 Article 51 of the UN Charter.

41 Article 2(4) of the Charter of the United Nations provides, '[a]ll Members shall refrain in their international relations from the threat or use of force against the territorial integrity or political independence of any State, or in any other manner inconsistent with the Purposes of the United Nations.'

42 Stanimir A Alexandrov, *Self-Defense Against the Use of Force in International Law* (Kluwer Law International 1996); Oscar Schachter, 'International Law: The Right of States to Use Armed Force' (1984) 82 Michigan Law Review 1620; Thomas Franck, *Recourse to Force: State Action Against Threats and Armed Attacks* (CUP 2002).

43 See Yoram Dinstein, *War, Aggression and Self-Defence* (4th edn, CUP 2005); Judith Gardam, *Necessity, Proportionality and the Use of Force by States* (CUP 2004); Christine D Gray, *International Law and the Use of Force* (2nd edn, OUP 2005); Natalia Ochoa-Ruiz and Esther Salamanca-Aguado, 'Exploring the Limits of International Law Relating to the Use of Force in Self-Defence' (2005) 16 European Journal of International Law 499.

(a) The Notion of an Armed Attack

Article 51 of the UN Charter speaks of the right of self-defence 'if an armed attack occurs' but does not define what an 'armed attack' is. The jurisprudence of the ICJ affirms that the scale of the force used, the target of the attack, and the military nature of the attack are the main factors to be considered when evaluating the occurrence of an armed attack.[44] Notably, there is a discrepancy between the language of Article 51 (safeguarding the right of self-defence if an armed attack occurs) and the words of Article 2(4) (prohibiting the threat or use of force). The clear implication is that while every use of force against the territorial integrity or political independence of another state is prohibited, not every such use of force constitutes an armed attack.[45] Indeed, the ICJ has distinguished between the most grave forms of the use of force and other less grave forms (such as a mere frontier accident).[46] Thus, only a use of force that meets a certain threshold of 'scale and effects', or gravity of harm, would constitute an armed attack. This approach has not been universally accepted. It has been argued that any use of force causing human casualties or serious damage to property constitutes an armed attack.[47] Furthermore, it has been held that an armed attack means any use of armed force and does not need to cross some threshold of intensity' to activate the right to act in self-defence.[48]

While affirming the need for an armed attack to occur to trigger the right to act in self-defence, the ICJ was also open to the possibility for an armed attack to be the result not only of a single event, but also of a series of events, through a doctrine that has been labelled as the 'theory of accumulation of events.'[49] In short, this theory argues that while one of the attacks by itself would be insufficient to meet the gravity threshold of an armed attack, the accumulation of more minor attacks potentially could.[50] The ICJ referred to this idea in the *Nicaragua* case when, in determining whether the gravity threshold had been met, it indicated that

44 Gray Christine, 'The International Court of Justice and the Use of Force' in Christian J Tams and James Sloan (eds), *The Development of International Law by the International Court of Justice* (OUP 2013); Laurie L Blanck, 'Irreconcilable Differences: The Threshold for Armed Attack and International Armed Attack' (2020) 96 Notre Dame Law Review 249.

45 David Kretzmer, 'The Inherent Right to Self-Defence and Proportionality in *Jus ad Bellum*' (2013) 24(1) European Journal of International Law 235.

46 See *Case Concerning Military and Paramilitary Activities in and Against Nicaragua* (*Nicaragua v. USA*) [1986] ICJ. Rep 94 (Nicaragua case), para 195; (*Islamic Republic of Iran v. United States of America*) [2003] ICJ Rep 161 (*Oil Platforms* case), para. 51. James A Green, *The International Court of Justice and Self-Defence in International Law* (Hart 2009) 27.

47 See Dinstein (n 43) 74.

48 Chatham House, 'Principles of International Law on Use of Force in Self-Defence' <www.chathamhouse.org.uk/publications/papers/view/-/id/308> accessed 11 July 2024.

49 Gray (n 43) 130, 155; Christian J, Tams, 'The Use of Force Against Terrorists' (2009) 20 European Journal of International Law 359; Monika Hakimi, 'Defensive Force Against Non-State Actors: The State of Play' (2015) 91 International Law Studies 1.

50 Chris Henderson, 'The 25 February 2021 Military Strikes and the "Armed Attack" Requirement of Self-Defence: From "*sina qua non*" to the Point of Vanishing?' (2022) 9 Journal on the Use of Force and International Law 55.

incursions 'may be treated for legal purposes as amounting, *singly or collectively*, to an 'armed attack.'[51] Even though the Court has never decided a case by relying on such a theory, there is some support by scholars, the ICJ, and, most importantly, by states.[52]

(b) The Timeframe for the Exercise of the Right of Self-Defence

The moment from which states can act in self-defence is extremely controversial.[53] Numerous scholars support a restrictive reading of Article 51 of the UN Charter, contending that the right of self-defence can only be exercised after an armed attack occurs.[54] This implicitly excludes any anticipatory acts of self-defence, either to impede an imminent attack or to deter future ones. Some scholars support a broader interpretation of Article 51 which allows a state to act preventively to impede an imminent attack to be launched against their territory. This is the so-called doctrine of anticipatory self-defence. Supporters of this doctrine bring forward historical, textual, and factual arguments to support it.[55] First, there is evidence that when drafting the UN Charter many states assumed that the inherent right of self-defence includes the right to use force against an imminent attack if the conditions of the *Caroline* test are met, namely that a state is faced with the threat of an armed attack which presents a 'necessity of self-defense, instant, overwhelming, leaving no choice of means and no moment of deliberation.'[56] Second, the use of the word 'inherent' in Article 51 signifies that the right of self-defence existed prior to the UN Charter and that the Charter was not meant to alter the already established interpretation of this right. Finally, considering the destructive power of modern weapons as well as the inability of the Security Council to

51 *Nicaragua* (merits) (n 7) para 231 (emphasis added). This was also accepted as a possibility in *Oil Platforms* (judgment) (n 34) para 64, and *Armed Activities on the Territory of the Congo* (Democratic Republic of the Congo v Uganda) (judgment) [2005] ICJ Reports 168, para 146.

52 The United States under the Biden Administration indirectly relied on this argument to justify as a self-defence measure the airstrikes undertaken by US force in eastern Syria following the 2021 rocket attacks on the Erbil airport. See, on this, Henderson (n 50) 58–60.

53 The International Law Association ('ILA') stated, '[w]hether or not a State may rely on self-defence in order to take forcible measures prior to an armed attack is one of the clearest instances in which the line between self-defence and unlawful use of force is most often debated.' International Law Association (ILA), Committee on the Use of Force, 'Final Report on Aggression and the Use of Force' (2018) <www.ila-hq.org/images/ILA/DraftReports/DraftReport_UseOfForce.pdf> accessed 11 July 2024.

54 Bruno Simma, *The Carter of the United Nations, Commentary*, vol I (2nd edn, OUP 2002) 805; James A Green, 'Article 51 Reporting Requirement for Self-Defense Actions' (2015) 55 Virginia Journal of International Law 568.

55 Dinstein (n 43) 76; Thomas M. Franck, 'The Power of Legitimacy and the Legitimacy of Power: International Law in an Age of Power Disequilibrium' (2006) 100 American Journal of International Law 88.

56 Note of Daniel Webster dated April 24, 1841 <http://avalon.law.yale.edu/19th_century/br-1842d.asp> accessed 11 July 2024. A description of the Caroline case is provided in Michael N Shaw, *International Law* (CUP 2008) 1131.

prevent aggression, it would be hard to request a state facing an imminent attack to sit by idly and wait for the attack to start before it could defend itself. Notably, the doctrine of anticipatory self-defence has gradually been accepted by a growing number of scholars.[57] Also, the High-Level Panel of Experts appointed by then UN Secretary-General Kofi Annan took a clear stand on this issue when it wrote, 'a threatened State, according to long established international law, can take military action as long as the threatened attack is imminent, no other means would deflect it and the action is proportionate.'[58] Even though there is growing support towards the legality of anticipatory actions of self-defence in the presence of an 'imminent' attack, this does not automatically signify that forms of anticipatory self-defence in outer space are legitimate or even desirable.

Indeed, there are several challenges to the hypothetical legitimacy of these actions in the space environment, such as the dual nature of space objects, the difficulties to determine the nature of the space activity undertaken, the question of whether the activity is of an offensive or defensive kind, and how to respond to it. For example, if we envision a situation where satellites from country A conduct unannounced proximity operations on satellites belonging to country B, how would it be possible to determine that the operations are of a hostile nature and constitute the prelude of an imminent attack? Starting from this latter remark, it is arguable that any attempt to justify anticipatory self-defence actions in outer space would have to meet a high threshold of proof that would be hard to achieve in practice. For instance, returning to the proximity operations example, a claimant state willing to act in an anticipatory manner would have to provide evidence that these proximity operations are not the result of a technical failure or miscommunication between the satellite and its control centre but are done purposefully, with the intention to harm and are irreversible. Realistically, the claiming state could only provide evidence that these conditions are met by showing that (1) any attempt to communicate with the operator of the satellites, either directly or indirectly, has failed; (2) any international call to de-escalate the situation has not reached any result; (3) the satellites are operating in a coordinated and consistent manner in proximity to the claimant State's satellites; and (4) the satellites are in such a proximity to the claimant state's satellites to see no other reason than a hostile intent. Even though all these conditions would be met, there would still be the open question of how the state could act to 'anticipate' this threat and the consequences of such actions on the space environment.

An additional interpretation of Article 51 has been suggested: the theory of pre-emptive self-defence. According to this theory states should be entitled to militarily intervene in order to prevent a future attack, even when there is no reason to believe that an attack is planned and no prior attack has occurred. Thus, unlike

57 Timothy LH McCormack, 'Anticipatory Self-Defence in the Legislative History of the United Nations Charter' (1991) 25 Israel Law Review 1; Kretzmer (n 45) 248. Franck (n 55) 107.

58 *A More Secure World: Our Shared Responsibility*, Report of the High-Level Panel on Threats, hallenges and Change (2004) UN Doc A/59/565, at para. 188 <www2.ohchr.org/English/bodies/hrcouncil/docs/gaA.59.565_En.pdf> accessed 11 July 2024.

anticipatory self-defence, pre-emptive self-defence is not triggered by any event but comes from a general apprehension of being attacked. This theory, which has been endorsed by the United States at the time of the G.W. Bush Administration[59] and by several writers,[60] is unlawful under international law and, not surprisingly, has been nearly universally rejected. Such a rejection is largely the result of the low threshold that a state should meet to act in self-defence, as opposed, for example, to forms of 'anticipatory' self-defence. Indeed, while in the latter case, a state must provide evidence of the imminence of an attack and the absence of an alternative solution to act in self-defence, in the former, the simple hypothetical threat of an attack is a sufficient reason to justify the use of force. Clearly, such a loose approach to the use of force does not translate well to the space environment, and there is no state that has ever formally claimed the legality of pre-emptive strikes of self-defence in outer space.

(c) The Scope of Self-Defence

The traditional and literal reading of Article 51 holds that the right of self-defence can be exercised only while an armed attack is in course and for the purpose of halting and repelling it.[61] Any military action undertaken after the attack is concluded would constitute a reprisal, hence illegal under the UN Charter.[62] The illegality of a reprisal stems from its scope, that is not to repel and halt an attack but to punish the aggressor. An opposite view argues that states can also act in self-defence after an attack is over.[63] The rationale behind this proposition is that it is not always possible to halt or repel an attack.[64] Indeed, such an attack can be unexpected and of short duration, making it technically impossible to halt. This, however, should not

59 The National Security Strategy of the United States of America, Washington, 17 September 2002 <http://www.whitehouse.gov/nsc/nss.html> accessed 11 July 2024; The National Military Strategy of the United States, 2004 <http://www.defenselink.mil/news/Mar2005/d20050318nms.pdf> accessed 11 July 2024; US National Security Strategy 2006 <http://georgewbush-whitehouse.archives.gov/nsc/nss/2006> accessed 11 July 2024.

60 Michael J. Glennon, 'Pre-Empting Terrorism; The Case for Anticipatory Self-Defense' *Weekly Standard* (28 January 2002); Thomas Franck, 'Terrorism and the Right of Self- Defense' (2001) 95 American Journal of International Law 839; but see Mary E O'Connell, 'The Myth of Preemptive Self-Defense' (2002) ASIL Task Force Paper.

61 Roberto Ago, Special Rapporteur to the International Law Commission, '*Eighth Report on State Responsibility*' (1980) Yearbooks of the International Law Commission ii, I, 13, UN Doc A/CN.4/318/ADD.5–7; at. para. 121; Antonio Cassese, *International Law* (2nd edn, OUP 2005), at 355; Antonio Canizzaro, 'Contextualizing Proportionality: *Jus Ad Bellum* and *Jus in Bello* in the Lebanese War' (2006) 88 International Review of the Red Cross 779; Olivier Corten, *The Law Against War: The Prohibition on the Use of Force in Contemporary International Law* (Hart Publishing 2010) 484–93.

62 Roberto Barsotti, 'Armed Reprisals' in A Cassese (ed), *The Current Legal Regulation of the Use of Force* (Martinus Nijhoff Publishers 1986), at 79; William O'Brien, 'Reprisals, Deterrence and Self-Defense in Counter Terror Operations' (1990) 30 Virginia Journal of International Law 421; Corten (n 61) 234–36.

63 Dinstein (n 43) 198; O'Brien (n 62) 426; Corten (n 61) 486; Daniel Mellow, 'Counterfactuals and the Proportionality Criterion' (2006) 20 Ethics and International Affairs 434.

64 Chris O' Meara, 'Reconceptualizing the Right of Self-Defence Against Imminent Armed Attacks' (2022) 9 Journal on the Use of Force and International Law.

alter the right to act in self-defence, even if at a later stage. Clearly, in this case the purpose of self-defence cannot be to stop the attack. Proponents of this view suggest that the response should not be moved by punitive intention, but by the goal of preventing or deterring future attacks.[65] Furthermore, the response must be proportionate to the scale and intensity of the attack. For example, a frontier incident should not lead to a military invasion of the territory of the attacker.

In practice, it might be problematic to demonstrate that a self-defence action undertaken after the conclusion of an attack is not guided by punitive intent. Many would classify it, regardless of its declared scope, as a reprisal. On the other hand, the claim that the sole aim of using force in self-defence is to halt and repel an armed attack seems out of touch with reality and does not reflect state practice.[66] Considering also the inability of the UN Security Council to take quick action, preventing *a priori* the possibility to act after an attack is concluded could eventually undermine the inherent right of a state to act in self-defence.[67] It could also be problematic to exactly determine if a response has been proportionate. In any case, decisive factors for claiming the legitimacy of an act in self-defence are (i) the actual occurrence of an armed attack; (ii) the scale of the attack; (iii) the necessity of recourse to force;[68] and (iv) the proportionality of the response.[69] First, self-defence requires the actual occurrence of an armed attack or the unquestionable proof of its imminence. Second, the attack must reach a certain magnitude to trigger the right of self-defence under Article 51 of the UN Charter. Third, recourse to force must be 'necessary'. In this context 'necessity' refers to situations where forceful action is *necessary* to defend against an armed attack.[70] Fourth, the response must be proportionate. Traditionally, 'proportionality' means that the amount of force used by state A as a countermeasure against state B must be proportionate to the force previously used by state B.[71] Other scholars argue that proportionality must be judged against the legitimate ends of using force (halt, repel, imminent, etc.) or in relation to the threat.[72] A response that is excessive compared to the legitimate ends would then be non-proportionate.

65 Mary Ellen O'Connell, 'The Popular but Unlawful Armed Reprisal' (2018) 44 Ohio Northern University Law Review 325.

66 Kretzmer (n 45) 262.

67 Vaughan. Lowe, '*The United Nations Security Council and War: The Evolution of Thought and Practice Since 1945*' (OUP 2008) 265–515.

68 As pointed out by the International Court of Justice, a state exercising the right of self-defence must comply with the principles of necessity and proportionality, see *Nicaragua Case*, at para. 176; *Legality of the Threat or Use of Nuclear Weapons*, Advisory Opinion [1996] ICJ Rep 226, at para. 41; Gray (n 43) 150.

69 On the issue of the proportionality of a self-defence response see generally Gardam (n 43) and Kretzmer (n 45); T Franck, 'On Proportionality of Countermeasures in International Law' (2008) 102 American Journal of International Law 715; Cassese (n 61) 355; The American Society of International Law, 22(5) *Newsletter*, September/October 2006, 1.

70 Oscar Schachter, 'The Right of States to Use Armed Force' (1984) 82 Michigan Law Review Festschrift in Honor of Eric Stein 1620.

71 Ago (n 61) 69; Noam Lubell, *Extraterritorial Use of Force Against Non-State Actors* (Oxford University Press 2010) 64.

72 D Rodin, *War and Self-Defense* (OUP 2005) 115; Gardam (n 43); Corten (n 61).

5 Space Law and the Right of Self-Defence

In today's world, satellites are increasingly at risk of being targeted either through a direct or indirect attack. This is not only due to their economic significance but also because of their relevance from a strategic and geopolitical perspective. Indeed, satellites perform crucial defence tasks, such as surveillance and early warnings, and contribute to enhancing the effectiveness of military operations, as the recent conflict in Ukraine has demonstrated. It is, thus, unsurprising that the need to protect space assets has become a part of the space narrative and a key element of the national defence strategies of space-faring countries. For instance, the 2020 National Space Policy of the United States affirms:

> [c]onsistent with the defense of those rights, the United States will seek to deter, counter, and defeat threats in the space domain that are hostile to the national interests of the United States and its allies. Any purposeful interference with or an attack upon the space systems of the United States or its allies that directly affects national rights will be met with a deliberate response at a time, place, manner, and domain of our choosing.[73]

Also, the Russian Federation and China, apart from constantly upgrading their counterspace capabilities,[74] view the protection of their space capabilities as a key component of their national defence strategies.[75] Notably, one of the policy goals of the newly established PLA Aerospace Force is, indeed, to safeguard China's security interests in outer space and ensure its capacity to access and use it.[76]

73 National Space Policy of the United States of America, Principles, 9th December, 2020 <https://trumpwhitehouse.archives.gov/wp-content/uploads/2020/12/National-Space-Policy.pdf> accessed 11 July 2024.

74 Secure World Foundation, 'Global Counterspace Capabilities' (2024) <https://swfound.org/media/207826/swf_global_counterspace_capabilities_2024.pdf> accessed 11 July 2024; Andrew Jones, 'China's Secretive Spaceplane Conducts Proximity Operations With Small Spacecraft' *SpaceNews* (13 June 2024) <https://spacenews.com/chinas-secretive-spaceplane-conducts-proximity-operations-with-small-spacecraft/> accessed 11 July 2024.

75 The 2019 China's White Paper on Defence states: '[o]uter space is a critical domain in international strategic competition. Outer space security provides strategic assurance for national and social development. China . . . and enhances the capacity to safely enter, exit and openly use outer space' <https://english.www.gov.cn/archive/whitepaper/201907/24/content_WS5d3941ddc6d08408f502283d.html> accessed 11 July 2024; Greg Hadley, 'Advancing in Space, China Poses Growing Threat, USSF Leaders Warn' *Air and Space Forces Magazine* (28 March 2024) <https://www.airandspaceforces.com/ussf-leaders-china-space-threaten-us/> accessed 11 July 2024; Anthony H Cordesman, 'Chinese Strategy and Military Modernization in 2016: A Comparative Analysis' (*Center for Strategic and International Studies*, 8 December 2016 <https://www.csis.org/analysis/chinese-strategy-and-military-modernization-2016> accessed 11 July 2024.

76 Namrata Goswami, 'The Reorganization of China's Space Force: Strategic and Organizational Implications' <https://thediplomat.com/2024/05/the-reorganization-of-chinas-space-force-strategic-and-organizational-implications/#:~:text=One%20of%20the%20Aerospace%20Force's,security%20interests%20in%20outer%20space.%E2%80%9D> May.

Attempting to envision how the right of self-defence[77] applies to outer space faces two immediate challenges, one linked to the special nature of the space environment and the other to the dual characteristics of space objects. Outer space explorers need to strike a very delicate balance, where one's actions may harm the environment as well as negatively affect other countries' activities.[78] For example, space debris generated by the destruction of a satellite not only puts at risk the safety of the space objects located near the explosion but also makes a section of the Earth's orbit virtually unusable. Second, many satellites have a dual function, meaning that they can perform the same service for both civil and military purposes.[79] Imagine a series of satellites providing navigation and Earth observation services to support civil navigation and disaster relief operations; the same satellites may be used to provide militaries with intelligence, surveillance, and reconnaissance data enabling them to identify adversary capabilities, track troop movements, and locate potential targets. The dual nature of satellites not only complicates the task of identifying where an attack has originated from, but it also raises the question of whether a satellite, which provides fundamental services to civilian populations, may become a legitimate target if it is used to support military operations. Another aspect of this dilemma is also the fact that some of the most recent technological developments in space have, at least in principle, a dual purpose. For instance, the technology to perform on-orbit servicing, refuelling, and active debris removal, while being created to serve benign purposes, may be repurposed to harm other space objects (the robotic arm intended to repair satellites may in turn be used to harm them).[80]

(a) Space Law and the Right of Self-Defence

Any legal analysis of how the right of self-defence may be exercised in outer space must start by determining if that right is applicable therein.[81] Notably, the main

77 Dio H Tobing and Olivia N Maryatmo, 'Celestial Anarchy: States' Right to Self-Defence'(2013) 4 Juris Gentium Law Review 9.

78 Marietta Benkö, 'A Valid Case Against the Use of Aggressive Military Systems in Outer Space?' in M Benkö and KU Schrogl (eds), *Current Problems and Perspectives for Future Regulation* (Eleven 2005) 155–75; Steve Mirmina, 'The Ballistic Missile Defense System and Its Effects on the Outer Space Environment' (2005) 31 Journal of Space Law 287.

79 Jakub Prazak, 'Dual-Use Conundrum: Towards the Weaponization of Outer Space?' (2021) 187 Acta Astronautica 397–405.

80 UNIDIR Statement at the Open-Ended Working Group on 'Reducing Space Threats Through Norms, Rules and Principles of Responsible Behaviours', Topic 3: Current and future space-to-space threats by States to space systems, Geneva, 14 September 2022 <https://documents.unoda.org/wp-content/uploads/2022/09/Azcarate-Ortega-Almudena-OEWG-dual-use-presentation-FINAL.pdf> accessed 11 July 2024.

81 On the applicability of the right of self-defence to outer space see Elisabeth S. Waldrop, 'Integration of Military and Civilian Space Assets: Legal and National Security Implications' (2004) 55 Air Force Law Review 157; Ricky J. Lee, 'The Jus ad Bellum in Outer Space: The Interrelationship Between Article 103 of the Charter of the United Nations and Article IV of the Outer Space Treaty' (2002) 45 Proceedings of the International Institute of Space Law 139; Brandon L. Hart,

instruments regulating activities in outer space, namely the 1967 Outer Space Treaty, does not specifically refer to the possibility for states to act in self-defence in outer space. This has led some to question whether this right can be exercised outside of Earth based on the argument that self-defence operations would clash with the idea of using space for peaceful purposes.[82] This view relies on a restrictive interpretation of the notion of peaceful purposes that is not accepted by the majority of states and scholars. Indeed, by virtue of Article III of the Treaty, it is instead arguable that the right to act in self-defence extends to the space realm. Article III formally codifies the applicability of public international law to outer space by providing: '[s]tates Parties to the Treaty shall carry on activities in the exploration and use of outer space, . . . in accordance with international law, including the Charter of the United Nations.'[83] This means that the scope of the obligations and rights laid down in the UN Charter, including the right of self-defence, extend to outer space. Some may reject this argument by pointing out that Article 51, as well as the whole Charter, never mentions outer space; however, there is nothing in the Charter that specifically excludes it either. Furthermore, the meaning of Article 51 must be ascertained in the light of the object and purpose of the UN Charter as well as of the meaning attributed to that article at the time of the signing of the Charter.[84] The purpose of Article 51 is to give states the right to react if attacked. This right is attributed to states regardless of where the attack takes place on land, air, sea, or even outer space.

Interestingly, the Outer Space Treaty contains limited provisions dealing with the military uses of space.[85] Besides the prohibition to place nuclear weapons or weapons of mass destruction in orbit or on the Moon, the Treaty does not provide any specific restriction on the use of space for military or defence purposes, meaning that the placing of conventional weapons in orbit around the Earth as well as the testing of anti-satellite technology is not specifically prohibited.[86] The Outer Space Treaty indicates that space should be used for 'peaceful purposes' without, however,

---

'Anti-Satellite Weapons: Threats, Laws and the Uncertain Future of Space' (2008) XXXIII Annals of Air & Space Law 345; early studies were conducted by John C. Cooper, 'Self-Defence in Outer Space and the United Nations' (1962) 5 Air Force and Space Digest 51; Hamilton DeSaussure and others, 'Self-Defence—A Right in Outer Space' (1965) 7 Air Force Law Review 38.

82 See Ian A Vlasic, 'Space Law and the Military Applications of Space Technology' in N Jasentuliyana (ed), *Perspectives on International law* (Martinus Nijhoff 1995) 394; Bruce Hurwitz, *The Legality of Space Militarization* (Elsevier 1986) 71.

83 On this point see Michel Bourbonniere, 'National Security Law in Outer Space: The Interface of Exploration and Security' (2005) 70 Journal of Air Law and Commerce 3, 7; Francis Lyall and Paul B Larsen, *Space Law: A Treatise* (Ashgate 2009) 501.

84 Art. 31(1), Vienna Convention on the Law of Treaties.

85 Isavella Maria Vasilogeorgi, 'Military Uses of Outer Space: Legal Limitations, Contemporary Perspectives' (2014) 39 Journal of Space Law 379.

86 Fabio Tronchetti. 'Legal Aspects of the Military Uses of Outer Space' in Frans G von der Dunk and Fabio Tronchetti (eds), *Handbook of Space Law* (Edward Elgar Publishing 2015) 331; Frans G von der Dunk, 'Armed Conflicts in Outer Space: Which Law Applies?' (2021) 97 International Law Studies 188.

explaining the meaning of this notion.[87] Usually, this has been interpreted not as a total prohibition on the use of force, but as a prohibition to use space, and space objects, for aggressive purposes in contradiction to the prohibition to use force set forth in Article 2(4) of the UN Charter (for instance the intentional destruction of another country's satellite).[88] From this perspective, the use of satellites to support military operations on Earth, via the provision of Earth observation data, communication, and navigation services, is generally regarded as a non-aggressive, peaceful, use of outer space.[89]

Another controversial provision included in Article IX of the Outer Space Treaty requires states to conduct their space operations taking into consideration the interests of other states. International consultations must be undertaken if they believe that their planned space activity is likely to cause harmful interference with other states' activities. Once again, the Treaty does not explain the notions of 'due regard' or 'harmful interference'. However, determining their meaning is important for ascertaining the potential triggering of the right of self-defence. For instance, is a series of unannounced proximity operations a sufficient reason to act in self-defence? One may also remember the language of the US National Space Policy that speaks of 'purposeful interference with US space assets' as a reason justifying a deliberate response.

6 Applying the Right of Self-Defence to Outer Space

Having established that the right of self-defence applies to outer space, it is now time to discuss when and how this right might be exercised. The starting point of this analysis is the determination of the occurrence of an armed attack which, as explained earlier, is the condition set by Article 51 of the UN Charter for the activation of the right to act in self-defence. Determining whether an 'armed attack' has occurred in, or in relation to, outer space might be an easy as well as a challenging task. Indeed, much depends on the nature of and circumstances surrounding the events that are claimed to amount to an 'armed attack'.

(a) Attack Against a Space Object by Kinetic (Destructive) Means

If a destructive means is used against another country's satellite and causes its destruction, the activation of the right to act in self-defence pursuant to Article

87 Martin Menter, 'Peaceful Uses of Outer Space and National Security' (1983) Proceedings 25th Colloquium on the Law of Outer Space 135; Carl Q. Christol, *The Modern International Law of Outer Space* (Pergamon Press 1982) 5; Marko G Markoff, 'Disarmament and "Peaceful Purposes" Provisions in the 1967 Outer Space Treaty' (1976) 4 Journal of Space Law 3.

88 Ram Jakhu and others, 'Threats to Peaceful Purposes of Outer Space: Politics and Law' (2020) 18 Astropolitics 22.

89 Air Force Doctrine Publication, Space support to operations (2021) <https://www.doctrine.af.mil/Portals/61/documents/AFDP_3-14/3-14-D06-SPACE-Support-Ops.pdf> accessed 11 July 2024; Frans von der Dunk, 'Armed Conflicts in Outer Space: Which Laws Apply?' (2021) 97 International Law Studies 189.

51 of the UN Charter seems to be rather automatic.[90] Indeed, in such a case the requirements foreseen by this provision as well as the criteria set by the ICJ in the *Nicaragua* and *Oil Platform* rulings would be fully met. First, the action must be armed. The satellite must be destroyed by using a device that is undoubtedly a 'weapon',[91] in the case of a kinetic, hit-to-kill device, or used as a 'weapon', in the case of a microsatellite. While it may be uncertain whether a microsatellite can be classified as a 'weapon' once it is removed from its original orbit and manoeuvred against another satellite, it would lose its peaceful/civil status and turn into an offensive weapon in the hands of the attacker. Second, the purpose of the action must be offensive. In the event of the use of a kinetic, direct-ascent device, the attacker could not claim the destruction of the satellite to be non-intentional or accidental, as the purely harmful intent of its action was clear from the moment the attack was launched. The same argument can be made in relation to a microsatellite, unless its operator can prove that the satellite has drifted unintentionally out of control and notification of the situation had been promptly made to the international community. Third, the satellite must be destroyed. Article 51 requires the offensive action to reach a certain degree of severity. If the ASAT destroys the satellite this parameter would be automatically met. In conclusion, if a state utilizes an ASAT weapon against another state's space object, the right of the latter to act in self-defence cannot be questioned. Such an approach is also confirmed by the military doctrines of the space powers.[92] More problematic is the determination of the forms and means of the state response to the attack. Any use of force in self-defence must meet the criteria of necessity and proportionality and be determined based on the scale and effects of the attack. In the event of an attack against a space object by kinetic (destructive) ASATs, a response could hardly be viewed as proportionate if, for example, the victim state either launched a military invasion of the territory of the attacker or targeted a constellation of its satellites. This is particularly true if the attack had been isolated, meaning that no other satellite had been targeted or that the attack had not been part of a larger military operation (for instance, one that simultaneously involved land, sea, air, and space forces). Instead, a

90 Hart (n 81) 358.

91 'Weapon' is defined as 'An instrument of attack or defense in combat, as a gun, missile', see at <http://www.thefreedictionary.com/weapon>.

92 See, for example, the National Security Space Strategy of the United States of America, Unclassified Summary, 2011, which states, 'Finally, the United States will retain the right and capabilities to respond in self-defense, should deterrence fail. We will use force in a manner that is consistent with longstanding principles of international law, treaties to which the United States is a party, and the inherent right of self defense.' Also the failed EU Draft Code of Conduct for Outer Space Activities provided, '[t]he Subscribing States resolve to abide by the following principles: . . . the inherent right of individual or collective self-defence in accordance with the United Nations' Charter (Section I.2, General Principles); The Subscribing States '[shall] refrain from any action which intends to bring about, directly or indirectly, damage, or destruction, of outer space objects unless such action is conducted to reduce the creation of outer space debris and/or is justified by the inherent right of individual or collective self-defence' (Section II, 4.2).

more proportionate response would arguably be to target a single satellite of the attacker (preferably a satellite performing similar functions to the satellite hit in the first initial attack).

Some could argue that the physical destruction of an enemy's satellites would not be proportionate because of its punitive intent. This argument would certainly have a level of validity in relation to isolated attacks. Indeed, in the absence of additional attacks or of their provable threat, an act of self-defence would have no scope other than a punitive one. A possible way out could be to argue that a self-defence response should aim at deterring future attacks. Following this reasoning, an arguably proportionate response would be to target the military base from which the attack was launched.[93] The lack of proportionality of a 'destructive' response could be further supported by claiming that the harmful effects deriving from such a destructive use of force largely outweighs the expected benefits of preventing future attacks. Indeed, the space-debris released into Earth's orbit following the destruction of a satellite would environmentally contaminate outer space and endanger, and possibly hit, third-party satellites. Additionally, one could refer to the fact that a state exercising the right to use force in self-defence must comply with *jus in bello* principles (also referred to as International Humanitarian Law or IHL).[94] IHL provides that 'an attack which might be expected to cause incidental loss of civilian life, injury to civilians, damage to civilian objects, or a combination thereof, which would be excessive in relation to the concrete and direct military advantage anticipated.'[95] Thus, if the victim state would deem the collateral civil damage deriving from disabling the enemy's satellite to be excessive compared to the advantages of doing so, it should explore alternative options to respond. In conclusion, if a satellite is destroyed or permanently damaged, the legality of a response that includes recourse to conventional weapons could be hardly questioned. The state acting in self-defence shall, however, take due care to avoid and reduce collateral damage as much as possible.

(b) Attack Against a Space Object by Non-Kinetic (Destructive) Means

In the event of an attack using non-kinetic (non-destructive) means, the determination of whether an 'armed attack' has occurred is quite challenging. Indeed, in this case the targeted satellite is normally not physically destroyed but temporarily disabled, and furthermore, there is no recourse to conventional weapons. Based on these factors, it is questionable if recourse to these means reaches the level of

93 Clearly, this approach falls short in case the attack was launched not from a specific military facility but from a submarine at sea.

94 *Nuclear Weapons Case, Legality of the Threat or Use of Nuclear Weapons*, Advisory Opinion [1996] ICJ Rep 226, at para. 42; Dinstein (n 43); Michel Bourbonniere, 'Law of Armed Conflict (LOAC) and the Neutralization of Satellites or *Jus in Bello Satellitis*' (2004) 9 Journal of Conflict and Security Law 43 (2004).

95 Articles 51(5) and 57(2 and 5), Additional Protocol I to the Geneva Conventions of 1949.

seriousness required to be classified as an 'armed attack'. This uncertainty might result in a situation where the victim state, having suffered a violation of its rights, might lack the right to act in self-defence under Article 51 of the UN Charter as the use of force it has suffered might not reach the threshold of 'gravity' set out by the ICJ in the *Nicaragua* and *Oil Platform* cases. Interestingly, while the functionality of satellites may have been affected through jamming or cyber-attacks in the past,[96] none of these events has led to a military response based on the right of self-defence.

As described, Article 51 of the UN Charter requires the occurrence of an 'armed attack'. This expression should be intended as the use of arms or military force of offensive, destructive, and illegal nature.[97] For the purpose of this chapter, the provisions of the 'Definition of Aggression' adopted by the UN General Assembly through Resolution 3314 are particularly useful.[98] Article 1 provides, '[a]ggression is the use of armed force by a state against the sovereignty, territorial integrity or political independence of another state, or in any other manner inconsistent with the Charter of the United Nations, as set out in the Definition.' Article 3 (b) gives examples of acts that amount to acts of aggression, inter alia: '[b]ombardment by the armed force of a state against the territory of another state of the use of any weapon by a state against the territory of another state.' Resolution 3314 is intended to guide the Security Council in assessing the existence of aggression under Article 39 and not as a definition of 'armed attack'.[99] However, if 'armed attack' is understood to be a kind of aggression that justifies self-defence under Article 51 of the UN Charter, then the Resolution's definition of aggression and the acts of aggressions listed in Article 3 are at least indicative of circumstances wherein recourse to force in self-defence is justified.[100]

Insofar as an attack by non-kinetic means on a state's satellite is commensurate with the use of armed force (an aggression) by a state against the sovereignty of another state, it can be deduced that it will constitute an armed attack within the scope of Article 51 and, thus, the right of self-defence will be triggered. Two criteria are used to make this determination: (1) the effect of the attack and (2) the intent of the attack. As to the former, if cyber operations lead to the loss of functionality of an object it is arguable that it would constitute an armed attack, under Article 51 of the UN Charter as well as Article 49 of Additional Protocol 1 of the Geneva Convention. Indeed, in such a case, recourse to these means would indeed equate to the use of weapons intended to permanently alter the ability of a satellite to operate,

96 For example, in July 2003 Iran 'jammed' a US geostationary satellite from a location inside of Cuba. The satellite had been broadcasting US government and private Persian-language television and radio broadcasts into Iran. In 1997 Tonga accused Indonesia of jamming the broadcast of transmissions from a Hong Kong satellite (Apstar 1A).

97 See JN Singh, *Use of Force Under International Law* (Harnam Publishers 1984) 15.

98 Definition of aggression, G.A. Res. 3314, UN GAOR, 29th Sess. Supp. No. at 142, UN Doc. A/9631 (1975), adopted without a vote at the 2319th plenary meeting, Dec. 14, 1974.

99 Definition of aggression (n 98) at Preamble (2, 4) and Art. 6. See also *The Charter of the United Nations: A Commentary*, B Simma (ed), at 668.

100 Simma (n 99) 668.

triggering the right to act in self-defence. As to the latter point, it is important to ascertain if the use of non-kinetic means, such as cyber-attacks, jamming, and interference, can be commensurate with the use of military force. Brownlie's discussion of the 'use of weapons which do not involve any explosive effect' deserves special attention.[101] He suggests that weapons which do not employ the force of shock waves and heat associated with more orthodox weapons may nevertheless be considered a use of force on two grounds: '[i]n the first place the agencies concerned are commonly referred to as "weapons" and forms of "warfare" . . . [and] the second consideration [is] the fact that these weapons are employed for the destruction of life and property.'[102] By analogy, a 'cyber-attack' is viewed as a weapon in the arsenal of 'information warfare',[103] and jamming and interference, if used for offensive purposes, might be indirectly qualified as 'weapons'.

More problematic is the situation where recourse to non-kinetic means does not permanently affect the functionality of a satellite or its ground station; for example, when a satellite or a cyber-attack interfere with or degrade the regular functionality of another satellite or cause the temporary interruption of its transmission with the respective ground station. First, it would be challenging to locate where the interference came from. Second, even when the 'attacker' is identified, it might declare the event to be accidental and reject any claim of hostile intent.[104] What is relevant for this analysis is the determination of what type of actions can trigger the right to act in self-defence. This question might be answered taking the following criteria into account: the repetitiveness of an action, its intent, the circumstances surrounding it, and parallel terrestrial events. 'Repetitiveness' is of relevance in this context. Indeed, if an interference or disruption of service is not occasional but occurs over an extended period and in a recurring fashion, the argument that such an action would constitute a mere 'accident' is fragile. To support the claim that repeated interferences constitute an 'armed attack', one may make use of the theory of 'accumulation of events'.[105] As explained, this theory views the idea that a series of low-scale attacks ultimately is equivalent to an armed attack.[106] Although the theory of accumulation of events has received a cold reception at the UN Security Council,[107] the International Court of Justice in the *Oil Platforms* case has

101 Ian Brownlie, *International Law and the Use of Force by States* (OUP 1963) 362.

102 Brownlie (n 101) 362.

103 See Robert G Hanseman, 'The Realities and Legalities of Information Warfare' (1997) 42 Air Force Law Review 173.

104 In 2022, the KA-Sat Network, owned by ViaSat, was the target of a cyber-attack that disrupted its services across Europe. Even though many suspected Russia to be the origin of the attack, the country strongly rejected these allegations. See Sylvester Kaczmarek, 'Cyber Security for Satellites is a Growing Challenge, as Threats to Space-Based Infrastructures Grow' *The Conversation* (20 February 2024) <Cybersecurity for satellites is a growing challenge, as threats to space-based infrastructure grow (theconversation.com)> accessed 7 August 2024.

105 Israel Ronen, 'Hezbollah and the Second Lebanon War' (2006) 9 Yearbook of International Humanitarian Law 362.

106 Ochoa-Ruiz and Salamanca-Aguado (n 43) 516.

107 Tams (n 49).

used language to suggest that the cumulative nature of a series of forcible actions could possibly turn them into an 'armed attack'.[108] Pursuant to this logic, a series of repeated interferences and harms to the transmissions or services of a satellite could eventually be considered an 'armed attack'. The 'accumulation of events' theory has received mixed reception by the international community, with some supporting its validity[109] and others questioning its consistency with customary international law and Article 51 of the UN Charter.[110]

This argument could be reinforced by proving the harmful intent of the attacker. It is likely that, in the case of interference, the victim state would demand the state causing it to cease and desist. Refusal to do so would provide further evidence to claim the harmful intention of the attacker and the planned nature of the harmful actions. Unsurprisingly, both the United States and China view the purposeful interference with space systems, including space infrastructure, as an infringement of a nation's rights.[111] The circumstances surrounding the events leading up to the initial attack also play a role in ascertaining whether the right to act in self-defence can be exercised. If the dispute involves two states already experiencing tense relations, recourse to non-destructive means against the other country's satellite could easily be interpreted as an intentional undertaking to hurt the adversary's interests. In addition, if the interference or cyber-attack is instrumental to support or complement operations occurring on the ground, such as border operations or unauthorized access to the adversary's territorial waters, their offensive nature could hardly be denied.[112] In short, even if there is room to argue that the use of non-kinetic means against a satellite constitutes an armed attack, further factors, such as repetitiveness and harmful intent, might need to be demonstrated to justify the right to act in self-defence under Article 51 of the UN Charter.

Once it is established that an action by non-kinetic means constitutes an 'armed attack', the victim state is legally entitled to act in self-defence, and, theoretically, also to use conventional force. It remains to be seen how a response that encompasses the use of conventional weapons could be viewed as proportionate to an attack that does not involve such weapons. Useful criteria to evaluate this question would be the consequences and the scale of the attack. If the end-result of the use of non-kinetic means is virtually the same to the one resulting from the use of kinetic ASATs, such as crippling the satellite and/or its function, than

108 Oil Platforms case (n 2) para. 63.

109 Yael Ronen, 'Israel, Hizbollah and the Second Lebanon War' (2006) 9 Yearbook of International Humanitarian Law 362; Ococha-Ruiz and Salamanca Aguado (n 43).

110 Tams (n 49); Kretzmer (n 45).

111 2020 National Space Policy of the United States of America, Principles; Kevin Pollpetter, 'Coercive Space Activities: A View From PRC Sources' (*China Aerospace Studies Institute Report*, February 2024) <https://www.airuniversity.af.edu/Portals/10/CASI/documents/Research/Space/2024-02-26%20Coercive%20Space%20Activities.pdf> accessed 7 August 2024.

112 This interpretation is also shared by Christopher Petras, 'The Use of Force in Response to Cyber-Attack on Commercial Space Systems—Reexamining Self-Defense in Outer Space in Light of the Convergence of U.S. Military and Commercial Space Activities' (2002) 67 Journal of Air Law and Commerce 1213.

recourse to conventional weapons as a self-defence measure could be considered a proportionate act of self-defence.[113] Similar reasoning could be also suggested in connection to 'attacks' against satellites that, while not resulting in their permanent loss of functionality or physical destruction, are repeated over an extensive period of time and show a clear harmful intent. More problematic would be to prove that recourse to conventional weapons is a proportionate response to an isolated cyber-attack, interference, or jamming that does not reach a certain threshold of gravity. Indeed, recourse to these weapons would have negative consequences (such as the permanent destruction of a satellite or the creation of space debris) that would largely outweigh the temporary interference suffered. On the contrary, in such a scenario a proportionate response would arguably be one that utilizes techniques and means like those used in the attack. Ultimately, it must be concluded that there are no fixed criteria to evaluate the proportionality of a response in self-defence and, until such criteria are internationally determined, this evaluation must be done on a case-by-case basis. Arguably, this is an insufficient state of affairs since it puts the stability of outer space at risk. Indeed, it opens the door to arbitrary legal interpretations of orbital behaviours and has negative implications for the safety of space objects and the long-term sustainability of space activities.

7 Conclusion

Satellites face an increasing level of risk. On the one hand, their strategic relevance renders them a valuable target in the event of a conflict, but on the other hand, their vulnerability renders them an easy object of attack by an adversary. Article 51 of the UN Charter recognizes the right of states to act in self-defence if an armed attack occurs. While there is a general understanding that this right extends to outer space, it remains uncertain when and how it might be exercised therein. This matter is complicated even further by the diverse nature of the existing means, kinetic and non-kinetic, that can be used to harm or disable a satellite. In particular, these factors challenge the determination of what constitutes an 'armed attack' in outer space and the forms and proportionality of a response.

This uncertainty undermines international security because it leaves open the possibility of arbitrary interpretations of the law and also unpredictable behaviour by states. This chapter was intended to provide a contribution to clarify this uncertainty, but much is still left to be determined to clarify how the right of self-defence applies and will apply in outer space. It is hoped that the international community will engage in serious discussions on this topic with the clear understanding that existing international rules need to be adapted to the specific characteristics of outer space and space objects. One, however, shall not overlook the fact that, in the

113 Clearly, also in this situation the victim state should take adequate measures to reduce interference with the space activities of other states and to prevent/reduce the contamination of the space environment.

present tense geopolitical environment, similar discussions face major challenges, as the failed Open-Ended Working Group on Reducing Space Threat Initiative showed. These challenges render more important than ever the role to be played by scholars in clarifying the meaning and application of the right of self-defence in space. Considering these difficulties, one way to avoid the use of force in outer space might be to increase reliance on SSA and SST capabilities.[114] Indeed, through recourse to these technologies, states will be able to achieve a better understanding of orbital events and set up mechanisms to timely share information about hazardous situations. This kind of mechanism will, in turn, contribute to enhancing the predictability of orbital behaviours and avoid unnecessary misunderstandings and tensions among space-faring nations.

Bibliography

A More Secure World: Our Shared Responsibility, Report of the High-Level Panel on Threats, Challenges and Change, (2004) UN Doc A/59/565, at para. 188 <www2.ohchr.org/English/bodies/hrcouncil/docs/gaA.59.565_En.pdf> accessed 11 July 2024.

Roberto Ago, Special Rapporteur to the International Law Commission, '*Eighth Report on State Responsibility*' (1980) Yearbooks of the International Law Commission ii, I, 13, UN Doc A/CN.4/318/ADD.5–7.

Stanimir A Alexandrov, *Self-Defense Against the Use of Force in International Law* (Kluwer Law International 1996).

Armed Activities on the Territory of the Congo (Democratic Republic of the Congo v Uganda) (judgment) [2005] ICJ Reports 168.

Roberto Barsotti, 'Armed Reprisals' in A Cassese (ed), *The Current Legal Regulation of the Use of Force* (Martinus Nijhoff Publishers 1986) 79.

LT. Gen Steven L Basham, 'The Critical Role of Space in Modern Warfare and the Imperative of Joint Space Capabilities in Europe' (9 February 2024) <https://www.eucom.mil/article/42685/the-critical-role-of-space-in-modern-warfare-and-the-imperative-of-joint-spacecapabilitie#:~:text=In%20today's%20rapidly%20evolving%20security,fabric%20of%20modern%20military%20operations> accessed 8 July 2024.

Marietta Benkö, 'A Valid Case Against the Use of Aggressive Military Systems in Outer Space?' in M Benkö and KU Schrogl (eds), *Current Problems and Perspectives for Future Regulation* (Eleven 2005) 155–75.

Laurie L Blanck, 'Irreconcilable Differences: The Threshold for Armed Attack and International Armed Attack' (2020) 96 Notre Dame Law Review 249.

Michel Bourbonniere, 'Law of Armed Conflict (LOAC) and the Neutralization of Satellites or *Jus in Bello Satellitis*' (2004) 9 Journal of Conflict and Security Law 43 (2004).

Michel Bourbonniere, 'National Security Law in Outer Space: The Interface of Exploration and Security' (2005) 70 Journal of Air Law and Commerce 3, 7.

Ian Brownlie, *International Law and the Use of Force by States* (OUP 1963) 362.

Matt Bruzzese and Peter Senger, 'Farewell to China's Strategic Support Force. Let's Meet Its Replacements' (*Defense One*, 28 April 2024) <https://www.defenseone.com/ideas/2024/04/farewell-chinas-strategic-support-force-lets-meet-its-replacement/396143/> accessed 11 July 2024.

114 Regina Peldszus/Pascal Faucher, 'European Union Space Surveillance and Tracking (SST): State of Play and Perspective' (2022) 62 Space Policy 1015; Secure World Foundation, 'Space Situational Awareness Factsheet' (2017) <https://swfound.org/media/205874/swf_ssa_fact_sheet.pdf> accessed 11 July 2024; European Union, 'EU SST' <https://www.eusst.eu/> accessed 11 July 2024.

Shanno Bugos, 'Russian ASAT Test Creates Massive Debris' (*Arms Control Today*, 1 December 2021) <https://www.armscontrol.org/act/2021-12/news/russian-asat-test-creates-massive-debris> accessed 11 July 2024.

Antonio Canizzaro, 'Contextualizing Proportionality: *Jus Ad Bellum* and *Jus in Bello* in the Lebanese War' (2006) 88 International Review of the Red Cross 779.

Case Concerning Military and Paramilitary Activities in and Against Nicaragua (*Nicaragua v. USA*) [1986] ICJ. Rep 94 (Nicaragua case).

Antonio Cassese, *International Law* (2nd edn, OUP 2005).

Chatham House, 'Principles of International Law on Use of Force in Self-Defence' <www.chathamhouse.org.uk/publications/papers/view/-/id/308> accessed 11 July 2024.

Gray Christine, 'The International Court of Justice and the Use of Force' in Christian J Tams and James Sloan (eds), *The Development of International Law by the International Court of Justice* (OUP 2013).

Carl Q Christol, *The Modern International Law of Outer Space* (Pergamon Press 1982) 5.

John C Cooper, 'Self-Defence in Outer Space and the United Nations' (1962) 5 Air Force and Space Digest 51

Anthony H Cordesman, 'Chinese Strategy and Military Modernization in 2016: A Comparative Analysis' (*Center for Strategic and International Studies*, 8 December 2016) <https://www.csis.org/analysis/chinese-strategy-and-military-modernization-2016> accessed 11 July 2024.

Olivier Corten, *The Law Against War: The Prohibition on the Use of Force in Contemporary International Law* (Hart Publishing 2010).

Dwayne A Day, 'Burning Frost, the View From the Ground: Shooting Down a Spy Satellite in 2008' *The Space Review* (21 May 2021) <https://www.thespacereview.com/article/4198/1> accessed 11 July 2024.

Hamilton DeSaussure and others, 'Self-Defence—A Right in Outer Space' (1965) 7 Air Force Law Review 38.

Department of Defense, '2020 National Space Defense Strategy' <https://media.defense.gov/2020/Jun/17/2002317391/-1/-1/1/2020_DEFENSE_SPACE_STRATEGY_SUMMARY.PDF> (DoD, June 2022) accessed 11 July 2024.

Yoram Dinstein, *War, Aggression and Self-Defence* (4th edn, CUP 2005).

Nader Elhefnawy, 'Making Sense of China's Weapons Test' *The Space Review* (2007) <https://www.thespacereview.com/article/801/1#:~:text=On%20Thursday%2C%20January%2011%2C%202007,its%20kind%20since%20the%201980s> accessed 11 July 2007.

European Union, 'EU SST' < https://www.eusst.eu/> accessed 11 July 2024.

Jeff Foust, 'More Countries Encouraged to Commit to Halt Destructive ASAT Tests' *SpaceNews* (15 June 2023) <https://spacenews.com/more-countries-encouraged-to-commit-to-halt-destructive-asat-tests/> accessed 6 August 2024.

Thomas M Franck, 'On Proportionality of Countermeasures in International Law' (2008) 102 American Journal of International Law 715.

Thomas M Franck, *Recourse to Force: State Action Against Threats and Armed Attacks* (CUP 2002).

Thomas M Franck, 'Terrorism and the Right of Self- Defense' (2001) 95 American Journal of International Law 839.

Thomas M Franck, 'The Power of Legitimacy and the Legitimacy of Power: International Law in an Age of Power Disequilibrium' (2006) 100 American Journal of International Law 88.

Judith Gardam, *Necessity, Proportionality and the Use of Force by States* (CUP 2004).

Michael J Glennon, 'Pre-Empting Terrorism; The Case for Anticipatory Self-Defense' (*Weekly Standard*, 28 January 2002).

Chelsea Gohd, 'Russia Anti-Satellite Missile Test Was the First of Its Kind' (*Space.com*, 10 August 2022) <https://www.space.com/russia-anti-satellite-missile-test-first-of-its-kind> accessed 7 August 2024.

Namrata Goswami, 'The Reorganization of China's Space Force: Strategic and Organizational Implications' May<https://thediplomat.com/2024/05/the-reorganization-of-chinas-space-force-strategic-and-organizational-implications/#:~:text=One%20of%20the%20Aerospace%20Force's,security%20interests%20in%20outer%20space.%E2%80%9D>

Christine D Gray, *International Law and the Use of Force* (2nd edn, OUP 2005).

James A Green, 'Article 51 Reporting Requirement for Self-Defense Actions' (2015) 55 Virginia Journal of International Law 568.

James A Green, *The International Court of Justice and Self-Defence in International Law* (Hart 2009) 27.

Greg Hadley, 'Advancing in Space, China Poses Growing Threat, USSF Leaders Warn' (*Air and Space Forces Magazine*, 28 March 2024) <https://www.airandspaceforces.com/ussf-leaders-china-space-threaten-us/> accessed 11 July 2024.

Monika Hakimi, 'Defensive Force Against Non-State Actors: The State of Play' (2015) 91 International Law Studies 1.

Robert G Hanseman, 'The Realities and Legalities of Information Warfare' (1997) 42 Air Force Law Review 173.

Brandon L Hart, 'Anti-Satellite Weapons: Threats, Laws and the Uncertain Future of Space' (2008) 33 Annals of Air & Space Law 345, 358.

Chris Henderson, 'The 25 February 2021 Military Strikes and the "Armed Attack" Requirement of Self-Defence: From "*sina qua non*" to the Point of Vanishing?' (2022) 9 Journal on the Use of Force and International Law 55.

Theresa Hitchens, 'LeoLabs: Russia, China Time Suspicious Space Activity for Some US Holidays' (*Breaking Defense*, 12 December 2023) <https://breakingdefense.com/2023/12/leolabs-russia-china-time-suspicious-space-activity-for-some-us-holidays/ accessed 7 August 2024.

Theresa Hitchens, 'Satellite Jamming Normal by Militaries During Conflict, Not Peacetime: State Dept. Official' (*Breaking Defense*, 21 March 2022) <Satellite jamming 'normal' by militaries during conflict, not peacetime: State Dept. official—Breaking Defense> accessed 7 August 2024.

Mark Holmes, 'The Growing Risk of a Major Satellite Cyber-Attack' (*Via Satellite*, 2024) <https://interactive.satellitetoday.com/the-growing-risk-of-a-major-satellite-cyber-attack/> accessed 11 July 2024.

Bruce Hurwitz, *The Legality of Space Militarization* (Elsevier 1986).

International Law Association (ILA), Committee on the Use of Force, 'Final Report on Aggression and the Use of Force' (2018) <www.ila-hq.org/images/ILA/DraftReports/DraftReport_UseOfForce.pdf> accessed 11 July 2024.

Islamic Republic of Iran v. United States of America [2003] ICJ Rep 161 (*Oil Platforms Case*), at para. 51.

Ram Jakhu and others, 'Threats to Peaceful Purposes of Outer Space: Politics and Law' (2020) 18 Astropolitics 22.

Joint Air Power Competence Centre, 'Space Support in Operations' <https://www.japcc.org/warfare-areas/space/> accessed 8 July 2024.

Andrew Jones, 'China's Secretive Spaceplane Conducts Proximity Operations with Small Spacecraft' *SpaceNews* (13 June 2024) <https://spacenews.com/chinas-secretive-spaceplane-conducts-proximity-operations-with-small-spacecraft/> accessed 11 July 2024.

David Kretzmer, 'The Inherent Right to Self-Defence and Proportionality in *Jus ad Bellum*' (2013) 24(1) European Journal of International Law 235.

Ricky J Lee, 'The Jus ad Bellum in Outer Space: The Interrelationship Between Article 103 of the Charter of the United Nations and Article IV of the Outer Space Treaty' (2002) 45 Proceedings of the International Institute of Space Law 139.

Ajey Lele, 'Indian ASAT: Mission Shakti Should Be a Comma, Not a Full Stop' *The Space Review* (27 March 2023) <https://www.thespacereview.com/article/4556/1#:~:text=On%20March%2027%2C%202019%2C%20India,US%2C%20Russia%2C%20and%20China> accessed 11 July 2024.

Vaughan Lowe, *The United Nations Security Council and War: The Evolution of Thought and Practice Since 1945* (OUP 2008) 265–515.

Noam Lubell, *Extraterritorial Use of Force Against Non-State Actors* (2010) 64.

Francis Lyall and Paul B Larsen, *Space Law: A Treatise* (Ashgate 2009) 501.

Marko G Markoff, 'Disarmament and 'Peaceful Purposes' Provisions in the 1967 Outer Space Treaty' (1976) 4 Journal of Space Law 3.

Anne Sophie Martin, 'State's Right to Self-Defence in Outer Space' (2020) 30 The Journal of the JAPCC.

Timothy LH McCormack, 'Anticipatory Self-Defence in the Legislative History of the United Nations Charter' (1991) 25 Israel Law Review 1.

Daniel Mellow, 'Counterfactuals and the Proportionality Criterion' (2006) 20 Ethics and International Affairs 434.

Martin Menter, 'Peaceful Uses of Outer Space and National Security' (1983) Proceedings 25th Colloquium on the Law of Outer Space 135.

Steve Mirmina, 'The Ballistic Missile Defense System and Its Effects on the Outer Space Environment' (2005) 31 Journal of Space Law 287.

National Defense Panel, 'Transforming Defense National Security in the 21st Century' (1997).

National Space Intelligence Center/National Air and Space Intelligence Center, *Competing in Space* (2nd edn, 2023) <https://www.spoc.spaceforce.mil/Portals/4/Images/2_Space_Slicky_11x17_Web_View_reduced.pdf> accessed 11 July 2024.

National Space Policy of the United States of America, Principles, 9 December 2020 <https://trumpwhitehouse.archives.gov/wp-content/uploads/2020/12/National-Space-Policy.pdf> accessed 11 July 2024.

Nicaragua Case [1986] ICJ Rep 14, 91.

North Atlantic Treaty Organization, 'NATO's Approach to Space' (*NATO*, 21 March 2024) accessed 6 August 2024.

North Atlantic Treaty Organization, 'NATO's Approach to Space' <https://www.nato.int/cps/en/natohq/topics_175419.htm>

North Atlantic Treaty Organization, 'NATO's Overarching Space Policy' (*NATO*, 30 May 2024) <https://www.nato.int/cps/en/natohq/official_texts_190862.htm>.

Note of Daniel Webster dated 24 April 1841 <http://avalon.law.yale.edu/19th_century/br-1842d.asp> accessed 11 July 2024. A description of the Caroline case is provided in Michael N Shaw, *International Law* (CUP 2008) 1131.

William O'Brien, 'Reprisals, Deterrence and Self-Defense in Counter Terror Operations' (1990) 30 Virginia Journal of International Law 421.

Mary Ellen O'Connell, 'The Myth of Preemptive Self-Defense' (2002) ASIL Task Force Paper.

Mary Ellen O'Connell, 'The Popular but Unlawful Armed Reprisal' (2018) 44 Ohio Northern University Law Review 325.

Chris O'Meara, 'Reconceptualizing the Right of Self-Defence Against Imminent Armed Attacks' (2022) 9 Journal on the Use of Force and International Law.

Jacob G Oakley, *Cybersecurity for Space: Protecting the Final Frontier* (Apress 2020).

Natalia Ochoa-Ruiz and Salamanca-Aguado, 'Exploring the Limits of International Law Relating to the Use of Force in Self-defence' (2005) 16(49) European Journal of International Law 499, 516.

Office of Space Commerce, 'National Space Policy of the United States of America, Principles' (*White House*, 9 December 2020) <https://trumpwhitehouse.archives.gov/wp-content/uploads/2020/12/National-Space-Policy.pdf> accessed 6 August 2024

Walter Peeters, 'Cyber Attacks on Satellites: An Underestimated Political Threat' (*London School of Economics Ideas*, 10 November 2022) <https://www.lse.ac.uk/ideas/projects/space-policy/publications/Cyberattacks-on-Satellites> accessed 7 August 2024.

Regina Peldszus and Pascal Faucher, 'European Union Space Surveillance and Tracking (SST): State of Play and Perspective' (2022) 62 Space Policy 1015.

Christopher Petras, 'The Use of Force in Response to Cyber-Attack on Commercial Space Systems—Reexamining Self-Defense in Outer Space in Light of the Convergence of U.S. Military and Commercial Space Activities' (2002) 67 Journal of Air Law and Commerce 1213.

Kevin Pollpetter, 'Coercive Space Activities: A View From PRC Sources' (*China Aerospace Studies Institute Report*, February 2024) <https://www.airuniversity.af.edu/Portals/10/CASI/documents/Research/Space/2024-02-26%20Coercive%20Space%20Activities.pdf> accessed 7 August 2024.

Jakub Prazak, 'Dual-Use Conundrum: Towards the Weaponization of Outer Space?' (2021) 187 Acta Astronautica 397.

D Rodin, *War and Self-Defense* (OUP 2005) 115.

Yael Ronen, 'Israel, Hizbollah and the Second Lebanon War' (2006) 9 Yearbook of International Humanitarian Law 362.

Russia's Defense Industry, 'Russia Establishes Aerospace Forces as New Armed Service' <http://tass.com/russia/812184> accessed 11 July 2024.

Oscar Schachter, 'The Right of States to Use Armed Force' (1984) 82 Michigan Law Review Festschrift in Honor of Eric Stein 1620.

Secure World Foundation, 'Global Counterspace Capabilities' (2024) <https://swfound.org/media/207826/swf_global_counterspace_capabilities_2024.pdf> accessed 11 July 2024.

Secure World Foundation, 'Global Counterspace Capabilities Report' (2024) <https://swfound.org/counterspace/> accessed 8 July 2024.

P Shakarian, *An Introduction to Cyber-Warfare: A Multidisciplinary Approach* (Syngress 2013).

Bruno Simma, *The Carter of the United Nations, Commentary*, vol I (2nd edn, OUP 2002) 805.

JN Singh, *Use of Force Under International Law* (Harnam Publishers 1984) 15.

Christian J Tams, 'The Use of Force Against Terrorists' (2009) 20 European Journal of International Law 359.

The National Military Strategy of the United States (2004) <http://www.defenselink.mil/news/Mar2005/d20050318nms.pdf> accessed 11 July 2024.

The National Security Strategy of the United States of America, Washington, 17 September 2002 <http://www.whitehouse.gov/nsc/nss.html> accessed 11 July 2024.

Brett Tingley, 'International Space Station Dodges Space Debris From Russian Anti-Satellite Test' (*Space.com*, 26 October 2022) <https://www.space.com/international-space-station-dodges-russian-space-debris> accessed 7 August 2024.

Dio H Tobing and Olivia N Maryatmo, 'Celestial Anarchy: States' Right to Self-Defence'(2013) 4 Juris Gentium Law Review 9.

Fabio Tronchetti. 'Legal Aspects of the Military Uses of Outer Space' in Frans G von der Dunk and Fabio Tronchetti (eds), *Handbook of Space Law* (Edward Elgar Publishing 2015) 331.

Fabio Tronchetti, 'The Right of Self-Defence in Outer Space: An Appraisal' (2014) 63 Zeitschrift für Luft-und Weltraumrecht 92.

UK Space Agency, 'Why Space Matters?' <https://www.gov.uk/government/publications/infographic-why-space-matters/why-space-matters> accessed 8 July 2024.

US Department of State, 'The Space Force's Critical Role in National Security' (9 May 2024) <https://www.state.gov/briefings-foreign-press-centers/the-space-forces-critical-role-in-national-security>

US National Security Strategy 2006 <http://georgewbush-whitehouse.archives.gov/nsc/nss/2006> accessed 11 July 2024.

Charlotte Van Camp and Walter Peeters, 'A World Without Satellite Data as a Result of a Global Cyber-Attack' (2022) 59 Space Policy 1.

Pavel Veskovsky, Jnani Mohan and Maxwell Simon, 'Satellite Jamming' (*Issue Briefs*, 3 April 2019) <https://ontheradar.csis.org/issue-briefs/satellite-jamming/#:~:text=For%20

example%2C%20interference%20with%20satellite,of%20the%20International%20Telecommunications%20Union> accessed 11 July 2024.
Ian A Vlasic, 'Space Law and the Military Applications of Space Technology' in N Jasentuliyana (ed), *Perspectives on International law* (Martinus Nijhoff 1995) 394.
Frans G von der Dunk, 'Armed Conflicts in Outer Space: Which Law Applies?' (2021) 97 International Law Studies 188.
Elisabeth S Waldrop, 'Integration of Military and Civilian Space Assets: Legal and National Security Implications' (2004) 55 Air Force Law Review 157.
World Economic Forum, 'The Space Economy Is Booking: What Benefits Can It Bring to Earth?' <https://www.weforum.org/agenda/2022/10/space-economy-industry-benefits/> accessed 8 July 2024.

Part II

Futures for Colonisation and Residence in Outer Space

5 Boots on the Moon

Managing the Return of Humans to the Moon

Melissa de Zwart

1 Introduction

Several states have announced their intention to establish a permanent human presence on the Moon in the coming decade. International space law provides that space is 'free for exploration and use by all States without discrimination of any kind' and that the Moon (and other celestial bodies) are 'not subject to national appropriation' by claim of sovereignty or any other means.[1] This broad international law framework has provided the scope for peaceful uses of space for over 50 years and has facilitated a great deal of scientific and diplomatic collaboration, but it gives little detail regarding co-habitation on the lunar surface. Therefore, it may be asked what specific rules and principles will regulate the sustained presence of humans on the Moon and their use of resources? How will competing uses of the Moon be governed and how can international law assist with managing any resulting conflicts or tensions?

The Artemis Accords announced by NASA in 2020 articulate some new concepts with respect to communal uses of the Moon.[2] Whilst modelled in part on the agreements which have successfully underpinned international collaboration on the International Space Station, the Artemis Accords will involve many more and different partners and new ways of working. China is also leading a multilateral project to establish a base on the Moon, which will involve 'complex experimental research facilities to be constructed. . . on the surface and/or in the orbit of the moon.'[3] How will these activities compete and co-operate in the context of the UN Space Treaties? What laws will regulate the *in situ* use of

1 Treaty on Principles Governing the Activities of States in the Exploration and Use of Outers Space, Including the Moon and Other Celestial Bodies, opened for signature 27 January 1967, 610 UNTS 205 (entered into force 10 October 1967) ('Outer Space Treaty'), Article I and Article II,

2 The Artemis Accords: Principles for Cooperation in the Civil Exploration and Use of the Moon, Mars, Comets, and Asteroids for Peaceful Purposes, 13 October 2020 <https://www.nasa.gov/wp-content/uploads/2022/11/Artemis-Accords-signed-13Oct2020.pdf?emrc=653a00>.

3 China National Space Administration, International Lunar Research Station (ILRS), 'Guide for Partnership' (16 June 2021) <https://www.cnsa.gov.cn/english/n6465652/n6465653/c6812150/content.html>.

DOI: 10.4324/9781003370499-7

resources and how will historic sites be protected? How will private operators respond to the current international law context of space law in their activities on the Moon?

This chapter will consider the legal frameworks that will be applied to the return of humans to the Moon and where gaps and discrepancies in those frameworks may give rise to international tensions. It will begin by briefly outlining the history of human missions to the Moon, identifying the cultural and historical motivations for missions to the Moon and addressing the context for the absence of clear laws which regulate use of the Moon's surface and resources. This section will also highlight the changing political and strategic contexts which are now guiding the space programs of the states engaged in the return to the Moon. It will then outline the features of the two multi-state projects to create permanent human habitations on the Moon, namely the US-led Artemis project and the China-led International Lunar Research Station. The next section will outline and apply current international space law to the proposed activities, providing the context for the analysis of their specific rules of participation of those projects in the following section. A consideration of the specific issue of *in situ* resource utilisation and some related matters of sustainability humans will encounter in managing a permanent presence on the Moon are addressed in the next section. The final section will conclude with a consideration of the fact that we are realising that creating a human habitation on the Moon will raise complex questions of what it means to be human in space and how we can ensure that our presence in space does not recreate mistakes of humanity's past.

2 Humans on the Moon

This section will provide a brief overview of the space programs of the US, USSR/Russia and China, as the key players in the current plans to return humans to the Moon, highlighting specific crises and achievements. In each case, issues of internal politics, as well as the external pressures of geopolitical rivalry, have shaped the evolution and nature of each state's space activities.[4] Despite the impediments to collaboration between these states, it is clear that the activities, successes and failures of each of them has driven unique responses of the others in their identification of their next space ambition.

Great space power rivalry commenced at the conclusion of World War II, with the capture of German rocket scientists by the US and the USSR. Wernher von Braun, a former Nazi SS junior officer and creator of the German V-2 rocket, was extracted from Bavaria along with many of his team and taken to the US, where they commenced work on the US ballistic missile program. In 1960, this work was transferred from the Army to the newly established National Aeronautics and

4 Tim Marshall, *The Future of Geography, How Power and Politics in Space Will Change Our World* (Elliott and Thompson Limited 2023) 111–88; Bleddyn Bowen, *War in Space: Strategy, Space Power, Geopolitics* (Edinburgh UP 2022) 158–87.

Space Administration (NASA) forming the basis for the development of the Saturn V rocket.[5] This powerful launch vehicle would take the US to the Moon later that decade and, if Von Braun had had his way, would also have taken NASA on to Mars.[6] Von Braun became the director of NASA's Marshall Space Flight Center and chief advocate of space flight to the Moon and beyond.[7] Von Braun retired from NASA in 1972, a date which also marks the shift in NASA ambition away from the Moon to low-Earth orbit.

The USSR had also acquired German missile technology, along with experienced rocket scientists.[8] Inevitably, in the context of nuclear competition, any co-operation between the former World War II allies quickly turned to suspicion and rivalry. The race for space was on, with each state heavily invested in demonstrating technical superiority in being the first to space. Despite the well-publicised US plans for Project Vanguard to orbit a scientific satellite as part of the International Geophysical Year (1 July 1957–31 December 1958), the USSR actually succeeded in being the first state to place an artificial satellite in orbit with the launch of Sputnik 1 on 4 October 1957.[9] As Vlasic notes, the launch by the USSR of Sputnik evidenced not a 'triumph for world science' but rather a demonstration of a 'revolutionary military instrument with potentially awesome strategic consequences.'[10] Whilst the US expressed little official concern regarding this important strategic achievement it exacerbated the already heightened technological and military rivalry between the Cold War rivals and prompted a renewed focus on space technology by the US.[11] The Sputnik orbit was also notable for creating the precedent for one of the few principles of space law that is regarded as customary international law: the free use of space by a state including transit in orbit above other states.[12]

In May 1961 President Kennedy announced that the US would be sending a manned mission to the Moon before the end of that decade.[13] The 1960s therefore

5 Roger D Launius, *Reaching for the Moon: A Short History of the Space Race* (Yale UP 2019) 1–11; Adam Mann, 'What Was the Space Race?' (*Space.com*, 14 May 2023) <https://www.space.com/space-race.html>.

6 David Baker, 'Wernher von Braun's Forgotten Mission to Mars' *BBC Sky at Night Magazine* (online) (16 July 2019) <https://www.skyatnightmagazine.com/space-missions/wernher-von-brauns-forgotten-mission-mars>.

7 Marshall (n 4) 33–34. NASA, *Wernher von Braun* <https://www.nasa.gov/people/wernher-von-braun/>.

8 Marshall (n 4) 34–35.

9 Roger Launius, 'Highlights of Human Spaceflight: The United States' in Lawrence Young and Jeffrey Sutton (eds), *Handbook of Bioastronautics* (Springer Nature Switzerland AG 2021) 677–89, 678.

10 IA Vlasic, 'Space Law and the Military Applications of Space Technology' in N Jasentuliyana (ed), *Perspectives on International Law* (Kluwer Law International 1995) 385.

11 Launius (n 9).

12 MN Schmitt, 'International Law and Military Operations in Space' in A von Bogdandy and R Wolfrum (eds), *Max Planck Yearbook of United Nations Law*, vol 10 (Brill 2006) 99.

13 Whilst the term 'crewed' is now preferred, the term 'manned' is used consciously here with respect to the Mercury, Gemini and Apollo missions, to highlight that only males were included in the astronaut training program at NASA until 1978.

witnessed the rapid scaling up of human spaceflight technology, with the Mercury, Gemini and the Apollo programs preparing for the Moon landing. Despite the intense efforts of the newly established NASA through Project Mercury (1958–1963), which was focused on launching a man into orbit and ensuring his safe return, the USSR also achieved the next significant first, sending Yuri Gagarin into orbit around the Earth on 12 April 1961.[14] Alan Shepard became the first American to reach (sub-orbital) space on 5 May 1961.[15] Shepard's achievement was followed by Gus Grissom in 1961, and by John Glenn, who became the first American to orbit the Earth in 1962.[16] Several more successful Mercury flights followed in 1962–1963. Project Gemini (1965–1966) completed ten human spaceflight missions, including prolonged periods in space, orbital rendezvous and docking and EVAs (extravehicular activities), developing a range of technology and experience that was needed for the mission to the Moon. Project Apollo (1967–1972) witnessed great achievement and great tragedy, with a fire during a ground test on 27 January 1967 causing the death of the three astronauts.[17] However, Kennedy's vision was realised on 20 July 1969 with the landing of the Lunar Module of Apollo 11, with two astronauts, Neil Armstrong and Buzz Aldrin, setting foot on the Moon's surface and planting the flag of the United States.[18] That mission and five subsequent Apollo missions (12, 14–17) saw a total of twelve American men walking (and driving) on the Moon, undertaking a number of scientific missions and collecting lunar samples.[19] No human has set foot on the Moon since 1972.

During this period, the USSR continued its human space program and succeeded in sending the first woman, Valentina Tereshkova, to space in 1963, and completing the first spacewalk in 1965 from the Voskhod 2.[20] The Soyuz program commenced in the early 1960s and was originally conceived as supporting a human mission to cislunar space, however no Moon landing was achieved by the USSR. Russian focus shifted to the development of a space station.[21] Interestingly, the 1975 Apollo-Soyuz mission witnessed a major step forward in space diplomacy, with the docking of the US Apollo capsule to the Soviet Soyuz module, culminating in a literal and figurative embrace between the two module commanders.[22] In order to

14 Sven Grahn and Carol Norberg, 'History of Human Spaceflight' in Carol Norbeg (ed), *Human Spaceflight and Exploration* (Springer-Verlag 2013) 11–63, 16.

15 Marshall (n 4) 38–42.

16 Launius (n 9) 679.

17 Launius (n 9) 681.

18 Anne M Platoff, 'Where No Flag Has Gone before: Political and Technical Aspects of Placing a Flag on the Moon' (August 1993) <https://www.nasa.gov/history/alsj/alsj-usflag.html#TX17>

19 Launius (n 9).

20 Grahn and Norberg (n 14) 11–63, 17–18.

21 Grahn and Norberg (n 14) 32–39.

22 Olga Krasnyak 'The Apollo–Soyuz Test Project: Construction of an Ideal Type of Science Diplomacy' (2018) 13 The Hague Journal of Diplomacy 410, 421–30; 'Obituary Thomas Stafford 1930–2024: Astronaut Whose Space Handshake with a Soviet Helped Thaw Cold War' *Sydney Morning Herald* (19 March 2024) <https://www.smh.com.au/national/astronaut-whose-space-handshake-with-a-soviet-helped-thaw-cold-war-20240319-p5fdku.html>.

achieve this embrace an 'androgynous' docking system had to be developed. That system had to not only link two previously incompatible systems, but also ensure that neither module was perceived as 'submissive' to the other.[23] This event highlights the fact that interoperability performs a political as much as an engineering role and the success of this project set the scene for more extensive collaboration to come on the International Space Station.[24]

It should also be noted that this same period of the 1950s and 1960s witnessed not only a race for who would be first to space, but also a growing realisation of the potential global threats posed by the detonation of a nuclear weapon in outer space. Any rocket that could send a satellite to outer space could also be used to deliver a nuclear warhead across continents. The V-2 ballistic missile was capable of speeds in excess of 5,300 km per hour and travelling distances of 320 km.[25] The potential for space to become a venue for conflict loomed as a real possibility. The first nuclear test detonation in space was undertaken by the Soviets on 27 August 1957, with the US following suit with six high-altitude nuclear detonations in 1958.[26] The US Air Force detonated 'Starfish Prime' a 2,200-pound W-49 nuclear warhead with a yield of 1.44 megatons 248 miles above the Pacific Ocean on 9 July 1962.[27] The blast produced an electromagnetic pulse which damaged electrical systems on Oahu, Hawaii, 800 miles away from the explosion, as well as creating a flash of light and red aurora visible over many parts of the Pacific.[28] These detonations revealed the significant and dispersed harm posed by nuclear weapons in space. There was concern not only with respect to their threat to life on Earth, but also potentially to astronauts travelling through the Van Allen belts on their way to the Moon.[29]

After the Apollo 17 mission in 1972, US space policy shifted its focus and expenditure to low-Earth orbit, with the development of the Space Shuttle, intended to be a workhorse, delivering regular payloads to space, including servicing foreshadowed commercial customers. The Shuttle was however plagued with problems and delays and ultimately terminated following two fatal accidents, the *Challenger* disaster of 1986 and the 2003 destruction of *Columbia* upon re-entry.[30] The Shuttle

23 Thomas Ellis, '"Howdy Partner!" Space Brotherhood, Détente and the Symbolism of the Apollo-Soyuz Test Project' (2019) 53(3) Journal of American Studies 744, 764–69.

24 William Stewart and Jason Dittmer, 'More-than-Human Space Diplomacy: Assembling Internationalism in Orbit' (2023) 18 Hague Journal of Diplomacy 219, 232–33.

25 NASA, *Wernher von Braun* (n 5); Everett C Dolman, *Astropolitik: Classical Geopolitics in the Space Age* (Frank Cass 2002) 107–9; Neil deGrasse Tyson and Avis Lang, *Accessory to War: The Unspoken Alliance between Astrophysics and the Military* (WW Norton 2018) 192–94; Richard Hollingham, 'V2: The Nazi Rocket that Launched the Space Age' *BBC Online* (8 September 2014) <https://www.bbc.com/future/article/20140905-the-nazis-space-age-rocket>.

26 Robert Ramey, 'Armed Conflict on the Final Frontier: The Law of War in Space' (2000) 48 Air Force Review 1, 12–13.

27 David SF Portree, 'Starfish and Apollo (1962)' *Wired* (21 March 2012) <https://www.wired.com/2012/03/starfishandapollo-1962/>.

28 Portree (n 27).

29 Portree (n 27).

30 Launius (n 9) 682–85; Grahn and Norberg (n 14) 41–45.

programme was closed in 2011, leaving the US reliant upon Russia to ferry crew to the International Space Station.

Until recent tensions created by the Russian invasion of Ukraine, the International Space Station has provided the best example of the capacity for space to facilitate international co-operation. It operates pursuant to the International Space Station Intergovernmental Agreement supported by four memoranda of understanding between NASA, the European Space Agency (ESA), the Canadian Space Agency (CSA), Roscosmos and the Japanese Space Agency (JAXA), and it is an exemplar of international co-operation in outer space.[31] Astronauts from the US, Russia, Japan, Canada, Italy, Belgium, Brazil, Denmark, UK, Israel, Kazakhstan, Malaysia, the Netherlands, South Africa, South Korea, Sweden and the UAE have all lived and worked together on scientific projects and fulfilled some of those aspirational statements of space as a place for peaceful co-operation.[32] However, the ISS is to be decommissioned by the end of this decade and replaced by commercial space stations. Notably, China has been formally excluded from participation in the ISS under the *Wolf Amendment*, which prohibits NASA from collaborating with any Chinese entity that uses government funding without specific Congressional permission.[33] Whilst this legislation was intended to prevent NASA from assisting China in advancing with their space program through the sharing of US technology, it has also created barriers to the use of space as a form of technological diplomacy.[34] In keeping China out of the International Space Station, it has spurred China to build a space station of its own and to pursue the exploration of the Moon as discussed later.

China's journey into space began later than either the US or Russia but its space program has acquired great significance as part of the 'China Dream.' Space technology may contribute to scientific and economic success, but it also provides an ideal platform for forging international partnerships and influence.[35] China's space program was born with the deportation of rocket scientist Qian Xuesen from the

31 Alexander Yakovenko 'The Intergovernmental Agreement on the International Space Station' (1999) 15(2) Space Policy 79–86 <http://doi.org/10.1016/S0265-9646(99)OOD11-9>; Agreement among the Government of Canada, Governments of Member States of the European Space Agency, the Government of Japan, the Government of the Russian Federation, and the Government of the United States of America concerning Cooperation on the Civil International Space Station. 29 January 1998 (entered into force 28 March 2001); Agreement among the Government of the United States of America, Governments of Member States of the European Space Agency, the Government of Japan, and the Government of Canada on Cooperation in the Detailed Design, Development, Operation, and Utilization of the permanently Manned Civil Space Station, 29 September 1988 (entered into force on 30 January 1992).

32 Marshall (n 4) 64–65.

33 Hannah Kohler 'The Eagle and the Hare: US-Chinese Relations, the Wolf Amendment, and the Future of International Cooperation in Space' (2015) 103(4) Georgetown Law Journal 1135.

34 Dennis Normile, 'NASA Opens Door to Cooperation With China on Moon Rock Research' *Science Insider* (7 December 2023) <https://www.science.org/content/article/nasa-opens-door-cooperation-china-moon-rock-research>.

35 Evgenlia Drozhashchikh, 'China's National Space Program and the "China Dream"' (2018) 16(3) Astropolitics 175–86, 175–76.

United States and his return to China in 1955.[36] With technical support from the USSR, China was able to launch its first satellite into orbit in 1970.[37] A human spaceflight programme was formally proposed in 1970. However, despite the development of plans and conduct of extensive biological experiments, resources were not available to undertake a human flight at that time.[38] China continued to undertake launches of satellites and further refine its space technology, with growing independence from the USSR. Plans for human spaceflight were revived in the 1980s, including designs for a crewed space station and the recruitment and training of taikonauts.[39] In 2003, China became the third state to achieve human spaceflight, when it sent taikonaut Yang Liwei to orbit on the Shenzhou 5.[40] A significant number of crewed launches have followed, with both male and female taikonauts undertaking orbital missions. China has also established a Space Station program, with the launch of *Tiangong-1* in 2011 and *Tiangong-2* in 2016. The current Tiangong space station is a modular design constructed during 2021–2022 and maintains a permanent human crew.[41]

China has undertaken several successful missions to lunar orbit Chang'e 1 (2007) and Chang'e 2 (2010) and to the surface of the Moon, including the deployment of rovers Chang'e 3 (2013) and Chang'e 4 (2018) and sample return Chang'e 5 (2020). Chang'e 6 was launched on 3 May 2024, with a mission to collect samples from the far side of the Moon.[42] Chang'e 6 was also carrying a number of international payloads and a rover. Further scheduled missions include sample return, lunar orbiter, rover, 'mini-flying detector,' 3D printing, *in situ* resource utilisation and infrastructure for a lunar base.[43] All of these missions have been conducted in preparation for a human landing on the Moon and the construction of a Moon base. As is evident from the history of these three spacefaring nations, they have adopted various strategies towards the fostering of a human spaceflight program which responds to specific domestic political needs. The plans discussed later demonstrate the belief of all three states in the growing strategic importance of human presence on the Moon, responding to both domestic and international pressures. The tensions and underlying geopolitical rivalries which underpin the history of these fragmented and competing space activities continue into the various proposals to return humans to the Moon. Despite some evidence of the success

36 S Chandrashekar, 'The Origins of China's Space Program (1956–1976)' in *China's Space Programme* (National Institute of Advanced Studies 2022) 3.
37 Drozhashchikh (n 35) 176.
38 Chandrashekar (n 36) 14–15.
39 Chandrashekar (n 36) 37–38.
40 Drozhashchikh (n 35) 180.
41 Andrew Jones and Daisy Dobrijevic, 'China's Space Station, Tiangong: A Complete Guide' (*Space.com*, 15 August 2023) <https://www.space.com/tiangong-space-station>.
42 Andrew Jones, 'China's Chang'e-6 Is Carrying a Surprise Rover to the Moon' *SpaceNews* (online) (6 May 2024) <https://spacenews.com/chinas-change-6-is-carrying-a-surprise-rover-to-the-moon/>.
43 Andrew Jones, 'China Outlines Pathway for Lunar and Deep Space Exploration' *SpaceNews* (online) (28 November 2022) <https://spacenews.com/china-outlines-pathway-for-lunar-and-deep-space-exploration/>.

of individual exercises of détente and willingness of individual astronauts and scientists to work together to overcome these restrictions, there are few signs that the Moon will witness a single approach to its settlement by humanity. Rather, projects will be rivalrous, creating points of tension for international space law to resolve. These projects will now be discussed in the next section.

3 Return to the Moon: Artemis and the International Lunar Research Station

In 2017, President Trump announced that US Space Policy was once again to focus on the Moon, stating, 'the United States will lead the return of humans to the Moon for long-term exploration and utilization, followed by human missions to Mars and other destinations.'[44] This policy marked the beginnings of the Artemis program, through which NASA will lead an international consortium of space agencies and commercial partners in building a new lunar Gateway space station in orbit around the Moon and a permanent human presence on the Moon.

A new vision for international collaboration in the expanded uses of outer space was announced by NASA in May 2020. With the publication of the Artemis Accords in October 2020, the US, through NASA, invited other states, through their respective space agencies, to participate via the Accords:

> to establish a common vision via a practical set of principles, guidelines, and best practices to enhance the governance of the civil exploration and use of outer space with the intention of advancing the Artemis Program.[45]

The Accords thus articulate the principles that NASA and other signatories agree to use in their ongoing use of outer space. A signatory of the Accords is not automatically included in the Artemis program activities. Rather, the Accords are higher-level principles which remain to be specifically implemented by partnership agreements and contracts between participants in specific projects. In this way, the provisions of the Accords may find their way to becoming fundamental conditions of many and diverse projects, even outside of the scope of Artemis itself. The Artemis program includes the Space Launch System rocket and the Orion spacecraft to deliver humans to the Moon, the Lunar Gateway, a space station servicing connection to the surface of the Moon and sustained robotic and human presence on the Moon, which will require exercise of *in situ* resource utilisation.[46] The first mission was the successful test of the uncrewed Artemis 1 in November 2022, with

44 President Donald Trump, 'Presidential Memorandum on Reinvigorating America's Human Space Exploration Program' 11 December 2017, amending Presidential Policy Directive-4 of June 28, 2010 (National Space Policy).

45 NASA, The Artemis Accords, Principles for Cooperation in the Civil Exploration and Use of The Moon, Mars, Comets, and Asteroids for Peaceful Purposes, Section 1.

46 Gabriel Swiney and Amanda Hernandez, *Policy and Strategy Lunar Landing and Operations Policy Analysis* (NASA Office of Technology 30 September 2022) 10.

Artemis 2 planned to send a crew around the Moon in late 2025. The landing of humans on the Moon is currently slated for 2026 but delays are likely.

The planned Artemis activities are so extensive that they will require the involvement of multiple commercial providers and other states. The number of state space agencies that have signed the Accords now greatly exceeds the number of state parties to the *Moon Agreement*, suggesting that the principles outlined in the Accords may start to acquire the status of customary international law, reflecting the rules that a large number of states choose to determine their actions and behaviour.[47] The 39 current signatories to the Accords are Angola, Argentina, Australia, Bahrain, Belgium, Brazil, Bulgaria, Canada, Colombia, Czech Republic, Ecuador, France, Germany, Greece, Iceland, India, Israel, Italy, Japan, Luxembourg, Mexico, Netherlands, New Zealand, Nigeria, Poland, the Republic of Korea, Romania, Rwanda, Saudi Arabia, Singapore, Slovenia, Spain, Sweden, Switzerland, Ukraine, the United Arab Emirates, the United Kingdom, the United States and Uruguay.[48] Thus, the space agencies of all four states with domestic laws permitting space resource activities (US, Luxembourg, Japan and UAE) are signatories to the Accords.[49]

China and its partners in the International Lunar Research Station (ILRS) have also announced ambitious plans to create a permanent habitation on the Moon. Building upon its original plans to establish a permanent base on the Moon in 2016, China initially announced the ILRS as a partnership with Russia in 2021. China has actively been seeking additional partners since that time.[50] The announcement of the partnership explicitly called for open participation:

> ILRS will be open to all interested international partners to cooperate in the areas of planning, substantiating, engineering, development, implementation and operation of ILRS, to strengthen scientific research exchanges and promote the peaceful exploration and use of outer space in the interests of all humankind.[51]

There remain some questions regarding the strength of the China/Russia partnership in the context of space co-operation. Certainly the Russian invasion of Ukraine

47 Walker Smith, 'Using the Artemis Accords to Build Customary International Law: A Vision for a U.S.-Centric Good Governance Regime in Outer Space' (2021) 86(4) Journal of Air Law & Commerce 661.

48 US Department of State, 'United States Welcomes Slovenia's Signing of the Artemis Accords' (22 April 2024) <https://www.state.gov/united-states-welcomes-slovenias-signing-of-the-artemis-accords/>.

49 US Commercial Space Launch Competitiveness Act, Pub L No 114–90, 129 Stat 704.; Journal officiel du Grand-Duché de Luxembourg, Loi du 20 juillet 2017 sur l'exploration et l'utilisation des ressources de l'espace; Federal Law No. 12 of 2019 on the Regulation of the Space Sector, United Arab Emirates; Space Resources Act (2021) (Japan).

50 Joint Statement Between CNSA and ROSCOSMOS Regarding Cooperation for the Construction of the International Lunar Research Station, 29 April 2021 <https://www.cnsa.gov.cn/english/n6465668/n6465670/c6811967/content.html>

51 Joint Statement (n 50).

has created some complexities for international partnerships in space, leading to observations that 'their partnership is stronger on paper than in reality.'[52] In fact, given the evolution of the Artemis program from the experience of the International Space Station, it was foreshadowed that Russia would become an Artemis participant. Russia (as a partner on the ISS) had initially indicated that it was open to participating in the Artemis program. However, following the release of the Artemis accords Russia declared it too 'US-centric.'[53]

In most recent statements on the ILRS, China is positioned as the managing party to the ILRS. This marks a profound shift in China's space science and diplomacy towards openness and international engagement. In 2023, a document was presented to UNCOPUOS which outlined China's intention that participating ILRS partners would establish an International Lunar Research Station Cooperation Organization (ILRSCO) to oversee the management of building the ILRS projects and facilities and which would be the vehicle by which partners would share research.[54] Interestingly, presumably as an incentive, it also stated that the first signatories will 'enjoy more favourable terms, more rights and more results as founding members of ILRSCO.'[55] That document also stated that the ILRSCO would be headquartered in Hefei Deep Space Science City, China. As of April 2024, nine states have joined the ILRS: China, Russia, Venezuela, Pakistan, Azerbaijan, Belarus, South Africa, Egypt and Thailand.[56] However, it has been observed that not all of these states have signed the same type of agreement, nor are the signatories uniform in terms of size, structure or space capabilities. A number of non-governmental entities, such as corporations, agencies, universities and astronomical associations, have also signed agreements with the ILRS, as well as the Asia-Pacific Space Cooperation Organization (APSCO).[57] This structure, whilst opening the door to various levels of participation in the ILRS, may undermine any arguments that activities of the ILRS provide strong evidence of state practice for the purposes of international law.

Current plans for the ILRS include facilities on the lunar surface, in lunar orbit and on Earth. As of April 2024, China announced that a lunar station would be constructed in the lunar south pole region by 2035.[58] That station would support

52 Xiaodan Wu, 'The International Lunar Research Station: China's New Era of Space Cooperation and Its New Role in the Space Legal Order' (2023) 65 Space Policy 101537, 6–7.

53 Jeff Foust, 'Russia Skeptical about Participating in Lunar Gateway' *SpaceNews* (online) (12 October 2020). <https://spacenews.com/russia-skeptical-about-participating-in-lunar-gateway/>.

54 International Lunar Research Station (ILRS) 23–05 <https://www.unoosa.org/documents/pdf/copuos/2023/TPs/ILRS_presentation20230529_.pdf>.

55 ILRS (n 54).

56 Andrew Jones, 'Thailand Joins China-led ILRS Moon Base Initiative' *SpaceNews* (online) (5 April 2024) <https://spacenews.com/thailand-joins-china-led-ilrs-moon-base-initiative/>.

57 Andrew Jones, 'China Adds New Moon Base Project Partners, but Struggles to Attract National-Level Participation' *SpaceNews* (online) (28 March 2024) <https://spacenews.com/china-adds-new-moon-base-project-partners-but-struggles-to-attract-national-level-participation/#:~:text=the%20Gateway.-,LRS%20Signatory,-Type>.

58 The State Council, 'The People's Republic of China, China Unveils International Lunar Research Station Details' (25 April 2024) <http://english.scio.gov.cn/m/chinavoices/2024-04/26/content_117152685.htm>.

humans to undertake scientific experiments, as well as *in situ* resource utilisation. By 2045, phase two of the of the ILRS would see the expansion of the lunar south pole station, as well as a facility in lunar orbit. Research undertaken by these activities, involving *in situ* resource utilisation, power systems, command, control navigation and information systems and transportation, would be used to support a human landing on Mars.[59] The Space China Dream positions China as a space leader and is based upon building legitimacy through alliances and collaborations.[60] The outlined approach positions China not only as a leader in space technology, but also as an exemplar of peaceful and inclusive space co-operation. The ILRS is expressed as being open to all states, including developing nations and, rather than imposing a set of principles upon its partners, China invites participants to contribute to designing the projects as well as the legal framework of the ILRS.[61] Strategically, the existence of the ILRS and the invitation for other states to join in the program provides an alternative to the US-led Artemis program and resists the Artemis Accords becoming the de facto rulebook for the Moon.

With so many projects now planned for the Moon, alongside an increasing number of national and private uncrewed missions, the Moon is about to become a busy domain. In 2022, NASA identified, '[j]ust within the next four years, we expect to see at least 22 lunar surface missions. Half of these missions will occur in the Moon's south polar region.'[62] With competing uses and users, there also comes the potential for conflict over locations, resources and landing spaces, as well as increased risk to heritage sites and sites of greater scientific interest. Clearly both projects have a strategic as well as a scientific mission. As Wu observes, 'the ILRS can act as a buffer zone to alleviate the negative impact of sole dependence on the United States in lunar exploration activities.'[63] Conversely, the opportunity for China to demonstrate its space expertise may open the path for scientific diplomacy and demonstration of the benefits of novel ways of working together.[64] Clearly the Moon has once again become the site of major geopolitical rivalry.[65] How do we avoid repeating mistakes of the past in destruction of novel environments? The next section will consider the application of international space law to the multilateral Moon projects outlined in this section.

59 The State Council (n 58).

60 Namrata Goswami and Peter Garretson, *Scramble for the Skies: The Great Power Competition to Control the Resources of Outer Space* (Lexington Books 2020) 211.

61 Fengna Xu and Jun Ou, 'Promoting International Cooperation on the International Lunar Research Station: Inspiration from the ITER' (2023) 203 Acta Astronautica 341, 344–45; Namrata Goswami, 'The Strategic Implications of the China-Russia Lunar Base Cooperation Agreement' *The Diplomat* (online) (19 March 2021) <https://thediplomat.com/2021/03/the-strategic-implications-of-the-china-russia-lunar-base-cooperation-agreement/>

62 Swiney and Hernandez (n 46) i.

63 Wu (n 52) 7.

64 Wu (n 52) 7.

65 Xu and Ou (n 61) 341, 348; Goswami (n 61).

3 International Space Law

International space law was crafted in the context of the great nuclear and space power rivalry of the Cold War. Following the conduct of Soviet space nuclear tests in 1957,

> the UN General Assembly (UNGA) adopted its first resolution directed at the use of outer space on 14 November 1957. Notably, that resolution urged states to adopt a disarmament agreement that included a mandate for 'the joint study of an inspection system designed to ensure that the sending of objects through outer space shall be exclusively for peaceful and scientific purposes.'[66] The reference to the use of space exclusively for peaceful purposes was to be repeated in subsequent resolutions, declarations and treaties, as well as becoming the language repeated by many states in the context of asserting their own 'good behaviour' whilst simultaneously casting doubt of that of other states.[67]

UNGA Resolution 1348 (XIII) concerned 'Questions of the Peaceful Use of Outer Space' and established the Committee on the Peaceful Uses of Outer Space (COPUOS) as an ad hoc committee of the UNGA. The UN General Assembly established COPUOS as a permanent committee on 12 December 1959, with a mandate to deal with matters related to the peaceful uses of outer space.[68] Matters related to military uses of space are referred to the UN Conference on Disarmament. This bifurcation has created some opportunity for delays and prevarication with respect to discussion on the prevention of weaponisation of outer space. Prevalent in discussions regarding space security was the focus on transparency, inspection and information sharing.

The Treaty on Principles Governing the Activities of States in the Exploration and Use of Outer Space, Including the Moon and Other Celestial Bodies 1967 ('Outer Space Treaty') established the international law which has regulated the use of space by states since the 1960s. It creates fundamental principles regarding the use of space and, in particular, places the responsibility on states to supervise and regulate the space activities of their nationals. The Outer Space Treaty is regarded as the most successful of the five UN space treaties and currently has 115 ratifying parties and 22 signatories.[69] The principles of the Outer Space Treaty were further elaborated upon in the subsequent space treaties: the Agreement on the Rescue of Astronauts, the Return of Astronauts and the Return of Objects Launched Into Outer Space, 1968 ('Rescue and Return Agreement'); the Convention on

66 UNGA Resolution 1148 (XII) 14 November 1957.

67 P.J. Blount, 'The Shifting Sands of Space Security: The Politics and Law of The Peaceful Uses of Outer Space' (2019) 17(1) Indonesian Journal of International Law 1–18.

68 UNGA Resolution 1472 (XIV) 12 December 1959.

69 Committee on the Peaceful Uses of Outer Space, Status of International Agreements relating to activities in outer space as at 1 January 2024, 15 April 2024, A/AC.105/C.2/2024/CRP.3 <https://www.unoosa.org/res/oosadoc/data/documents/2024/aac_105c_22024crp/aac_105c_22024crp_3_0_html/AC105_C2_2024_CRP03E.pdf>, plus ratification from Columbia (15 April 2024).

International Liability for Damage Caused by Space Objects, 1972 ('Liability Convention'); and the Convention on Registration of Objects Launched Into Outer Space, 1975 (Registration Convention). The Agreement Governing the Activities of States on the Moon and Other Celestial Bodies, which deals with the arrangements needed for space resource activities, has attracted only 17 parties, with the withdrawal of Saudi Arabia, effective 5 January 2024. Each of these treaties is relevant to the activities of the proposed activities on the Moon and will be discussed in the context of the Artemis Accords and the ILRS framework in the next section. First, it is important to highlight the key elements of international space law which will need to be considered and applied in each of those projects.

Article I of the Outer Space Treaty sets the background and context for all human uses of outer space. It affirms that the 'exploration and use of outer space, including the Moon and other celestial bodies, shall be carried out for the benefit and in the interests of all countries, irrespective of their degree of economic or scientific development, and shall be the province of all mankind.'[70] Further, it confirms that space 'including the Moon and other celestial bodies, shall be free for exploration and use by all States without discrimination of any kind, on a basis of equality and in accordance with international law, and there shall be free access to all areas of celestial bodies.'[71] It explicitly confirms, 'There shall be freedom of scientific investigation in outer space, including the Moon and other celestial bodies, and States shall facilitate and encourage international cooperation in such investigation.'[72] Hence, Article I establishes two fundamental principles: that space is free and open to all states and that such uses and activities must be undertaken in compliance with international law.

Article III of the Outer Space Treaty further affirms, 'activities in the exploration and use of outer space' must be undertaken 'in accordance with international law. . .in the interest of maintaining international peace and securing and promoting international cooperation and understanding.'[73] Fundamentally Article I recognises the rights of states to explore and use space, and the subsequent provisions prescribes the 'limitations and restrictions on such use and exploration.'[74] It is important also to recall the specific circumstances under which the Outer Space Treaty was negotiated and concluded, reflecting the Cold War rivalry of the two nuclear states, the United States and the USSR. Prior to the successful orbit of Sputnik around the Earth, it was not even certain that orbital overflight would not infringe the rights of states.[75] With the desire of both states to ensure that space

70 Outer Space Treaty, Article I.

71 Outer Space Treaty, Article I.

72 Outer Space Treaty, Article I.

73 Outer Space Treaty, Article III.

74 Andrea Harrington, 'Due Regard as the Prime Directive for Responsible Behavior in Space' (2024) 20(1) Loyola University Chicago International Law Review 57, 58.

75 Małgorzata Polkowska, 'Limitations in the Airspace Sovereignty of States in Connection With Space Activity' (2018) 20(3) Security and Defence Quarterly 42–56, William E Burrows, *This New Ocean: The Story of the First Space Age* (Random House 1998).

remained open for their endeavours, the freedom of use and exploration of space had to be confirmed.

Other articles which are of importance to the activities of humans in space include Article II, which establishes the principle of non-appropriation: 'Outer space, including the Moon and other celestial bodies, is not subject to national appropriation by claim of sovereignty, by means of use or occupation, or by any other means.' Article V deems astronauts 'envoys of mankind in outer space,' a designation which has generated significant academic debate regarding its content and meaning. The general consensus appears to conclude that the designation is 'political rhetoric'[76] or a 'figure of speech.'[77] Perhaps reflecting the heroic role of astronauts and cosmonauts of the era in undertaking extremely dangerous missions, as well as the honour and national prestige that was created by those who completed successful missions, it is not regarded as creating any diplomatic status under international law, subject to the following specific obligations:

- States must render to astronauts 'all possible assistance in the event of accident, distress, or emergency landing on the territory of another [State] or on the high seas';[78]
- Astronauts 'shall be safely and promptly returned to the State of registry of their space vehicle';[79]
- When undertaking space activities, astronauts of one state 'shall render all possible assistance to the astronauts' of another state;[80] and
- States must notify the United Nations of 'any phenomena they discover in outer space. . . which could constitute a danger to the life or health of astronauts.'[81]

These obligations are further elaborated on the Rescue and Return Agreement, which uses the terminology 'personnel of a spacecraft' in place of the term astronaut.

Article VI requires states to 'bear international responsibility for national activities in outer space' whether such activities are undertaken by government or commercial entities. States must authorise and continually supervise the activities of non-governmental entities and ensure that they comply with the provisions of the Outer Space Treaty. This authorisation may be conducted by a state in whatever manner is compatible with its domestic processes and may involve comprehensive space laws, the creation of national space agencies and the enactment of a range

76 GS Sachdeva, 'Outer Space Treaty: An Appraisal' in Ajey Lele (ed), *50 Years of the Outer Space Treaty* (Pentagon Press 2017) 24–47, 24.

77 Frans von der Dunk and Gerardine Goh, 'Article V' in Stephen Hobe, Bernhard Schmidt-Tedd and Kai-Uwe Schrogl (eds), *Cologne Commentary on Space Law*, vol 1 (Carl Heymanns Verlag 2009) 94–102, 94.

78 Outer Space Treaty, Article V.

79 Outer Space Treaty, Article V.

80 Outer Space Treaty, Article V.

81 Outer Space Treaty, Article V.

of related laws, such as those relating to corporate governance and national security.[82] Article IX creates several principles which have heightened relevance in the context of increasingly congested uses of space, including the potential for lunar bases co-existing in close proximity.[83] It requires that states shall conduct their space activities 'with due regard to the corresponding interests' of other states.[84] States must also conduct their space activities in such a manner as to avoid the harmful contamination of space and adverse changes of the Earth's environment. Where states consider that their activities may cause harmful interference with the activities of other states, it must undertake consultation regarding that activity. As yet, no agreed methodology has been developed for such consultation, and this lack of consensus may lead to misunderstandings and dispute regarding whether the requirement of consultation has been complied with.

In addition to these specific provisions, clearly the entire body of international space law, as well as relevant domestic laws, will apply in the context of the proposed Moon habitats. There is not sufficient scope in this chapter to outline them all. These particular laws have been highlighted as they have been applied or interpreted in a particular way in the Artemis Accords and the ILRS Cooperation Guidelines.

4 The Artemis Accords and ILRS Cooperation Guidelines

This section will outline the provisions which form the basis of each of the Artemis Accords and the ILRS and consider how they operate within (and may continue to shape) the scope of international space law.

The Artemis Accords are intended to 'establish a common vision via a practical set of principles, guidelines, and best practices to enhance the governance of the civil exploration and use of outer space with the intention of advancing the Artemis Program.'[85] Signatories are expected to undertake 'a political commitment to the principles' articulated in the document, and signature of the Accords does not equate to participation in any part of the Artemis program.[86] The Artemis Accords do not purport to be a treaty nor to create international law, confirming that the principles 'are intended to apply to civil space activities conducted by civil space agencies.'[87] The Accords specifically envisage that activities to be undertaken by Artemis signatories will be implemented through appropriate agreements which reference and implement the principles contained in the Accords. Certainly, the principles present a gloss on the provisions of the Outer Space Treaty. Some of

82 Frans von der Dunk, *Advanced Introduction to Space Law* (Edward Elgar Publishing 2020) 115–25. See further, UNOOSA, National Space Law Database <https://astro.unoosa.org/astro/national-space-law-landing-page.html>.

83 Harrington (n 74).

84 Outer Space Treaty, Article IX.

85 Artemis Accords, Section 1.

86 Artemis Accords, Section 1.

87 Artemis Accords, Section 1.

the provisions provide specific operational guidance on how certain principles of the Outer Space Treaty may be interpreted, whilst others articulate new concepts which extend beyond the Treaty.

Provisions that repeat or affirm principles of the Outer Space Treaty are:

- Section 3: Peaceful Purposes rephrases the obligations of Article III of the Outer Space Treaty, requiring signatories to conduct any cooperative activities under the Accords for 'peaceful purposes and in accordance with relevant international law.' The phrase 'peaceful purposes' appears four times in the Outer Space Treaty, twice in the preamble and twice in Article IV. As the Artemis program is conceived as a partnership between civilian space agencies and commercial partners, this section affirms the peaceful, co-operative and lawful nature of those activities.
- Section 4: Transparency restates obligations under Article XI of the Outer Space Treaty, regarding transparency of space policies and exploration plans and sharing of scientific information.
- Section 6: Emergency Assistance echoes the obligations of Article V of the Outer Space Treaty and the Rescue and Return Agreement. It requires signatories to 'commit to taking all reasonable efforts to render necessary assistance to personnel in outer space who are in distress.'[88] As outlined earlier, the Outer Space Treaty creates a special regime for the treatment of astronauts, including rendering them assistance in event of accident, distress or emergency landing. The Rescue and Return Agreement extends these obligations and adopts the term 'personnel of a spacecraft.' The Moon Agreement goes further to impose obligations with respect to protection and rescue of people in space, deeming all people on or in orbit around the Moon or other celestial body to be both an 'astronaut' and 'personnel of a spacecraft.'[89]
- Section 7: Registration of Space Objects requires signatories to address their obligations under the Registration Convention. This provision is relevant to the responsible uses of space and ensures that state responsibility can be attributed to different elements in use as part of Artemis activities.
- Section 8: Release of Scientific Data reflects the information sharing principles of Articles X, XI and XII, providing for signatories to 'communicate and release information to the public' and make scientific results available 'to the public and international scientific community,' subject to a number of specific provisos. These limitations include protection of proprietary and export-controlled information, necessary prior consultation with other partners and recognition that open sharing of scientific data does not apply to the private sector, unless their operations are being conducted on behalf of an Artemis signatory.

88 Artemis Accords, Section 6.

89 Melissa de Zwart and Joel Lisk, 'The Effect of Space Tourism on the Concept of "Astronaut" Under International Law' in Sandeepa Bhat B (ed), *Space Tourism: Legal and Policy Aspects* (Routledge 2024) 28, 30–32.

- Section 12: Orbital Debris obliges signatories to engage in mitigation of orbital debris, including plans for end-of-mission disposal and the avoidance of creating debris through accidents and conjunctions. Like the Long-Term Sustainability Guidelines,[90] this section is focused on orbit rather than surface activities, nevertheless it is clear that consideration will also need to be given to sustainability related to resource extraction and other surface activities.

Novel provisions address the following:

- Section 5: Interoperability. Recognising that there will be a need for Artemis partners to be able to share communications, equipment, power, fuel, transport, landing and other facilities, the signatories commit to use 'reasonable efforts' to develop and apply common interoperability standards. As noted earlier, once of the most significant impediments to co-operation in space will simply be the incompatibility of equipment. The ability to overcome these restrictions has created some fundamental opportunities for space-based diplomacy, such as the International Space Station.[91] Further, the involvement of commercial space operators will likely lead to greater use of lower cost off-the-shelf solutions than high-value bespoke products.
- Section 9: Preserving Outer Space Heritage. Building upon recent work in the US to preserve the heritage of the Apollo landing sites on the Moon, Artemis signatories agree to 'preserve outer space heritage, which they consider comprising historically significant human or robotic landing sites, artifacts, spacecraft, and other evidence of activity on celestial bodies in accordance with mutually developed standards and practices.' They also commit to contribute to the development of new multilateral efforts to 'develop international practices and rules applicable to preserving outer space heritage.' Notably, this focus is only on the US historic sites and reflects the work being done in the US to protect such sites.[92]
- Section 10: Space Resources. The utilisation of *in situ* resources will be vital for sustaining the long-term presence of humans on the Moon. In this section, Artemis Accords signatories affirm the critical nature of space resources and emphasise that the extraction and use of space resources must be undertaken in accordance with the Outer Space Treaty and 'in support of safe and sustainable

90 Guidelines for the Long-Term Sustainability of Outer Space Activities, UN Doc A/AC.105/2018/CRP.20 (27 June 2018).

91 Stewart and Dittmer (n 24) 219–52.

92 NASA, 'NASA's Recommendations to Space-Faring Entities: How to Protect and Preserve the Historic and Scientific Value of US Government Lunar Artifacts' (20 July 2011) <https://www.nasa.gov/wp-content/uploads/2017/10/617743main_nasa-usg_lunar_historic_sites_reva-508.pdf>; Public Law 116—275 One Small Step to Protect Human Heritage in Space Act, 31 December 2020; Michelle Hanlon, 'Apollo Landers, Neil Armstrong's Boot Print and Other Human Artifacts on Moon Officially Protected by New US Law' *The Conversation* (online) (13 January 2021) <https://theconversation.com/apollo-landers-neil-armstrongs-bootprint-and-other-human-artifacts-on-moon-officially-protected-by-new-us-law-152661>.

space activities.' Noting the lingering question regarding the effect of Article II's prohibition on appropriation, this section also states that the signatories 'affirm that the extraction of space resources does not inherently constitute national appropriation under Article II of the Outer Space Treaty.' Further, it requires that all 'contracts and other legal instruments relating to space resources should be consistent with that Treaty.'[93] Notably, the signatories commit to information sharing with the UN, the public and the international scientific community with respect to their space resource activities and 'intend to use their experience under the Accords to contribute to multilateral efforts to further develop international practices and rules applicable to the extraction and utilization of space resources, including through ongoing efforts at the COPUOS.'

- Section 11: Deconfliction of Space Activities. Possibly the most contentious provision of the Artemis Accords, this section commits signatories to contribute to multilateral efforts to develop 'international practices, criteria, and rules applicable to the definition and determination of safety zones and harmful interference.' Activities undertaken on the Moon may create a range of hazards, including landings and other activities generating dust particle plumes, the use of autonomous equipment, heavy machinery and unfamiliar operating environments, including navigation across the lunar surface.[94] While the concept of safety zones is not new and draws upon precedents from air and maritime laws, it does raise again the issue of whether it permits appropriation by another means. This section explicitly scaffolds the justification for safety zones in Article IX concepts of due regard and the avoidance of harmful contamination. Signatories commit to provide notification of their own activities and to 'commit to coordinating with any relevant actor to avoid harmful interference.' That area of activity which is identified as necessary to avoid the creation of harmful interference to any 'public and private personnel, equipment, and operations' will be designated as a 'safety zone.' Whilst the full details of how safety zones will be developed, designated and operated remain to be developed, further provisions state that size, scope and operation of safety zones should reflect:

  a. the fact that all safety zones are temporary and end when the related operation ceases;
  b. 'the nature of the operations being conducted and the environment that such operations are conducted in';
  c. 'commonly accepted scientific and engineering principles';
  d. changes in function of activities over time;
  e. the need to provide information and consultation to others regarding the establishment, alteration and cessation of a safety zone.

93 Artemis Accords, Section 10.

94 Swiney and Hernandez (n 46).

The two provisions regarding space resources and safety zones are potentially the most contentious elements and will be considered further in the next section on *in situ* space resources.

Rather than providing high-level rules or principles, as outlined in the Artemis Accords, the Cooperation Guidelines of the ILRS identify Cooperation Domains, which include technical, strategic and legal planning and collaboration, such as:

- 'Strategy development and coordination related to the Moon exploration and use, defining of areas of cooperation and planning including development of the roadmap with regard to the exploration and use of the Moon.'[95]
- 'Joint development of the legal documents regulating relations, including the involvement of third parties, in the framework of the creation of the ILRS.'[96]
- 'Review of existing standards in the field of launch vehicle and spacecraft technology development and potential definition of future standards that may be used during the creation of ILRS.'[97]

All partners to the ILRS 'are encouraged to join the ILRS based on their own situation.' The Guidelines place an emphasis on 'joint development' and negotiation of the terms of their participation:

> Any Partner willing to contribute to the ILRS, through a jointly coordinated negotiation with China and Russia, can participate including co-lead status in any part of the project. The objective, plan, interface, standards, interoperability and scientific application of the participating project(s) or missions shall be aligned with general architecture and functions of ILRS.[98]

Projects are envisaged to encompass cooperation on complete missions, specific systems (such as space nuclear or solar power), subsystems, equipment and ground segment or other specific application, such as data analysis.[99]

The ILRS does not prescribe adherence to any mandatory terms or principles to participants. Rather there is expressed to be scope for states and other participants to adopt binding and non-binding agreements and to build upon bilateral and multilateral agreements in working towards a binding treaty. This ability for partners to have input into projects and the guiding principles is being positioned by China as creating a more open and democratic project. China has described this as inviting partners to 'advance hand in hand' to develop a project 'on the basis of equality, mutual benefit and peaceful use, practicing the concepts of extensive

95 China National Space Administration, *International Lunar Research Station (ILRS) Guide for Partnership*, V1.0 (June 2021) <https://www.cnsa.gov.cn/english/n6465652/n6465653/c6812150/content.html>, 12.
96 China National Space Administration (n 95).
97 China National Space Administration (n 95).
98 China National Space Administration (n 95).
99 China National Space Administration (n 95) 13.

consultation, joint contribution and sharing, and providing new opportunities for world development.'[100] Therefore, a significant amount of work remains to be done to develop the 'rules of the road' for the Moon. Neither project provides clear guidance yet on how human and robotic operators will be able to live and work safely on the Moon and navigate a range of potentially competing uses. Nor is there any guidance on how any disputes over sites or resources may be managed. One clear point of tension will be the access to and use of vital *in situ* resources, such as water, sunlight, fuel and other minerals.

5 *In situ* Resource Utilisation

The Artemis Accords affirm that *in situ* resource utilisation will be a vital component of sustained human presence on the Moon and plans to use the Moon to travel further into the solar system. Noting that none of the major spacefaring powers are signatories to the Moon Agreement and that the US has clearly asserted that it will object to 'any attempt to treat the 1979 Moon Agreement as expressing customary international law,' it appears that the principles outlined in that treaty will have little impact of resource allocation on the Moon.[101] However, several Artemis Accords signatories are also signatories to the Moon Agreement, including Australia, Mexico, Netherlands, France and India. This suggests that their participation in Artemis will be undertaken in accordance with obligations they may have under the Moon Agreement.[102]

As is clear from the Chang'e missions discussed earlier, China is also focused on resource identification, extraction and return. The ILRS missions explicitly make reference to *in situ* resource utilisation. Until recently, it has been unclear what China's legal and policy position on the utilisation of space resources would be. Wu notes, 'a conservative interpretation of and adherence to the common understanding of the space treaties would help build confidence in the ILRS and encourage consensus among partners.'[103] Certainly, as many authors have noted, the development of broad consensus principles of the use of outer space, through

100 China: The 74th International Astronautical Congress—International Lunar Research Station—International Major Science and Engineering Global Network Forum was successfully held, 7 October 2021 <https://www.proquest.com/wire-feeds/china-74th-international-astronautical-congress/docview/2873823000/se-2?accountid=8203>.

101 President Donald J Trump, 'Executive Order 13914 of April 6, 2020: Encouraging International Support for the Recovery and Use of Space Resources' (2020) 85 Federal Register 20381; 'Fact Sheet: Encouraging International Support for the Recovery and Use of Space Resources' (*The White House*, 6 April 2020) <https://trumpwhitehouse.archives.gov/wp-content/uploads/2020/04/Fact-Sheet-on-EO-Encouraging-International-Support-for-the-Recovery-and-Use-of-Space-Resources.pdf>.

102 63rd session of the Legal Subcommittee, 15–26 April 2024, Statement by Australia: 'Australia considers that the Artemis Accords are consistent with Australia's international obligations. Australia considers that the Moon Agreement and the Artemis Accords provide frameworks that will guide and enable Australia's planned future activities on the Moon' <https://www.unoosa.org/documents/pdf/copuos/lsc/2024/Statements/9_Australia.pdf>.

103 Wu (n 52) 8.

agreements such as the Artemis Accords, will have an influence on the evolution of customary international law.[104] Practices adopted by states in conformity with the Artemis Accords or principles developed under the ILRS will contribute to the shaping of space law through the development of state practice.

In a Submission to the UNCOPUOS Working Group on Legal Aspects of Space Resource Activities in March 2024, China outlined a clearer articulation of its position on space resources. First, it affirms China's position that any rules governing space resource activities must be developed within the framework of international space law, and especially the provisions of the Outer Space Treaty, including peaceful uses of space 'for the benefit and in the interests of all humankind, non-appropriation, international cooperation, due regard and compliance with international law.'[105] It then elaborates in further detail how these principles apply to space resources:

- Non-appropriation: the submission clarifies that 'the exploration, exploitation and utilization of space resources shall be in conformity with the principle of non-appropriation.'[106]
- Freedom of scientific investigation: 'space resource activities are in line with the principle of exploration and use of outer space for the benefit and in the interests of all humankind' and results and data are eligible for benefit sharing.[107]
- Due regard: referencing the principle of co-operation, mutual assistance and due regard under Article IX, China suggests that the Working Group formulate principles 'to implement the principle of cooperation and mutual assistance in space resource activities, which would ensure the safe and orderly conduct of such activities, and promote coordination among relevant States.'[108]
- Supervision of non-governmental entities: noting the Article VI requirements that states bear international responsibility for national activities in outer space and must ensure that the activities of non-governmental entities are authorised and supervised by the relevant state, China suggests that the Working Group develop standards for authorisation and supervision of non-governmental entities carrying out space resource activities.

104 Guoyu Wang, 'NASA's Artemis Accords: The Path to a United Space Law or a Divided One?' *The Space Review* (24 August 2020) <www.thespacereview.com/article/4009/1>; Rossana Deplano, 'The Artemis Accords: Evolution or Revolution in International Space Law?' (2021) 70 International and Comparative Law Quarterly 799–819; Goswami (n 61); Melissa de Zwart, 'To the Moon and Beyond: The Artemis Accords and the Evolution of Space Law' in *Commercial and Military Uses of Outer Space* (Springer 2021) 65–80; Athar ud Din, 'The Artemis Accords: The End of Multilateralism in the Management of Outer Space?' (2022) 20(2–3) Astropol 136.

105 Submission by the Delegation of China to the Working Group on Legal Aspects of Space Resource Activities of the Legal Subcommittee of the Committee on the Peaceful Uses of Outer Space <https://www.unoosa.org/documents/pdf/copuos/lsc/space-resources/LSC2024/English_Chinas_submission_to_the_working_group_on_space_resources.pdf>, n.d., submitted March 2024.

106 Submission by the Delegation of China (n 105).

107 Submission by the Delegation of China (n 105).

108 Submission by the Delegation of China (n 105).

The Chinese Submission to the UNCOPUOS Working Group states that space resource activities should be conducted 'with full consideration of the sustainability of resources, and ensure the freedom of exploration and use of outer space for future generations with the aim of intergenerational equity.' Further, the Working Group should consider developing principles which 'prevent depletive exploitation of space resources which fails the requirements of sustainability.'[109] These principles are consistent both with the provisions of the Outer Space Treaty and other evolving space resource frameworks being developed by various working groups discussed later.

There are several initiatives working on developing frameworks for space resource utilisation. In addition to the domestic laws in place in the US, Luxembourg, the UAE and Japan noted previously, there are multiple proposals which seek to address some of the uncertainties identified earlier. The Hague International Space Resources Governance Working Group produced the 'Building Blocks for the Development of an International Framework on Space Resource Activities' in 2019.[110] The Building Blocks do not purport to provide a complete rule set to be applied to resource activities, but rather they intend to provide recommendations and guidelines regarding the issues that need to be clarified before activities commence. The Global Expert Group on Sustainable Lunar Activities (GEGSLA) released its 'Recommended Framework and Key Elements for Peaceful and Sustainable Lunar Activities' in 2022.[111] These principles promote concepts of sustainability and reduction of environmental impact. These and other proposals are being considered as part of the work of the UNCOPUOS Working Group on Legal Aspects of Space Resources, which was established in 2021 to develop a set of recommended principles for the exploration, exploitation and use of space resources and has a five-year work plan.[112] At its meeting in Luxembourg in April 2024, the chair and the vice-chair of the Working Group stated that an initial draft of recommended principles for space resource activities would be disseminated to members of the Committee in early January 2025.[113]

109 Submission by the Delegation of China (n 105).

110 The Hague International Space Resources Governance Working Group, 'Building Blocks for the Development of an International Framework on Space Resource Activities' (2019) <https://www.universiteitleiden.nl/binaries/content/assets/rechtsgeleerdheid/instituut-voor-publiekrecht/lucht-en-ruimterecht/space-resources/bb-thissrwg-cover.pdf>.

111 Global Expert Group on Sustainable Lunar Activities, 'Recommended Framework and Key Elements for Peaceful and Sustainable Lunar Activities' (2022) <https://moonvillageassociation.org/gegsla/documents/gegsla-recommended-framework/>.

112 UNCOPUOS Legal Sub-Committee Working Group on Legal Aspects of Space Resource Activities <https://www.unoosa.org/oosa/en/ourwork/copuos/lsc/space-resources/index.html>.

113 Draft Report, Committee on the Peaceful Uses of Outer Space, Legal Subcommittee, Sixty-third session, Vienna, 15–26 April 2024, Annex II, Report of the Chair and Vice-Chair of the Working Group on Legal Aspects of Space Resource Activities, A/AC.105/C.2/2024/SRA/L.1, 23 April 2024 <https://www.unoosa.org/res/oosadoc/data/documents/2024/aac_105c_2sral/aac_105c_22024sral_1_0_html/AC105_C2_2024_SRA_L01E.pdf>.

This work and these proposals will build upon the principles outlined in both the Artemis Accords and the ILRS Cooperation Guidelines (and any resulting work done by the relevant subgroups). However, in order for habitation to proceed effectively and safely there will need to be consensus on the applicable principles. It is likely that where there is any divergence between the two (or potentially more) models there will be scope for conflict. Hence it is vital that these projects move towards a consistent approach and one that avoids political claims. The Outer Space Treaty provides a clear framework for future space activities. However, these various initiatives are required to fill in the detailed rules which need to operate to ensure predictable, sustainable and co-ordinated space activities. It is likely that a diversity of operators, both governmental and commercial, will commence activities on the Moon before the end of this decade. They may bring with them competing rule sets for operation. However, with the consolidation of two large multilateral coalitions focused on activities on the Moon and beyond, which will require resource extraction and use, there is some possibility that practical requirements will create the context for consensual development of rules of operation for the safe and sustainable conduct of activities.

6 Conclusions

As alliances are forged across the two projects, it is clear that the impact of these partnerships and rivalries will be felt on Earth, as well as in space. Given the significant (and growing) number of parties to these two projects, it is inevitable that the Artemis Accords and any similar principles articulated by the ILRS will perform a major role in influencing the development, interpretation and application of international space law. It is also vital to acknowledge that human life in space is likely to be even more fragile than it is on Earth. Resources such as oxygen and water cannot be easily replicated or sourced on the Moon, and it will be difficult to imagine how provisions such as the emergency assistance provisions of Article V of the Outer Space Treaty will scale to large lunar habitations. The key legal principles which require clarification have been outlined earlier and should form the basis of any reviews undertaken to determine issues requiring urgent clarification, alongside the relevant technical issues. Time should also be taken to ensure that these questions are considered in the light of what we can do better. How can the rules be framed in a way that improves and supports the human experience on the Moon, rather than simply replicate Earth-based problems?

This chapter has outlined the journey that China, Russia and the US have taken to be on the verge of returning humans to the Moon, to stay, and then on to Mars. Whilst this has taken a relatively short period of time, it highlights the reliance of each space program on political support. This support comes at the cost of the perceived value of the space program in terms of tangible outcomes and national prestige. These two factors create a tension with the stated aims of the Outer Space Treaty in creating space as a domain which offers the capacity for the peaceful exploration and scientific purposes and the 'benefit of all peoples regardless of their economic or scientific development.' To ensure that the

Moon's environment is utilised in a sustainable manner, these rules of the road need to be developed and agreed on a global basis, very soon.

Bibliography

David Baker, 'Wernher von Braun's Forgotten Mission to Mars' *BBC Sky at Night Magazine* (online) (16 July 2019) <https://www.skyatnightmagazine.com/space-missions/wernher-von-brauns-forgotten-mission-mars>

P.J. Blount, 'The Shifting Sands of Space Security: The Politics and Law of the Peaceful Uses of Outer Space' (2019) 17(1) Indonesian Journal of International Law 1–18.

Bleddyn Bowen, *War in Space: Strategy, Space Power, Geopolitics* (Edinburgh UP 2022).

William E Burrows, *This New Ocean: The Story of the First Space Age* (Random House 1998).

S Chandrashekar, 'The Origins of China's Space Program (1956–1976)' in *China's Space Programme* (National Institute of Advanced Studies 2022) 3.

China: The 74th International Astronautical Congress—International Lunar Research Station–International Major Science and Engineering Global Network Forum was successfully held, 7 October 2021 <https://www.proquest.com/wire-feeds/china-74th-international-astronautical-congress/docview/2873823000/se-2?accountid=8203>.

China National Space Administration, *International Lunar Research Station (ILRS) Guide for Partnership*, V1.0 (June 2021) <https://www.cnsa.gov.cn/english/n6465652/n6465653/c6812150/content.html>, 12.

Committee on the Peaceful Uses of Outer Space, Status of International Agreements relating to activities in outer space as at 1 January 2024, 15 April 2024, A/AC.105/C.2/2024/CRP.3, https://www.unoosa.org/res/oosadoc/data/documents/2024/aac_105c_22024crp/aac_105c_22024crp_3_0_html/AC105_C2_2024_CRP03E.pdf, plus ratification from Columbia (15 April 2024).

Melissa de Zwart, 'To the Moon and Beyond: The Artemis Accords and the Evolution of Space Law' in *Commercial and Military Uses of Outer Space* (Springer 2021) 65–80.

Melissa de Zwart and Joel Lisk, 'The Effect of Space Tourism on the Concept of "Astronaut" Under International Law' in Sandeepa Bhat B (ed) *Space Tourism: Legal and Policy Aspects* (Routledge 2024) 28.

Rossana Deplano, 'The Artemis Accords: Evolution or Revolution in International Space Law?' (2021) 70 International and Comparative Law Quarterly 799.

Athar ud Din, 'The Artemis Accords: The End of Multilateralism in the Management of Outer Space?' (2022) 20(2–3) Astropol 136.

Everett C Dolman, *Astropolitik: Classical Geopolitics in the Space Age* (Frank Cass 2002).

Draft Report, Committee on the Peaceful Uses of Outer Space, Legal Subcommittee, Sixty-third session, Vienna, 15–26 April 2024, Annex II, Report of the Chair and Vice-Chair of the Working Group on Legal Aspects of Space Resource Activities, A/AC.105/C.2/2024/SRA/L.1, 23 April 2024 <https://www.unoosa.org/res/oosadoc/data/documents/2024/aac_105c_2sral/aac_105c_22024sral_1_0_html/AC105_C2_2024_SRA_L01E.pdf>.

Thomas Ellis, '"Howdy Partner!" Space Brotherhood, Détente and the Symbolism of the Apollo-Soyuz Test Project' (2019) 53(3) Journal of American Studies 744, 764–69.

Evgenlia Drozhashchikh, 'China's National Space Program and the "China Dream"' (2018) 16(3) Astropolitics 175.

'Fact Sheet: Encouraging International Support for the Recovery and Use of Space Resources' (*The White House*, 6 April 2020) <https://trumpwhitehouse.archives.gov/wp-content/uploads/2020/04/Fact-Sheet-on-EO-Encouraging-International-Support-for-the-Recovery-and-Use-of-Space-Resources.pdf>

Jeff Foust, 'Russia Skeptical about Participating in Lunar Gateway' *SpaceNews* (online) (12 October 2020) <https://spacenews.com/russia-skeptical-about-participating-in-lunar-gateway/>.

Global Expert Group on Sustainable Lunar Activities, 'Recommended Framework and Key Elements for Peaceful and Sustainable Lunar Activities' (2022) <https://moonvillageassociation.org/gegsla/documents/gegsla-recommended-framework/>.

Namrata Goswami, 'The Strategic Implications of the China-Russia Lunar Base Cooperation Agreement' *The Diplomat* (online) (19 March 2021) <https://thediplomat.com/2021/03/the-strategic-implications-of-the-china-russia-lunar-base-cooperation-agreement/>

Namrata Goswami and Peter Garretson, *Scramble for the Skies: The Great Power Competition to Control the Resources of Outer Space* (Lexington Books 2020) 211.

Sven Grahn and Carol Norberg 'History of Human Spaceflight' in Carol Norberg (ed), *Human Spaceflight and Exploration* (Springer-Verlag 2013) 11–63, 17–18.

'Guidelines for the Long-Term Sustainability of Outer Space Activities' UN Doc A/AC.105/2018/CRP.20 (27 June 2018).

Andrea Harrington, 'Due Regard as the Prime Directive for Responsible Behavior in Space' (2024) 20(1) Loyola University Chicago International Law Review 57.

Richard Hollingham, 'V2: The Nazi Rocket That Launched the Space Age' *BBC Online* (8 September 2014) <https://www.bbc.com/future/article/20140905-the-nazis-space-age-rocket>.

International Lunar Research Station (ILRS) 23–05 <https://www.unoosa.org/documents/pdf/copuos/2023/TPs/ILRS_presentation20230529_.pdf>

Joint Statement Between CNSA and ROSCOSMOS Regarding Cooperation for the Construction of the International Lunar Research Station, 29 April 2021 <https://www.cnsa.gov.cn/english/n6465668/n6465670/c6811967/content.html>

Andrew Jones, 'China Adds New Moon Base Project Partners, but Struggles to Attract National-Level Participation' *SpaceNews* (online) (28 March 2024) <https://spacenews.com/china-adds-new-moon-base-project-partners-but-struggles-to-attract-national-level-participation/#:~:text=the%20Gateway.-,LRS%20Signatory,-Type>

Andrew Jones, 'China's Chang'e-6 Is Carrying a Surprise Rover to the Moon' *SpaceNews* (online) (6 May 2024) <https://spacenews.com/chinas-change-6-is-carrying-a-surprise-rover-to-the-moon/>

Andrew Jones, 'China Outlines Pathway for Lunar and Deep Space Exploration' *SpaceNews* (online) (28 November 2022) <https://spacenews.com/china-outlines-pathway-for-lunar-and-deep-space-exploration/>

Andrew Jones, 'Thailand Joins China-led ILRS Moon Base Initiative' *SpaceNews* (online) (5 April 2024) <https://spacenews.com/thailand-joins-china-led-ilrs-moon-base-initiative/>

Andrew Jones and Daisy Dobrijevic, 'China's Space Station, Tiangong: A Complete Guide' (*Space.com*, 15 August 2023) https://www.space.com/tiangong-space-station.

Hannah Kohler, 'The Eagle and the Hare: US-Chinese Relations, the Wolf Amendment, and the Future of International Cooperation in Space' (2015) 103(4) Georgetown Law Journal 1135.

Olga Krasnyak, 'The Apollo–Soyuz Test Project: Construction of an Ideal Type of Science Diplomacy' (2018) 13 The Hague Journal of Diplomacy 410, 421–30.

Roger D Launius, 'Highlights of Human Spaceflight: The United States' in Lawrence Young and Jeffrey Sutton (eds), *Handbook of Bioastronautics* (Springer Nature Switzerland AG 2021) 677–89.

Roger D Launius, *Reaching for the Moon: A Short History of the Space Race* (Yale UP 2019).

Adam Mann, 'What Was the Space Race?' (*Space.com*, 14 May 2023) <https://www.space.com/space-race.html>.

Tim Marshall, *The Future of Geography, How Power and Politics in Space Will Change Our World* (Elliott and Thompson Limited 2023).

NASA, The Artemis Accords, Principles for Cooperation in the Civil Exploration and Use of The Moon, Mars, Comets, and Asteroids for Peaceful Purposes, Section 1.

NASA, 'Wernher von Braun' <https://www.nasa.gov/people/wernher-von-braun/>.

Dennis Normile, 'NASA Opens Door to Cooperation With China on Moon Rock Research' *Science Insider* (7 December 2023) <https://www.science.org/content/article/nasa-opens-door-cooperation-china-moon-rock-research>.

'Obituary Thomas Stafford 1930–2024: Astronaut Whose Space Handshake with a Soviet Helped Thaw Cold War' *Sydney Morning Herald* (19 March 2024) <https://www.smh.com.au/national/astronaut-whose-space-handshake-with-a-soviet-helped-thaw-cold-war-20240319-p5fdku.html>.

Anne M Platoff, 'Where No Flag Has Gone Before: Political and Technical Aspects of Placing a Flag on the Moon' (August 1993) <https://www.nasa.gov/history/alsj/alsj-usflag.html#TX17>

Małgorzata Polkowska, 'Limitations in the Airspace Sovereignty of States in Connection With Space Activity' (2018) 20(3) Security and Defence Quarterly 42–56.

David SF Portree, 'Starfish and Apollo (1962)' *Wired* (21 March 2012).

President Donald J Trump, 'Executive Order 13914 of April 6, 2020: Encouraging International Support for the Recovery and Use of Space Resources' (2020) 85 Federal Register 20381.

President Donald Trump, 'Presidential Memorandum on Reinvigorating America's Human Space Exploration Program' 11 December 2017, amending Presidential Policy Directive-4 of June 28, 2010 (National Space Policy).

Robert Ramey, 'Armed Conflict on the Final Frontier: The Law of War in Space' (2000) 48 Air Force Review 1.

GS Sachdeva, 'Outer Space Treaty: An Appraisal' in Ajey Lele (ed), *50 Years of the Outer Space Treaty* (Pentagon Press 2017) 24.

MN Schmitt, 'International Law and Military Operations in Space' in A von Bogdandy and R Wolfrum (eds), *Max Planck Yearbook of United Nations Law*, vol 10 (Brill 2006) 99.

Walker Smith, 'Using the Artemis Accords to Build Customary International Law: A Vision for a U.S.-Centric Good Governance Regime in Outer Space' (2021) 86(4) Journal of Air Law & Commerce 661.

William Stewart and Jason Dittmer, 'More-than-Human Space Diplomacy: Assembling Internationalism in Orbit' (2023) 18 Hague Journal of Diplomacy 219–52.

Gabriel Swiney and Amanda Hernandez, *Lunar Landing and Operations Policy Analysis* (NASA Office of Technology, Policy and Strategy 30 September 2022).

Gabriel Swiney and Amanda Hernandez, *Policy and Strategy Lunar Landing and Operations Policy Analysis* (NASA Office of Technology 30 September 2022) 10.

The Artemis Accords: Principles for Cooperation in the Civil Exploration and Use of the Moon, Mars, Comets, and Asteroids for Peaceful Purposes, 13 October 2020 <https://www.nasa.gov/wp-content/uploads/2022/11/Artemis-Accords-signed-13Oct2020.pdf?emrc=653a00>.

Treaty on Principles Governing the Activities of States in the Exploration and Use of Outers Space, Including the Moon and Other Celestial Bodies, opened for signature 27 January 1967, 610 UNTS 205 (entered into force 10 October 1967) ('Outer Space Treaty').

Neil deGrasse Tyson and Avis Lang, *Accessory to War: The Unspoken Alliance between Astrophysics and the Military* (WW Norton 2018) 192–94.

'UNCOPUOS Legal Sub-Committee Working Group on Legal Aspects of Space Resource Activities' <https://www.unoosa.org/oosa/en/ourwork/copuos/lsc/space-resources/index.html>.

US Commercial Space Launch Competitiveness Act, Pub L No 114–190, 129 Stat 704.; Journal officiel du Grand-Duché de Luxembourg, Loi du 20 juillet 2017 sur l'exploration et l'utilisation des ressources de l'espace; Federal Law No. 12 of 2019 on the Regulation of the Space Sector, United Arab Emirates; Space Resources Act (2021) (Japan).

US Department of State, 'United States Welcomes Slovenia's Signing of the Artemis Accords' (22 April 2024) <https://www.state.gov/united-states-welcomes-slovenias-signing-of-the-artemis-accords/>

IA Vlasic, 'Space Law and the Military Applications of Space Technology' in N Jasentuliyana (ed), *Perspectives on International Law* (Kluwer Law International 1995) 385.

Frans von der Dunk, *Advanced Introduction to Space Law* (Edward Elgar Publishing 2020) 115–25. See further, UNOOSA, National Space Law Database <https://astro.unoosa.org/astro/national-space-law-landing-page.html>.

Frans von der Dunk and Gerardine Goh, 'Article V' in Stephen Hobe, Bernhard Schmidt-Tedd and Kai-Uwe Schrogl (eds), *Cologne Commentary on Space Law*, vol 1 (Carl Heymanns Verlag 2009) 94–102, 94.

Guoyu Wang, 'NASA's Artemis Accords: The Path to a United Space Law or a Divided One?' *The Space Review* (24 August 2020) <www.thespacereview.com/article/4009/1>

Xiaodan Wu, 'The International Lunar Research Station: China's New Era of Space Cooperation and Its New Role in the Space Legal Order' (2023) 65 Space Policy 101537, 6–7.

Fengna Xu and Jun Ou, 'Promoting International Cooperation on the International Lunar Research Station: Inspiration from the ITER' (2023) 203 Acta Astronautica 341.

Alexander Yakovenko, 'The Intergovernmental Agreement on the International Space Station' (1999) 15(2) Space Policy 79–86 <http://doi.org/10.1016/S0265-9646(99)OOD11-9>

6 The Moondust Kingdom

Jurisdiction Over 3D-Printed Stations Created on Celestial Bodies

Danny Johansen

1 Introduction

Humanity is on the brink of going multi-planetary. However, the laws we have set out for ourselves are from a time when Star Trek may have been bound for the final frontier, but humanity had just started to touch the Moon. The drafters of the Treaty on Principles Governing the Activities of States in the Exploration and Use of Outer Space, Including the Moon and Other Celestial Bodies[1] (OST) had to deal with an altogether different reality than Captain Kirk. New marvelous technological advancements were made at a fantastic speed, promising a new dawn for a humankind that was otherwise largely occupied with threatening itself with all-annihilating atomic destruction.[2] Thus, the OST was unsurprisingly written using broad language that left room for advancements in the years to come, and with a focus on cooperation and peace. The legal framework of outer space revolving around the OST and the four subsequent treaties have worked incredibly well for more than 50 years. However, as society and technology have developed significantly since the treaties' negotiations, cracks have started to show in the framework. One of these cracks emerged when the United States famously allowed its spacefaring entities to own abiotic resources retrieved from outer space and profit from them.[3] This legislation was followed by Luxembourg,[4] the United Arab Emirates,[5] and recently Japan.[6] This has been further stated in the Artemis Accords, in which the signatories have declared that they do not view the

1 Treaty on Principles Governing the Activities of States in the Exploration and Use of Outer Space, Including the Moon and Other Celestial Bodies (adopted 27 January 1967, entered into force 10 October 1967) 610 UNTS 205.

2 History.com Editors, 'Arms Race' (*history.com*, 14 October 2009) <https://www.history.com/topics/cold-war/arms-race> accessed 14 December 2022.

3 114th Congress (2015–2016): U.S. Commercial Space Launch Competitiveness Act, H.R.2262 (51 USC 10101) §§ 51301 and 51303.

4 Law of July 20th 2017 on the Exploration and Use of Space Resources. Article 1.

5 Federal Law No. (12) of 2019 On the Regulation of the Space Sector Article 18.

6 Act No. 83 of December 23, 2021 Act on the Promotion of Business Activities for the Exploration and Development of Space Resources (Tentative Translation).

DOI: 10.4324/9781003370499-8

extraction of resources in outer space as inherently constituting appropriation in violation of Article II of the OST.[7] These developments have spawned discussions on what the non-appropriation principle entails.[8] Is it considered a breach of the non-appropriation principle to claim ownership of the resources beneath the crust of celestial bodies, or does the right to free use in Article I of the OST permit them to be mined and sold?

The question of space resource ownership will greatly affect tomorrow's world. The amount of metal and water in nearby asteroids is, in all probability, vast.[9] Water could also be potentially turned into fuel to reach farther into space.[10] Space resources could vastly improve human life, make all of Earth richer, and even be used to construct stations on other planets.[11] The last of the options, the construction of space stations on other planets, is another legal vacuum that may slip through the cracks in the legal framework of outer space. The OST allows outer space, including the celestial bodies, to be used and explored.[12] It also permits a state to have jurisdiction over objects launched from Earth,[13] and even that stations may be built on celestial bodies.[14] What happens, however, when the station on the Moon is created from local materials which, contrary to materials launched from Earth, are not necessarily subject to the jurisdiction of the launching state? Insightful work by scholars has discussed the problem of jurisdiction in outer space and on

7 NASA, 'The Artemis Accords—Principles for Cooperation in the Civl Exploration and Use of the Moon, Mars, Comets and Asteroids for Peaceful Purposes' (2020) <https://www.nasa.gov/specials/artemis-accords/index.html> Section 10(2).

8 See for example Ram Jakhu and Steven Freeland, 'The Relationship Between the Outer Space Treaty and Customary International Law' (2016) SSRN Electronic Journal 11; John G Wrench, 'Non-Appropriation, No Problem: The Outer Space Treaty Is Ready for Asteroid Mining' (2019) 51 Case Western Reserve Journal of International Law 437; Wian Erlank, 'Property and Ownership in Outer Space' in Yanal Abul Failat and Anél Ferreira-Snyman (eds), *Outer Space Law: Legal Policy and Practice* (2nd edn, Globe Law and Buisness Ltd 2022) 141; Sandeepa Bhat B, 'Legal Issues Surrounding Human Settlements on the Moon and Other Celestial Bodies Session 2: Moon and Mars Settlement: Open Legal Issues' (2020) 63 Proceedings of the International Institute of Space Law 91 98.

9 Laszlo P Keszthelyi and others, *Feasibility Study for the Quantitative Sssessment of Mineral Resources in Asteroids* (Open-File Report 2017) 2017–1041 11.

10 Neel V Patel, 'Here's How We Could Mine the Moon for Rocket Fuel' *MIT Technology Review* (www.technologyreview.com) <https://www.technologyreview.com/2020/05/19/1001857/how-moon-lunar-mining-water-ice-rocket-fuel/>.

11 Lee Mohon, 'NASA Looks to Advance 3D Printing Construction Systems for the Moon and Mars' (*www.nasa.gov*, 1 October 2020) <https://www.nasa.gov/centers/marshall/news/releases/2020/nasa-looks-to-advance-3d-printing-construction-systems-for-the-moon.html> accessed 10 June 2024; European Space Agency, 'Building a Lunar Base With 3d Printing' (*www.esa.int*, 31 January 2013) <https://www.esa.int/Enabling_Support/Space_Engineering_Technology/Building_a_lunar_base_with_3D_printing> accessed October 2023.

12 The Outer Space Treaty, Article I.

13 The Outer Space Treaty, Article VIII.

14 The Outer Space Treaty, Article XII.

space stations generally.[15] However, little writing seems to address the jurisdiction problem of stations built of celestial materials.

This chapter will, therefore, examine whether states can exercise jurisdiction over 3D-printed stations on celestial bodies. This chapter is structured into two parts. Part 2 will examine the general principles of jurisdiction in public international law. Once the applicable jurisdiction principles are established, the chapter will consider the special jurisdiction situation in outer space and why 3D-printed stations present a problem. Part 2 of the chapter will conclude by examining whether an analogy can be made to artificial islands and the legal implications if this is the case. Part 3 will then examine three potential situations where 3D-printed materials could be used to construct a space station and how this will influence the question of jurisdiction. Materials will likely be used not only to repair the station and construct extensions but also to build the entire station from scratch. The chapter will focus on state-owned facilities, as opposed to non-governmentally owned stations, because states will most likely create the first stations on celestial bodies. Moreover, the potential for non-governmental entities, such as corporations, to create stations on celestial bodies raises numerous legal questions that deserve their own unique examination. Furthermore, the article concentrates on how state jurisdiction can be argued instead of how it may be lost.[16]

2 Space Stations and the Law

It has been a dream since early science fiction that humanity would one day have space stations on other planets. While the OST does not explicitly state that space stations are allowed, they are assumed within the treaty. First, Article IV declares that establishing military bases is forbidden, indicating that a civilian base would be fine. Subsequently, Article XII declares that stations and installations on the Moon and celestial bodies must be open to the representatives of other states based on reciprocity.[17] With innovative 3D printing technology, this is becoming more feasible than ever, and almost every major spacefaring state is looking to construct

15 For example Frans von der Dunk, '"For All Moonkind"—Legal Issues of Human Settlements on the Moon: Jurisdiction, Freedom and Inclusiveness Session 2: Moon and Mars Settlement: Open Legal Issues' (2020) 63 Proceedings of the International Institute of Space Law 77; Danielle Ireland-Piper and Steven Freeland, 'Star Laws: Criminal Jurisdiction in Outer Space' (2020) 44 Journal of Space Law 44; P.J. Blount, 'Jurisdiction in Outer Space: Challenges of Private Individuals in Space' (2007) 33(2) Journal of Space Law 299; Jan Ondrej, 'Problems of Jurisdiction in Connection With Settlements on the Moon and Mars Legal Aspects of Settlements on the Moon and Mars' (1991) 34 Proceedings of the Colloquia on the Law of Outer Space 71; Ernst Fasan, 'Human Settlements on Planets: New Stations or New Nations' (1994) 22 Journal of Space Law 47.

16 See for example on the possibility for self-determination Fasan, (n 15); Kuan-Wei Chen, 'The Principle of Self-Determination in Outer Space: An Age-Old Right for New Age Activities? Part II: Shorter Articles and Comments' (2020) 45 Annals of Air & Space Law 471.

17 See Gisela Suess, 'Article XII' in Stephan Hobe and others (eds), *Cologne Commentary on Space Law—Outer Space Treaty: Кёльнский Комментарий К Космическому Праву—Договор По Космосу*, vol 1 (Berliner Wissenschafts-Verlag 2017).

buildings on the Moon.[18] It goes without saying that states constructing stations of this kind will seek to maintain jurisdiction and control over them. First, the state will want to ensure that activities at these stations conform to its wishes. Second, there is a general obligation in Article VI of the OST that provides that the state will be responsible for the national activities of both the state and its non-governmental entities in outer space. Thus, not only is there a desire for a right to wield jurisdiction over the activities, but there is perhaps even an obligation to do so. However, as there is no territory in outer space, and the space actors may consist of collaborations of different nationalities, the customary rules on jurisdiction tied to the territory or the citizens of the state may not be as easily wielded in space as on Earth. To compensate for this, the OST offers a jurisdiction regime, especially for outer space. However, even this regime may be challenged when the space station is created from resources extracted from the celestial bodies.

This section of the chapter will delve into these problems; this will be done with the first section clarifying the general scope of the international legal principles concerning jurisdiction to establish the general rules. The following section will then first explain the special regime for outer space and then analyze how 3D-printed space stations may frustrate the application of both the general international law jurisdiction principles and those special for outer space. The final section will consider whether an analogy to artificial islands found in the law of the sea may resolve the problem.

(a) Jurisdiction in Public International Law

Jurisdiction as a concept can broadly be boiled down to a state's lawful power to create and enforce rules on its territory and over its nationals.[19] A state within its own territory is able to create laws and impose them on all who reside within its territory.[20] While jurisdiction is thus closely connected to the territory of the state, it does not mean that the state cannot apply its laws outside the state.[21] A crime may, for example, have been initiated outside a state territory and still have an effect within that territory; a criminal may flee a state, and a national of the state may be the victim of a crime while in another state. While a state's jurisdiction covers many areas that may be of significance for stations on the Moon, such as the state's ability to make administrative laws for the operation of space stations, criminal law may be the most important. As of yet, no known crimes have been committed

18 Jan Woerner, 'Moon Village' (*www.esa.int*, 2016) <https://www.esa.int/About_Us/Ministerial_Council_2016/Moon_Village> accessed 22 February 2022; Mike Wall, 'Not Just Artemis: China And Russia Plan to Put Boots on the Moon, Too' (*www.space.com*, 3 September 2022) <https://www.space.com/china-russia-moon-base-ilrs> accessed 5 April 2022.

19 Bernard H Oxman, 'Jurisdiction of States' in Anne Peters and Rüdiger Wulfrum (eds), *Max Planck Encyclopedias of International Law* (Online edn, OUP 2007) 1; Christopher Staker, 'Jurisdiction' in Malcolm D Evans (ed), *International Law* (4th edn, OUP 2014) 309.

20 Staker (n 19) 316.

21 Malcolm N Shaw, *International Law* (9th edn, CUP 2021) 556, Oxman (n 19) 11.

in space. While an astronaut was accused of a domestic crime while stationed at the International Space Station in 2019,[22] the allegation, turned out to be false, and the accuser was charged with making false statements to the authorities.[23] The fact that there have been no crimes in space may be due to the low number of state personnel in outer space that are highly trained. Due to Article VI of the OST, the state is responsible for national activities, whether the state's own or those of its non-governmental entities. Therefore, the state will need to be able to enforce its criminal laws to control its nationals effectively. It should be acknowledged that there might be difficulties in enforcing the law in the future when humanity moves beyond the Moon due to the simple fact of distance.[24] Whether the solution to this will be establishing a local court system on Mars, faster and cheaper rockets, or simply that Mars will be self-governed[25] remains to be seen at this time. For now, the Moon is not far enough away to make enforcement impossible,[26] and furthermore, all missions to outer space still need to return to Earth for the time being. So, at least for now, all activities in outer space require jurisdiction.

Jurisdiction in public international law is divided into three different categories: territory, nationality, and universality.[27] Where both the territorial and nationality principle can be considered a linking point between the state and the conduct governed,[28] universality is the "odd one out" in that it requires no connection to the state.[29] Universal jurisdiction is limited to the most heinous crimes, such as genocide, crimes against humanity, war crimes, and piracy.[30] It has been suggested that this principle may be relevant in the future for possible space pirates or war crimes committed in space.[31] However, as of now, the principle does not have much practicable use in space and will not be further elaborated upon here.

The first category of principles upon which jurisdiction can be based is territorial principles. Territorial principles can be divided into three generally acknowledged principles. Two of these principles, subjective and objective, can be said to be two sides of the same coin. The subjective principle is applicable when the activity,

22 Mike Baker, 'NASA Astronaut Anne McClain Accused by Spouse of Crime in Space' *The New York Times* (New York, 23 August 2019) <https://www.nytimes.com/2019/08/23/us/astronaut-space-investigation.html>.

23 Christina Zdanowicz, 'NASA Astronaut's Estranged Wife Charged With Lying About Claim That Spouse Improperly Accessed Account From Space' *CNN* (Atlanta, GA, 8 April 2020) <https://edition.cnn.com/2020/04/08/us/nasa-astronaut-anne-mcclain-estranged-wife-charged-trnd/index.html>.

24 Fasan (n 15) 51.

25 Starlink, 'Starlink (US) Terms of Service' (*SpaceX*, 2022) Section 11 <https://www.starlink.com/legal/documents/DOC-1020-91087-64?regionCode=US> accessed 4 November 2022.

26 Fasan (n 15) 51.

27 Ireland-Piper and Freeland (n 15) 56.

28 Staker (n 19) 315.

29 Alexander Orakhelashvili, *Akehurst's Modern Introduction to International Law* (8th edn, Routledge 2019) 221; James Crawford, *Brownlie's Principles of Public International Law* (8th edn, OUP 2012) 467.

30 Shaw (n 21) 575; Crawford (n 29) 468.

31 Blount (n 15) 309; Ireland-Piper and Freeland (n 15) 57.

for example, a crime, being governed is started within the state.[32] The objective principle is when the effect of the activity is fulfilled within the state.[33] A classic example is the case of criminal jurisdiction, where a shooter fires a weapon across a state border and injures someone.[34] The state where the shooter resides would have subjective jurisdiction, and the state that has become bullet-richer would have objective jurisdiction. The final territorial jurisdiction principle is the protective principle, where an act committed by a foreign person in State A threatens the national security of State B.[35] A classic example of this is a counterfeit operation in State A, creating false tender of State B, thus threatening the financial stability and trust in money in State B.[36]

The final group of jurisdiction principles is that of nationality.[37] Where the territorial principles are by their very nature tied to the territory of the state, the nationality principles are tied to the nationals of that state. Thus, the nationality principles allow the state to claim jurisdiction over crimes related to the citizens of the state. As nationals may move outside the territory of the state, the need to regulate their behavior may follow, and thus, the nationality principle may be applied outside the state's borders (also called extra-territorial).[38] As this can result in a national needing to have regard for a plethora of jurisdictions including the jurisdiction of the home state, the state visited, and the states of other parties to a crime, some nations have put limits on the nationality principles. However, due to the states' right to determine their internal laws, there are, however, no requirements in public international law to have such limitations.[39]

The primary principle based on nationality is the active nationality principle,[40] where the state has jurisdiction over its nationals who commit crimes outside of the state's border. The second principle, the passive nationality principle, is a little more controversial.[41] According to this principle, the state of the victim can claim jurisdiction over a crime that happened abroad.[42] Thus, the state can claim jurisdiction over a national of another state for a crime that occurred outside of the victim state's territory. The principles have become more or less accepted, especially in cases related to terrorism.[43] Thus, as can be seen, there is a variety of jurisdictional principles that may apply in general public international law. When the eyes are turned upwards to outer space, however, jurisdiction is similar in some points and very different in others.

32 Crawford (n 29) 458; Shaw (n 21) 563; Orakhelashvili (n 29) 218; Staker (n 19) 317.
33 Crawford (n 29) 458; Shaw (n 21) 563; Orakhelashvili (n 29) 218; Staker (n 19) 317.
34 Crawford (n 29) 458; Shaw (n 21) 563; Orakhelashvili (n 29) 218; Staker (n 19) 317.
35 Crawford (n 29) 462; Shaw (n 21) 573; Orakhelashvili (n 29) 220; Staker (n 19) 321.
36 Ireland-Piper and Freeland (n 15) 57; Staker (n 19) 321.
37 Crawford (n 29) 459; Shaw (n 21) 567; Orakhelashvili (n 29) 220; Staker (n 19) 318.
38 Crawford (n 29) 459; Orakhelashvili (n 29) 220.
39 Crawford (n 29) 460.
40 Orakhelashvili (n 29) 220; Ireland-Piper and Freeland (n 19) 56.
41 Shaw (n 21) 572; Crawford (n 29) 461; Staker (n 19) 326.
42 Orakhelashvili (n 29) 220; Crawford (n 29) 461; Staker (n 19) 326; Shaw (n 21) 571.
43 Crawford (n 29) 461; Orakhelashvili (n 29) 220; Staker (n 19) 327; Shaw (n 21) 573.

(b) Jurisdiction in Space

Besides being in a realm other than Earth, outer space also has some special rules that affect jurisdiction. Article II of the OST declares, "[o]uter space, including the Moon and other celestial bodies, is not subject to national appropriation by claim of sovereignty, by means of use or occupation, or by any other means." This is the so-called non-appropriation principle, which is one of the most important and basic principles of the OST.[44] It was one of the first principles of the OST that was agreed upon by the negotiating states, who feared that outer space and its celestial bodies would become a battleground for territory.[45] As no part of outer space can be made a part of state territory, no territorial jurisdiction can be created in space. However, this does not mean that the state will be entirely limited to the nationality principle, as Article VIII of the OST declares that a state on whose registry a space object is carried has jurisdiction and control over the object and its personnel while in space or on a celestial body.

While no part of outer space and the celestial bodies can be appropriated, ownership of an object from Earth does not evaporate when it touches outer space. Article VIII thus creates jurisdiction over an object in a sovereignty-free area.[46] This means that a station constructed from materials brought from Earth belongs to whatever state owns the materials on Earth. Moreover, the state that registers the station has jurisdiction and control over it. Bin Cheng describes jurisdiction found in Article VIII as quasi-territorial jurisdiction, meaning that a state has authority over ships, aircraft, and spacecraft and also extends to all personnel and things aboard, including the activities of the personnel.[47] Quasi-territory is thus like the territorial principle in that it applies to the "territory" of the space object and everyone upon it. However, considering the jurisdiction not as territorial but rather quasi-territorial avoids a conflict with the non-appropriation principle in that no territorial jurisdiction is created in space, but rather, a jurisdiction is brought from Earth.

Regarding stations on celestial bodies built from materials brought by a spacecraft from Earth, it must be assumed that the quasi-territorial jurisdiction "sticks" to the materials. First, they are launched from Earth, and second, they have been on the spacecraft. Therefore, when the materials carry jurisdiction with them, the state can exercise jurisdiction over the station it has created based on quasi-territory. However, this may not necessarily be the case when stations are

44 Fabio Tronchetti, 'Legal Aspects of Space Resource Utilization' in Frans von der Dunk and Fabio Tronchetti (eds), *Handbook of Space Law* (Edward Elgar Publishing 2015) 778; Ram Jakhu and Steven Freeland, 'Article II' in Stephan Hobe and others (eds), *Cologne Commentary on Space Law—Outer Space Treaty: Кёльнский Комментарий К Космическому Праву—Договор По Космосу*, vol 1 (Berliner Wissenschafts-Verlag 2017) 48.

45 Tronchetti (n 44) 778.

46 Bernhard Schmidt-Tedd and Stephan Mick, 'Article VIII' in Stephan Hobe and others (eds), *Cologne Commentary on Space Law—Outer Space Treaty: Кёльнский Комментарий К Космическому Праву—Договор По Космосу*, vol 1 (Berliner Wissenschafts-Verlag 2017) para 2.

47 Bin Cheng, *Studies in International Space Law* (Clarendon Press 1997) 73.

3D printed on the Moon, as its component parts will not have been launched from Earth. It is straightforward to argue that the printer launched from Earth is owned by the launching state. However, if one agrees with those states that have declared that the extraction and ownership of resources from celestial bodies is not in conflict with the non-appropriation principle, ownership over the resources could also exist. Owning resources and constructing stations with them is one legal issue, but exercising jurisdiction in an area where no jurisdiction can be created is another, as nothing in the OST suggests that jurisdiction over something not launched from Earth can exist.

Article III of the OST declares that international law applies to outer space, which also encompasses jurisdictional principles. Indeed, nothing in the non-appropriation principle of Article II or the space object jurisdiction principle in Article VIII of the OST hinders the application of general principles of jurisdiction to outer space.[48] However, these principles do not bestow jurisdiction over the 3D-printed space station. Looking first at the territorial principles, as they would be the most obvious to look to for jurisdiction over an area, it is clear that they would, in reality, offer little help. The first principle, the subjective, granting jurisdiction over a crime started within the territory of the state, is not relevant as there is no territory, not even a quasi-territory. The objective principle, giving jurisdiction over crimes started elsewhere but fulfilled within the territory, as well as the protective principle, giving jurisdiction over crimes threatening the integrity of the state, could have limited use.[49] A crime may start on a Moon station and end in the territory of a state, such as counterfeiting money or loading a bomb into a rocket and exploding on Earth. Both of these principles are, however, tied to the effect of the conduct on the territory of Earth and would not be able to provide jurisdiction in any way over a space station. Nationality principles, on the other hand, might apply, but only to the individual and not the station. If a 3D-printed space station is used by astronauts from different nations, and one or more states involved have limitations on applying their jurisdiction extra-territorially, this could result in crimes falling between two jurisdictions.[50] Thus, at the very least, an agreement between the states that primarily use the space station would need to be created regarding how they would apply their national jurisdiction principles. This would not solve all problems, however, as Article XII of the OST declares that all stations on the celestial bodies shall be open to representatives from other states. The visiting representative must give notice in advance, and as such, there would be time for agreeing on jurisdiction rules. It is, however, in no way certain that such an agreement would be possible to conclude, as states may not be willing to allow jurisdiction over their representatives. Furthermore, were a state to declare general jurisdiction principles over the station, this would be close to an appropriation in violation of Article II.

48 Blount (n 15) 311.

49 Ireland-Piper and Freeland (n 15) 71.

50 See for example discussion on a theoretical mugging on the Moon in Blount (n 15) 316.

It is hard to believe that it was the intention of the drafters of the OST to enable a situation where jurisdiction over a space station would be an impossibility. It is, however, hard to find a direct solution to the problem, as allowing quasi-territorial jurisdiction to be created in space conflicts with the non-appreciation principle. The non-appropriation principle endeavors to foster peaceful cooperation amongst nations in outer space.[51] Article VIII of the OST works to this end, ensuring that no state can create territorial jurisdictions, as it must bring quasi-territorial jurisdiction from Earth.[52] If humankind ventures deeper into outer space, space stations will be needed to facilitate this exploration. There will most likely also be a need to build these stations with 3D-printing equipment using local materials extracted from celestial bodies. Imposing a legal requirement that all materials should be brought from Earth to build these stations is unfeasible and would restrict human space exploration due to its need to be within range of new resources from Earth. To find a solution, this chapter will now delve into an analysis of the law of the sea and the Moon to determine whether they could provide any possible legal solution to the challenges already discussed.

(c) The Sea and the Moon

Space law is often said to have elements resembling the law of the sea.[53] For example, both legal fields regulate international common spaces. Furthermore, the launching state of Article VIII of the OST is not too different from the regime of the flag state under Article 91 of UNCLOS,[54] in that they both create a link between a vessel and the state and give the right to wield jurisdiction. However, even though Article III of the OST states that international law applies to outer space, it is only the parts that make sense to apply.[55] So, while the law of the sea, for obvious reasons, is not directly applicable, it could provide inspiration for legal solutions to dilemmas with regards the regulation of outer space. Indeed, there are similarities between the concept of artificial islands in the sea and space stations. Both could be created in areas where no sovereignty is allowed.[56] Furthermore, both are specifically allowed in their legal regime—space stations in Article XII of the OST and artificial islands in Article 87(1d) of the UNCLOS. There are also differences, the

51 Jakhu and Freeland (n 44) para 12.

52 Schmidt-Tedd and Mick (n 46) 520; Christopher Johnson, 'International Law Governing Outer Space Activities' in Yanal Abul Failat and Anél Ferreira-Snyman (eds), *Outer Space Law: Legal Policy and Practice* (2nd edn, Globe Law and Buisness Ltd 2022) 20.

53 Stephan Hobe, *Space Law* (1st edn, Hart Publishing 2019) 69 Frans von der Dunk, 'International Space Law' in Frans von der Dunk and Fabio Tronchetti (eds), *Handbook of Space Law* (Edward Elgar Publishing 2015).

54 Hobe (n 53) 88; Schmidt-Tedd and Mick (n 46) 498.

55 Manfred Lachs, *The Law of Outer Space: An Experience in Contemporary Law-Making* (Sijthoff 1972).

56 The Outer Space Treaty, Article II: *United Nations Convention on the Law of the Sea* (adopted 10 December 1982, entered into force 16 November 1994) 1833 UNTS 3 1834 UNTS 3 1835 UNTS 3, Article 89.

main one being that one is created on Earth and the other is created outside Earth. Access to our seas and oceans is relatively straightforward, but travel in outer space puts great strain on the human body and demands high levels of training. It is also harder to reach, whereas the sea has a deep, interconnected history with humankind. Moreover, the sea, while expansive, is limited and directly influences our survival by being a valuable source of food. On the other hand, outer space is infinite, and it remains unclear whether it is possible to produce food on celestial bodies.

The sea is divided into different maritime zones, with jurisdictions varying and weakening the farther the zone is from the territorial boundaries of the state. The maritime zones recognized under international law are internal waters,[57] the territorial sea,[58] the contiguous zone,[59] the exclusive economic zone,[60] and the high seas.[61] The internal waters zone has the highest degree of jurisdiction, and the high seas zone is an area where no state may lay claim.[62] The exclusive economic zone is an area where the coastal state may enjoy the right to exploit natural resources and create artificial islands.[63] Article 60(2) of UNCLOS declares that the coastal state shall have exclusive jurisdiction over artificial islands in its exclusive economic zones. However, when moving farther out to the high seas, Article 87(1)(d) of UNCLOS states that it is a freedom of the high seas for all states to construct artificial islands in this area. Article 87 of UNCLOS, contrary to Article 60(2), does not mention anything about jurisdiction over artificial islands. Thus, we fall back to Article 89 of the UNCLOS, which states that no part of the high seas can be subjected to sovereignty. This situation is perhaps similar to outer space: artificial islands can be built, but there seems to be no way that jurisdiction other than the nationality principle can be applied, just as with 3D-printed space stations. It can thus be argued that when acting in an area where no sovereignty can be created, a state may create installations, but the jurisdiction over the installation is lacking and non-appropriation principles prevail.

Therefore, an analysis of the law of the sea does not provide much guidance on how jurisdiction may be exercised over 3D-printed space stations. As a result, the next section will explore how jurisdiction might be exercised by states over space stations by examining different scenarios where degrees of space stations are being 3D printed, offering an interpretation of the articles of the OST, and suggesting an analogy from international human rights law.

3 Moondust Bricks

It is important to remember that the use of outer space and celestial bodies is allowed according to Article I of the OST. For example, water may be extracted

57 UNCLOS, Article 8.
58 UNCLOS, Article 2.
59 UNCLOS, Article 33.
60 UNCLOS, Part V.
61 UNCLOS, Part VII.
62 UNCLOS, Article 89.
63 UNCLOS, Article 56(1).

from moon ice and drunk by astronauts, moon rocks may be used for science, and materials can be extracted to create the equipment necessary for science and exploration. As such, there is nothing legally to hinder that these resources can be used.[64] The question is mainly on jurisdiction. To ascertain whether jurisdiction over a 3D-printed space station can be ensured, the following sections will explore three different scenarios, each with a suggested method for working towards a solution. The first two scenarios are similar in both the problem and the solution proposed. These consist of a space station that is created of materials brought from Earth and subsequently either repaired or expanded with resources extracted from the celestial body. In both these cases, it is suggested that an interpretation of the articles of the OST would allow for the quasi-territorial properties of the materials from Earth to seep into the resources of the celestial body. The final scenario, which consists of a space station created entirely from materials extracted from the celestial body, will explore an analogy to a concept of effective control over an area outside of the territory, as found in human rights law.

(a) Moondust Duct Tape

In the scenario where a station has been built using materials from Earth, it is likely that wear and tear will require the station to be repaired from time to time. Repairs of a station neither add nor take away the quasi-territorial status of the station; they merely prolong the period of time they will be in use and operation on the celestial body. A reading of the OST indicates that there is no time limit on how long a station can be in place on a celestial body without it constituting appropriation. No other state can demand that the station be removed due to the freedom of outer space principle,[65] and even if the station is abandoned, no other state can take over the station or destroy it. As long as the ground beneath the station is not claimed as territory and it is not argued that the station, due to it being there, is creating territorial jurisdiction, there should be no problem because the station, at least in theory, is considered a temporary structure, not creating permanent jurisdiction. So, there should be no initial problem with the repairs. Indeed, it could be argued that it is in the interest of all states that local resources are used to construct space stations to reduce the number of spaceships launched into space. This, in turn, would greatly reduce the environmental impact of rocket fuel.

It could be discussed whether there should be a limit to the size of the repairs, similar to the philosophical question concerning the Ship of Theseus, which asks whether the ship is still the same despite every rotten part of the ship being replaced

64 Stephan Hobe, 'Article I' in Stephan Hobe and others (eds), *Cologne Commentary on Space Law—Outer Space Treaty: Кёльнский Комментарий К Космическому Праву—Договор По Космосу*, vol 1 (Berliner Wissenschafts-Verlag 2017) 195; Phillip De Man, 'The Exploitation of Natural Resources in Outer Space' in Yanal Abul Failat and Anél Ferreira-Snyman (eds), *Outer Space Law: Legal Policy and Practice* (2nd edn, Globe Law and Business Ltd 2022) 202. Here it is suggested that the scarcity of the resource may be a factor.

65 The Outer Space Treaty, Article 1; De Man (n 64) 201.

with new components.[66] We can also ask whether it is still the same station when many parts are replaced over time. If a section of a station falls into disrepair, is it only the station that collapses, or is it also the quasi-territorial jurisdiction that exists on the station due to it being constructed of materials brought from Earth? Can the quasi-territorial jurisdiction seep into whenever a part is replaced, so the already established jurisdiction now covers the new part? Or should every part changed be noted down in a registry so that it can be concluded at some point that so much of the station has been repaired, as the jurisdiction would effectively be lost?

Where the Ship of Theseus is an entirely philosophical question, the reparations of space stations are more of a treaty interpretation question. As already discussed, objects launched into outer space are more than the actual object; it is also the quasi-territorial jurisdiction it represents. Were it the other way around that a state would not wish to repair it, the state would not be able to deregister the space object (unless another state takes over its registry); there is no way for deregistering an object in space in any of the treaties. As a result, the state will always be liable for the object,[67] even the parts that may fall off it.[68] It is also not possible for an abandoned space object to be claimed by others as it still belongs to the state of registry;[69] this might even apply to the debris of a smashed space object if it is still recognizable enough to identify the owner. The same must be true for objects being repaired; the state would not be able to evade liability or responsibility for the station just by exchanging the parts, and thus, jurisdiction and control cannot dissolve either. Thus, repair, no matter the size, should be viewed as just upholding a state's quasi-territorial jurisdiction.

(b) Moondust Porches

If resources extracted from outer space can be used to repair stations, what about modifications in the form of extensions? This is relevant should the mission to the station be expanded by the launching state. It could be argued that so long as the newly created station did not contain human life, the question was more academic than important. Thus, if there were no human actors to enforce the laws of the state there would be no need for jurisdiction. In this scenario, the station may still be owned, and the extension of the law to it is of less importance. However, article VIII of the OST talks of jurisdiction and control. Jurisdiction means that there is an ability to make laws and enforce them over humans and objects alike.[70] Control

66 S Marc Cohen, 'Identity, Persistence, and the Ship of Theseus' (*faculty.washington.edu*, 10 June 2004) <https://faculty.washington.edu/smcohen/320/theseus.html> accessed 9 December 2021.

67 Lotta Viikari, 'Enviromental Aspects of Space Activities' in Frans von der Dunk and Fabio Tronchetti (eds), *Handbook of Space Law* (Edward Elgar Publishing 2015) 728.

68 Convention on Registration of Objects Launched Into Outer Space (adopted 12 November 1974, entered into force 15 September 1976) 1023 UNTS 15, Article 1(b).

69 Viikari (n 67) 728.

70 Schmidt-Tedd and Mick (n 46) para 48.

means the exclusive right and ability to supervise the activities of a space object, as well as direct and modify elements of the space object, all of which are rights that cannot be distinguished from the jurisdiction.[71] Seeing that the two concepts cannot be entirely separated, and Article VIII of the OST also ties control to the object that is launched, the question of rights regarding the space station being expanded is still relevant.

It could be argued that Article VIII does not necessarily state that a space object must be launched from Earth and thus that an extension to a station could be "launched" from the station. There are, however, a few problems with this reasoning. First, the Vienna Convention on the Law of Treaties Article 31 describes the general rules on treaty interpretation and declares in that article that the initial step of treaty interpretation is to look at the ordinary meaning given to the words.[72] Article VIII of the OST states that the criterion is that "A State Party to the Treaty on whose registry an object launched into outer space." The rudimentary definition of launching an object is to throw forward, catapult, or send off.[73] There is a general understanding that launch in Article VIII of the OST per Article II of the Registration Convention means that the object must be launched into Earth orbit or beyond.[74] There is a practice of launch being performed in space. For example, the United States has registered space objects launched from the International Space Station ("ISS"),[75] and Cubesats have been transported as cargo to the ISS for launch from the Japanese module.[76] Rideshares on rockets, where a rocket carries objects for different clients, have also been released into outer space.[77] An important question to consider here is whether there is a difference between the examples already outlined and the building of an extension to a space station on the Moon. To answer this question, it must first be noted that the objects launched from the ISS and rockets in outer space were brought from Earth and thus had quasi-territorial jurisdiction inherent in them. On the other hand, objects built on the Moon do not have quasi-territorial jurisdiction inherent in them. Article VIII of the OST declares that the state that has the object in its register "retains" jurisdiction and control; thus, the jurisdiction and control must have been there in the first place. Second, those objects launched from the ISS and rockets were meant to be released into outer space, whereas a space station built on the Moon is not meant to be launched. If it is allowed to consider an object launched, if it has been in space without a plan to launch the object, this could mean, in theory, that when a satellite

71 Schmidt-Tedd and Mick (n 46) para 48.

72 Vienna Convention on the Law of Treaties, Article 31(1).

73 *Merriam-Webster.com* "Launch" (Online Edition).

74 Schmidt-Tedd and Mick, (n 46) para 33.

75 Michael C Mineiro and Bhavya Lal, 'Legal Uncertainties Related to Additive Manufacturing in Space' (International Astronautical Congress, 2015—International Institute of Space Law Symposium IAC-14E7210 2014) 238.

76 Alessandra Matteis, 'Legal Challenges of the Deployment of Cubesats From the International Space Station, 64th IISL Colloquium on the Law of Outer Space Sessions: Session 1: Young Scholars Session' (2021) 64 Proceedings of the International Institute of Space Law 15 17.

77 Matteis (n 76).

breaks apart, every fragment could be considered a new launch. This could mean chaos for the liability regime for those fragments of the satellite.

A space station for which there are built extensions is not as much creating a new quasi-territorial area as it is "merely" stretching the quasi-jurisdiction area that already exists. This is close to the discussion in Section 2(a) on whether the quasi-territorial jurisdiction of Article VIII can seep into the materials used for repairing a space station. This is one area where Article VIII is ambiguous. On the one hand, when building materials are brought by a spaceship, they carry quasi-territorial jurisdiction properties, and when the building materials are assembled, they expand the quasi-territorial jurisdiction to the station built without conflicting with Article II. On the other hand, if quasi-territorial jurisdiction is allowed to seep into 3D-printed materials used to extend the station, there must be a limit to this. If there is no limitation set for the extension of a space station, in theory, one brick brought from Earth could be supplied with Moon materials to extend the brick into a wall surrounding the Mare Tranquillitatis.[78] The crucial question is, what should the limit be? Would it ever be feasible for a state, even with a 3D printer, to make a station much bigger than it actually needs? Article IX requires that the state performs its activities in space and on celestial bodies with due regard to the interest of other states, which could be interpreted as a requirement not to construct a space station to occupy an area on the Moon more than what is necessary. Thus, the general rule would be that the state can extend its space station to the size that is needed and no more.

(c) Moondust Palaces

Making the station entirely from materials found on the Moon, or at least in part, seems to be the long-term best solution. Every kilogram brought by a rocket costs a vast amount of fuel. Thus, making the station from resources present on the Moon would cut costs and ensure that priority is given to launching equipment for survival and science from Earth instead.[79] However, this provides for problems regarding jurisdiction as, unlike under Sections 3(a) and 3(b) of this chapter, there is no quasi-territorial jurisdiction that can be used as a starting point. The first and most direct way of resolving this problem would be to amend the OST to allow for jurisdiction over 3D-printed stations. Amendments are allowed per Article XV of the OST, so an amendment to Article VIII could be done to include facilities made from materials extracted from the celestial bodies. However, there do not seem to be any forthcoming changes to the OST in the foreseeable future. Furthermore, changes to the OST only enter into force for the states accepting the

78 Julius Dasch (ed), *The Hutchinson Dictionary of Space Exploration* (1st edn, Helicon 2005) "Sea of Tranquility."

79 Fuel price per kg ranges drastically, in the last 10 years it has ranged from 1,500 dollars to 34,500 dollars. Our World in Data, 'Cost of Space Launches to Low Earth Orbit, 1961 to 2019' (*ourworldindata.org*, 2022) <https://ourworldindata.org/grapher/cost-space-launches-low-earth-orbit> accessed 22 February 2022.

amendments, and with tensions between the major spacefaring nations on the rise, it seems unlikely that an agreement is possible at the moment.

Jurisdiction is, however, not a static construct but rather a living concept that can slowly adapt to modern-day situations. New forms of jurisdiction are thus being developed within specific public international law systems, which may be looked to for analogies and suggestions for solutions. A relevant example is human rights law, having developed obligations to exercise jurisdiction over areas within their "effective control." Article 2(1) of the International Covenant on Civil and Political Rights[80] (ICCPR), Article 1 of the Convention for the Protection of Human Rights and Fundamental Freedoms[81] (ECHR), and Article 1 of the American Convention on Human Rights[82] (ACHR) all require the member states to ensure the rights and freedoms of everyone within their jurisdiction. This has been interpreted as being applicable extra-territorially when the state has effective control over an area.[83] The Human Rights Committee has commented that the state has an obligation to ensure the rights of the ICCPR when its forces are in control of an area outside the territory, regardless of how the forces came to be in control.[84] The European Court of Human Rights has also, in its case law, found that jurisdiction regarding the obligation in Article 1 of the ECHR is not restricted to the state's national territory but may also extend outside the territory when the state, through its military activity, has effective control over an area.[85] To this extent, it does not matter whether the control is exercised through the armed forces or local administration. The fact that the state has dominating control makes it responsible for upholding the rights of the ECHR.[86] The American human rights system, however, approaches the obligation differently. Instead of effective control, it has a concept of "authority and control" over a person or situation, which is also possible through the forces of the state.[87]

Moving outside the conventions, the International Committee of the Red Cross also describes the concept of effective control in its database on customary

80 *International Covenant on Civil and Political Rights* (adopted 16 December 1966, entered into force 23 March 1976) 999 UNTS 171.

81 *Convention for the Protection of Human Rights and Fundamental Freedoms* (adopted 4 November 1950, entered into force 3 September 1953) 213 UNTS 221.

82 *American Convention on Human Rights "Pact of San José, Costa Rica"* (adopted 22 November 1969, entered into force 18 July 1978) 1144 UNTS 123.

83 Ibrahim Kanalan, 'Extraterritorial State Obligations Beyond the Concept of Jurisdiction International Law' (2018) 19 German Law Journal 43, 47.

84 Human Rights Committee, General Comment No. 31 [80] The Nature of the General Legal Obligation Imposed on States Parties to the Covenant adopted on 29 March 2004 (2187th meeting) (HUMAN RIGHTS COMMITTEE Eightieth session 2004) CCPR/C/21/Rev.1/Add. 13 26 May 2004.

85 *Case of Loizidou v. Turkey (Preliminary Objections)* [1995] ECtHR, (App 15318/89) Judgement, para 62.

86 *Case of Loizidou* (n 85). See also *Al-Skeini and Others v. The United Kingdom* [2011] ECtHR (App 55721/07) Judgement, para 138.

87 *Alejandre Jr. v. Cuba* case 11589 Inter-Am CHR, Report No 86/99, OEA/SerL/V/II106, doc 6 rev (1999), para 23.

international law.[88] Furthermore, the concept of effective control has also found its way into some military manuals recognizing this principle. It must be mentioned that the US military manual, however, does not recognize the obligation to uphold human rights in occupied areas, but speaks instead of a right to exercise temporary jurisdiction in an occupied area from a necessity to ensure law and order.[89] Thus, it would seem that there is broad acceptance that jurisdiction may be established on the basis of effective control; even the US Army manual, which does not recognize a human rights obligation, does acknowledge a temporary jurisdiction over an area that it has control over. There is, therefore, little doubt that effective control of an area can bestow a temporary jurisdiction, which, for the most part, comes from an obligation to uphold basic human rights for humans within the area.

The inherent jurisdiction under the effective control principle, however, seems to be tied to an obligation upon the state rather than a right, in that when the state is in effective control, it is required to ensure fundamental rights and freedoms. Thus, the question is whether an obligation to ensure fundamental human rights can be transferred to a right to wield jurisdiction over a space station. Is an important area such as human rights law even comparable to areas such as space law? One is aimed at ensuring the health and life of individuals and even protecting them against the state; the other area sets up the rules between states in outer space. Rather than moving along such a discussion, it may be more prudent not to compare legal fields but to take a broader view of the elements of the principle. Looking broadly at the basic elements of the effective control jurisdiction principle, two elements are discernable. First, there has to be temporary effective control over an area. Second, there has to be an obligation that the state must ensure the fulfillment of legal obligations within the area.

If these criteria, as an analogy, are applied to space stations on the Moon, it could be argued that effective control could provide a solution to a station being entirely 3D printed. The state that 3D prints the station and provides personnel would, in this case, be in temporary effective control of the area of the station. This cannot be military control because Article IV prohibits the establishment of military bases and the conduct of military operations on celestial bodies. However, astronauts, as representatives of the state, will arguably exercise this temporary control. As to the second element of an obligation upon the state, there are a couple in the OST. The primary obligation in Article VI declares that the state is responsible for all its activities, no matter whether they are performed by governmental or non-governmental entities. This obligation in itself argues that the state needs to control these entities, also on a space station. Furthermore, the obligation in Article VI specifically requires that all activities, including those of non-governmental entities, conform to the OST. Thus, there is, for example, a requirement that these activities are for the benefit of all states according to Article I, that they are done in

88 International Committee of the Red Cross, 'Customary IHL Database' (2005) 'Introduction to Fundamental Guarantees' <https://ihl-databases.icrc.org/customary-ihl/eng/docs/home> accessed 29 November 2022.

89 International Committee of the Red Cross (n 88) 772 at 11.4.1.

accordance with public international law following Article III, and that due regard is shown to the interest of other states following Article IX. Therefore, the second criterion of an obligation upon the state could also be said to be fulfilled.

This solution would allow jurisdiction to be wielded over a 3D-printed space station without violating the non-appropriation principle of Article II of the OST. If more states become involved in the creation and maintenance of the station, this would require an agreement on jurisdiction. This agreement, however, could apply directly to the station and could thus also encompass guests from other states, therefore avoiding having to rely on the nationality principles. On the other hand, applying the effective control jurisdiction on a 3D-printed space station would mean that if the space station were to be abandoned, the state would lose jurisdiction over the station. As the other form of jurisdiction over the station, based on Article VIII, requires that the station, or at least its elements, is launched, the jurisdiction would truly only be temporary. Thus, effective control jurisdiction allows for a flexible and living instrument to wield jurisdiction without violating Article II of the OST and with the possibility to easily extinguish the jurisdiction when the mission is done.

4 Some Concluding Thoughts: A Kingdom From (or to) Moondust?

Law is, in general, retrospective and made for the world as we know it, not the one of tomorrow. At the same time, there is little doubt that the future of humankind is closely tied to outer space and that these are formative years. The OST was made at a different time, and concepts such as 3D printing on the Moon are starting to show this. It is thus tempting to declare that the OST is obsolete and that new rules must be either drafted or chiseled out through state practice. However, the OST has been a stable regulatory tool for outer space since the beginning of the space age, and in that time, it has ensured that space is used for the benefit of all states and that humanity's exploration of outer space has been peaceful, and thus the OST should not be easily dismissed. A new set of rules would also merely reflect the state of outer space affairs at present, and no one can predict the technologies that will arrive in just a couple of years, which may again shake the rules in place. Instead, new ways to understand the OST must be found, as well as flexible interpretations that ensure that the world can continue onwards.

Space stations built on celestial bodies from local materials is a future that will allow humanity to venture further into space and live on celestial bodies. It will not only be a cheaper option than sending everything from Earth but also much more efficient. It would also protect the Earth from more pollution emitted from rocket launches. Finally, it would reduce the likelihood of a celestial body being contaminated by a constant flow of rockets bringing materials, bacteria, and trash from other planets. At the same time, a literal interpretation of the OST suggests that these stations are in a legal deadlock where there is no good way to establish jurisdiction over the station. This interpretation of the OST would not only result in the need for huge amounts of resources brought from Earth but also most likely result in states ignoring the rules. But the treaty rules are not set in stone and do not need to be read needlessly rigorously. The non-appropriation principle is still a sensible rule to avoid conflict; it is also sensible to only allow jurisdiction over objects launched from Earth to avoid appropriation in any way. It does also make sense, however, to consider new solutions to handle the fast-developing area of outer space, solutions that do not violate the legal regime in place and still allow for progress, which is what this chapter aims to do.

As shown in Section 2 of the chapter, the general jurisdiction principles of public international law do not apply well to 3D-printed space stations. Territorial principles are limited in outer space because territory is not possible, and nationality principles do not bestow jurisdiction over a station. In Section 3 the quasi-territorial jurisdiction of Article VIII of the OST is discussed. It can be seen that when a space station is built of materials brought from Earth, they are able to bring a quasi-territorial jurisdiction with them. This quasi-territorial jurisdiction is then able to flow into 3D-printed materials made from resources extracted from the celestial bodies, allowing for jurisdiction over the station to be maintained. A space station built from scratch using 3D-printed materials offers some conundrums in regard to jurisdiction, but a slight modification of the effective control principle from human rights law would be a useful solution. Thus, extracting the basic criterion from the effective control principle being that there has to be control over an area, and an obligation upon the state that the state must enforce, enables a pragmatic and flexible solution for jurisdiction over space stations without violating the non-appropriation principle.

Bibliography

114th Congress (2015–2016): U.S. Commercial Space Launch Competitiveness Act, H.R.2262 (51 USC 10101) §§ 51301 and 51303.

Act No. 83 of December 23, 2021 Act on the Promotion of Business Activities for the Exploration and Development of Space Resources (Tentative Translation).

Al-Skeini and Others v. The United Kingdom [2011] ECtHR, (App 55721/07) Judgement.

Alejandre Jr. v. Cuba Case 11589 Inter-Am CHR, Report No 86/99, OEA/SerL/V/II106, doc 6 rev (1999).

Mike Baker, 'NASA Astronaut Anne McClain Accused by Spouse of Crime in Space' *The New York Times* (New York, 23 August 2019) <https://www.nytimes.com/2019/08/23/us/astronaut-space-investigation.html>

Sandeepa Bhat B, 'Legal Issues Surrounding Human Settlements on the Moon and Other Celestial Bodies Session 2: Moon and Mars Settlement: Open Legal Issues' (2020) 63 Proceedings of the International Institute of Space Law 91.

P.J. Blount, 'Jurisdiction in Outer Space: Challenges of Private Individuals in Space' (2007) 33(2) Journal of Space Law 299.

Case of Loizidou v. Turkey (Preliminary Objections) [1995] ECtHR, (App 15318/89) Judgement.

Kuan-Wei Chen, 'The Principle of Self-Determination in Outer Space: An Age-Old Right for New Age Activities? Part II: Shorter Articles and Comments' (2020) 45 Annals of Air & Space Law 471.

Bin Cheng, *Studies in International Space Law* (Clarendon Press 1997).

S Marc Cohen, 'Identity, Persistence, and the Ship of Theseus' (*faculty.washington.edu*, 10 June 2004) <https://faculty.washington.edu/smcohen/320/theseus.html> accessed 9 December 2021.

Convention for the Protection of Human Rights and Fundamental Freedoms (adopted 4 November 1950, entered into force 3 September 1953) 213 UNTS 221.

Convention on Registration of Objects Launched Into Outer Space (adopted 12 November 1974, entered into force 15 September 1976) 1023 UNTS 15, Article 1(b).

James Crawford, *Brownlie's Principles of Public International Law* (8th edn, OUP 2012).

Phillip De Man, 'The Exploitation of Natural Resources in Outer Space' in Yanal Abul Failat and Anél Ferreira-Snyman (eds), *Outer Space Law: Legal Policy and Practice* (2nd edn, Globe Law and Buisness Ltd 2022) 202.

Wian Erlank, 'Property and Ownership in Outer Space' in Yanal Abul Failat and Anél Ferreira-Snyman (eds), *Outer Space Law: Legal Policy and Practice* (2nd edn, Globe Law and Buisness Ltd 2022) 141.

European Space Agency, 'Building a Lunar Base With 3d Printing' (*www.esa.int*, 31st January 2013) <https://www.esa.int/Enabling_Support/Space_Engineering_Technology/Building_a_lunar_base_with_3D_printing> accessed October 2023.

Ernst Fasan, 'Human Settlements on Planets: New Stations or New Nations' (1994) 22 Journal of Space Law 47.

Federal Law No. (12) of 2019 On The Regulation Of The Space Sector Article 18.

History.com Editors, 'Arms Race' (*history.com*, 14 October 2009) <https://www.history.com/topics/cold-war/arms-race> accessed 14 December 2022.

Stephan Hobe, 'Article I' in Stephan Hobe and others (eds), *Cologne Commentary on Space Law—Outer Space Treaty: Кёльнский Комментарий К Космическому Праву—Договор По Космосу*, vol 1 (Berliner Wissenschafts-Verlag 2017) 195.

Stephan Hobe, *Space Law* (1st edn, Hart Publishing 2019).

International Covenant on Civil and Political Rights (adopted 16 December 1966, entered into force 23 March 1976) 999 UNTS 171.

Danielle Ireland-Piper and Steven Freeland, 'Star Laws: Criminal Jurisdiction in Outer Space' (2020) 44 Journal of Space Law 44.

Ram Jakhu and Steven Freeland, 'Article II' in Stephan Hobe and others (eds), *Cologne Commentary on Space Law—Outer Space Treaty: Кёльнский Комментарий К Космическому Праву—Договор По Космосу*, vol 1 (Berliner Wissenschafts-Verlag 2017) 48

Ram Jakhu and Steven Freeland, 'The Relationship Between the Outer Space Treaty and Customary International Law' (2016) *SSRN Electronic Journal* 11.

Christopher Johnson, 'International Law Governing Outer Space Activities' in Yanal Abul Failat and Anél Ferreira-Snyman (eds), *Outer Space Law: Legal Policy and Practice* (2nd edn, Globe Law and Buisness Ltd 2022) 20.

Ibrahim Kanalan, 'Extraterritorial State Obligations Beyond the Concept of Jurisdiction International Law' (2018) 19 German Law Journal 43.

Laszlo P Keszthelyi and others, *Feasibility Study for the Quantitative Assessment of Mineral Resources in Asteroids* (Open-File Report 2017) 2017–1041 11.

Manfred Lachs, *The Law of Outer Space: An Experience in Comtemporary Law-Making* (Sijthoff 1972).

Law of July 20th 2017 on the Exploration and Use of Space Resources. Article 1.

Alessandra Matteis, 'Legal Challenges of the Deployment of Cubesats From the International Space Station, 64th IISL Colloquium on the Law of Outer Space Sessions: Session 1: Young Scholars Session' (2021) 64 Proceedings of the International Institute of Space Law 15.

Michael C Mineiro and Bhavya Lal, 'Legal Uncertainties Related to Additive Manufacturing in Space' (International Astronautical Congress, 2015—International Institute of Space Law Symposium IAC-14E7210 2014) 238.

Lee Mohon, 'NASA Looks to Advance 3D Printing Construction Systems for the Moon and Mars' (*www.nasa.gov*, 1 October 2020) <https://www.nasa.gov/centers/marshall/news/releases/2020/nasa-looks-to-advance-3d-printing-construction-systems-for-the-moon.html> accessed 10 June 2024.

NASA, *The Artemis Accords—Principles for Cooperation in the Civl Exploration and Use of the Moon, Mars, Comets and Asteroids For Peaceful Purposes* <https://www.nasa.gov/specials/artemis-accords/index.html 2020> Section 10(2).

Jan Ondrej, 'Problems of Jurisdiction in Connection With Settlements on the Moon and Mars Legal Aspects of Settlements on the Moon and Mars' (1991) 34 Proceedings of the Colloquia on the Law of Outer Space 71.

Alexander Orakhelashvili, *Akehurst's Modern Introduction to International Law* (8th edn, Routledge 2019).

Bernard H Oxman, 'Jurisdiction of States' in Anne Peters and Rüdiger Wulfrum (eds), *Max Planck Encyclopedias of International Law* (Online edn, OUP 2007) 1.

Neel V Patel, 'Here's How We Could Mine the Moon for Rocket Fuel' *MIT Technology Review* (www.technologyreview.com) <https://www.technologyreview.com/2020/05/19/1001857/how-moon-lunar-mining-water-ice-rocket-fuel/>.

Bernhard Schmidt-Tedd and Stephan Mick, 'Article VIII' in Stephan Hobe and others (eds), *Cologne Commentary on Space Law—Outer Space Treaty: Кёльнский Комментарий К Космическому Праву—Договор По Космосу*, vol 1 (Berliner Wissenschafts-Verlag 2017).

Malcolm N Shaw, *International Law* (9th edn, CUP 2021) 556.

Christopher Staker, 'Jurisdiction' in Malcolm D Evans (ed), *International Law* (4th edn, OUP 2014) 309.

Starlink, 'Starlink (US) Terms of Service' (*SpaceX,* 2022) Section 11 <https://www.starlink.com/legal/documents/DOC-1020-91087-64?regionCode=US> accessed 4 November 2022.

Gisela Suess, 'Article XII' in Stephan Hobe and others (eds), *Cologne Commentary on Space Law—Outer Space Treaty: Кёльнский Комментарий К Космическому Праву—Договор По Космосу*, vol 1 (Berliner Wissenschafts-Verlag 2017).

Treaty on Principles Governing the Activities of States in the Exploration and Use of Outer Space, Including the Moon and Other Celestial Bodies (adopted 27 January 1967, entered into force 10 October 1967) 610 UNTS 205.

Fabio Tronchetti, 'Legal Aspects of Space Resource Utilization' in Frans von der Dunk and Fabio Tronchetti (eds), *Handbook of Space Law* (Edward Elgar Publishing 2015) 778.

Lotta Viikari, 'Enviromental Aspects of Space Activities' in Frans von der Dunk and Fabio Tronchetti (eds), *Handbook of Space Law* (Edward Elgar Publishing 2015) 728.

Frans von der Dunk, '"For All Moonkind"—Legal Issues of Human Settlements on the Moon: Jurisdiction, Freedom and Inclusiveness Session 2: Moon and Mars Settlement: Open Legal Issues' (2020) 63 Proceedings of the International Institute of Space Law 77.

Frans von der Dunk, 'International Space Law' in Frans von der Dunk and Fabio Tronchetti (eds), *Handbook of Space Law* (Edward Elgar Publishing 2015).

Mike Wall, 'Not Just Artemis: China And Russia Plan to Put Boots on the Moon, Too' (*www.space.com*, 3 September 2022) <https://www.space.com/china-russia-moon-base-ilrs> accessed 5 April 2022.

Jan Woerner, 'Moon Village' (*www.esa.int*, 2016) <https://www.esa.int/About_Us/Ministerial_Council_2016/Moon_Village> accessed 22 February 2022

John G Wrench, 'Non-Appropriation, No Problem: The Outer Space Treaty Is Ready for Asteroid Mining' (2019) 51 Case Western Reserve Journal of International Law 437.

Christina Zdanowicz, 'NASA Astronaut's Estranged Wife Charged With Lying About Claim That Spouse Improperly Accessed Account From Space' *CNN* (Atlanta, Georgia, 8 April 2020) <https://edition.cnn.com/2020/04/08/us/nasa-astronaut-anne-mcclain-estranged-wife-charged-trnd/index.html>

7 Living Amongst the Stars

Conceptualising Freedom of Movement to and From Future Extraterrestrial Human Settlements

Anna Marie Brennan

1 Introduction

With a tentative launch date of September 2025, NASA's Artemis 2 mission will mark the first time since the Apollo 17 mission in December 1972 that humans have been brought within the vicinity of the Moon.[1] Utilising the Space Launch System mega rocket and Orion spacecraft the mission will orbit Earth twice as a 'hybrid free return' to pick up speed for its trans-lunar injection.[2] Following an orbit around the Moon on a 'free-return trajectory,' the mission will return to Earth.[3] While the mission is only expected to last between eight and ten days,[4] the crew will be the farthest people have travelled from Earth since Apollo 13, presupposing that Artemis 2 attains its planned maximum altitude of 8,889 km above the Moon's surface.[5] As part of the mission, the crew will also collect data to evaluate how primed the Artemis program is to land humans on the Moon's surface.[6] Concern about Earth's capacity to sustain a predicted human population of 12 billion by the end of the 21st century[7] has catalysed ambitions to establish a permanent installation on the Moon as part of a long-term strategy to facilitate missions and human settlements on Mars.[8] While it will take scientists and engineers several months to evaluate the Artemis 2 mission's data, Artemis 3 is already being planned to land

1 E Howell, 'Will Artemis 2 Launch to the Moon in 2024? NASA Has a Lot of Work Ahead' (*Space.com*, 27 December 2023) <https://www.space.com/artemis-2-moon-mission-countdown-astronaut-ground-team-safety> accessed 1 November 2024.

2 E Howell, 'NASA's Artemis 2 Mission: Everything You Need to Know' (*Space.com*, 23 June 2023) <https://www.space.com/artemis-2-humans-moon-orbit> accessed 1 November 2024.

3 Howell (n 2).

4 Howell (n 2).

5 Howell (n 2).

6 Howell (n 2).

7 Vladimir Krapivin, Costas Varotsos and Vladimir Soldatov, 'The Earth's Population Can Reach 14 Billion in the 23rd Century Without Significant Adverse Effects on Survivability' (2017) 14 International Journal of Environmental Research and Public Health 885, 897 at Figure 10.

8 Elizabeth Leahy Madsen, 'UN Further Refines Population Projections: 80 Percent Probability of 10–12 Billion People by 2100' (*New Security Beat* [blog], 16 October 2014) online: New Security Beat. See also Ram Jakhu and J Pelton, 'Space Migration and Colonisation' in Ram Jakhu and Joseph Pelton (eds), *Global Space Governance: An International Study* (Springer 2017) 479, 483.

DOI: 10.4324/9781003370499-9

on the surface of the Moon as early as September 2026.[9] As the 11th administrator of NASA, Michael Griffin reasons, 'if we humans want to survive for hundreds of thousands or millions of years, we must ultimately populate other planets. . . . One day . . . there will be more human beings who live off the Earth than on it.'[10]

However, the United States is not the only country with ambitions to establish interstellar bases. On 3 May 2024, China launched Chang'e 6, a multi-component spacecraft which successfully placed a lander/ascender in the South Pole-Aitken (SPA) basin on 1 June 2024 and maintained a spacecraft in orbit around the Moon.[11] Within 48 hours of successfully landing, Chang'e 6 collected 'a targeted 2 kilograms (4.4 pounds) of lunar samples from the surface, as well as material drilled from up to 2 meters (6.5 feet) underground.'[12] After being safely stowed in the re-entry module of the Chang'e 6 orbiter, a probe containing the samples returned to Earth on 25 June 2024, marking the end of its 54-day mission.[13] According to Wu Weiran, the chief designer of China's lunar program, this latest endeavour marks the dawn of an

> international lunar research station [that] will provide a platform for long-term scientific research, work and habitation paving the way for future human exploration into deeper space. It will serve as a technological, material and intellectual reservoir, preparing us for future missions to Mars and other distant destinations in space.[14]

Humankind is clearly 'in the preparatory stages of a new form of mass migration,' but the possibility of becoming a multi-planetary species in the continued absence of a coherent human rights framework tailored to outer space activity, and extraterrestrial settlements more specifically, raises questions about the future responsible and sustainable exploration of celestial bodies.[15] Crucially, will

9 NASA, Artemis II <https://www.nasa.gov/mission/artemis-iii/> accessed 1 November 2024.

10 Michael D Griffin, 'NASA's Griffin: 'Humans Will Colonize the Solar System' *The Washington Post* (25 September 2005), online: Washington Post <www.washingtonpost.com/wpdyn/content/article/2005/09/23/AR2005092301691.html> accessed 1 November 2024.

11 Simon McCarthy, 'China's Chang'e-6 Probe Successfully Lands on Far Side of the Moon' *CNN* (1 June 2024) <https://edition.cnn.com/2024/06/01/china/china-change6-moon-landing-intl-hnk-scn/index.html#:~:text=World%20%2F%20China-,China%27s%20Chang%27e%2D6%20probe%20successfully%20lands%20on,far%20side%20of%20the%20moon&text=The%20Long%20March%205%20rocket,province%20on%20May%203%2C%202024> accessed 1 November 2024.

12 Josh Dinner, 'China's Chang'e 6 Mission to Collect Samples of the Far Side of the Moon Enters Lunar Orbit (Video)' (*Space.com*, 9 May 2024) <https://www.space.com/china-change-6-moon-sample-return-mission-enters-lunar-orbit> accessed 1 November 2024.

13 Laura Bicker and Kelly Ng, 'China Space Probe Returns With Rare Moon Rocks' (*BBC.com*, 25 June 2024) <https://www.bbc.com/news/articles/c04447venm1o> accessed 1 November 2024.

14 Andrew Jones, 'China Unveils Video of Its Moon Base Plans, Which Weirdly Includes a NASA Space Shuttle' (*SpaceX.com*, 1 May 2024).

15 For an example of general commentary on some of the concerns raised by scientists see R Zubrin, 'Colonising the Red Planet: Humans to Mars in Our Time' (2014) 84(6) Architectural Design 46–53; Jacques Arnold, 'Colonising Mars: A Time Frame for Ethical Questions' in Konrad Szocik

individuals enjoy freedom of movement to and from future settlements as well as within the settlements themselves? If this right will exist in outer space, what will be its precise parameters and how will it be enforced in a realm that lacks a bespoke human rights enforcement mechanism? Scholars have only recently turned their attention to hypothesising the future intersection of human rights law with outer space law, but a determination of whether freedom of movement will exist as a right in extraterrestrial settlements and to what extent has yet to be delineated.[16] While the Outer Space Treaty 1967 was drafted and negotiated around the same time as the International Covenant on Civil and Political Rights (ICCPR), the development of outer space law and human rights law have remained separate and distinct.[17] It was inconceivable at the time both treaties were drafted and negotiated that humans would eventually develop the scientific and technological capacity to survive and, more importantly, thrive long term in outer space. Consequently, no explicit reference to human rights is included in the five outer space treaties,[18] and of course, any reference in the five declarations and principles relating to outer space is not legally binding.[19]

(ed), *The Human Factor in a Mission to Mars* (Springer 2019) 133–44; Charles Cockell, 'Mars Is an Awful Place to Live' (2002) 27(1) Interdisciplinary Science Review 32–38; Konrad Szocik, Tomasz Wojtowicz and Leszek Baran, 'War or Peace? The Possible Scenarios of Colonising Mars' (2017) 42 Space Policy 31–36; Maurizio Balistreri and Steven Umbrello, 'Modifying the Environment or Human Nature? What Is the Right Choice for Space Travel and Mars Colonisation?' (2023) 17(5) Nanoethics 1–13; Maurizio Balistreri and Steven Umbrello, 'Should the Colonisation of Space Be Based on Reproduction? Critical Considerations on the Choice of Having a Child in Space' (2022) 11 Journal of Responsible Technology 1–7.

16 Andrew Simon-Butler, 'Freedom of Movement in Outer Space as an Individual Human Right' (2017) 42 Annals of Air & Space Law 253; Aram Kerkonian, 'The Legal Aspects of Permanent Human Settlement on Celestial Bodies' (2019) 44 Annals of Air & Space Law 415; Saskia Vermeylen, 'The Iconography of the Astronauts as a Critical Enquiry of Space Law' in Juan Salazar and A Gorman, *The Routledge Handbook of Social Studies in Outer Space* (Routledge 2023) 172.

17 Danielle Ireland-Piper and Steven Freeland, 'Human Rights and Space: Reflections on the Implications of Human Activity in Outer Space on Human Rights Law' (2021) 9(1) Groningen Journal of International Law 101, 104. See also Steven Freeland and Ram Jakhu, 'The Intersection Between Space Law and International Human Rights Law' in Ram Jakhu and Paul Dempsey (eds), *Routledge Handbook of Space Law* (Routledge 2016) 225, 226.

18 The five treaties are the following: Treaty on Principles Governing the Activities of States in the Exploration and Use of Outer Space, Including the Moon and Other Celestial Bodies (adopted 27 January 1967, entered into force 10 October 1967) 610 UNTS 205 (Outer Space Treaty); Agreement on the Rescue of Astronauts, the Return of Astronauts and the Return of Objects Launched Into Outer Space (adopted 22 April 1968, entered into force 3 December 1969) 672 UNTS 119 (Rescue Agreement); Convention on International Liability for Damage Caused by Space Objects (adopted 29 March 1972, entered into force 1 September 1972) 961 UNTS 187 (Liability Convention); Convention on Registration on Objects Launched Into Outer Space (adopted 14 January 1975, entered into force 15 September 1976) 1023 UNTS 15 (Registration Convention); see Agreement Governing the Activities of States on the Moon and Other Celestial Bodies (adopted 18 December 1979, entered into force 11 July 1984) 1363 UNTS 3 (Moon Agreement).

19 Anna Brennan, 'Human Rights Due Diligence in the Final Frontier: The Quandary of Private Corporations and Future Extraterrestrial Human Settlements' in I Bratu and S Freeland (eds), *Space Security* (Routledge, forthcoming in 2025). The five core declarations are: the UNGA Res 1962

No guidance on this issue continues to be forthcoming from the United Nations Office for Space Affairs, which is the main international organisation tasked with supporting states to implement legal frameworks to regulate their use and exploration of outer space. Perhaps then, is some scholars' unease about how human rights will be protected and enforced on extraterrestrial human settlements warranted? Ram Jakhu and Joseph Pelton assert that the enforcement of human rights in outer space is critical for protecting it as a 'shared international commons' and 'province of all [hu]mankind.'[20] Simultaneously, they advocate, 'simply transposing Earth-based laws . . . to outer space [would be] . . . a lazy exercise failing to consider the multiple scientific differences that will necessarily carry legal implications.'[21] Of course, failing to factor the unique and perilous environment of outer space, as well as the complex science, engineering, and technology needed to sustain life, into an examination of the contours of future human rights approaches in outer space would indeed be fallible. But surely, Earth-based human rights systems could provide at least a starting point for constructing future outer-space based human rights systems? Some scholars believe that maintaining outer space as a relatively 'regulation-free environment is sufficient' while others opine that 'careful rule-setting, established by international treaties and implementation by national law, is essential for the orderly movement of human activities into space beyond the reach of Earth's orbit.'[22]

With regards freedom of movement, this chapter advocates for a hybrid approach. While some initial studies have provided some guidance about how extraterrestrial settlements will be potentially administered, organised, and governed, it is not possible to foresee every possible future scenario. Section 2 of this chapter will consider the implications of the non-appropriation principle for freedom of movement

---

(XVII) (13 December 1963) GAOR 18th Session Supp 15 (Declaration of Legal Principles); UNGA Res 37/92 (1982) GAOR 37th Session Supp 51 (Broadcasting Principles) principles 2, 6, 11; UNGA Res 41/65 (1986) GAOR 41st Session Supp 53 (Remote Sensing Principles) Principles II, IX, XII, XIII; UNGA Res 47/68 (14 December 1992) UN Doc A/SPC/47/L.6 (Principles to Use of Nuclear Power Sources in Outer Space) Principle 7(2)(b); UNGA Res 51/122 (1996) GAOR 51st Session (Use of Space for Benefit and Interest of All States).

20 Ram Jakhu and Joseph Pelton, 'Space Migration and Colonisation' in Ram Jakhu and Joseph Pelton (eds), *Global Space Governance: An International Study* (Springer 2017) 479, 489. See also Outer Space Treaty, Article I.

21 Jakhu and Pelton (n 20).

22 Jakhu and Pelton (n 20) 488. Simon-Butler (n 16) 253, 255. Other scholars who have examined this issue are as follows: Marc M Harold, 'Asylum-Seekers in Outer Space, A Perspective on the Intersection Between International Space Law and US Immigration Law' (2006) 32(1) Journal of Space Law 15; Hamilton Desaussure, 'The Freedoms of Outer Space and Their Marine Antecedents' in Nandasiri Jasentuliyana (ed), *Space Law: Development and Scope* (Praeger 1992) 1, 12–13; George S Robinson, 'Humankind Space Migration: While Nero "Fiddles", Will Space Lawyers "Muse"' (2013) 38 Annals of Air & Space Law 563; George Robinson, 'Space Law, Secularism, and the Survival of Humankind "Essence"' (2013) 2(1) Journal of Space Philosophy 35; George Robinson, 'Space Jurisprudence and the Need for a Transglobal Cybernation: The Underlying Biological Dictates of Humankind Dispersal, Migration, and Settlement in Near and Deep Space' (2014) 39 Annals of Air & Space Law 487.

in outer space. In particular, the section will suggest that a balance between an individual's freedom of movement and humankind's overall aspiration to establish viable and long-lasting settlements will be imperative. Following on from this, Section 3 of the chapter will consider the potential parameters of an individual's freedom of movement in isolated extraterrestrial settlements millions of miles from Earth. In particular, the circumstances where it might be deemed legitimate and indeed permissible to restrict this right within the extraterrestrial human settlement will be analysed. If the contours of the right will be more limited in scope than on Earth, what safeguards will be possible to ensure that extraterrestrial settlements do not descend into tyranny leading to abuses such as forced detention, displacement, and expulsion? The final part of this chapter will examine the right of individuals to return to Earth following extended periods of time inhabiting extraterrestrial settlements. Will individuals, who are descendants of the first settlers of extraterrestrial settlements, be permitted to migrate to Earth or another extraterrestrial settlement? Since this question has not yet been explored in the scholarly literature, this chapter will conclude with an examination of the potential application and scope of the right to return in the context of extraterrestrial settlements and outer space more broadly.

2 Freedom of Movement to and From Future Extraterrestrial Human Settlements: Exploring the Implications of the Non-Appropriation Principle

Recently, a number of astronauts have met the United Nations definition of 'long-term migrant' by residing continuously for more than a year off Earth.[23] On 4 February 2024, Russian cosmonaut Oleg Kononenko set a new world record for the longest time spent continuously residing in outer space by breaking Gennady Padalka's record of 878 days on board the International Space Station.[24] By 5 June 2024, Kononenko had accumulated 1,000 days and by late September 2024, he surpassed a staggering 1,110 days.[25] Indeed, the habitation of humans in outer space for over 35 years has enabled medical and psychological researchers to intently study the impact of space travel on human health and well-being in preparation for a permanent base on the Moon as part of a long-term strategy to facilitate missions to Mars.[26] While residents of future extraterrestrial settlements will likely

23 Miles O'Brien and Kate Tobin, 'Astronaut Who Spent a Year in Space Discusses Readjusting to Life Back on Earth' *PBS News* (26 January 2024) <https://www.pbs.org/newshour/show/astronaut-who-spent-a-year-in-space-discusses-readjusting-to-life-back-on-earth> accessed 1 November 2024. See also UN Data: Glossary at: <https://data.un.org/Glossary.aspx?q=long-term+migrant> accessed 1 November 2024.

24 Alec Luhn, 'Russian Cosmonaut Beats Record for Career Time Spent in Space' *The Guardian* (29 June 2015).

25 Luhn (n 24).

26 Chayakrit Krittanawong and others, 'Human Health During Space Travel: State-of-the-Art Review' (2023) 12(1) Cells 40; Ramsha Mahmood and others, 'Cardiovascular Challenges Beyond Earth: Investigating the Impact of Space Travel on Astronauts' Cardiovascular Health' (2024) 10

face dangers such as famine, disease, violent insurrection, and environmental disasters, it remains unclear whether states will have a precise duty under international law to render assistance to them. Article 1 of the Outer Space Treaty clearly provides, '[o]uter space . . . shall be free for exploration and use by all States without discrimination of any kind,'[27] but immigration law stringently empowers states to exercise discretion with regards who can and cannot reside within its territorial borders.[28] Simon-Butler argues for a paradigm shift[29] by asserting that the phrase 'the province of all mankind' in Article 1 of the Outer Space Treaty should be construed 'with the full territorial implications ordinarily associated with the word 'province.'[30] This is similar to Aldo Armando Cocca's stance that humanity should 'be a permanent subject of law, created by active members of the international community for the exploration and utilization of outer space and celestial bodies for peaceful purposes, and with a full juridical capacity.'[31] So all areas of outer space explored and used by humans constitute the province of all humankind and, as a result, sovereignty over these areas is vested in humankind as a legal entity.[32]

Arguably, Simon-Butler's contention conflicts with Article II of the Outer Space Treaty which provides, '[o]uter space . . . is not subject to national appropriation by claim of sovereignty, by means of use or occupation, or by any other means.'[33] In deciphering the precise meaning of the phrase 'national appropriation,' Article 31(1) of the Vienna Convention on the Law of Treaties (VCLT) states that it should be discerned 'in good faith in accordance with the ordinary meaning to be given to the terms of the treaty in [its] context and in the light of its object and purpose.'[34]

Cardiology in Review 1097; Marta Gimunová and others, 'The Effect of Space Travel on Human Reproduction: A Systemic Review' (2024) 10 NPJ Microgravity 10; T Cahill and G Hardiman, 'Nutritional Challenges and Countermeasures for Space Travel' (2020) 45(1) Nutrition Bulletin 98.

27 Article 1 of the Outer Space Treaty.

28 Article 1 of the Outer Space Treaty. See also Simon-Butler (n 16) 253, 257.

29 Joanne Gabrynowicz, 'The Province and Heritage of Mankind Reconsidered' (Paper delivered at the Second Conference on Lunar Bases and Space Activities of the 21st Century, Houston, 5–7 April 1988) 692, online: NASA <ntrs.nasa.gov/search.jsp?R=19930004830> accessed 1 November 2024. See also Simon-Butler, (n 16) 258.

30 Simion-Butler (n 16) 258.

31 Aldo Armando Cocca, 'Mankind as a New Legal Subject: A New Juridical Dimension Recognized by the United Nations' in Mortimer D Schwartz (ed), *Proceedings of the 13th Colloquium on the Law of Outer Space* (Fred B Rothman & Co 1971) 211, 214. See also Aldo Armando Cocca, 'The Advances in International Law Through the Law of Outer Space' (1981) 9 Journal of Space Law 13, 14; Ernst Fasan, 'The Meaning of the Term 'Mankind' in Space Legal Language' (1974) 2 Journal of Space Law 125, 131.

32 Simon-Butler (n 16) 259.

33 Article II of the Outer Space Treaty. This principle is echoed in Article 11(2) of the Agreement Governing the Activities of States on the Moon and Other Celestial Bodies 1979 (Moon Agreement) 1979 1363 UNTS 22, 18 I.L.M. 1434 (1979) which also declares non-appropriation with respect to the Moon and other celestial bodies. See also Art. 1(1) of the Moon Agreement which stipulates, '[t]he provisions of this Agreement relating to the Moon shall also apply to other celestial bodies within the solar system . . . except insofar as specific legal norms enter into force with respect to any of these celestial bodies.'

34 Article 31(1) of the Vienna Convention on the Law of Treaties 1135 UNTS 331 (1980).

According to *Black's Law Dictionary*, the 'ordinary meaning' of the term 'appropriation' includes '[t]he exercise of control over property.'[35] So there is very little room for scholars to contend that Article II of the Outer Space Treaty does not prohibit the appropriation of territory in outer space *lato sensu*.[36] The inclusion of the phrase 'by claim of sovereignty, by means of use or occupation, or by any other means' in Article II substantiates this contention.[37] Long-standing state practice of not claiming sovereignty over any part of outer space, accompanied by *opinio juris sive necessitates*, means that the non-appropriation principle has arguably achieved customary law status and, thus, outer space is *res communis omnium*.[38] In the first instance, perhaps Simon-Butler's argument that the non-appropriation principle does not apply to humankind can be challenged since outer space *lato sensu* is *res communis omnium* and thus not subject to territory acquisition or occupation.

However, it is contended that a distinction can be drawn between the concept of 'national appropriation' as specified in Article II and the concept of appropriation more generally.[39] In Simon-Butler's view, the inclusion of the word 'national' in Article II has a 'limitative' effect on the scope of the provision.[40] Thus, the prohibition only applies to states, commercial entities, and individuals.[41] Humankind 'as an emerging subject of international law, is explicitly conferred with title and legal/residual sovereignty over areas of outer space by the overt declaration of 'the province of all mankind' in Article I of the Outer Space Treaty.[42] This is a plausible argument since a simple reading of Article II does indeed confine prohibition to 'national appropriation' and does not rule out appropriation entirely. So, while states, commercial entities, and private individuals are not permitted to engage in territorial acquisition of areas of outer space humankind, as an emerging subject of international law, is permitted to do so on the proviso that an 'accepted means of legally acquiring title over new territory here on Earth' is used.[43] While scholars have not yet considered the scope and nature of activity required for humanity to establish territorial acquisition of areas of outer space, it will no doubt differ significantly from means and methods used over millennia here on Earth. If the territorial conception of the humankind province is embraced, it is highly possible that quite a broad range of activity will eventually be regarded as acquisition of

35 Bryan Garner (ed), *Black's Law Dictionary* (12th edn, LexisNexis 2005) 84.

36 Steven Freeland and Ram Jakhu, 'Article II' in Stephan Hobe, Bernhard Schmidt-Tedd and Kai-Uwe Schrogl (eds), *Cologne Commentary on Space Law: Volume 1* (Carl Heymanns Verlag 2009) 44, 53; Vladen Vereshchetin, 'On the Principle of State Sovereignty in International Space Law' (1977) 2 Annals of Air & Space Law 429, 430. See also Zachos Paliouras, 'The Non-Appropriation Principle: The Grundnorm of International Space Law' (2014) 27 Leiden Journal of International Law 37, 44.

37 Article II of the Outer Space Treaty.

38 Paliouras (n 36) 44.

39 Simon-Butler (n 16) 260.

40 Simon-Butler (n 16) 260.

41 Simon-Butler (n 16) 261.

42 Simon-Butler (n 16) 261.

43 Simon-Butler (n 16) 262.

territory including the sending of probes to visit celestial bodies.[44] For now, the geographical scope of humankind is confined to the Moon and the void of space between it and Earth.

There is no doubt that as science and technology develop at an exponential pace over the next century extraterrestrial settlements on Mars will become reality and, with that, humankind's province into the depths of outer space will grow. Some scholars contend that the territorial conception of the humankind province would benefit every human engaged in spacefaring.[45] If outer space territorially comprises the province of all humankind, then 'all members of humankind . . . collectively share ultimate title, a corollary of this is that as a co-proprietor and member of humanity's body politic, every individual should be endowed with freedom of movement throughout space.'[46] However, with so few states currently engaged in outer space activity, concerns are emerging that mobility may become the subject of a 'birthright lottery' where only a few select nationalities will enjoy the right to travel in outer space.[47] States may also restrict foreign nationals from accessing commercial launch facilities within their territorial boundaries thereby cutting off their ability to travel and perhaps even migrate to extraterrestrial settlements.[48] As a consequence, individuals who are not nationals or residents of spacefaring states could find themselves constrained or even cut off from accessing outer space. If the territorial conception of humankind province is generally recognised, then the right to freedom of movement should be extended to all individuals in the outer space realm. Thus, 'every individual is a member of humankind . . . [and] holds legal/residual sovereignty and title over those areas of outer space where humanity's presence extends.'[49] Consequently, 'no human being should be considered to be unlawfully present in humankind's province.'[50] The use and exploration of outer space as framed within Article I of the Outer Space Treaty is a freedom bestowed on all human beings and 'not relegated as a right only exercisable through a State.'[51] Even though

> State control is appropriate in regulating most space activities, this is not so when it comes to individual migration and mobility as the political equality of all people and the promotion of personal autonomy call for an open border regime wherever humanity's explorations and use of outer space is conducted.'[52]

44 Simon-Butler (n 16) 263.
45 Simon-Butler (n 16) 264.
46 Simon-Butler (n 16) 264.
47 Ayelet Shachar, *The Birthright Lottery: Citizenship and Global Inequality* (Harvard UP 2009) 28. See also Simon-Butler (n 16) 264.
48 Simon-Butler (n 16) 267.
49 Simon-Butler (n 16) 265.
50 Simon-Butler (n 16) 265.
51 Simon-Butler (n 16) 266.
52 Simon-Butler (n 16) 267.

Simon-Butler's analysis is compelling, but how freedom of movement will be observed in extraterrestrial human settlements remains unclear. Harsh and unpredictable living conditions on celestial bodies will undoubtedly necessitate limitations on the exercise of this right to safeguard the health, safety, and well-being of the community. Undoubtedly, striking a balance between respect for freedom of movement and humankind's overall aspiration to establish viable and long-lasting settlements will be crucial, but it remains to be seen how this will be achieved.

3 Freedom of Movement and Extraterrestrial Human Settlements: Hypothesising a Future Approach for International Human Rights Law

Article 1 of the Outer Space Treaty affirms, '[t]here shall be free access to all areas of celestial bodies,' but as discussed in the previous section of this chapter the extent to which an individual will enjoy freedom of movement in extraterrestrial settlements remains unclear.[53] Article 13 of the Universal Declaration of Human Rights affirms not only an individual's freedom of movement 'within the borders of each state' but also the right to return to their own state.[54] These fundamental principles are also reiterated in Article 12 of the ICCPR which confirms not only that '[e]veryone lawfully within the territory of a State shall, within that territory, have the right to liberty of movement,' but also that they have the right to return to their country.[55] As a result, an initial reading of Article 1 of the Outer Space Treaty in tandem with Article 12 of the ICCPR suggests that freedom of movement will be an absolute right and not subject to limitations despite the location of extraterrestrial settlements in perilous, remote environments. Recognition of Article 12 of the ICCPR will be especially pertinent for individuals who wish to leave the extraterrestrial settlement of their own volition to travel either to Earth or other celestial bodies since the provision guarantees persons the freedom 'to leave any country, including [their] own.'[56] Within the settlement itself, the individual would also enjoy the freedom to choose the location of their residence.[57] Thus, 'the right to remain, or the right to stay, or even the right to return, are [all] expressions of the freedom of movement.'[58] If residents of an extraterrestrial settlement are displaced or forced to leave due to disasters, famine, or armed conflict, the ICCPR seems to guarantee individuals the right to return to the settlement even if it is impractical or costly for the governing authority of the settlement to facilitate this. Given the

53 Article 1 of the Outer Space Treaty.

54 Article 13 of the Universal Declaration of Human Rights.

55 Article 12 of the ICCPR. General Comment No. 31 also provides, 'every State Party has a legal interest in the performance by every State Party of its obligations.' For further analysis please see General Comment No. 31, The Nature of the General Legal Obligation imposed on States Parties to the Covenant, CCPR/C/21/Rev.1/Add. 13, 26 May 2004.

56 Article 12(2) of the ICCPR.

57 Article 12(2) of the ICCPR.

58 M Stavropoulou, 'The Right Not to Be Displaced' (1994) 9(3) American University International Law Review 689, 739.

perilous environment of outer space and the likelihood that the financial cost of spacefaring will remain exorbitantly high, it is unclear how and the extent to which states will be required to guarantee freedom of movement, especially the right to return to extraterrestrial settlements.

During the drafting and negotiation process of the ICCPR a number of states objected to the classification of freedom of movement as a fundamental guarantee while other states defined it as 'an important human right and one which was an essential part of the right to personal liberty.'[59] The UN Human Rights Committee recognising that '[l]iberty of movement is an indispensable condition for the free development of a person' noted that '[t]he right to move freely relates to the whole territory of a State.'[60] In addition, the Committee concluded, '[t]he enjoyment of this right must not be made dependent on any particular purpose or reason for the person wanting to move or to stay in a place.'[61] So if an individual is lawfully resident on an extraterrestrial settlement a rudimentary analysis would suggest that they 'have a de facto absolute right of residence' and the right to relocate to another part of the settlement if they choose to do so.[62] However, the logistics involved in facilitating an individual's relocation within an extraterrestrial settlement are likely to be hazardous and highly complex so it remains to be seen whether there will be any restrictions on the exercise of this right.

Indeed, Article 12(3) of ICCPR, which outlines the circumstances which permit the restriction of freedom of movement, will likely be deployed to limit movement to and from an extraterrestrial settlement as well as within the settlement itself. However, such restrictions will need to strike a balance between individual rights and the state interest 'to protect national security, public order (ordre public), public health or morals or the rights and freedoms of others.'[63] Since the restrictions outlined in Article 12(3) are articulated in such general and broad terms there is a strong possibility that individuals in extraterrestrial settlements will be limited in their movements where it is deemed necessary for the subsistence and survival of the community.[64] Of course, to achieve peaceful co-existence on extraterrestrial settlements, respect and not denial of human rights will be crucial, but questions remain about how freedom of movement will be exercised if multiple extraterrestrial human settlements are established on a celestial body. There is a strong possibility that individuals will be restricted from freely moving between settlements to reside, work, and engage in commerce since communities will be vulnerable not

59 MJ Bossuyt, *Guide to the 'Travaux Preparatoires' of the International Covenant on Civil and Political Rights* (Martinus Nijhoff Publishers 1987) 253 as quoted by Elena Proukaki. See further Elena Proukaki, 'The Right to Return Home and the Right to Property Restitution Under International Law' in Elena Proukaki (ed), *Armed Conflict and Forcible Displacement: Individual Rights Under International Law* (Routledge 2018) 46 at page 52.

60 General Comment No. 27, Article 12 (Freedom of Movement), CCPR/C/21/Rev.1/Add.9, 2 November 1999, at paras. 1 and 4.

61 General Comment No. 27 (n 60) para. 5.

62 M Nowak, *U.N. Covenant on Civil and Political Rights: CCPR Commentary* (2nd edn, N.P. Engel Publisher 2005) 263.

63 Article 12(3) of the ICCPR.

64 Proukaki (n 59) 53.

only to the perilous environment but also to the risk of disease which could thwart the long-term health and well-being of sustainable settlements.[65] If that is indeed the case, it will be necessary 'to be extremely cautious when human rights are being sacrificed [in extraterrestrial communities] to ensure that the strict, specific, and free from discrimination restrictions, when allowed, are indeed justified.'[66]

According to General Comment No. 27 any 'permissible limitations . . . imposed . . . must not nullify the principle of liberty of movement'[67] and states 'should always be guided by the principle that the restrictions must not impair the essence of the right.'[68] The UN Human Rights Committee endeavoured to provide more in-depth guidance by stipulating that any restrictions 'must be provided by law, must be necessary in a democratic society for the protection of these purposes and must be consistent with all other rights recognised in the Covenant.'[69] Arguably, any restrictions to freedom of movement not only within and between extraterrestrial human settlements but also between extraterrestrial settlements and Earth will need to be proportionate to the interest sought to be protected.[70] Luteran defines proportionality as 'a test comprised of four inquiries addressing: (1) the legitimacy of governmental aims, (2) the suitability of the means chosen to achieve those aims, (3) the necessity of the means chosen to achieve the aims, and (4) the overall balance of a state action.'[71] All four criteria will need to be 'satisfied for a derogation from the full implementation of a human right to be considered acceptable.'[72] While the Outer Space Treaty declares that 'free access' must prevail on celestial bodies the principle of proportionality could require 'differing implementations' of the freedom of movement between extraterrestrial settlements compared to between Earth and extraterrestrial settlements.[73] Moreover, Article 12 of the ICCPR is subject to Article 4 which provides:

> [i]n time of public emergency which threatens the life of the nation [states] . . . may take measures derogating from their obligations under the . . . Covenant to the extent strictly required by the exigencies of the situation provided that such measures are not inconsistent with their other obligations under international law.[74]

65 Further analysis on this point please see Charles Cockell, *Interplanetary Liberty: Building Free Societies in the Cosmos* (OUP 2022) 27–68.

66 Proukaki (n 59) 53.

67 General Comment No. 27 (n 60) para. 2.

68 General Comment No. 27 (n 60) para. 13.

69 General Comment No. 27 (n 60) para. 11.

70 Gregoire Webber, 'Proportionality and Absolute Rights' in Vicki Jackson and Mark Tushnet (eds), *Proportionality: New Frontiers, New Challenges* (CUP 2017) 75, 77.

71 Martin Luteran, 'The Lost Meaning of Proportionality' in Grant Huscroft, Bradley Miller and Gregoire Webber (eds), *Proportionality and the Rule of Law: Rights, Justification, Reasoning* (CUP 2014) 21.

72 Simon-Butler (n 16) 269.

73 Simon-Butler (n 16) 269.

74 Article 4 of the ICCPR.

Derogations can only be implemented on a temporary basis, and they must also 'not provide a *carte blanche* on the state to act arbitrarily and without legal restraint.'[75] Instead, derogations 'must meet the conditions of legality and must be justified and exceptional and necessary measures to take a serious situation.'[76] While it is likely that derogations will be permitted in future extraterrestrial settlements in situations such as disasters, epidemics, and internal disturbances once the situation is over, they will no longer be justified.[77]

However, with so few states currently engaged in outer space activity, concerns are emerging that mobility may become the subject of a 'birthright lottery' where only a few select nationalities will enjoy the right to travel in outer space.[78] States may also restrict foreign nationals from accessing commercial launch facilities within their territorial boundaries thereby cutting off their ability to travel and perhaps even migrate to extraterrestrial settlements.[79] As a consequence, individuals who are not nationals or residents of spacefaring states could find themselves constrained or even cut off from accessing outer space. Given the remoteness and isolation of proposed extraterrestrial human settlements there is an increased likelihood that the governing authority may implement prolonged and indefinite restrictions on freedom of movement. While initially a restriction may be necessary, it will need to be reviewed on a regular basis to curb 'as far as possible its scope and territorial applicability and the associated derogation of rights.'[80] It remains to be seen how this will be achieved given that multiple states may partner together to establish the first extraterrestrial human settlement. A practical solution would be to establish an independent human rights review mechanism not only to examine the general scope of human rights on extraterrestrial settlements but also to regularly review the scope, duration, and application of any proposed restrictions. Given the inevitable challenges of sustaining future communities on celestial bodies one question this review mechanism would need to consider is whether residents will retain a right to return to Earth either temporarily or indefinitely. The subsistence of such a right may prove contentious especially for individuals born on extraterrestrial settlements, who will be in effect descendants of the first wave of settlers. Undoubtedly, there is a likelihood that Earth-based authorities will seek to limit the scope of this right not only to reduce space debris and preserve public health but also to realise humankind's ambition for multi-planetary societies. The final section of this chapter will analyse the potential scope of this right and why its parameters need to be discerned before extraterrestrial settlements are established.

75 Proukaki (n 59) 54.

76 Proukaki (n 59) 54.

77 Proukaki (n 59) 54.

78 Ayelet Shachar, *The Birthright Lottery: Citizenship and Global Inequality* (Harvard UP 2009) 28. See also Simon-Butler (n 16) 264.

79 Simon-Butler (n 16) 267.

80 Consideration of reports submitted by states parties under Article 40 of the Covenant, Concluding Observations of HRC, Israel, CCPR/C/79/Add. 93, 18 August 1998 at para. 11. For further analysis please see Consideration of reports submitted by states parties under Article 40 of the Covenant, Concluding observations of HRC, Israel, CCPR/C/ISR/CO/3, 3 September 2010, para. 7.

4 Developing a Future Right to Enter/Return to Earth From Outer Space: Resolving the Dilemma of Future Generations Born on Extraterrestrial Settlements

Customary international law recognises a right to enter one's country which is reflected in several international human rights treaties, most notably the ICCPR. In particular, Article 12(4) ensures, '[n]o one shall be arbitrarily deprived of the right to enter [their] . . . own country.'[81] An intervention by some states during the treaty's drafting process ensured, 'the right applies equally to citizens and permanent residents' and individuals can 'return from a journey abroad to what had in effect become their country.'[82] Thus, 'citizenship and nationality [are] not the final determinants' of a right to enter a country.[83] Instead, [t]he final determinant is whether . . . [the country] was the [individual's] permanent home.'[84] Delineating the precise circumstances under which an individual can be legitimately deprived of the right to either enter or return to Earth will be difficult to predict. The wording of Article 12(4) suggests that the right to enter is an individual as opposed to a collective right, 'the significance of which lies in the fact that any agreement concluded enabling the return of some but not all . . . could be challenged as being in violation of this provision.'[85] Arbitrary interference with the right to return to Earth could possibly occur whenever an individual is denied entry in a way that is 'incompatible with the objective of protection.'[86] The right to freedom of movement within the territorial boundaries of a state, the right to leave the state, and the right to return cannot be subject to restrictions under the ICCPR. As outlined in the *travaux preparatoires*, '[t]he general consensus was, however, that, while the right was not absolute, it should not be made subject to the same kind of restrictions as the other rights' outlined in Article 12 (1) and (2).[87] The UN Human Rights Committee would seem to be of a similar view asserting, 'there are few, if any circumstances in which deprivation of the right to enter one's own country could be reasonable.'[88] Indeed, the drafting records of the ICCPR indicate that perhaps the only legitimate ground to refuse a person entry is if they have already been lawfully exiled.[89]

81 Article 12(4) of the ICCPR.

82 United Nations Commission on Human Rights, Summary Record of the 151st Meeting, E/CN.4/SR.151, 10 April 1950, para. 52.

83 United Nations Commission on Human Rights, Summary Record of the 315th Meeting, E/CN.4/SR.315, 29 May 1950, para. 12.

84 United Nations Commission on Human Rights (n 83).

85 Proukaki (n 59) 57.

86 Hurst Hannum, *The Right to Leave and Return in International Law and Practice* (Martinus Nijhoff Publishers 1987) 44–45. See also Proukaki (n 59) 57.

87 United Nations General Assembly Draft International Covenants on Human Rights: Report of the Third Committee, A/4299, 3 December 1959, para 3.

88 General Comment No. 27 (n 60) para. 41.

89 Stig Jagerskold, 'The Freedom of Movement' in Louis Henkin, ed., *The International Bill of Rights: The Covenant on Civil and Political Rights* (Columbia UP 1981) 182.

In the context of individuals seeking to either enter or return to Earth from extraterrestrial settlements, how will the concept of 'his own country' under Article 12(4) be construed and who will be bestowed with legal protection? Will descendants of the first generation of settlers also be entitled to exercise this right or will they be subject to restrictions? Article 12(4) refers to the right to enter as opposed to the right to return. In Proukaki's view, this suggests that Article 12(4) 'is not intended to be restricted to those individuals who lived in the state of origin as opposed to individuals who never lived there.'[90] Thus, the fact that a descendant of the first generation of settlers has never set foot on a state on Earth may not restrict them from exercising this right. This interpretation finds support in General Comment 27 of the UN Human Rights Committee which affirms:

> [t]he right of a person to enter his or her own country recognises the special relations of a person to that country. The right has various facets. It implies the right to remain in one's own country. It includes not only the right to return after having left one's own country; it may also entitle a person to come to the country for the first time if he or she was born outside the country.[91]

While some states have endeavoured to argue to the contrary, a person's right to enter under Article 12(4) is not limited to the state of which they are a citizen. Instead, what matters most 'is the effectiveness of the links that an individual has with the said country.'[92] It remains to be seen how the right to enter will be interpreted and applied to individuals ordinarily resident on extraterrestrial settlements, but it is conceivable that they will retain a right to enter specific states on Earth if they can demonstrate an effective link to them.

Ancestry, place of birth, family/community bonds, and prolonged domicile before moving to the extraterrestrial settlement may be decisive factors in determining this effective link. As Joseph, Schultz, and Castan contend,

> an individual who, because of his or her special ties to or claims in relation to a given country, cannot be considered to be a mere alien. This would be the case . . . [if] individuals whose country of nationality has been incorporated in or transferred to another national entity.[93]

Their argument finds support in the decision of the UN Human Rights Committee in *Stewart* v. *Canada*.[94] Here, the applicant was a permanent resident of Canada, having lived in Ontario since he was seven years old.[95] Following his

90 Proukaki (n 59) 57. See also Hannum (n 86) 56.

91 General Comment No. 27 (n 60) para. 19.

92 Proukaki (n 59) 58.

93 Sarah Joseph, Jenny Schultz and Melissa Castan, *The International Covenant on Civil and Political Rights: Cases, Materials and Commentary* (OUP 2000) 2.

94 *Stewart v. Canada*, CCPR/C/58/D/538/1993 (16 December 1996).

95 *Stewart* v. *Canada* (n 94) para. 2.1.

conviction for 42 criminal offences, immigration officials sought to deport him to the United Kingdom, where he had been born.[96] The applicant argued, 'for all practical purposes, Canada [was] his own country' within the meaning of Article 12(4) of the ICCPR.[97] The United Kingdom was not the applicant's 'own country' as he had emigrated as a young child and had spent his whole life in Canada.[98] While 'not Canadian in a formal sense, [it was argued that] he must be considered de facto a Canadian citizen.'[99] The UN Human Rights Committee agreed, concluding, '[f]or the rights set forth in [A]rticle 12, the existence of a formal link to the State is irrelevant; the Covenant is here concerned with the strong personal and emotional links an individual may have with the territory where he lives and with the social circumstances obtaining in it.'[100] As long as an enduring personal link to the state can be demonstrated, an individual residing on an extraterrestrial settlement could arguably retain a right to enter that particular state even if they are not a citizen.

This interpretation also finds support in *Stefan Lars Nystrom* v. *Australia*, where it was determined that the phrase 'his own country' in Article 12(4) includes not just an individual's formal nationality links to the country but also 'special ties to or claims in relation to a given country.'[101] In addition, it comprises 'close and enduring connections between a person and a country, connections [particularly family] which may be stronger than those of nationality.'[102] So far, the international community has been silent on the issue of citizenship/residency rights in the context of future extraterrestrial settlements.[103] The case law analysed previously indicates that if an individual resident on an extraterrestrial settlement is able to maintain 'close and enduring connections' with a state on Earth their right to enter would be potentially enforceable. While international human rights law may eventually evolve to recognise a broad right for residents of extraterrestrial settlements to enter Earth, no matter how tenuous their connection, an overarching framework outlining the future migration rights of individuals who choose to reside off-Earth needs to be developed. With several states, as well as corporations, seeking to establish extraterrestrial settlements within the next 50 years this framework is needed sooner rather than later. One of the core questions which will need consideration is the definition of 'close and enduring connections' in the context of outer space. If the first generation of settlers, as well as their future descendants, are unable to maintain 'close and enduring connections' to Earth, what potential legal consequences will ensue? Some states and scholars may argue that individuals, aware of the technological challenges of moving to an extraterrestrial settlement,

96 *Stewart v. Canada* (n 94) paras. 2.2 and 2.4.

97 *Stewart v. Canada* (n 94) para. 3.4.

98 *Stewart v. Canada* (n 94) para 3.4.

99 *Stewart v. Canada* (n 94) para 3.4.

100 *Stewart v. Canada* (n 94) Part C, para. 5.

101 *Stefan Lars Nystrom v. Australia*, Communication No. 1557/2007, CCPR/C/102/D/ 1557/2007, paras. 7.4–7.6.

102 *Stefan Lars Nystrom v. Australia* (n 101).

103 Article 12 (4) of the ICCPR.

have accepted the risk that this could potentially sever their 'close and enduring connections.' Consequently, their right to enter a state on Earth could potentially be unenforceable.[104]

As already mentioned, it remains to be seen whether customary law will eventually evolve to recognise a broad right to return to Earth as opposed to a right to return to a specific country only. Certainly, it would resolve some of the dilemmas discussed earlier in relation to the varying approaches adopted by states with regards their interpretation of the phrase 'his own country.' Another foreseeable challenge is that individuals seeking to migrate to extraterrestrial settlements may need to satisfy stringent health and skills criteria to safeguard and develop a sustainable community off-Earth. While these definitive criteria have not yet been envisaged it is conceivable that individuals seeking to enter Earth may also have to satisfy similar criteria, especially with regards health. Due to the risks involved with space travel and the harsh and potentially restrictive living conditions of celestial bodies, it would not be incongruous to propose that customary law may evolve to require the governing authorities of extraterrestrial settlements to apprise potential and selected candidates for residency that if they voluntarily choose to reside on an extraterrestrial settlement, there is a strong possibility they will be unable to return to Earth.

5 Conclusion

As stated in the introduction, outer space law has so far had extraordinarily little to do with human rights, especially freedom of movement, and this chapter has examined a fundamental consequence of that actuality with reference to extraterrestrial settlements. It has explored the potential impact of the continued lack of migratory regulations for outer space and made proposals for how freedom of movement could be protected and monitored. This chapter has also highlighted how outer space law is lagging despite rapid developments in technology and engineering which will make extraterrestrial settlements a reality soon. The discussion has also analysed the potential application of the ICCPR to this dilemma. While the ICCPR provides the foundation upon which the freedom of movement will be enjoyed in outer space states, it will need to carefully explore a range of policy and regulatory approaches with regards migration to and from extraterrestrial settlements. Article 12 of the ICCPR provides, '[e]veryone lawfully within the territory of a State shall . . . have the right to liberty of movement and freedom to choose his residence,' yet it remains unclear how and, indeed, if this right will be enforceable in extraterrestrial settlements. As explored in this chapter, the perilous and complex nature of extraterrestrial settlements may require limits on the exercise of this right to safeguard the well-being of the community. International human rights law still provides no guidance on how the international community can monitor and enforce compliance with human rights in outer space and investigate alleged human rights

104 *Stefan Lars Nystrom* (n 101) paras. 7.4–7.6.

violations. An additional challenge is that nearly all corporations, seeking to establish extraterrestrial settlements by the end of the 21st century, are registered in the United States. The United States is regarded as a major spacefaring nation and while it is a signatory party to the ICCPR it has consistently refuted its extraterritorial application. Indeed, it curtly withdrew from the negotiations for the UN Draft Treaty on Business and Human Rights for this reason.

Consequently, efforts to encourage state and corporate compliance with freedom of movement principles in outer space will be challenging at best. This chapter could therefore appear to be quite demoralising: like a lot of research, it attempts to identify ambiguities in outer space law and critically analyses why any solutions to assuage it are likely to be difficult. Nonetheless, the consequences of restricting freedom of movement in outer space, and in extraterrestrial settlements, are likely to be far-reaching. Without a coherent human rights framework specifically tailored to extraterrestrial settlements it is unlikely that individuals will choose to reside there due to concerns that grave human rights violations and international crimes may be perpetrated in the quest for profit maximisation. Thus, the adoption of a comprehensive legal framework would enable individuals contemplating a move to an extraterrestrial settlement to fully evaluate the impact this would potentially have on their human rights, especially freedom of movement. Indeed, to encourage individuals to reside on celestial bodies, states in partnership with corporations will need to proactively demonstrate to potential residents that they will have an exercisable right to return to Earth if they wish to do so. Risk assessments as well as mitigation and remediation processes will not only need to be transparent but will also need to comprehensively assess the potential consequences of their activities on residents' freedom of movement. It remains to be seen whether the international community will succeed in grappling with these issues and, indeed, the governance of an extraterrestrial settlement by either a commercial entity, state, or commercial-state hybrid will undoubtedly have a significant bearing on how the right to liberty of movement will be interpreted, monitored, and protected. Given that the proposed Artemis Base and the International Lunar Research Station will be located in close proximity on the Moon and governed by different states, finding a solution to this dilemma is perhaps needed sooner rather than later.

Bibliography

Agreement Governing the Activities of States on the Moon and Other Celestial Bodies (adopted 18 December 1979, entered into force 11 July 1984) 1363 UNTS 3 (Moon Agreement).

Agreement on the Rescue of Astronauts, the Return of Astronauts and the Return of Objects Launched Into Outer Space (adopted 22 April 1968, entered into force 3 December 1969) 672 UNTS 119 (Rescue Agreement).

Jacques Arnold, 'Colonising Mars: A Time Frame for Ethical Questions' in Konrad Szocik (ed), *The Human Factor in a Mission to Mars* (Springer 2019) 133–44.

Maurizio Balistreri and Steven Umbrello, 'Modifying the Environment or Human Nature? What Is the Right Choice for Space Travel and Mars Colonisation?' (2023) 17(5) Nanoethics 1–13.

Maurizio Balistreri and Steven Umbrello, 'Should the Colonisation of Space Be Based on Reproduction? Critical Considerations on the Choice of Having a Child in Space' (2022) 11 Journal of Responsible Technology 1–7.

Laura Bicker and Kelly Ng, 'China Space Probe Returns With Rare Moon Rocks' (*BBC.com*, 25 June 2024) <https://www.bbc.com/news/articles/c04447venm1o> accessed 1 November 2024.

Anna Brennan, 'Human Rights Due Diligence in the Final Frontier: The Quandary of Private Corporations and Future Extraterrestrial Human Settlements' in I Bratu and S Freeland (eds), *Space Security* (Routledge, forthcoming in 2025).

T Cahill and G Hardiman, 'Nutritional Challenges and Countermeasures for Space Travel' (2020) 45(1) Nutrition Bulletin 98.

Charles Cockell, *Interplanetary Liberty: Building Free Societies in the Cosmos* (OUP 2022).

Aldo Armando Cocca, 'Mankind as a New Legal Subject: A New Juridical Dimension Recognized by the United Nations' in Mortimer D Schwartz (ed), *Proceedings of the 13th Colloquium on the Law of Outer Space* (Fred B Rothman & Co 1971) 211, 214.

Aldo Armando Cocca, 'The Advances in International Law Through the Law of Outer Space' (1981) 9 Journal of Space Law 13.

Charles Cockell, 'Mars Is an Awful Place to Live' (2002) 27(1) Interdisciplinary Science Review 32–38.

Convention on International Liability for Damage Caused by Space Objects (adopted 29 March 1972, entered into force 1 September 1972) 961 UNTS 187 (Liability Convention).

Convention on Registration on Objects Launched Into Outer Space (adopted 14 January 1975, entered into force 15 September 1976) 1023 UNTS 15 (Registration Convention).

Hamilton Desaussure, 'The Freedoms of Outer Space and Their Marine Antecedents' in Nandasiri Jasentuliyana (ed), *Space Law: Development and Scope* (Praeger 1992) 1.

Josh Dinner, 'China's Chang'e 6 Mission to Collect Samples of the Far Side of the Moon Enters Lunar Orbit (Video)' (*Space.com*, 9 May 2024) <https://www.space.com/china-change-6-moon-sample-return-mission-enters-lunar-orbit> accessed 1 November 2024.

Ernst Fasan, 'The Meaning of the Term 'Mankind' in Space Legal Language' (1974) 2 Journal of Space Law 125.

Steven Freeland and Ram Jakhu, 'Article II' in Stephan Hobe, Bernhard Schmidt-Tedd and Kai-Uwe Schrogl (eds), *Cologne Commentary on Space Law: Volume 1* (Carl Heymanns Verlag 2009) 44.

Steven Freeland and Ram Jakhu, 'The Intersection Between Space Law and International Human Rights Law' in Ram Jakhu and Paul Dempsey (eds), *Routledge Handbook of Space Law* (Routledge 2016) 225.

Joanne Gabrynowicz, 'The Province and Heritage of Mankind Reconsidered' (Paper delivered at the Second Conference on Lunar Bases and Space Activities of the 21st Century, Houston, 5–7 April 1988) 692, online.

Bryan Garner (ed), *Black's Law Dictionary* (12th edn, LexisNexis 2005).

Marta Gimunová and others, 'The Effect of Space Travel on Human Reproduction: A Systemic Review' (2024) 10 NPJ Microgravity 10.

Michael D Griffin, 'NASA's Griffin: 'Humans Will Colonize the Solar System' *The Washington Post* (25 September 2005) <www.washingtonpost.com/wpdyn/content/article/2005/09/23/AR2005092301691.html> accessed 1 November 2024.

Hurst Hannum, *The Right to Leave and Return in International Law and Practice* (Martinus Nijhoff Publishers 1987).

Marc M Harold, 'Asylum-Seekers in Outer Space, A Perspective on the Intersection Between International Space Law and US Immigration Law' (2006) 32(1) Journal of Space Law 15.

E Howell, 'NASA's Artemis 2 Mission: Everything You Need to Know' (*Space.com*, 23 June 2023) <https://www.space.com/artemis-2-humans-moon-orbit> accessed 1 November 2024.

E Howell, 'Will Artemis 2 Launch to the Moon in 2024? NASA Has a Lot of Work Ahead' (*Space.com*, 27 December 2023) <https://www.space.com/artemis-2-moon-mission-countdown-astronaut-ground-team-safety> accessed 1 November 2024.

Danielle Ireland-Piper and Steven Freeland, 'Human Rights and Space: Reflections on the Implications of Human Activity in Outer Space on Human Rights Law' (2021) 9(1) Groningen Journal of International Law 101.

Stig Jagerskold, 'The Freedom of Movement' in Louis Henkin (ed), *The International Bill of Rights: The Covenant on Civil and Political Rights* (Columbia UP 1981) 182.

Ram Jakhu and Joseph Pelton, 'Space Migration and Colonisation' in Ram Jakhu and Joseph Pelton (eds), *Global Space Governance: An International Study* (Springer 2017) 479.

Andrew Jones, 'China Unveils Video of Its Moon Base Plans, Which Weirdly Includes a NASA Space Shuttle' (*SpaceX.com*, 1 May 2024).

Sarah Joseph, Jenny Schultz and Melissa Castan, *The International Covenant on Civil and Political Rights: Cases, Materials and Commentary* (OUP 2000).

Aram Kerkonian, 'The Legal Aspects of Permanent Human Settlement on Celestial Bodies' (2019) 44 Annals of Air & Space Law 415.

Vladimir Krapivin, Costas Varotsos and Vladimir Soldatov, 'The Earth's Population Can Reach 14 Billion in the 23rd Century Without Significant Adverse Effects on Survivability' (2017) 14 International Journal of Environmental Research and Public Health 885.

Chayakrit Krittanawong and others, 'Human Health During Space Travel: State-of-the-Art Review' (2023) 12(1) Cells 40.

Alec Luhn, 'Russian Cosmonaut Beats Record for Career Time Spent in Space' *The Guardian* (29 June 2015).

Martin Luteran, 'The Lost Meaning of Proportionality' in Grant Huscroft, Bradley Miller and Gregoire Webber (eds), *Proportionality and the Rule of Law: Rights, Justification, Reasoning* (CUP 2014) 21.

Elizabeth Leahy Madsen, 'UN Further Refines Population Projections: 80 Percent Probability of 10–12 Billion People by 2100' (*New Security Beat* [blog], 16 October 2014), online: New Security Beat.

Ramsha Mahmood and others, 'Cardiovascular Challenges Beyond Earth: Investigating the Impact of Space Travel on Astronauts' Cardiovascular Health' (2024) 10 Cardiology in Review 1097.

Simon McCarthy, 'China's Chang'e-6 Probe Successfully Lands on Far Side of the Moon' *CNN* (1 June 2024) <https://edition.cnn.com/2024/06/01/china/china-change6-moon-landing-intl-hnk-scn/index.html#:~:text=World%20%2F%20China-,China%27s%20Chang%27e%2D6%20probe%20successfully%20lands%20on,far%20side%20of%20the%20moon&text=The%20Long%20March%205%20rocket,province%20on%20May%203%2C%202024> accessed 1 November 2024.

M Nowak, *U.N. Covenant on Civil and Political Rights: CCPR Commentary* (2nd edn, N.P. Engel Publisher 2005).

Miles O'Brien and Kate Tobin, 'Astronaut who Spent a Year in Space Discusses Readjusting to Life Back on Earth' *PBS News* (26 January 2024) <https://www.pbs.org/newshour/show/astronaut-who-spent-a-year-in-space-discusses-readjusting-to-life-back-on-earth> accessed 1 November 2024.

Zachos Paliouras, 'The Non-Appropriation Principle: The Grundnorm of International Space Law' (2014) 27 Leiden Journal of International Law 37.

Elena Proukaki, 'The Right to Return Home and the Right to Property Restitution Under International Law' in Elena Proukaki (ed), *Armed Conflict and Forcible Displacement: Individual Rights Under International Law* (Routledge 2018) 46.

George S Robinson, 'Humankind Space Migration: While Nero "Fiddles", Will Space Lawyers "Muse"' (2013) 38 Annals of Air & Space Law 563.

George S Robinson, 'Space Jurisprudence and the Need for a Transglobal Cybernation: The Underlying Biological Dictates of Humankind Dispersal, Migration, and Settlement in Near and Deep Space' (2014) 39 Annals of Air & Space Law 487.

George S Robinson, 'Space Law, Secularism, and the Survival of Humankind "Essence"' (2013) 2(1) Journal of Space Philosophy 35.
Ayelet Shachar, *The Birthright Lottery: Citizenship and Global Inequality* (Harvard UP 2009).
Andrew Simon-Butler, 'Freedom of Movement in Outer Space as an Individual Human Right' (2017) 42 Annals of Air & Space Law 253.
M Stavropoulou, 'The Right Not to Be Displaced' (1994) 9(3) American University International Law Review 689.
Stefan Lars Nystrom v. Australia, Communication No. 1557/2007, CCPR/C/102/D/ 1557/ 2007.
Stewart v. Canada, CCPR/C/58/D/538/1993 16 December 1996.
Konrad Szocik, Tomasz Wojtowicz and Leszek Baran, 'War or Peace? The Possible Scenarios of Colonising Mars' (2017) 42 Space Policy 31–36.
Treaty on Principles Governing the Activities of States in the Exploration and Use of Outer Space, Including the Moon and Other Celestial Bodies (adopted 27 January 1967, entered into force 10 October 1967) 610 UNTS 205 (Outer Space Treaty).
UN Doc A/SPC/47/L.6 (Principles to Use of Nuclear Power Sources in Outer Space).
UNGA Res 1962 (XVII) (13 December 1963) GAOR 18th Session Supp 15 (Declaration of Legal Principles).
UNGA Res 37/92 (1982) GAOR 37th Session Supp 51 (Broadcasting Principles).
UNGA Res 41/65 (1986) GAOR 41st Session Supp 53 (Remote Sensing Principles).
UNGA Res 47/68 (14 December 1992).
UNGA Res 51/122 (1996) GAOR 51st Session (Use of Space for Benefit and Interest of All States).
Vladen Vereshchetin, 'On the Principle of State Sovereignty in International Space Law' (1977) 2 Annals of Air & Space Law 429.
Saskia Vermeylen, 'The Iconography of the Astronauts as a Critical Enquiry of Space Law' in Juan Salazar and A Gorman (eds), *The Routledge Handbook of Social Studies in Outer Space* (Routledge 2023) 172.
Gregoire Webber, 'Proportionality and Absolute Rights' in Vicki Jackson and Mark Tushnet (eds), *Proportionality: New Frontiers, New Challenges* (CUPs 2017) 75.
R Zubrin, 'Colonising the Red Planet: Humans to Mars in Our Time' (2014) 84(6) Architectural Design 46–53.

Part III

Futures for Contemporary Problems

8 Emerging Principles on Safety Zones Around Space Resource Utilisation Activities on Celestial Bodies

Lachlan Blake and Matthew Stubbs

1 Introduction

Space resource utilisation (SRU) will be essential to humankind's anticipated expanded exploration and use of outer space in the coming decades.[1] SRU is not merely, or even primarily, about space mining for direct profit—it is about utilisation of resources located in outer space to expand the horizons of humankind's endeavours in outer space.[2] There are many important legal issues raised by space resource utilisation.[3] In this chapter, we focus on just one of those issues—the emerging norms that will regulate the declaration of safety zones around SRU activities.[4] Our inquiry commences from the 'constitution' of outer

1 NASA, 'Using Space-Based Resources for Deep Space Exploration' (*web page*, 26 July 2023) <https://www.nasa.gov/overview-in-situ-resource-utilization/>; JN Rasera and others, 'The Beneficiation of Lunar Regolith for Space Resource Utilisation: A Review' (2020) 186 Planetary and Space Science 104879; The Hague International Space Resources Governance Working Group, 'Building Blocks for the Development of an International Framework on Space Resource Activities' (2019) <https://www.universiteitleiden.nl/en/law/institute-of-public-law/institute-of-air-space-law/the-hague-space-resources-governance-working-group> [11.3].

2 NASA (n 1); Rasera and others (n 1); The Hague International Space Resources Governance Working Group (n 1).

3 For example, the question of the legality of SRU itself under the non-appropriation principle found in Art II of the *Outer Space Treaty* (see discussion later at page 167); the question whether SRU for commercial purposes is permissible (see, e.g., statements on national appropriation in Belarussian Delegation, submission to the Working Group on Legal Aspects of Space Resource Activities, 62nd session of the COPUOS Legal Subcommittee, 20–31 March 2023 UN Doc A/AC.105/C.2/2023/CRP.10, 3; United Kingdom Delegation, submission to the Working Group on Legal Aspects of Space Resource Activities, 62nd session of the COPUOS Legal Subcommittee, 20–31 March 2023, UN Doc A/AC.105/C.2/2023/CRP.21, 2–3); and the question whether the permanent placement of facilities on celestial bodies abrogates principles of free exploration and non-appropriation (see discussion later at page 165).

4 In this paper, we examine only civil safety zones, and do not address security or warfare zones. For an analysis of the latter zones, see Matthew Stubbs, 'The Legality of Keep-Out, Operational and Safety Zones in Outer Space' in Cassandra Steer and Matthew Hersch (eds), *War and Peace in Outer Space: Law, Policy and Ethics* (OUP 2021) 199. One example of a treaty-based safety zone is found in *United Nations Convention on the Law of the Sea*, opened for signature 10 December 1982,

DOI: 10.4324/9781003370499-11

space,[5] the 1967 Treaty on Principles Governing the Activities of States in the Exploration and Use of Outer Space, Including the Moon and Other Celestial Bodies (Outer Space Treaty).[6] Although the treaty does not expressly address SRU or safety zones, it establishes a set of key principles which must guide any assessment of the legality of safety zones around SRU activities and which will determine the permissible nature of such zones if they are lawful. Using orthodox principles of treaty interpretation, we examine the relevant provisions of the Outer Space Treaty in light of their object and purpose,[7] referring to the *travaux préparatoires* where appropriate,[8] considering the interaction of these provisions with other relevant rules of international law,[9] and taking into account the subsequent practice of states in the interpretation of the provisions.[10]

We approach the task of determining the rules governing safety zones around SRU activities by examining relevant principles of space law set out in the Outer Space Treaty. We refer to these as legal principles because the Outer Space Treaty is a document establishing foundational principles for the law of outer space but is not a treaty containing highly detailed rules on particular topics. It is an anticipatory treaty, intended to establish foundational principles, the understanding of its drafters being that 'future developments would give rise to new problems requiring subsequent solution.'[11] These key principles will guide the assessment of the lawfulness of safety zones around SRU activities and will provide the outer limits within which the permissible nature of safety zones and other deconfliction measures will be determined by subsequent practice. The relevant principles that we examine are:

- freedom of exploration, use and access;[12]
- non-appropriation;[13]

1833 UNTS 397 (entered into force 16 November 1994) art 60(4) which permits a coastal state to establish within its exclusive economic zone a 'reasonable safety zones around . . . artificial islands, installations and structures in which it may take appropriate measures to ensure the safety both of navigation and of the artificial islands, installations and structures'. See, e.g., Sebastian tho Pesch, 'Coastal State Jurisdiction around Installations: Safety Zones in the Law of the Sea' (2015) 30(3) International Journal of Marine and Coastal Law 512, 512–14; Gemma Andreone, 'The Exclusive Economic Zone' in Donald Rothwell and others (eds), *The Oxford Handbook of the Law of the Sea* (OUP 2015) 159–60, 173.

5 Ram Jakhu and Yaw Nyampong, 'International Regulation of Emerging Modes of Space Transportation' in Joseph N Pelton and Ram Jakhu (eds), *Space Safety Regulations and Standards* (Elsevier 2010) 220.

6 Treaty on Principles Governing the Activities of States in the Exploration and Use of Outer Space, Including the Moon and Other Celestial Bodies, *opened for signature* 27 January 1967, 610 UNTS 205 (entered into force 10 October 1967) ('Outer Space Treaty').

7 Vienna Convention on the Law of Treaties, *opened for signature* 23 May 1969, 1155 UNTS 331 (entered into force 27 January 1980) art 31(1) ('VCLT').

8 Vienna Convention on the Law of Treaties (n 7) Art 32.

9 Vienna Convention on the Law of Treaties (n 7) Art 31(3)(c).

10 Vienna Convention on the Law of Treaties (n 7) Art 31(3)(b).

11 UNGAOR, 4th Comm, 5th Sess, 63rd mtg, Summary Record of the 63rd Mtg, UN Doc A/AC.105/c.2/SR/63 (20 October 1966) at 4–5 (UNCOPUOS 63rd Meeting) 10. See discussion of the 'anticipatory' approach in Rossana Deplano, 'The Artemis Accords: Evolution or Revolution in International Space Law' (2021) 70(3) International and Comparative Law Quarterly 799, 813–14.

12 Outer Space Treaty (n 6) Art I.

13 Outer Space Treaty (n 6) Art II.

- registry-state jurisdiction and control over space objects;[14]
- due regard and the avoidance of harmful interference;[15]
- information-sharing requirements;[16] and
- rules regarding visits to facilities on celestial bodies.[17]

Having examined these principles of the Outer Space Treaty, we will then turn to recent practice that provides insights into the emerging, more specific, norms that will be needed to regulate safety zones around SRU activities. In particular, we analyse the 2019 Building Blocks for the Development of an International Framework on Space Resources developed by the (non-government) Hague Space Resources Governance Working Group, relevant provisions of the Artemis Accords signed by civil space agencies in 2020 and subsequently (which, at the time of writing, had 36 states parties),[18] and state contributions across 2022 and 2023 to the Working Group on Legal Aspects of Space Resources Utilization of the UN Committee on the Peaceful Uses of Outer Space (COPUOUS) (Working Group) and the Open-Ended Working Group on Reducing Space Threats Through Norms, Rules and Principles of Responsible Behaviours (OEWG) established by the UN General Assembly.

In light of this recent practice, we conclude that the declaration of safety zones around SRU activities is likely to be lawful, provided that safety zones are declared in such a way as to ensure respect for the key principles of the Outer Space Treaty. We suggest criteria that may be used in considering the nature of any safety zone to be declared and which can serve as a means of determining the legality of potential future safety zones around SRU activities.

2 Outer Space Treaty Principles Relevant to Safety Zones

(a) Freedom of Exploration, Use and Access

> The exploration and use of outer space . . . shall be the province of all mankind . . . Outer space . . . shall be free for exploration and use by all States . . . and there shall be free access to all areas of celestial bodies.[19]

Article I of the Outer Space Treaty thus enshrines the fundamental principles of free exploration, access and use of outer space and celestial bodies by states and their nationals. It is abrogable only in limited circumstances based on principles contained in other parts of the Outer Space Treaty: notably Article II which

14 Outer Space Treaty (n 6) Art VIII.

15 Outer Space Treaty (n 6) Art IX.

16 Outer Space Treaty (n 6) Art IX.

17 Outer Space Treaty (n 6) Art XII.

18 'The Artemis Accords: Principles for Cooperation in the Civil Exploration and Use of the Moon, Mars, Comets, and Asteroids for Peaceful Purposes' *National Aeronautics and Space Administration* (13 October 2020) <https://www.nasa.gov/wp-content/uploads/2022/11/Artemis-Accords-signed-13Oct2020.pdf> ('Artemis Accords').

19 Outer Space Treaty (n 6) Art I.

proscribes the 'national appropriation' of space,[20] and Article III which requires that 'activities in the exploration and use of outer space' be carried on 'in accordance with international law.'[21] The plain wording of the 'free use' principle appears to permit SRU, and this has been accepted by a range of (but certainly not all) states and space law scholars.[22] On this view, Article I is considered to be 'permissive'[23] in that it naturally ought to be interpreted broadly and is only subject to minor limitations, including that found in Article II as well as those articles that prescribe obligations on states to observe the rights and interests of other actors and that bestow quasi-jurisdictional rights over facilities and space objects, for practical and operational reasons. Indeed, Stephan Hobe has expressed the view that the word 'use' in Article I:

> basically means the non-economic and economic use of outer space. . . . the use of outer space for economic ends can include exploitation of outer space and/or the celestial bodies with the goal of making economic profit. . . . freedom of outer space is thus generally granted to exercise economic activities in outer space and on celestial bodies and to profit from these activities. . . . 'use' . . . certainly includes exploitation of outer space and of celestial bodies.[24]

Even more relevant to SRU, Steven Freeland and Ram Jakhu have concluded, 'the exploitation of the natural resources of the moon and other celestial bodies constitutes a "use" of outer space that is contemplated by the freedom principle' in Article I.[25] However, naturally, use and exploration cannot always occur in the same place at one time. This necessitates the development of legal principles surrounding the

20 A. Martin and S Freeland, 'From One to Many: "Mega" (Constellation) Challenges to the Legal Framework for Outer Space' (2021) 46 McGill University Annals of Air & Space Law 131, 139–40; Charles O Brichet, 'Commercial Exploitation: Lessons From the Law of the Sea' (2021) 46 McGill University Annals of Air & Space Law 255, 270–73.

21 Olivier Ribbelink, 'Article III' in Stephan Hobe, Bernhard Schmidt-Tedd and Kai-Uwe Schrogl (eds), *Cologne Commentary on Space Law* (Carl Heymanns Verlag 2009) 64.

22 Micah Hill-Smith, 'Ending Poverty With Space Mining: The Global Space Resources Dividend' (2021) 46 McGill University Annals of Air & Space Law 221, 234; Brichet (n 20) 270–73; Australian Delegation, submission to the Working Group on Legal Aspects of Space Resource Activities, 62nd session of the COPUOS Legal Subcommittee, 20–31 March 2023 UN Doc A/AC.105/C.2/2023/CRP.7, 7; Canadian Delegation, submission to the Working Group on Legal Aspects of Space Resource Activities, 62nd session of the COPUOS Legal Subcommittee, 20–31 March 2023 UN Doc A/AC.105/C.2/2023/CRP.11, 3; Japanese Delegation, submission to the Working Group on Legal Aspects of Space Resource Activities, 62nd session of the COPUOS Legal Subcommittee, 20–31 March 2023 UN Doc A/AC.105/C.2/2023/CRP.33, 2; French Delegation, submission to the Working Group on Legal Aspects of Space Resource Activities, 62nd session of the COPUOS Legal Subcommittee, 20–31 March 2023, UN Doc A/AC.105/C.2/2023/CRP.12, 4.

23 Australian Delegation (n 22) 2; Canadian Delegation (n 22) 3; Japanese Delegation (n 22) 3.

24 Stephan Hobe, 'Article I' in Stephan Hobe, Bernhard Schmidt-Tedd and Kai-Uwe Schrogl (eds), *Cologne Commentary on Space Law* (Carl Heymanns Verlag 2009) 25, 35.

25 Steven Freeland and Ram Jakhu, 'Article II' in Stephan Hobe, Bernhard Schmidt-Tedd and Kai-Uwe Schrogl (eds), *Cologne Commentary on Space Law* (Carl Heymanns Verlag 2009) 44, 53.

deconfliction of an outer space environment where all states and private actors are permitted to use, access and explore all parts of space. It begs the question of how to avoid conflicts regarding the placement of space infrastructure such as stations, equipment and other facilities whilst maintaining these freedoms.[26] The Outer Space Treaty provides the following principles to guide states parties in the deconfliction of activities carried out in the exercise of their freedoms in outer space.

- *Non-Appropriation*

There has been significant debate over the legality and permissible scope of SRU as regards Article II's non-appropriation principle. UNCOPUOS material demonstrates that it is a relatively widely held belief among states that SRU, even for commercial purposes, is merely curtailed (and not proscribed) by the Outer Space Treaty.[27] We agree with Freeland and Jakhu that the 'primary intent' of Article II is to confirm 'that principles of territorial sovereignty do not apply to outer space.'[28] Our concern in this chapter is with deconfliction and constraining access to certain areas of celestial bodies. Generally, our view (which we expand upon later) is that whilst Article II proscribes 'national appropriation,' it will not prevent the lawful exercise of jurisdiction over objects in outer space, nor will it proscribe the construction of facilities on celestial bodies and the establishment of safety zones around such facilities, so long as they are established for legitimate purposes.[29] It is possible that a safety zone could abrogate the non-appropriation principle in effect if it is not framed consistently with the legitimate and lawful bases enumerated in the articles discussed later.

- *Registry-State Jurisdiction and Control Over Space Objects*

Article VIII provides that a state party shall retain jurisdiction and control over space objects on its registry, and over any personnel thereof, while in outer space or on a celestial body. This article permits a state to exercise a level of prescriptive

---

The authors do note, however, that such 'use' may have limits if it threatens to exploit a celestial body 'out of existence.'

26 For example see Russian Delegation, submission to the Working Group on Legal Aspects of Space Resource Activities, 62nd session of the COPUOS Legal Subcommittee, 20–31 March 2023 UN Doc A/AC.105/C.2/2023/CRP.20, 4, 7.

27 Australian Delegation (n 22) 6–7. See also commentary on draft law in Luxembourg Delegation, submission to the Working Group on Legal Aspects of Space Resource Activities, 62nd session of the COPUOS Legal Subcommittee, 20–31 March 2023, UN Doc A/AC.105/C.2/2023/CRP.16, 6; see also the domestic law cited in Japanese Delegation (n 22) 2–3. See also New Zealand Delegation, submission to the Working Group on Legal Aspects of Space Resource Activities, 62nd session of the COPUOS Legal Subcommittee, 20–31 March 2023, UN Doc A/AC.105/C.2/2023/CRP.18, 2.

28 Freeland and Jakhu (n 25) 48.

29 Lachlan Blake, 'Jurisdiction on the Final Frontier: Facilities, Jurisdiction and Control in International Space Law' (2022) 46 McGill University Annals of Air & Space Law 188–89; see Russian Delegation (n 26) 6–7.

and enforcement jurisdiction over and within a space object on its registry and therefore represents another fetter on the free use of outer space.[30] That is, states may prescribe and enforce the nature and type of activities occurring within and on space objects that are on their registry. Beyond this, Article VIII does not provide much practical basis upon which rules surrounding deconfliction of space activities may be developed. First, that is because it applies only to 'space objects,' being objects launched into space. Moreover, it applies to the object itself, including its surface and interior, and not to activities occurring in the object's immediate surrounds.[31] Second, an Article VIII 'space object' is arguably distinguishable from objects permanently located on, or constructed upon, a celestial body. Such space infrastructure is dealt with in Article XII.[32] Those facilities are subject to distinct deconfliction rules, which are discussed later. It is relevant to note here that this deliberate distinction was inserted by the drafters, who expressly contemplated whether 'platforms' in orbit around celestial bodies would be subject to the principles contained in Article XII.[33] The drafters concluded that only facilities located on a celestial body on an ongoing or permanent basis would be subject to Article XII.

- *Due Regard and the Avoidance of Harmful Interference*

Article IX obliges states to conduct activities in outer space with 'due regard' for the 'corresponding interests' of all other parties to the Outer Space Treaty, and to avoid 'harmful contamination' through the adoption of necessary and appropriate measures. It further provides that states shall 'undertake appropriate international consultations' before proceeding with activities that may cause 'potentially harmful interference' with the activities of other states parties. The purpose of these consultations is implicitly to ensure that states take 'appropriate preventive measures to avoid such harm' where possible,[34] and in our view the parties to any consultation would at a minimum have to display good faith in seeking to avoid

30 Dale Stephens and Lachlan Blake, 'Good Fences Make Good (Space) Neighbours' (2021) 8(2) Griffith Journal of Law and Human Dignity 213, 220–22; Blake (n 29) 197–98. See discussion of these principles in respect of the ISS Agreement in Stacy J Ratner, 'Establishing the Extraterrestrial: Criminal Jurisdiction and the International Space Station' (1999) 22(2) Boston College International and Comparative Law Review 330–32; Cestmir Cepelka and Jamie HC Gilmour, 'The Application of General International Law in Outer Space' (1970) 36(1) Journal of Air Law & Commerce 30, 34–35; Imre Anthony Csafabi, *The Concept of State Jurisdiction in International Space Law: A Study in the Progressive Development of Space Law in the United Nations* (Martinus Nijhoff 1971) 113; Ogunsola O Ogunbanwo, *International Law and Outer Space Activities* (Martinus Nijhoff 1975) 80.

31 Blake (n 29) 197; Stephens and Blake (n 30) 220–21 See also United States Delegation, submission to the Working Group on Legal Aspects of Space Resource Activities, 62nd session of the COPUOS Legal Subcommittee, 20–31 March 2023, UN Doc A/AC.105/C.2/2023/CRP.37, 3.

32 Blake (n 29) 196–200; Stephens and Blake (n 30) 221–22.

33 Blake (n 29) 196; Stephens and Blake (n 30) 221–22.

34 Sergio Marchisio, 'Article IX' in Stephan Hobe, Bernhard Schmidt-Tedd and Kai-Uwe Schrogl (eds), *Cologne Commentary on Space Law* (Carl Heymanns Verlag 2009) 169, 180.

harm.[35] This article provides important insights into how activities conducted in space, including the construction of space infrastructure such as stations located on celestial bodies, can occur whilst maintaining the general principle of free access, exploration and use. Sergio Marchisio has expressed the view that the 'due regard' obligation in Article IX means:

> Outer space is to be explored and used with due diligence . . . taking into account the interests and rights of other States. States are bound to ensure that the exercise of their rights and freedoms in outer space does not interfere with, or compromise the safety of, space operations.[36]

Further, statements made in the drafting process indicate that the obligation of 'due regard' was intended as a means of balancing the rights and interests of different states.[37] Thus, the Japanese representative supported an earlier version of Article IX, explaining, 'Freedom in the use of outer space should be recognized in so far as it did not prejudice the interests of other States in the peaceful uses of outer space.'[38] Similar observations were made more generally during discussions. For example, the representative of Morocco observed, 'the interests of each nation and of the international community as a whole must be protected against any abuse,'[39] and the Czechoslovakian representative stated, 'the activities of one country should not endanger those of others in outer space.'[40]

From the treaty's plain wording the principle of due regard would entail a positive duty to understand the nature and location of other states' interests and activities in space, to plan activities in space with respect for those interests and to consult other states where those interests may be interfered with.[41] In a similar vein, Carpanelli posits that the principle of due regard contains within it several procedural duties, including duties to 'undertake appropriate consultation'; 'cooperate'; and 'undertake a prior impact assessment.'[42] While they are correctly characterised as a

35 See for example *Affaire du lac Lanoux (France v Spain)* (1957) 12 RIAA 281, 307: 'sanctions can be applied in the event, for example, of an unjustified breaking off of the discussions, abnormal delays, disregard of the agreed procedures, systematic refusals to take into consideration adverse proposals or interests.' See also *Tacna-Arica Question* (*Chile v Peru*) (1925) 2 RIAA 921, 929–30; *Case of Railway Traffic Between Lithuania and Poland (Railway Sector Landwarów-Kaisiadorys)* (Advisory Opinion) (1931) PCIJ Series A/B, No 42, 108, 116.

36 Marchisio (n 34) 175.

37 Blake (n 29) 201–2; Elana Carpanelli, 'Unweaving the Tangled Web: The Due Regard Obligation Under Article IX of the Outer Space Treaty' (2024) 49(1) Air & Space Law 35, 42; Cepelka and Gilmour (n 30) 33–34; Walker A Smith, 'Using the Artemis Accords to Build Customary International Law: A Vision for a U.S.-Centric Good Governance Regime in Space' (2021) 86(4) Journal of Air Law and Commerce 661, 685–86; See also French Delegation (n 22) 3–4.

38 UN Doc A/AC.105/C.2/SR.22 (24 April 1963) (Japan).

39 UN Doc A/AC.105/C.2/SR.24 (29 April 1963) (Morocco).

40 UN Doc A/AC.105/C.2/SR.28 (3 May 1963) (Czechoslovakia).

41 Melissa de Zwart, Stacey Henderson and Michelle Neumann, 'Space Resource Activities and the Evolution of International Space Law' (2023) 211 Acta Astronautica 155, 157.

42 Elana Carpanelli (n 37) 48–55.

'genuine innovation in space law,'[43] safety zones are a suitable and adapted mechanism for implementing and operationalising the principles of Article IX. These zones would permit states to notify other states of their ongoing activities in areas of space and coordinate movement through and use of space in those areas.[44] In that way, states may understand and have due regard for their corresponding interests, avoid harmful interference and engage in consultations in respect of those interests. In any event, Article IX circumscribes the activities permitted in the exercise of Article I freedoms. States must not only exercise reasonable care in preventing interference in the activities of other states but must respect the interests and rights of other states to conduct activities, including SRU, in space.

- *Information Sharing*

Article XI provides for a practical mechanism for deconfliction of space activities. It stipulates that states will make information regarding the nature, conduct and locations of activities occurring in space (necessarily including SRU activities) available to a central registry.[45] The purpose of Article XI, as noted by Jean-François Mayence and Thomas Reuter, is 'to promote international cooperation.'[46] As they observe, the value of Article XI lies in its emphasis on 'the importance of exchanges of information as the key element for a smooth and harmonious international co-operation in outer space.'[47] There is some obvious synergy here with Articles IX and XII. States naturally must share information as to the nature, location and scope of their activities and facilities in space in order to perform their obligations under the due regard and non-interference principles found in those articles. As we will demonstrate later, states increasingly mention Article XI in their deliberations and submissions to the UN Committee on the Peaceful Uses of Outer Space (UNCOPUOS) as a key principle in operationalising the Outer Space Treaty and in promoting the deconfliction of outer space activities.[48]

- *Visits to Facilities*

Article XII is another mechanism by which states may seek to deconflict their space activities. It provides that 'stations, installations, equipment and space vehicles' on the moon and other celestial bodies shall be open to visitation by other states parties 'on a basis of reciprocity.'[49] The article helpfully articulates some

43 Deplano (n 11) 808–9.

44 Mike Gold, 'Artemis Accords—Enabling International Partnerships for Lunar Exploration' (U.S. Department of State, Foreign Press Center, 15 May 2020) 5.

45 Outer Space Treaty (n 6) Art XI.

46 Jean-François Mayence and Thomas Reuter, 'Article XI' in Stephan Hobe, Bernhard Schmidt-Tedd and Kai-Uwe Schrogl (eds), *Cologne Commentary on Space Law* (Carl Heymanns Verlag 2009) 189, 197.

47 Mayence and Reuter (n 46) 206.

48 See discussion later at page 179.

49 Outer Space Treaty (n 6) art XII.

practical considerations in respect of such visits, including that 'appropriate consultations' must be held prior to any visit, and that 'maximum precautions' be taken to 'assure safety and to avoid interference with normal operations in the facility to be visited.'[50] The negotiations surrounding the development of this article make clear that the principle of free access and open facilities may be tempered by a number of considerations, which in effect allow states to restrict access to space infrastructure. The employment of safety zones, encompassing a reasonable area surrounding a facility for the purposes of safety and non-interference, is a reasonable and adapted measure for states to observe their rights and responsibilities under this article.[51] As will be discussed later in this chapter, the Russian delegation to UNCOPUOS seemingly foreshadowed these considerations by referring to 'infrastructure facilities' when stating that freedom to explore and access all areas of outer space must necessarily be tempered in certain circumstances:

> Certain space resources, such as areas of the lunar surface favorable to the placing of space infrastructure facilities in exploitation projects, might be limited, that is, finite. Consequently, space resources can be limited either in terms of volume or in terms of location, to which access is limited.[52]

The drafters of Article XII emphasised that safety and non-interference must be ensured through the employment of 'maximum precautions.'[53] This language implies a strict standard and guides the interpretation of the priorities to be observed in the avoidance of interference.[54] It suggests that states may deny access to areas (or perhaps a reasonable safety zone around the area in question) in space in the interests of safety and maintaining normal operations of state facilities in such areas (including, necessarily, SRU activities). This naturally implies that states may 'close' their installations to other states if maximum precautions cannot or will not be guaranteed. It would also imply that visitation by other states may be geographically restricted in circumstances where visits to an existing operation may justifiably raise safety concerns or interfere in the activities conducted by a state in a given facility.[55]

Two statements which ultimately led to the deletion of the words 'at all times' from the free access provision by the Soviet delegate, Mr Morozov, are particularly instructive.[56] First, the peculiar circumstances attending space operations presented practical safety and operational considerations in respect of the timing of visits such that the USSR 'could not agree that a space vehicle must open its doors at

50 Outer Space Treaty (n 6) art XII.
51 Stephens and Blake (n 30) 224–25; Blake (n 29) 214.
52 Russian Delegation (n 26) 6–7.
53 Blake (n 29) 209, 213; Summary Record of the 64th Meeting, UN GAOR, 4th Comm, 5th session, 64th mtg UN Doc A/AC.105/C.2/SR.64 (24 October 1966) 7 ('UN COPUOS 64th Meeting') 8.
54 Blake (n 29) 209, 213; Stephens and Blake (n 30) 223–24.
55 Stephens and Blake (n 30) 223; Blake (n 29) 195, 209; UNCOPUOS 64th Meeting (n 53) 6–7.
56 See UNCOPUOS 63rd Meeting (n 11) 5–7. See discussion in Blake (n 29) 210–13.

any time, without regard to the measures that might have to be taken to ensure the safety of the crew and the normal operation of installations.'[57] Second, 'even on earth' it was customary for visits to 'be preceded by agreement between the guest and the host and in the extremely difficult conditions of outer space such a rule was especially important from the viewpoint of the safety of personnel in space vehicles and installations.'[58]

Moreover, Article XII states that space infrastructure shall be open on the 'basis of reciprocity.'[59] The drafters considered that this may provide a ground for the denial of access by states into certain areas of space where, for example, there is a 'poor international relationship' between the owning and visiting states, where a state 'was affected by the refusal of another State to grant access' or where a state lacks an interest in engaging in visits to similar facilities and installations of other states.[60] Mr Vici, the Italian representative, suggested that if the intention of the drafters was to disallow these interpretations, 'free access should be allowed at any time' and 'it should therefore be specified that access to all [facilities] would be allowed at all times.'[61] This discussion continued, with delegations highlighting the importance of safety and non-interference over that of free access at all times, with Mr Morozov stating that it seemed 'physically difficult to apply' the expression 'at all times,' and that visitation of facilities would be better effected if treated as 'a matter simply of agreeing on a date for a visit, to suit the convenience of the host Government and the visitor.'[62] Ultimately, the Soviet draft text was adopted, and no expression regarding 'free access at all times' was included in Article XII.

While it is important not to overstate the strength of the obligation contained in Article XII (which is strikingly weak compared with inspection obligations in arms control contexts),[63] it is significant for understanding the deconfliction of space activities for two reasons. First, it demonstrates that visits to facilities can be an important part of cooperation to ensure that space activities do not conflict with each other. Second, its drafting history suggests that states accepted the idea that Article I's freedom of access would be limited where appropriate to ensure the safe operation of particular facilities. The relevance of these points to the declaration of safety zones around SRU activities will be further explored later.

57 UNCOPUOS 63rd Meeting (n 11) 6–7.

58 UNCOPUOS 63rd Meeting (n 11) 5.

59 Francesco Paris and Nita Chei, 'The Role of Reciprocity in International Law' (2003) 33(1) Cornell International Law Journal 93; Robert O Keohane, 'Reciprocity in International Relations' (1986) 40(1) *International Organization* 1.

60 UNCOPUOS 63rd Meeting (n 11) 6–7; UNCOPUOS 64th Meeting (n 53) 6–7.

61 UNCOPUOS 64th Meeting (n 53) 4–5.

62 UNCOPUOS 64th Meeting (n 53) 9–10.

63 For example, Treaty Between the United States of America and the Union of Soviet Socialist Republics on the Elimination of Their Intermediate-Range and Shorter-Range Missiles, opened for signature 8 December 1987, 1657 UNTS 2 (entered into force 1 June 1988) ('INF Treaty'); Antarctic Treaty, opened for signature 1 December 1959, 402 UNTS 71 (entered into force 23 June 1961) art VII. For further discussion of this point see Blake (n 29) 206–7.

Taken together, the articles of the Outer Space Treaty that we have analysed in this section envisage an outer space environment in which states must recognise rights to engage in space activity without interference and provide both impetus and guidance for the establishment of safety zones as a practical means of deconflicting space activities. In particular, rules established by states parties in developing standards to maintain safety and non-interference in normal operations of facilities in giving effect to Article XII rights and obligations will be relevant when states are implementing the principle of due regard under Article IX. It is against this background of relevant principles found in the Outer Space Treaty that we next set out to examine emerging state practice that demonstrates how these principles might support and constrain the declaration of safety zones around SRU activities.

3 Emerging State Practice Regarding Safety Zones

(a) International Space Station

One instance in which steps have been taken towards identifying a safety zone in outer space (albeit not on a celestial body) concerns the international space station (ISS).[64] Two complementary zones have been prescribed in order to avoid collisions and manage safety concerns—a 200 m 'Keep-Out Sphere' around the ISS centre-of-mass, and a 4 km by 2 km 'Approach Ellipsoid' outside which visiting space vehicles may initiate an approach to the ISS but must comply with orbit trajectory and timing requirements prior to entering the ellipsoid.[65] These zones delimit an area within which permission is required for visiting space vehicles to enter. 'Defined corridors' for approach are prescribed and a vehicle may not move 'closer than 6 feet to any ISS structure' and must comply with specific requirements for capture of approaching vehicles and ISS attachment points.[66]

Whilst little has been officially stated as regards their legality, these zones can be taken as state practice under the Outer Space Treaty, particularly in respect of Articles IX and XI. Their purpose is to share information regarding the location of space vehicles (manned and unmanned) in the vicinity of the ISS and to effect due regard obligations in the interests of maintaining safety and avoiding collisions. This use of specific delimitation measurements is presently unique in state practice in outer space, and the physical scope and ongoing duration of these zones appear to be well adapted in the context of the ISS.

64 Stubbs (n 4) 199, 199.

65 Rebecca Reesman and Andrew Rogers, 'Getting in Your Space: Learning From Past Rendezvous and Proximity Operations', Center for Space Policy and Strategy (2018) 5, citing Al Dupont, 'ISS Rendezvous, Proximity Operations, Docking, and Berthing Considerations' NAZA/JSC/Aeroscience and Flight Mechanics Division (2015); Lucas Mallowan, Lucien Rapp and Maria Topka, *Reinventing Treaty Compliant 'Safety Zones' in the Context of Space Sustainability'* (Elsevier 2021) 11–12; Diane Koons and others, *Risk Mitigation Approach to Commercial Resupply to the International Space Station* (NASA 2010) 4.

66 Reesman and Rogers (n 65) 5.

(b) The Hague Building Blocks

One source of potential future norms relating to SRU are the Building Blocks for the Development of an International Framework on Space Resources ('Building Blocks') published in 2019 by The Hague Space Resources Governance Working Group.[67] It is important to note that these Building Blocks are not the product of state views on the law but represent the outcome of several years of deliberations in a civil society initiative led by the Institute of Air and Space Law at Leiden University. Their value lies not in any legal status in themselves but as an example of expert views about how the law relating to SRU may develop. This value has not gone unnoticed by states, with many delegations to the COPUOS Legal Subcommittee citing The Hague Building Blocks as useful guidance (particularly in respect of the rules surrounding jurisdiction in space, the responsibility for space activities and the definition of space resources contained in The Hague Building Blocks).[68] It can be inferred that at least some states broadly concur with the principles put forth in The Hague Building Blocks (as well as the Artemis Accords, discussed later): indeed, as we address further later, Australia, the Netherlands and Austria (the first two of whom are parties to the Artemis Accords) submitted a guidance document for the development of deconfliction measures, citing the Artemis Accords as well as the Building Blocks.[69] The critical passage in the Building Blocks would permit:

> States and international organizations responsible for space resource activities to establish *a safety zone*, or other area-based safety measure, around an area identified for a space resource activity as necessary to assure safety and to *avoid any harmful interference* with that space resource activity. Such safety measure shall *not impede the free access*, in accordance with international law, to any area of outer space by personnel, vehicles and equipment of another operator. In accordance with the area-based safety measure, a State or international organization may *restrict access for a limited period of time*, provided that *timely public notice* has been given setting out the reasons for such restriction.[70]

A number of points may be made about this statement. First, the ability to declare a safety zone is expressly linked to the obligation under Article IX of the Outer Space Treaty to avoid harmful interference. While this does not give any indication of how the principles of due regard and the avoidance of harmful interference shape safety zones, it does suggest that they will do so. Second, the suggestion that a safety zone could not impede free access appears to suggest a special understanding of

67 De Zwart, Henderson and Neumann (n 41) 159; Stubbs (n 4) 225.

68 See Draft Report of the Legal Subcommittee on its 62nd session, 31 May–9 June 2023, UN Doc AC.105/L.332.Add.3 (13 April 2023), [174]–[175]. Australian Delegation (n 22) 7. See also building blocks annexed to Belgian Delegation (n 103) 5–6; Luxembourg Delegation (n 27) 3, 7; French Delegation (n 22) 3.

69 Australian, Austrian and Netherlands Delegations (n 22).

70 The Hague Building Blocks (n 1) [11.3] (emphasis added).

free access. However, the statement does point to temporal limitations as being an important feature of safety zones, which may be the means through which compliance with the free access principle is maintained. While the Building Blocks have no legal status, they do suggest the views of some relevant actors as to possible future norms.

(c) Artemis Accords

More significant as an indicator of state practice are the Artemis Accords. In form, the Artemis Accords are a non-binding 'political commitment' between 'civil space agencies.'[71] However, they are also expressly intended to:

> establish a common vision via a practical set of principles, guidelines, and best practices . . . increase the safety of operations, reduce uncertainty, and promote the sustainable and beneficial use of space for all humankind.[72]

This language points to a potential normative function. Moreover, the Artemis Accords have grown rapidly from eight original parties in 2020[73] to 36 parties as of February 2024. Their value as an indication of state practice is already significant and will grow as states put these commitments into practice. Reinforcing that significance, the Legal Subcommittee of COPUOS noted that many delegations considered that the Artemis Accords (having reached 23 signatory states by the time of the 62nd session), provided 'clear, non-legally binding guidance for space exploration and established a useful set of principles based on the Outer Space Treaty.'[74] The continuing increase in the number of parties to the Artemis Accords further underlines their importance.

Section 11 of the Artemis Accords addresses 'Deconfliction of Space Activities.' The section begins by expressly linking deconfliction to Article IX of the Outer Space treaty and the concepts of due regard and the avoidance of harmful interference.[75] Article XI is also invoked in respect of information-sharing and transparency obligations.[76] Section 11 of the Artemis Accords goes on to state, '[t]he Signatories intend to use their experience under the Accords to . . . further develop international practices, criteria, and rules applicable to the definition and determination of safety zones.'[77] The Artemis Accords then outline in more detail the legal basis and structure of safety zones, making several important points. First, there is a definition: a safety zone is 'the area wherein' parties will 'provide notification of

71 Artemis Accords (n 18) s 1. See, e.g., Rachel Neef, 'Artemis Accords: A New Path Forward for Space Lawmaking?' (2021) 42(2) Adelaide Law Review 569.

72 Artemis Accords (n 18) s 1. Neef (n 71).

73 Australia, Canada, Italy, Japan, Luxembourg, UAE, UK, USA.

74 Draft Report of the Legal Subcommittee (n 68) [32], see also [185].

75 Artemis Accords (n 18) s 11(1).

76 Artemis Accords (n 18) s 11(7)(d); Deplano (n 11) 802–3, 808. See also Gold (n 44) 5.

77 Artemis Accords (n 18) s 11(6).

their activities and commit to coordinating with any relevant actor to avoid harmful interference.'[78] This again expressly links safety zones to Article IX of the Outer Space Treaty. Second, a safety zone will be defined by the extent of potential harmful interference—the Artemis Accords indicate, '[a] safety zone should be the area in which nominal operations of a relevant activity or an anomalous event *could reasonably cause harmful interference*.'[79] Moreover, '[t]he Signatory establishing, maintaining, or ending a safety zone should do so in a manner that protects public and private personnel, equipment, and operations from harmful interference.'[80]

The parties to the Artemis Accords then commit to observing a range of 'principles related to safety zones.' Third, insofar as the 'size and scope of the safety zone' is concerned, this should 'be determined in a *reasonable manner* leveraging commonly accepted scientific and engineering principles' and 'reflect the nature of the operations being conducted and the environment that such operations are conducted in.'[81] Fourth, safety zones should change in response to conditions and be temporary:

> The nature and existence of safety zones is expected to change over time reflecting the status of the relevant operation. If the nature of an operation changes, the operating Signatory should alter the size and scope of the corresponding safety zone as appropriate. *Safety zones will ultimately be temporary*, ending when the relevant operation ceases.[82] . . . safety zones . . . will be expected to change, evolve, or end based on the status of the specific activity.[83]

Fifth, the parties recognise a range of notification and information-sharing requirements. Thus, they should 'promptly notify each other as well as the Secretary-General of the United Nations of the establishment, alteration, or end of any safety zone,'[84] 'upon request . . . provide any Signatory with the basis for the area'[85] and 'make relevant information regarding such safety zones, including the extent and general nature of operations taking place within them, available to the public as soon as practicable and feasible.'[86] There is also an express obligation of notification and coordination regarding activities: signatories commit to 'providing prior notification to and coordinating with each other before conducting operations in a safety zone.'[87]

78 Artemis Accords (n 18) s 11(7).
79 Artemis Accords (n 18) s 11(7) (emphasis added).
80 Artemis Accords (n 18) s 11(9).
81 Artemis Accords (n 18) s 11(7)(a) and (b) (emphasis added).
82 Artemis Accords (n 18) s 11(7)(c) (emphasis added).
83 Artemis Accords (n 18) s 11(11).
84 Artemis Accords (n 18) s 11(7)(d).
85 Artemis Accords (n 18) s 11(8).
86 Artemis Accords (n 18) s 11(9).
87 Artemis Accords (n 18) s 11(10).

Sixth, signatories may use safety zones, 'in a manner that encourages scientific discovery and technology demonstration, as well as the safe and efficient extraction and utilization of space resources in support of sustainable space exploration and other operations. . . . [and] respect the principle of free access to all areas of celestial bodies.'[88] Seventh, the parties 'commit to respect reasonable safety zones to avoid harmful interference with operations.'[89] These quite detailed provisions relating to safety zones advance our understanding of the potential norms governing the declaration of safety zones around SRU activities on celestial bodies. They maintain the link to Article IX of the Outer Space Treaty and its principles of due regard and harmful interference, as well as to Article XI's information-sharing requirements. They further stress factors going to deconfliction so as to enable a range of different activities to co-exist as far as possible, including notification and information-sharing requirements, and to limit safety zones to what is reasonable in order to protect against harmful interference. Factors that would limit safety zones are also taken into account—not merely through the link to harmful interference, but also through emphasis on the temporally limited nature of safety zones, the necessity of their being updated as circumstances change, the indication that these are not keep-out zones but instead zones within which coordination of activities is required, and that the principle of free access shall be respected.

Notwithstanding the increasing number of parties, opposition to the Artemis Accords from some states must also be noted. One (anonymous) delegation to the COPUOS Legal Subcommittee explicitly repudiated the concept of 'exclusionary safety zones around space resource installations' and described national measures purporting to 'legalize' the national appropriation of space resources as not being recognised as legitimate by the 'international community.'[90] Some delegations considered that an assumption of legal permissibility and the unilateral approach represented by the Artemis Accords could create monopolies and would go against the spirit of the Outer Space Treaty and, potentially, international customary law.[91]

(d) Working Group on Space Resource Activities

Comments of some significance to safety zones around SRU activities have also been made in materials related to the COPUOS Working Group on Legal Aspects of Space Resource Activities (Working Group). The goal of the Working Group is to explore the application of the existing international space law regime to SRU

88 Artemis Accords (n 18) s 11(11).
89 Artemis Accords (n 18) s 11(10).
90 Draft Report of the Legal Subcommittee (n 68) [171]. See discussion concerning Chinese and Russian opposition to the Accords in Walker A Smith (n 37) 694–98 and the citations therein.
91 See Draft Report of the Legal Subcommittee (n 68) [189], [190].

and consider the development of a further legal framework specifically for SRU.[92] From some of this material, we can infer states' views about the future development of deconfliction norms in space law. The Draft Report of the Legal Subcommittee[93] foreshadows agreements and rifts in states' legal opinions regarding the sufficiency of the existing space law regime and attendant legal principles to render SRU and related activities, including establishing safety zones, both lawful and practical. This section analyses developments in respect of the deconfliction of SRU activities.

Statements to the Working Group have largely supported the view that SRU is consistent with the Article II non-appropriation principle. In its submission to the Working Group, the US delegation reiterated its position that SRU does not breach the non-appropriation principle under Article II of the Outer Space Treaty[94] and that the existing robust principles contained within the current international space law regime, as well as non-binding instruments (in particular, the Artemis Accords) were sufficient to support novel SRU activities.[95] The Chinese Delegation also considered that 'the exploration, exploitation and utilization of space resources [is] in conformity with the principle of non-appropriation' which ought to be considered by the Legal Subcommittee in order to operationalise the article's application to various SRU activities.[96]

The Outer Space Treaty principles most commonly cited by states expressing similar views to the Legal Subcommittee were the same as those cited in the Artemis Accords, namely 'free exploration and use, non-appropriation, protection of the outer space environment, and the observance of due regard for the corresponding interests of all other States parties.'[97] The US delegation also restated its long-standing position that the non-appropriation principle in Article II is tempered by other articles, including the deconfliction principles found in Articles VIII, IX and XI.[98] This approach was mirrored by other Artemis Accords signatory delegations. The Australian delegation expressed the view that the Outer Space Treaty contained 'permissive' terms as described previously.[99] The Canadian delegation similarly described Article I as a broad right subject to minor limitations found

92 UNCOPUOS 64th Meeting (n 53) 61–62. See discussion of the Working Group in De Zwart, Henderson and Neumann (n 41) at 159.

93 Draft Report of the Legal Subcommittee (n 68).

94 US Delegation (n 31) 3–4.

95 US Delegation (n 31) 4.

96 Chinese Delegation, submission to the Working Group on Legal Aspects of Space Resource Activities, 62nd session of the COPUOS Legal Subcommittee, 20–31 March 2023, UN Doc A/AC.105/C.2/2024/CRP.5, 2.

97 See Report of the Legal Subcommittee on its 62nd Session, 13 April 2023, AC.105.1285, 27—28 [196], [198] (Report of the Legal Subcommittee). See similar statements from the Greek Delegation's submission to the Working Group on Legal Aspects of Space Resource Activities, 62nd session of the COPUOS Legal Subcommittee, 20–31 March 2023, UN Doc A/AC.105/C.2/2024/CRP.14; Chinese Delegation (n 96) 2. See reference to Art I in Japanese Delegation (n 22) 2. See US Delegation (n 31) 3–6.

98 US Delegation (n 31) 2–3.

99 Australian Delegation (n 22) 2.

under Articles II and IX and that the Outer Space Treaty therefore contemplated lawful SRU activities.[100] The French delegation stated, 'France considers that the [Outer Space Treaty] fully applies to [SRU].'[101] Further, the Japanese delegation similarly expressed that the exploration, development and use of space resources fell within the freedom contained within Article I.[102]

However, some states opposed the US approach in respect of non-appropriation and free access and use. The Belgian delegation implied that the application of national laws to space may have a 'territorial basis' and that an overly permissive interpretation of the Outer Space Treaty would, among other things, 'render Article II largely meaningless.'[103] The Russian delegation stressed the urgent need to clarify rules surrounding the legal basis for use of territories on celestial bodies and how the principle of free access applies to 'the placement of space infrastructure.'[104] This foreshadows a new focus on deconfliction in respect of space infrastructure and the activities that such infrastructure permits.

Whilst concerns remain among a minority of states, it is clear that the majority view is that Article II does not proscribe SRU, nor attendant deconfliction measures, but maintains its importance in preventing states from claiming territorial sovereignty in outer space. Article IX has gained in prominence in state discussions surrounding SRU. Whilst no definitive statements were made within the Working Group, and there is still a lack of cohesion among states as to the practical implications of the article, many states regard Article IX as providing a basis to develop legal and policy frameworks for deconfliction.[105] Germany, for instance, put forth 'due regard and conflict prevention, including a potential framework for dispute resolution' as a 'pressing' topic that must be addressed at the UNCOPUOS.[106] Similarly, the Chinese delegation referred to Article IX in the context of 'enhancing the coordination of Space Resources Activities,' stating that the article would be important in deconflicting 'certain specific areas of the Moon' that would be targeted for SRU activities.[107] The Chinese Delegation emphasised the importance of the article in promoting coordination and 'safe and orderly conduct' in these areas.[108] This would seem to compound the importance of safety zones in

100 Canadian Delegation (n 22) 3.
101 French Delegation (n 22) 4.
102 Japanese Delegation (n 22) 2.
103 Belgian Delegation, submission to the Working Group on Legal Aspects of Space Resource Activities, 62nd session of the COPUOS Legal Subcommittee, 20–31 March 2023, UN Doc A/AC.105/C.2/2023/CRP.35, 2–3.
104 Russian Delegation (n 26) 6–7.
105 See Draft Report of the Legal Subcommittee (n 68) 27–28. See reference to these principles in Belgian Delegation (n 103) at 5; Canadian Delegation (n 22) 3; German Delegation, submission to the Working Group on Legal Aspects of Space Resource Activities, 62nd session of the COPUOS Legal Subcommittee, 20–31 March 2023, UN Doc A/AC.105/C.2/2023/CRP.13, 5; Japanese Delegation (n 22) 2; US Delegation (n 31) 3. For an analysis of OEWG statements in 2022 see Carpanelli (n 37) 53–54.
106 German Delegation (n 105) 4, 5.
107 Chinese Delegation (n 96) 3.
108 Chinese Delegation (n 96) 3.

practically implementing Article IX in respect of SRU activities in specific, resource-rich areas in space. Further, it may indicate that China is relaxing its apparent opposition to the United States' interpretation of the principle of due regard as regards SRU under the Artemis Accords.[109]

Information sharing has also continued to expand in importance, with states expressing the need for the development of information-sharing practices under Article XI of the Outer Space Treaty.[110] The Legal Subcommittee's decisions and recommendations paper emphasised the need to develop a 'standardized way to submit information under Article XI of the Outer Space Treaty' and recommended that 'the development of dedicated tools and practices should be considered.'[111] Further, the draft report of the 62nd session noted that states engaging in SRU 'should engage in the systematic and regular sharing of information on the scope, nature and location of their space resource activities,' both for transparency and so that these activities complied with the Outer Space Treaty and general international law.[112] This is an oblique reference to the principles of due regard and non-interference discussed earlier, and perhaps also to the prominence states give to the principle of information sharing under Article XI to the deconfliction of SRU activities. Instructively, Australia, Austria and the Netherlands jointly submitted a comparative study concerning the relevant articles of The Hague Building Blocks, Artemis Accords, Outer Space Treaty and *Moon Agreement* to be used in guiding the development of principles surrounding SRU to the Working Group.[113] These principles were considered by the three submitting states as important guidance for the development of a broader legal framework for deconfliction and to contain broad and mutually reconcilable themes that reflected the wording of the two citied treaties.[114] This paper noted the provisions relating to safety zones in both the Building Blocks and the Artemis Accords.[115] Safety zones were also expressly addressed in the paper submitted by Luxembourg.[116]

Finally, the US noted that Article VIII ownership rights will extend to 'equipment' in space, and stated, 'noninterference rights flow from those ownership interests even though they will not acquire ownership interests in the ground beneath

109 Walker A Smith (n 37) 698.

110 See Draft Report of the Legal Subcommittee (n 68) at [72], [177]–[180], [198]. See also the Romanian Delegation proposal to the Working Group of the Whole, 61st session of the COPUOS Science and Technical Subcommittee, 29 January–9 February 2024, UN Doc A/AC.105/C.1/2024/CRP.30; German Delegation (n 105) 4; US Delegation (n 31) 2.

111 Draft Report of the Legal Subcommittee (n 68) [12].

112 Draft Report of the Legal Subcommittee (n 68) at [176].

113 Australian, Austrian and Netherlands Delegations, 'Relevant considerations for developing a set of initial recommended principles for the exploration, exploitation and utilisation of space resources' (submission to the Working Group on Legal Aspects of Space Resource Activities, 62nd session of the COPUOS Legal Subcommittee, 20 March 2023) UN Doc A/AC.105/C.2/2023/CRP.6, 3.

114 Australian, Austrian and Netherlands Delegations (n 113).

115 Australian, Austrian and Netherlands Delegations (n 113) 18–19.

116 Luxembourg Delegation (n 27) 7.

their equipment.'[117] These statements indicate an understanding that 'equipment' in outer space constitutes both an Article VIII 'space object' and 'equipment' for the purposes of Article XII (with attendant 'non-interference rights'). Moreover, this statement justifies the inference that states consider areas of space activity outside of facilities and space objects to be subject to principles of non-interference. The use of equipment on the 'ground' of celestial bodies, therefore, would grant states a right to take exclusionary measures (such as the invocation of a safety zone) to ensure maximum precautions are taken to avoid interference, without abrogating the principle of non-appropriation. The Canadian delegation specifically noted that international law and the Charter of the United Nations also regulates the conduct of states in outer space, including SRU.[118] This express invocation of general international law could have implications in expanding the breadth of applicable law to draw on when exploring rules for deconfliction in outer space.

In sum, views expressed in the Working Group suggest significant support for the idea that SRU does not breach the non-appropriation principle in Article II. There is also widespread acceptance of the important role that Article IX's principle of 'due regard' will play in deconfliction of SRU activities, as well as of the importance of information sharing under Article XI and the relevance of Articles VIII and XII. Moreover, the concept of safety zones around SRU activities was expressly countenanced by Australia, Austria, Luxembourg and the Netherlands.

(e) Open-Ended Working Group on Reducing Space Threats Through Norms, Rules and Principles of Responsible Behaviours

The interaction of states with the OEWG in 2022 and 2023 has led to some important views being expressed regarding deconfliction of activities in outer space. While none of the relevant comments have directly addressed safety zones, there have been clear indications of views in respect of the meaning of due regard in Article IX of the Outer Space Treaty which are relevant to safety zones. The most significant development at the OEWG has been the use of the meaning of due regard in the law of the sea to inform the meaning of due regard in the Outer Space Treaty.[119] This link was first drawn in a paper submitted by the Philippines to the OEWG in 2022. This paper, drawing in the passage emphasised next from the

117 US Delegation (n 31) 3.

118 Canadian Delegation (n 22) 3.

119 *United Nations Convention on the Law of the Sea*, opened for signature 10 December 1982, 1833 UNTS 397 (entered into force 16 November 1994) arts 56(2), 58(3) and 87(2). See, e.g., Blake (n 29) 202–4; Deplano (n 11) 812; Rolf Einar Fife, 'Obligations of "Due Regard" in the Exclusive Economic Zone: Their Context, Purpose and State Practice (2019) 34(1) International Journal of Marine and Coastal Law 43, 54–55; Julia Gaunce, 'On the Interpretation of the General Duty of "Due Regard"' (2017) 32 Ocean Yearbook 1; Danielle Kroon, '"Due Regard" in the High Seas: The Tension Between Submarine Cables and Deep Seabed Mining' (2018) 24(1) Australian International Law Journal 35, 49–50.

judgment of the International Tribunal for the Law of the Sea ('ITLOS') in the *Chagos Marine Protected Area Arbitration*,[120] stated:

11.1. While the duty of 'due regard' does not constitute a blanket limit on state conduct, it also does not permit states to merely note other states' rights and still do as they wish. Instead, its application depends upon *the nature of the rights and duties involved, their importance, the extent of the anticipated impairment, the nature and importance of the activities contemplated, and the availability of alternative approaches*.

11.2. In most cases, the duty of 'due regard' would necessarily involve consultations on the basis of good faith, and require that the avenues for such consultations are exhausted. Such consultations, which is already provided for under Article IX of the 1967 [Outer Space Treaty], should encompass a conscious balancing of rights and interests, including extensive concern regarding the other party's reaction; suggestions of compromise and willingness to offer assurances; and an understanding of other parties' concerns in connection with any proposed activities.

11.3. The duty of 'due regard' imposes 'due diligence obligation' upon states over the conduct of their nationals and vessels, with the view to ensuring that their conduct do not prejudice the rights and interest of other states.[121]

A 2023 joint paper submitted by the Philippines and Germany again linked due regard in the Outer Space Treaty with the ITLOS interpretation noted earlier.[122] The Chairperson's Summary after the September 2023 meeting of the OEWG similarly indicated:

> Many States noted that jurisprudence on the law of the sea has opined that, in the maritime context, the duty of due regard represents a balancing of rights and interests between and among States, and between States and the international community as a whole.[123]

Addressing SRU, Italy noted that it would regard as 'irresponsible' any behaviour on celestial bodies which resulted in 'harmful interference with other ongoing space

120 *Chagos Marine Protected Area Arbitration (Mauritius v United Kingdom) (Award)* (Permanent Court of Arbitration, Case No 2011–03, 18 March 2015) [519]: 'the extent of the regard required by the Convention will depend upon the nature of the rights held by Mauritius, their importance, the extent of the anticipated impairment, the nature and importance of the activities contemplated by the United Kingdom, and the availability of alternative approaches. In the majority of cases, this assessment will necessarily involve at least some consultation with the rights-holding State.'

121 Philippines, 'The duty of "due regard" as a foundational principle of responsible behavior in space' (11 May 2022) UN Doc A/AC.294/2022/WP.12 (emphasis added).

122 Germany and Philippines, 'Recommendations on possible norms, rules and principles of responsible behaviours relating to threats by States to space systems' UN Doc A/AC.294/2023/WP.1 (19 January 2023) [4].

123 'Chairperson's Summary' UN Doc A/AC.294/2023/WP.22 (1 September 2023) [18].

activities, including other space resource activities.'[124] Italy further encouraged states to develop rules for coordination of space activities based on the Building Blocks.[125] As noted earlier, Australia, Austria and the Netherlands jointly explicitly endorsed those articles of The Hague Building Blocks and Artemis Accords that relate to safety zones as lawful under the Outer Space Treaty and *Moon Agreement* and appropriate deconfliction mechanisms that ought to guide the development of a future space law regime.[126]

This emerging practice contributes significantly to our understanding of the meaning of the key principles of the Outer Space Treaty relevant to the declaration of safety zones around SRU activities on celestial bodies. While the detailed insights to be drawn from this practice will be assessed in the next section, for now it is sufficient to note the broad contours of what this practice appears to indicate. First, there is an emerging majority view that declaring safety zones around SRU activities is likely to be lawful, subject to compliance with the various principles that will regulate the nature of such zones. Second, consistently with the insights from the *travaux préparatoires* noted previously, the concept of 'due regard' as requiring a balancing of the interests of states whose activities might otherwise conflict has become much clearer with the link drawn by a number of states between the concept of due regard in the law of the sea and the meaning of that same phrase in the Outer Space Treaty. Third, the specific criteria proposed in the Building Blocks and the Artemis Accords in respect of safety zones appear to be receiving considerable support from states. The result of these developments is that a picture is starting to emerge of the permissible nature of safety zones around SRU activities on celestial bodies—as the next section demonstrates.

4 Criteria for Determining the Permissible Nature and Legality of Safety Zones

In this section, we suggest several criteria which may be used in developing, or assessing the lawfulness of, a safety zone in the context of SRU. These criteria were developed with reference to the key principles of the Outer Space Treaty and subsequent state practice already discussed and articulate what we consider to be the general principles for the creation of safety zones in space.

(a) Scope

A safety zone must be connected to a specific object or area selected for use in an SRU activity. This is consistent with state practice and *opinio juris* in relation to deconfliction surrounding SRU, which uniformly characterises safety zones as

124 Italy, 'IT Contribution to the report of the UN Secretary-General following UNGA Resolution 75/36 on "Reducing Space Threats Through Responsible Behaviours"' <https://front.un-arm.org/wp-content/uploads/2021/05/Italy_contribution_to_the_report_of_the_UN_Secretary-1.pdf> 5.

125 Italy (n 124) 10.

126 Australian, Austrian and Netherlands Delegations (n 113).

relating to a specific activity that is either ongoing or planned to occur.[127] For three examples, the Artemis Accords envisage declarable safety zones around 'operations' occurring in space, the US declared that non-interference rights flow from ownership interests in particular pieces of 'equipment,' and The Hague Building Blocks contemplate a safety zone being declared around 'an area identified for [an SRU] activity.'[128] This means that an area in space cannot be arbitrarily selected where there is no or only a remote chance of SRU activity occurring in that area, or to pre-emptively take control of an area in order to prevent another state from conducting SRU activities in that area.

The physical scope of a safety zone is limited to what is required for safety and non-interference purposes. That is consistent with the aims of the Outer Space Treaty and with state practice and ensures that safety zones fall short of becoming de facto national appropriation.[129] States are not required to respect a safety zone established in an area unreasonably, or of an unreasonable physical scope.[130] Without a sufficient nexus between the scope of the zone and reasonable precautions for safety and non-interference in respect of an operation or facility, a zone would likely be unlawful under the Outer Space Treaty.

The state practice of the Artemis Accords seems to provide particularly useful guidance in this respect, establishing that the physical scope of the zone will reflect the area in which harmful interference is likely to be caused, to be determined 'in a reasonable manner leveraging commonly accepted scientific and engineering principles' reflecting the nature of operations and the environment therein.[131] An extant safety zone that demonstrates this 'nexus' principle in practice is that of the ISS, discussed earlier, which extends for 200 m around the space station and is proportional to the attendant safety requirements (that is, to avoid a collision between a space vehicle and the ISS).[132] The type of interference to be avoided through the use of a safety zone is 'harmful interference.'[133] That is interference which is harmful to crew, equipment and operations of any state in that area. It should be noted that the Outer Space Treaty stresses 'maximum precautions' ought to be taken in relation to safety of crews and non-interference with ordinary operations in relation to visits to 'stations, installations, equipment and space vehicles,' being Article XII facilities,[134] so naturally there should be considerable latitude as regards the type and extent of harm to be avoided as well as the physical scope of safety zones where required for safety and non-interference. Each of these considerations require that the safety zone must change in scope to accommodate changes

127 Artemis Accords (n 18) s 11(1).

128 Artemis Accords (n 18) s 11(1); US Delegation (n 31) 3; The Hague Building Blocks (n 1) [11.3].

129 See discussion above at page 167. See also concerns articulated in Belgian Delegation (n 103) 2–4.

130 See Artemis Accords (n 18) s 11(10); Stephens and Blake (n 30) 224–25; Blake (n 29) 214.

131 See Artemis Accords (n 18) s 11(7) (a) and (b).

132 See discussion at page 173, and Reesman and Rogers (n 65) 5.

133 See discussion in Part II D at 7; Artemis Accords (n 18) s 11(1); The Hague Building Blocks (n 1) [11.3].

134 See discussion in Part II F at page 9 and Outer Space Treaty (n 6) art XI.

in the operations and location it surrounds and the relevant safety considerations thereof.[135] The principle of due regard would also require that states consider and balance the interests of other states when declaring safety zones. A zone must not unreasonably impinge upon those rights and interests, and a balancing exercise is required where establishing a safety zone may affect the rights of other states.[136]

(b) Duration

In order not to breach the non-appropriation principle, and to be consistent with the aforementioned 'nexus' principle, a safety zone must be temporary and of a duration that is linked to that of the relevant operation or facility. This is consistent with the Outer Space Treaty and avoids the trap of rendering Article II of the treaty meaningless, as foreshadowed in the Working Group.[137] A safety zone may therefore extend indefinitely in that it attends an activity or facility that is ongoing or in use on an ongoing basis but cannot extend beyond the time for which that activity or facility is operating. For example, the safety zone surrounding the ISS is of an indefinite duration, so long as it is required for the safe operation of the station but will naturally not outlast the life of the station itself.[138] This is consistent with state practice contained in the Artemis Accords and is complementary with the need for zones to change over time.[139]

(c) Restrictions and Prescriptions

The restrictions imposed within a safety zone will be limited to what is required for the purposes of safety and non-interference. Importantly, this means that a safety zone will not necessarily be a keep-out zone. In accordance with state practice, evinced in The Hague Building Blocks and Artemis Accords, as well as in practice concerning the ISS, this will largely relate to restrictions on access to the area within the zone or restrictions on the activities that can be conducted within that area.[140] In crafting both the scope and the nature of the restrictions within a safety zone, states will need to consider a proportionate balance between their desire to undertake space activities and the rights of other states to also undertake activities in accordance with their Article I freedoms. As explained previously, the analogy to the meaning of due regard in the law of the sea suggests that relevant factors will include the nature of the rights and duties involved, their importance, the extent of the anticipated impairment, the nature and importance of the activities contemplated and the availability of alternative approaches.

135 See discussion in Part III C at page 12; Artemis Accords (n 18) s 11(7)(c).
136 See discussion in Part II D at 7 and III E at page 19.
137 See discussion above at page 179. Again, see concerns articulated in Belgian Delegation (n 103) 2–4.
138 See discussion at page 179, and Reesman and Rogers (n 65).
139 See discussion in Section 3(c) at page 175; Artemis Accords (n 18) s 11(7)(c).
140 The Hague Building Blocks (n 1) [11.3] (emphasis added); Reesman and Rogers (n 65) 5.

A safety zone may permit access to an area whilst restricting a visiting state from performing activities which may potentially cause harmful interference with operations. For example, ISS safety zones prescribe rules concerning the movement of space vehicles within a safety zone, including by specifying appropriate orbit trajectory and timing of approaches, and specific corridors through which a vehicle may move to avoid harmful interference.[141] Activities which may impact on the environment around an operation, causing harmful interference, could also be restricted. A zone establishing state may also give effect to principles contained in Article XII to restrict access to Article XII facilities within a safety zone.[142] Where a safety zone is established around such a facility, rather than a mere 'area identified for a [SRU] activity' maximum precautions must be observed in respect of safety and non-interference in normal operations.[143] In such circumstances, a state may have more latitude to impose restrictions and prescribe conditions regarding the visitation of its Article XII facilities and the surrounding area, consistent with the taking of 'maximum precautions.' This may impact the 'reasonableness' test implied in state practice such as the Artemis Accords.[144] Consistent with state practice in this context, a safety zone may require that visiting states engage in consultations in order to effect any relevant restrictions.[145]

(d) Information Sharing

State practice makes clear that safety zones are subject to strict information-sharing requirements and their establishment, alteration or ends must be 'promptly' notified 'as soon as practicable and feasible.'[146] The information that must be shared includes the scope of the zone, the nature and scope of the operations taking place within the zone and the location of the zone and of operations occurring within the zone.[147] That information is to be shared with a central registry (at present, the secretary-general of the United Nations)[148] and with other states and 'the public.'[149] It is important that states establishing a safety zone comply with transparency obligations, and thus withholding relevant information about a safety zone would be unlawful.[150] Moreover, the material considered earlier suggests that consultation prior to the declaration of a safety zone could be a requirement of the due regard

141 See discussion at page 170, and Reesman and Rogers (n 65).
142 See discussion at page 173.
143 See discussion at page 181; Outer Space Treaty (n 6) art XII.
144 Artemis Accords (n 18) s 11(7), 11(10).
145 Outer Space Treaty (n 6) art IX. See also discussion at pages 180 and 181.
146 Outer Space Treaty (n 6) art XI; The Hague Building Blocks (n 1) [14]; Artemis Accords (n 18) 11(d).
147 Artemis Accords.
148 But, at some stage, a future registry may be developed within UNCOPUOS (see the Romanian Delegation (n 110); and "building blocks" contained within Belgian Delegation (n 103)).
149 Romanian Delegation (n 110) s 11(9).
150 See emphasis on transparency at Report of the Legal Subcommittee (n 68) at [170], [176]; Artemis Accords (n 18) s 11; Deplano (n 11) 802–3, 808. See also Gold (n 44) 5.

principle—such consultation can only occur meaningfully in the presence of information sharing from all interested parties.

5 Conclusion

In assessing the emerging norms that will regulate the declaration of safety zones around SRU activities, some clarity is beginning to emerge as regards the legal principles informing the creation of these zones and their permissible scope. The Outer Space Treaty, true to its anticipatory nature, enumerates key principles which guide innovations in space law. The text of the treaty, along with its *travaux préparatoires* and subsequent state practice, indicate that safety measures which restrict the broad application of the freedoms found in Article I of the Outer Space Treaty may legitimately be based on principles articulated in Articles II, VIII, IX, XI and XII (amongst others). Specifically, principles of due regard and the avoidance of harmful interference, information sharing and maximum precautions during visits to state facilities in space provide a clear basis for the establishment of safety zones and accompanying restrictions and conditions surrounding entry into or activities undertaken within these zones.

We consider it clear that emerging state practice and legal opinion in relation to safety zones broadly endorses the approaches encapsulated in The Hague Building Blocks and the Artemis Accords (which has at the time of writing reached 36 states parties), and this is evident in state contributions across 2022 and 2023 to COPUOUS, the Working Group and the OEWG. Few states persist in objecting to the lawfulness of proposed safety zones under the Outer Space Treaty.

Given this growing state practice, we consider that criteria for the establishment of a safety zone, or the assessment of the lawfulness of a safety zone, are starting to emerge with some clarity. In Section 4 of this chapter (above), we articulated these criteria as relating to the following features of a safety zone:

- Scope;
- Duration;
- Restrictions and Prescriptions; and
- Information Sharing responsibilities.

Broadly, a safety zone must have a defined physical scope that is reasonable and proportionate for the safety and non-interference with the operation, facility or area contained within. It must be of a duration linked to those operations. It must restrict or prescribe activities within the zone only to the extent required for safety and non-interference with the operations taking place therein. Finally, it must effect information sharing requirements found in the Outer Space Treaty.

Bibliography

Gemma Andreone, 'The Exclusive Economic Zone' in Donald Rothwell and others (eds), *The Oxford Handbook of the Law of the Sea* (OUP 2015) 159.

Affaire du lac Lanoux (France v Spain) [1957] 12 RIAA 281, 307.

Australian, Austrian and Netherlands Delegations, 'Relevant Considerations for Developing a Set of Initial Recommended Principles for the Exploration, Exploitation and Utilisation of Space Resources' (submission to the Working Group on Legal Aspects of Space Resource Activities, 62nd session of the COPUOS Legal Subcommittee, 20 March 2023) UN Doc A/AC.105/C.2/2023/CRP.6, 3.

Belgian Delegation, submission to the Working Group on Legal Aspects of Space Resource Activities, 62nd session of the COPUOS Legal Subcommittee, 20–31 March 2023, UN Doc A/AC.105/C.2/2023/CRP.35, 2–3.

Lachlan Blake, 'Jurisdiction on the Final Frontier: Facilities, Jurisdiction and Control in International Space Law' (2022) 46 McGill University Annals of Air & Space Law 188.

Elana Carpanelli, 'Unweaving the Tangled Web: The Due Regard Obligation Under Article IX of the Outer Space Treaty' (2024) 49(1) Air & Space Law 35.

Case of Railway Traffic Between Lithuania and Poland (Railway Sector Landwarów-Kaisiadorys) (Advisory Opinion) (1931) PCIJ Series A/B, No 42, 108, 116.

Cestmir Cepelka and Jamie HC Gilmour, 'The Application of General International Law in Outer Space' (1970) 36(1) Journal of Air Law & Commerce 30.

Chagos Marine Protected Area Arbitration (Mauritius v United Kingdom) (Award) (Permanent Court of Arbitration, Case No 2011–03, 18 March 2015).

'Chairperson's Summary' UN Doc A/AC.294/2023/WP.22 (1 September 2023).

Imre Anthony Csafabi, *The Concept of State Jurisdiction in International Space Law: A Study in the Progressive Development of Space Law in the United Nations* (Martinus Nijhoff 1971).

Melissa de Zwart, Stacey Henderson and Michelle Neumann, 'Space Resource Activities and the Evolution of International Space Law' (2023) 211 Acta Astronautica 155.

Rossana Deplano, 'The Artemis Accords: Evolution or Revolution in International Space Law' (2021) 70(3) International and Comparative Law Quarterly 799.

Rolf Einar Fife, 'Obligations of "Due Regard" in the Exclusive Economic Zone: Their Context, Purpose and State Practice (2019) 34(1) International Journal of Marine and Coastal Law 43.

Steven Freeland and Ram Jakhu, 'Article II' in Stephan Hobe, Bernhard Schmidt-Tedd and Kai-Uwe Schrogl (eds), *Cologne Commentary on Space Law* (Carl Heymanns Verlag 2009) 44.

Julia Gaunce, 'On the Interpretation of the General Duty of "Due Regard"' (2017) 32 Ocean Yearbook 1.

German Delegation, submission to the Working Group on Legal Aspects of Space Resource Activities, 62nd session of the COPUOS Legal Subcommittee, 20–31 March 2023, UN Doc A/AC.105/C.2/2023/CRP.13, 5.

Germany and Philippines, 'Recommendations on Possible Norms, Rules and Principles of Responsible Behaviours Relating to Threats by States to Space Systems' UN Doc A/AC.294/2023/WP.1 (19 January 2023) [4].

Mike Gold, 'Artemis Accords—Enabling International Partnerships for Lunar Exploration' (*U.S. Department of State, Foreign Press Center*, 15 May 2020) 5.

Micah Hill-Smith, 'Ending Poverty With Space Mining: The Global Space Resources Dividend' (2021) 46 McGill University Annals of Air & Space Law 221.

Stephan Hobe, 'Article I' in Stephan Hobe, Bernhard Schmidt-Tedd and Kai-Uwe Schrogl (eds), *Cologne Commentary on Space Law* (Carl Heymanns Verlag 2009) 25.

Italy, 'IT Contribution to the Report of the UN Secretary-General Following UNGA Resolution 75/36 on "Reducing Space Threats Through Responsible Behaviours"' <https://front.unarm.org/wp-content/uploads/2021/05/Italy_contribution_to_the_report_of_the_UN_Secretary-1.pdf> 5

Ram Jakhu and Yaw Nyampong, 'International Regulation of Emerging Modes of Space Transportation' in Joseph N Pelton and Ram Jakhu (eds), *Space Safety Regulations and Standards* (Elsevier 2010) 220.

Danielle Kroon, '"Due Regard" in the High Seas: The Tension Between Submarine Cables and Deep Seabed Mining' (2018) 24(1) Australian International Law Journal 35.

Lucas Mallowan, Lucien Rapp and Maria Topka, *Reinventing Treaty Compliant 'Safety Zones' in the Context of Space Sustainability* (Elsevier 2021).

Sergio Marchisio, 'Article IX' in Stephan Hobe, Bernhard Schmidt-Tedd and Kai-Uwe Schrogl (eds), *Cologne Commentary on Space Law* (Carl Heymanns Verlag 2009) 169.

A Martin and S Freeland, 'From One to Many: "Mega" (Constellation) Challenges to the Legal Framework for Outer Space' (2021) 46 McGill University Annals of Air & Space Law 131.

Jean-François Mayence and Thomas Reuter, 'Article XI' in Stephan Hobe, Bernhard Schmidt-Tedd and Kai-Uwe Schrogl (eds), *Cologne Commentary on Space Law* (Carl Heymanns Verlag 2009) 189.

NASA, 'Using Space-Based Resources for Deep Space Exploration' (*web page*, 26 July 2023) <https://www.nasa.gov/overview-in-situ-resource-utilization/>;

Rachel Neef, 'Artemis Accords: A New Path Forward for Space Lawmaking?' (2021) 42(2) Adelaide Law Review 569.

Charles O Brichet, 'Commercial Exploitation: Lessons From the Law of the Sea' (2021) 46 McGill University Annals of Air & Space Law 255.

Robert O Keohane, 'Reciprocity in International Relations' (1986) 40(1) International Organization 1.

Ogunsola O Ogunbanwo, *International Law and Outer Space Activities* (Martinus Nijhoff 1975).

Francesco Paris and Nita Chei, 'The Role of Reciprocity in International Law' (2003) 33(1) Cornell International Law Journal 93.

Sebastian Pesch, 'Coastal State Jurisdiction around Installations: Safety Zones in the Law of the Sea' (2015) 30(3) International Journal of Marine and Coastal Law 512.

Philippines, 'The Duty of "Due Regard" as a Foundational Principle of Responsible Behavior in Space' (11 May 2022) UN Doc A/AC.294/2022/WP.12.

JN Rasera and others, 'The Beneficiation of Lunar Regolith for Space Resource Utilisation: A Review' (2020) 186 Planetary and Space Science 104879.

Stacy J Ratner, 'Establishing the Extraterrestrial: Criminal Jurisdiction and the International Space Station' (1999) 22(2) Boston College International and Comparative Law Review 330.

Rebecca Reesman and Andrew Rogers, 'Getting in Your Space: Learning From Past Rendezvous and Proximity Operations' (2018) 5 *Center for Space Policy and Strategy*.

Olivier Ribbelink, 'Article III' in Stephan Hobe, Bernhard Schmidt-Tedd and Kai-Uwe Schrogl (eds), *Cologne Commentary on Space Law* (Carl Heymanns Verlag 2009) 64.

Romanian Delegation proposal to the Working Group of the Whole, 61st session of the COPUOS Science and Technical Subcommittee, 29 January–9 February 2024, UN Doc A/AC.105/C.1/2024/CRP.30.

Walker A Smith, 'Using the Artemis Accords to Build Customary International Law: A Vision for a U.S.-Centric Good Governance Regime in Space' (2021) 86(4) Journal of Air Law and Commerce 661.

Matthew Stubbs, 'The Legality of Keep-Out, Operational and Safety Zones in Outer Space' in Cassandra Steer and Matthew Hersch (eds), *War and Peace in Outer Space: Law, Policy and Ethics* (OUP 2021) 199.

Tacna-Arica Question (*Chile v Peru*) [1925] 2 RIAA 921, 929–30.

'The Artemis Accords: Principles for Cooperation in the Civil Exploration and Use of the Moon, Mars, Comets, and Asteroids for Peaceful Purposes' (*National Aeronautics and Space Administration*, 13 October 2020) <https://www.nasa.gov/wp-content/uploads/2022/11/Artemis-Accords-signed-13Oct2020.pdf> ('Artemis Accords').

The Hague International Space Resources Governance Working Group, 'Building Blocks for the Development of an International Framework on Space Resource Activities' (2019)

<https://www.universiteitleiden.nl/en/law/institute-of-public-law/institute-of-air-space-law/the-hague-space-resources-governance-working-group>.
Treaty Between the United States of America and the Union of Soviet Socialist Republics on the Elimination of Their Intermediate-Range and Shorter-Range Missiles, opened for signature 8 December 1987, 1657 UNTS 2 (entered into force 1 June 1988).
Treaty on Principles Governing the Activities of States in the Exploration and Use of Outer Space, Including the Moon and Other Celestial Bodies, opened for signature 27 January 1967, 610 UNTS 205 (entered into force 10 October 1967).
United Nations Convention on the Law of the Sea, opened for signature 10 December 1982, 1833 UNTS 397 (entered into force 16 November 1994) arts 56(2), 58(3) and 87(2).
Vienna Convention on the Law of Treaties, opened for signature 23 May 1969, 1155 UNTS 331 (entered into force 27 January 1980).

9 It's Not My Fault! The Looming Danger of Space Debris and the Quest Towards a Future International Legal Framework

William P. Schonberg and Anna Marie Brennan

1 Introduction: The Scope of Space Debris Regulation Under Outer Space Law

Despite a continuing dearth of jurisprudence, outer space law is quickly becoming entrenched within the discipline of public international law. The well-established principle that the 'exploration and use of outer space . . . shall be carried out for the benefit and in the interests of all countries . . . in accordance with international law' is at the focal point of the discipline, but there continues to be no comprehensive legal framework regulating the impact of human activity on the fragile and often perilous outer space environment.[1] An innovative edited collection of essays on the future direction of outer space law cannot underestimate how the rise of corporate actors over the last decade has upended the *status quo* that prevailed in the 20th century. However, such actors will lead and demand new ways of regulating and managing our environmental impact in the outer space realm. This chapter seeks to critique the path for upcoming research challenges beyond the lure of a fashionable legal subject.

While several definitions of space debris have been proposed, it can generally be described as 'all tangible [hu]man-made materials in space which do not serve a useful purpose.'[2] The number of commercial entities contributing to the space sector has grown exponentially in recent years with companies such as Rocket Lab, Maxar Technologies and SpaceX increasingly investing in ever more sophisticated

1 Treaty on Principles Governing the Activities of States in the Exploration and Use of Outer Space, Including the Moon and Other Celestial Bodies (adopted 27 January 1967, entered into force 10 October 1967) 610 UNTS 205 (Outer Space Treaty), Article I.

2 Lotta Viikari, 'Environmental Aspects of Space Activities' in Frans von der Dunk and Fabio Tronchetti (eds), *Handbook of Space Law* (Edward Elgar Publishing 2017) 717–68, 719. See also Lotta Viikari, *The Environmental Element in Space Law* (Brill 2008) 31–36; International Academy of Astronautics, *The Updated IAA Position Paper on Orbital Debris* (3rd European Conference on Space Debris 2001) 3; International Academic of Astronautics, *Situation Paper on Space Debris 2016*, Technical Report on Space Debris, UNCOPUOS STSC (1999), para. 6; Inter-Agency Debris Coordination Committee, *Mitigation Guidelines* (2007), Sec. 31.

DOI: 10.4324/9781003370499-12

technologies to launch space objects.[3] As the cost of space exploration decreases, the number of space objects being launched has increased exponentially over the last ten years. The space economy is expected to be valued at $1.8 trillion U.S. dollars by 2035,[4] but there is still no international treaty or convention dedicated to the protection of the outer space environment. Instead, the outer space industry is navigated by a plethora of guidelines, domestic laws and industry-driven best practice. As a result, state and space companies circumnavigate legal ambiguity with regards their precise duties to mitigate and manage space debris. Several difficulties continue to arise including ambiguity about whether it is legally permissible for a state or space company to remove another state's or space company's object from outer space if it poses a risk not only to the environment of outer space but also to Earth.[5] Despite increasing acknowledgement that an international regulatory framework, beyond the Outer Space Treaty, the Moon Agreement and the Space Mitigation Guidelines of the UN Committee on the Peaceful Uses of Outer Space (UNCOPUOS), is needed to address this dilemma, no international treaty specifically focused on the management and prevention of space debris is on the horizon.[6]

To analytically approach the subject matter of this chapter, the relationship between outer space law and environmental law needs to be delineated. As Manfred Lachs posits, outer space law refers to the regulation of 'relations between [s]tates to determine their rights and duties resulting from all activities directed towards outer space and within it—and to do so in the interest of [hu]mankind

3 Sandra Erwin and Debra Wener, 'Maxar Technologies Reorganises as Two Separate Businesses' *SpaceNews* (20 September 2023) <https://spacenews.com/maxar-technologies-to-reorganize-under-two-separate-businesses/> accessed 1 November 2024; Anusuya Datta, 'Airbus Eyes American Geospatial Market With New U.S. Entity' (*GeoSpatial World*, 16 July 2020) <https://spacenews.com/maxar-technologies-to-reorganize-under-two-separate-businesses/> accessed 1 November 2024; Sandra Erwin, 'Blacksky Inks $50 Million Deal to Supply Imagery Services and Satellites to Indonesia' *SpaceNews* (8 February 2024) <https://spacenews.com/blacksky-inks-50-million-deal-to-supply-imagery-services-and-satellites-to-indonesia/>accessed 1 November 2024; RocketLab, 'Lunar Photon: Rocket Lab's Mission to the Moon' (August 2022) <https://www.rocketlabusa.com/assets/Uploads/EXC22_017%20-%20Photon%20Doc_%C6%92%20[Web].pdf> accessed 1 November 2024.

4 Gayle Markovitz, 'Space Is Booming: Here's How Embrace the $1.8 Trillion Opportunity' (*World Economic Forum*, 8 April 2024) <https://www.weforum.org/agenda/2024/04/space-economy-technology-invest-rocket-opportunity/> accessed 1 November 2024.

5 For further academic commentary on this question see Peter Stubbe, *State Accountability for Space Debris: A Legal Study of Responsibility for Polluting the Space Environment and Liability for Damage Caused by Space Debris* (Brill Nijhoff 2018); Abbas Sheer and Shouping Li, 'Space Debris Mounting Global Menace Legal Issues Pertaining to Space Debris Removal: Ought to Revamp Existing Space Law Regime' (2018) 10(3) Beijing Law Review 4230440.

6 Space Debris Mitigation Guidelines of the UN Committee on the Peaceful Uses of Outer Space, endorsed by the UN General Assembly in its Resolution 62/217 <https://www.unoosa.org/pdf/publications/st_space_49E.pdf> accessed 1 November 2024. Please note that the Inter-Agency Space Debris Coordination Committee (IADC) Space Debris Mitigation Guidelines are similar to the UN Space Debris Mitigation Guidelines. As a result, the IADC Guidelines are not examined in depth in this chapter.

as a whole, to offer protection to life, terrestrial and non-terrestrial, wherever it may exist.'[7] This body of principles range from those concerning liability for damage caused by space objects to the regulation of satellite remote sensing to space resource utilization. Moreover, running alongside this body of law, an institutional superstructure prevails which seeks to not only negotiate and adopt new outer space regulations and policies but also to foster cooperation and friendly relations among both states and space companies in outer space activity. It includes organizations such as the United Nations (UN), the International Telecommunications Union (ITU), the Word Trade Organization (WTO), the International Institute for the Unification of Private Law (UNIDROIT) and a myriad of others. While this basic definition of outer space law offers a springboard from which to define the scope of the present chapter, it will exclusively consider substantive space debris regulation. The parameters of our chapter are deliberately narrow to avoid intersecting with the substance of the other chapters in this book that discuss significant topics in outer space law more generally.

Moreover, it must be emphasized that space debris law analyses have thus far been overlooked in the outer space law discipline more generally unless they refer specifically to the protection of satellite infrastructure. For example, studies on the application of space debris regulations to proposed future extraterrestrial settlements have thus far been sidestepped.[8] Rapid developments in technology such as reusable spacecraft have spurred on a private-company space race and thereby the potential for future extraterrestrial human settlements on Mars and the Moon by the end of the 21st century. Yet very little research has been conducted to understand how the international community should address the protection of the environment in these contexts.[9] Despite not being included within the scope of this chapter,

7 Manfred Lachs, 'The International Law of Outer Space' (1986-III) 113 *Receuil des Cours* 33. See also Frans von der Dunk, 'International Space Law' in Frans von der Dunk with Fabio Tronchetti (eds), *Handbook of Space* (Edward Elgar Publishing 2017) 29. See also Peter Malanczuk, 'Space Law as a Branch of International Law' (1994) 25 Netherlands Yearbook of International Law 143; Clarence Jenks, 'International Law and Activities in Space' (1956) 5 International and Comparative Law Quarterly 99; Diego Zannoni, 'Out of Sight, Out of Mind? The Proliferation of Space Debris and International Law' (2022) 35(2) Leiden Journal of International Law 295–314; Annie Handmer and Steven Freeland, 'The Use of Law to Address Space Debris Mitigation and Remediation: Looking Through a Science and Technology Lens' (2022) 87(3) Journal of Air Law and Commerce 375; Anton de Waal Alberts, 'The Degree of the Lack of Regulation of Space Debris within the Current Space Law Regime and Suggestions for a Prospective Legal Framework and Technological Interventions' in Annette Froehlich (ed), *Space Security and Legal Aspects of Active Debris Removal* (Springer 2019) 93–106; Emily Nevala, 'Waste in Space: Remediating Space Debris Through the Doctrine of Abandonment and the Law of Capture' (2017) 66(6) American University Law Review 1495–531; Seyed Hosseini, Fatemeh Fathpour and Subhrajit Chanda, 'Space Debris Mitigation; Some Lessons From International Environmental Law' (2021) 51(6) Environmental Law and Policy 391–401.

8 M.Z. Naser, 'Extraterrestrial Construction Materials' (2019) 105 Progress in Materials Science 100577.

9 For example, Leslie Tennen and Margaret Race, 'Protection of Celestial Environments and the Laws of Outer Space,' 38th COSPAR Scientific Assembly (Bremen, 15–18 July 2010).

future duties and responsibilities of states and space companies to safeguard the environment of celestial bodies is imperative to the field. It will greatly assist in examining how and the degree to which environmental law can be widened to outer space to strengthen it as a 'shared international commons' and 'province of all [hu] mankind.'[10]

From a research perspective, although this chapter will concentrate on the legal regulation of space debris, it is important to highlight that this subject has a strong interdisciplinary component despite liability for this type of hazard still being relatively underexplored. As noted elsewhere, substantive outer space law is closely related to and influenced by non-legal fields of study such as engineering, science, commerce, industry and politics. Arguably, these disciplines are in continuous interaction with each other as well as outer space law. From the perspective of space debris, it needs to be accentuated that the predominant approach for research on space debris has been the interpretation and sufficiency of current regulations and policies to outer space policy propositions based on normative standards, or a blend of both. Over the last couple of years, several spacefaring nations have started to evaluate the efficiency of their domestic outer space laws to reduce debris in their use and exploration of outer space, but like many other subjects of outer space law, perhaps interpretation-based research continues to predominate policy-based research. A comprehension of this demarcation is necessary to consider the future scope, structure and direction of legal research on space debris, and the chapter will be structured as follows. Section 2 provides an overview of the emergence of space debris as a phenomenon and how state and space companies have approached its management and mitigation. Section 3 provides a briefing on the evolution of the regulation of space debris under outer space law to provide context for the current situation. Following a basic examination of the existing research in this area, Section 4 will determine the latest developments in the field which will enable an analysis of topics for future legal research.

2 A Briefing on the Emergence of Space Debris as a Phenomenon in Outer Space Use and Exploration

The objective of this section is to present a brief analysis on the prevalence of space debris as a hazard that will enable the authors to better demarcate the future of legal research in the field. In particular, it will examine not only how space debris is defined from a scientific perspective but also how states and space companies have endeavored to detect, model, predict and mitigate the impact of space debris on the environment of outer space.

Since 1957, the near-Earth population of trackable space objects has grown from one to an estimated 26,000, ranging from softball size to larger.[11] Of these

10 Treaty on Principles Governing the Activities of States in the Exploration and Use of Outer Space, Including the Moon and Other Celestial Bodies (adopted 27 January 1967, entered into force 10 October 1967) 610 UNTS 205 (Outer Space Treaty), Article I.

11 European Space Agency, 'Space Debris—Evolution in Pictures' <https://www.esa.int/About_Us/ESOC/Space_debris_-_evolution_in_pictures#:~:text=Since%201957%2C%20more%20than%20

trackable objects, only several hundred are operational spacecraft while the remaining 94% are classified as space debris, that is, objects which 'no longer serve any useful purpose.'[12] Some of these objects are 'fragments from explosions while others are from the breakup of satellites or rocket boosters.'[13] In addition to trackable objects, there are several hundred thousand objects the size of marbles and several million objects the size of sand grains.[14] Since space debris can no longer be controlled or maneuvered, all spacecraft that travel through or operate in low-Earth orbit (LEO) are subject to high-speed impacts by pieces of this space debris.[15] The risk of 'damage from high-speed orbital debris particle impacts has become a significant design consideration in the development and construction of long duration earth-orbiting spacecraft—[e]ven a marble-size piece of space debris can inflict considerable damage or possibly destroy an orbiting operational spacecraft or satellite.'[16] For example, on 10 February 2009, the Iridium 33, an operational 560 kg communications satellite launched by Russia but owned by the United States corporation Motorola, collided with the defunct 900 kg Russian military communications satellite Kosmos 2251 approximately 790 km above northern Siberia, resulting in the destruction of both satellites.[17] The collision resulted in nearly 2,000 pieces of debris measuring approximately 10 cm in diameter and thousands of other smaller pieces as well.[18]

Scientists believe the debris resulting from this incident will remain in orbit for decades posing a collision risk to active space objects in LEO.[19] No warning that a potential collision could occur was issued despite the United States

---

4900,longer%20serve%20any%20useful%20purpose> accessed 1 November 2024. For further commentary see Paul Dickson, *Sputnik: The Shock of the Century* (Walker Books 2011) and Benjamin Bastida Virgili and others, 'Risk to Space Sustainability From Large Constellations of Satellites' (2016) 126 Acta Astronautica 154–62.

12 European Space Agency (n 11); Dickson (n 11); Virgili and others (n 11). See also Phillip Anz-Meador, 'U.S. National Space Council Announces Update to the USG ODMSP, JSC-E-DAA-TN77633'(2020)<https://sma.nasa.gov/news/articles/newsitem/2019/12/09/national-space-council-announces-update-to-usg-odmsp> accessed 1 November 2024 and Heather Cowardin, 'The Intentional Destruction of Cosmos 1408' (2022) 26(1) Orbital Debris Quarterly News 1 <https://orbital debris.jsc.nasa.gov/quarterly-news/pdfs/odqnv26i1.pdf> accessed 1 November 2024.

13 William Schonberg, 'The Sky Is Falling: A Brief Primer on the Problem of Space Debris' *American Institute of Aeronautics and Astronautics* (7 October 2021) <https://engage.aiaa.org/sydney/events/event-description?CalendarEventKey=ed6ee0ff-f6f0-4904-89f7-3e87a01fe7ef&CommunityKey=5f5c4710-61c1-42ab-8f88-b51893c47072&Home=%2Fhome> accessed 1 November 2024.

14 Tomasz Nowakowski, 'Space Debris Expert Warns About the Dangers of Orbital Junk' (*Phys. Org*, 10 January 2015) <https://phys.org/news/2015-01-space-debris-expert-dangers-orbital.html> accessed 1 November 2024.

15 Schonberg (n 13).

16 Schonberg (n 13).

17 Nicholas Johnson, *The Collision of Iridium 33 and Cosmos 2251: The Shape of Things to Come* (International Astronautical Congress 16 October 2009).

18 Brian Weeden, *2009 Iridium-Cosmos Collision Fact Sheet* (Secure World Foundation 10 November 2010) <https://swfound.org/media/6575/swf_iridium_cosmos_collision_fact_sheet_updated_2012.pdf> accessed 1 November 2024.

19 Weeden (n 18).

and Russia both having the technology and means necessary to track both satellites.[20] More recently, India conducted an anti-satellite test on Microsat-R during an operation known as Mission Shakti on 27 March 2019 leading to the creation of around 400 pieces of orbital debris.[21] Despite India's assertions that the resulting debris would not last for long, experts widely believe that it will jeopardize the viability of space objects.[22] Indeed, on 24 August 2023, the International Space Station's 'Zveda service module engines were fired for 21.5 seconds . . . to maneuver the [orbiting] complex away from the predicted path of an orbital debris fragment.'[23] As a consequence of incidents such as these, the LEO and geostationary orbits (GEO) where the vast majority of satellites operate is becoming increasingly overcrowded with debris, with some particles travelling at speeds of 7 km/s to 15 km/s.[24] The increasing frequency of these incidents is fueling concerns about 'Kessler Syndrome,' hypothesized by Donald Kessler and Burton Cour-Palais, which posits that rising levels of space debris will increase the risk of collisions such as Iridium-33 which will in turn create even more debris and amplify the risks of collisions even further.[25] Collisions such as these can 'set off a catastrophic chain reaction, jeopardizing all existing satellites and filling orbits with high-velocity debris.'[26]

To further complicate matters, several corporations have launched several thousand satellites into Earth orbit, mainly for communication purposes, but also to provide a space-based World Wide Web.[27] Individual satellites provide limited coverage areas, whereas a satellite system (or constellation) provides a more

20 Weeden (n 18).

21 A Molayath and V Sanal Kumar, 'Studies on Space Debris Tracking and Elimination' in *46th AIAA/ASME/SAE/ASEE Joint Propulsion Conference and Exhibit* (Nashville, TN, USA, July 2010).

22 Brian Weeden and Victoria Samson, 'India's ASAT Test of Wake-Up Call for Norms of Behaviour in Space' *SpaceNews* (8 April 2019) <https://spacenews.com/op-ed-indias-asat-test-is-wake-up-call-for-norms-of-behavior-in-space/> accessed 1 November 2024.

23 Mar Garcia, 'Station Preps for New Cargo, Crew and Avoids Space Debris' (*NASA Space Station Blog*, 24 August 2023) <https://blogs.nasa.gov/spacestation/2023/08/24/station-preps-for-new-cargo-crew-and-avoids-space-debris/> accessed 1 November 2024.

24 Shenyan Chen, 'The Space Debris Problem' (2011) 35(4) Asian Perspective 537–88; Alessandro Rossi, 'Population Models of Space Debris' (2004) Proceedings of the International Astronomical Union 427–38.

25 Donald Kessler and Burton Cour-Palais, 'Collision Frequency of Artificial Satellites: The Creation of a Debris Belt' (1978) 83(A6) Journal of Geophysical Research: Space Physics 2637–46; V. Adushkin and others, 'The Small Orbital Debris Population and Its Impact on Space Activities and Ecological Safety' (2020) 176 Acta Astronautica 591–97.

26 Amrith Maraippan and John Crassidis, 'Kessler's Syndrome: A Challenge to Humanity' (2023) (4) *Frontiers in Space Technologies* 1–12, page 2. See also Jer Liou and Nicholas Johnson, 'Risks in Space From Orbiting Debris' (2006) 311(5759) Science 340–41.

27 Tom Metcalfe, 'SpaceX Wants to Bring the World Wide Web to the Whole Wide World' (*NBC News*, 6 March 2018) <https://www.nbcnews.com/mach/science/how-spacex-aims-bring-high-speed-internet-whole-world-ncna853766> accessed 1 November 2024; Jonathan Amos, 'OneWeb Launch Completes Space Internet Project' *BBC News* (26 March 2023) <https://www.bbc.com/news/science-environment-65066669> accessed 1 November 2024.

extended coverage area.[28] According to plans released to the public (and frequently updated), approximately 25,000 new satellites are expected to be launched into Earth orbit over the next decade.[29] Thus, the question arises, what benefits, if any, can these large satellite constellations provide, and what deleterious effects might they have on other space activities? There are, of course, many arguments in favor of large satellite constellations and why they should replace current, aging satellite networks.[30] For example, modern-day individual satellites provide limited coverage areas—either narrow bands around the Earth (if in LEO) or small circles (if in GEO).[31] Alternatively, a satellite system, or constellation, extends coverage area to nearly the entire globe. Demand for ever-faster broadband internet connections is maxing out the capabilities of today's satellites. Netflix, streaming video games, HDTV, and so on are 'bandwidth hogs,' and current satellites are unable to keep pace.[32]

Additionally, traditional satellites are cost exorbitant and take too long to build and launch and thus, by necessity, have a long operational life span.[33] Due to the exceedingly long lead time ahead of their launch, traditionally conceived and built satellites are obsolete before they are even launched. If one of these 'old school' satellites is lost (for whatever reason), the likelihood of retrieving it is slim at best.[34] Constellation satellites, on the other hand, are much cheaper and faster to build and design, and if one is lost due to a collision, malfunction or some other reason, the loss is not as financially detrimental.[35] Overall, satellite constellations will result in improved internet access and communication to places where the internet is slow

28 Ronald Freeman, 'Overview: Satellite Constellations' (2020) 17(2) Journal of Space Operations and Communicator 1–16.

29 NovaSpace, 'Satellite Demand to Quadruple Over the Next Decade' (*NovaSpace Press Release*, 12 December 2022) <https://nova.space/press-release/satellite-demand-to-quadruple-over-the-next-decade/> accessed 1 November 2024; Tereza Pultarova, 'SpaceX Starlink Satellites Had to Make 25,000 Collision-Avoidance Maneuvers in Just 6 Months—And It Will Only Get Worse' (*Space.com*, 7 July 2023) <https://www.space.com/starlink-satellite-conjunction-increase-threatens-space-sustainability> accessed 1 November 2024.

30 NovaSpace (n 29) at page 2.

31 Shkelzen Cakaj, 'The Coverage Analysis for Low Earth Orbiting Satellites at Low Elevation' (2014) 5(6) International Journal of Advanced Computer Science and Applications 6–10 at page 7.

32 PJ Hughes, 'Bandwidth Hogs Slows Internet (Unless You Have Fiber) (*FastNet*, 4 April 2023) <https://www.4cfastnet.com/bandwidth-hogs-slows-internet/> accessed 1 November 2024.

33 Alexandra Evans and others, 'Space Strategic Stability: Assessing U.S. Concepts and Approaches' (*Rand Research Report*, 2024) <https://www.rand.org/content/dam/rand/pubs/research_reports/RRA2300/RRA2313-1/RAND_RRA2313-1.pdf> accessed 1 November 2024; Christian Davenport, 'The Revelation in Satellite Technology Means There Are Swarms of Spacecraft No Bigger Than a Loaf of Bread in Orbit' *The Washington Post* (6 April 2021) <https://www.washingtonpost.com/technology/2021/04/06/small-satellites-growth-space/> accessed 1 November 2024.

34 Jonathan Amos, 'Somebody Moved UK's Oldest Satellite, and No-One Knows Who or Why' *BBC News* (9 November 2024) <https://www.bbc.com/news/articles/cpwrr58801yo>

35 Caleb Henry, 'Leo and MEO Broadband Constellations Mega Source of Consternation' *SpaceNews* (13 March 2018) <https://spacenews.com/divining-what-the-stars-hold-in-store-for-broadband-mega constellations/> accessed 1 November 2024.

or non-existent and in faster and more efficient disaster management.[36] It will also enable enhanced astronomical studies without atmospheric interference such as the BRITE/CANX-3 satellite-based research program, which has on-orbit observation precision that is more than ten times better than ground-based observations.[37] To effectively deal with a variety of different disasters and natural hazards, disaster managers need data collected in a variety of different wavebands.[38] Agricultural droughts, for example, require optical and near infrared data, while tracking a hurricane or monitoring flooded areas beneath clouds require microwave sensors.[39] Conversely, landslide studies depend on accurate high-resolution digital elevation models involving stereo-viewing optical sensors, interferometric synthetic aperture radars and light detection instruments, while fires and volcanoes require thermal imagery.[40] It is clear, then, that disaster managers need satellites with sensors that collect data in all regions of the electromagnetic spectrum. This can only be accomplished by a satellite system with a suite of sensors.[41]

The potential benefits of satellite constellations are clear, but launch operators, who are now predominantly space companies, need to ensure that satellites do not collide or interfere with already resident and fully functional space objects. The potentially serious deleterious impact of launching this many satellites is the increase in the number of close approaches (CAs) that organizations such as the North American Aerospace Defense Command (NORAD) will have to track and report to satellite owners.[42] Using today's thresholds, more than 25,000 warnings could be issued daily by NORAD alone, all of which would need to be adjudicated by the launch operators that receive them.[43] At present, NORAD does not require that launch operators take any action to avoid a collision or interference such as an orbit change or an avoidance maneuver. This decision must be made by the

36 Berna Gur, 'Equitable Access to Satellite Broadband Services: Challenges and Opportunities for Developing Countries' (2024) 48(5) Telecommunications Policy 102731.

37 Otto Koudelka, 'The BRITE Nanosatellite Constellation' (Proceedings of the 49th Session of UNCOPUOS-STSC, 6–17 February 2012).

38 Moez Krichen and others, 'Managing Natural Disasters: An Analysis of Technological Advancements, Opportunities and Challenges' (2024) 4 Internet of Things and Cyber-Physical Systems 99–109, 100.

39 Krichen and others (n 38) 103.

40 Krichen and others (n 38) 103. See also Mohamed Abdalzaher and Hussein Elsayed, 'Employing Data Communication Networks for Managing Safer Evacuation During Earthquake Disaster' (2019) 94 Simulation Modelling Practice and Theory 379–94.

41 R Navalgund, 'Disaster Management Needs Satellite Constellations' (*SciDev Net*, 29 October 2019) <https://www.scidev.net/global/opinions/disaster-management-needs-satellite-constellations-1/> accessed 1 November 2024.

42 Michael Dawson, 'NORAD: Remaining Relevant' (*University of Calgary School of Public Policy Briefing Paper*, November 2019) <https://d3n8a8pro7vhmx.cloudfront.net/cdfai/pages/4315/attachments/original/1574210059/NORAD_Remaining_Relevant.pdf?1574210059> accessed 1 November 2024.

43 Glenn Peterson and others, 'Implications of Proposed Small Satellite Constellations on Space Traffic Management and Long-Term Debris Growth in Near-Earth Environment' (67th International Astronautical Congress Paper, 2016).

satellite launch operators themselves, and the wrong decision could lead to a collision and the creation of several thousands of pieces of space debris. Unfortunately, the UN Space Debris Mitigation Guidelines do not provide in-depth guidance on the duty of launch operators to avoid CAs and collisions. While they may eventually acquire customary international law status in a similar vein to the UN Remote Sensing Principles, soft law approaches are perhaps more likely to emerge than 'hard law' options.[44] Nevertheless, Section 3 of this chapter will highlight the need for an effective multilateral system to counteract the challenge of space debris.

3 The Legal Quandary of Space Debris and the Future Protection of the Environment of Outer Space

The most obvious focus for scholarly research into space debris has been in the design and operation of the substantive principles. As discussed in the previous section, space debris can be described as 'spent satellites and rocket bodies, their fragments and parts, material released during space operations, as well as leaking fuel, paint flakes, microparticulate matter and such like, orbiting earth uncontrolled.'[45] Essentially, if it is not reusable and cannot be safely returned to Earth, anything and everything launched into outer space may eventually become space debris.[46] At the international level, there continues to be no treaty or convention to regulate space debris. Consequently, the rules are underdeveloped, and as discussed in Section 1 of this chapter, the significant question that has been considered in a large volume of legal literature has pivoted on 'what are the rules?' rather than the dilemma of 'do they work?' and 'what reforms could be made to bring those most responsible for space debris to account?' Unfortunately, the latter question has not yet been considered at length by legal scholars, but the question of the right of states to retain jurisdiction and control over objects launched in outer space has been examined at length.

Some legal researchers highlight an indirect reference to space debris in Article 1 of the Outer Space Treaty which maintains:

> the exploration and use of outer space . . . shall be carried out for the benefit and in the interests of all countries, irrespective of their degree of economic and scientific development . . . [and] without discrimination of any kind, on a basis of equality in accordance with international law.[47]

Even though Article 1 asserts that states are free to engage in the use and exploration of outer space as long as they comply with international law, such activities

44 Anna Brennan and Alex Davies, 'Space Law, Remote Sensing and Disaster Law: Future Steps Towards an International Legal Framework' in Dug Cubie (ed), *A Research Agenda for Disaster Law* (Edward Elgar Publishing, forthcoming in 2025).

45 Viikari (n 2) 719.

46 Viikari (n 2) 719.

47 Outer Space Treaty, Article 1.

will inevitably lead to the creation of space debris.[48] The only provision that perhaps alludes to this actuality is Article IX of the Outer Space Treaty, which proclaims that states, in conducting their

> exploration and use of outer space, including the Moon and other celestial bodies . . . [must act] with due regard to the corresponding interests of all other State Parties to the Treaty. States . . . [must] avoid their harmful contamination and also adverse changes in the environment of the Earth resulting from the introduction of extraterrestrial matter.[49]

Since this provision only refers to extraterrestrial matter, as opposed to human-made matter, space debris does not fall within the scope of Article IX. Consequently, several scholars posit that states do not have a duty under the Outer Space Treaty to avoid causing harm to the Earth environment when engaged in the use and exploration of outer space.[50]

Neither is guidance provided on the duty of states and space companies to safeguard the environment of outer space from harm caused by their activities. In a resolute attempt to provide this much-needed guidance, the Scientific and Technical Sub-Committee (STSC) of UNCOPUOS established a Working Group on Space Debris in 2004 to draft space debris mitigation guidelines that are largely based on the Space Debris Mitigation Guidelines of the Inter-Agency Debris Coordination Committee (IADC). Following their endorsement by UNCOPUOS, the UN General Assembly followed suit on 22 December 2007 and encouraged member states to implement the guidelines in their domestic legislation.[51] It remains unclear whether the principles have customary status and are 'evidence of a general practice accepted as law' under Article 38(1(b) of the Statute of the International Court of Justice.[52] Encouraging cooperation among states is at the core of the UN Space Debris Mitigation Guidelines, with Principle 3 providing that states and international organizations 'should voluntarily take measures, through national mechanisms . . . to ensure that these guidelines are implemented.'[53] Nevertheless, the guidelines are not legally binding, and as outlined by the Legal Subcommittee in its report to the UNCOPUOS during its 58th session, states have an inherent interest 'in preserving the safety and long-term sustainability of space activities . . . [and thus] took sound approaches to mitigating the problem of space debris.' As a result, it was concluded that since approaches to debris mitigation are continuously

48 Viikari (n 2) 727.

49 Outer Space Treaty, Article IX.

50 S Gorove, 'Pollution and Outer Space: A Legal Analysis and Appraisal' (1972) New York University Journal of International Law and Politics 53–66, at 62.

51 UN General Assembly Resolution 62/217 of 22 December 2007, UN Doc. A/RES/62/217 at para. 27.

52 *Statute of the International Court of Justice*, 18th April 1946 (33 UNTS 993, UKTS 67 (1946) Cmd 7015, 3 Bevans 1179, 59 Stat 1055, 145 BSP 832, TS No 993), Article 38.

53 UN Space Debris Mitigation Principles, Principle 3.

evolving because of advancements in technology, 'it was not necessary to develop legally binding space debris mitigation standards at present.'[54] However, this contradicts the view of some states: 'the strict application of space debris mitigation measures during all missions was mandatory . . . that it was necessary to expand the scope of international agreements to include space debris so as to ensure security and public safety.'[55] Indeed, some states believe that the 'major contributors to space debris must take appropriate responsibility in its removal under an internationally agreed framework.'[56] With no clear consensus on how space debris can be mitigated, an international legal framework is not on the horizon in the near future,[57] leaving it to individual states to determine how to manage the issue within their domestic legal systems. Thus, the legislative approaches adopted by states to mitigate space debris is ripe for scholarly exploration.

While satellites have been regarded as critical infrastructure for several decades, many states have until recently adopted a rather laissez-faire approach to assessing the harmfulness of their outer space activity on the environment and its potential to cause damage to this infrastructure. It was not until 1 November 2023 that the United States Senate passed the *Orbital Sustainability (ORBITS) Bill* in a unanimous vote. The Bill, which seeks to reduce the volume of space debris in outer space,[58] places an obligation on NASA to establish a debris removal program 'with the intent to close commercial capability gaps and enable potential future remediation missions for such orbital debris.'[59] At the U.S. Department of Commerce, the duty to create a list of space debris which needs to be removed falls on the Office of Space Commerce.[60] It also has the responsibility to design a Traffic Coordination System for Space (TraCSS) which will be responsible for the management of civil space traffic.[61] While scholars have welcomed the legislation as 'an excellent example of commitment to improve global behaviour and rulemaking in a key domain,'[62] it is interesting that not many states have so far followed suit.

Without an international treaty or convention outlining the duties and responsibilities of states to the outer space environment perhaps this legal reality will persist. Indeed, the UN Space Debris Mitigation Guidelines provide that member

54 Report of the Legal Subcommittee on its Fifty-Eighth Session, UN Doc. A/AC.105/1203 (2019), at 24, para. 163.
55 Report of the Scientific and Technical Subcommittee on its Fifty-Sixth Session, UN Doc. A/AC.105/1202 (2019), at 21, paras. 124 and 125.
56 Report of the Scientific and Technical Subcommittee on its Fifty-Seventh Session, UN Doc. A/AC.105/1224 (2020) at 19, para. 105.
57 Zannoni (n 7) 296.
58 S.447–118th Congress (2023–2024): Orbits Act of 2023, S.447, 118th Cong. (2023) <https://www.congress.gov/bill/118th-congress/senate-bill/447/text>
59 S.447–118th Congress (2023–2024) (n 58) at section 4 (b) (4).
60 S.447–118th Congress (2023–2024) (n 58) at section 7.
61 S.447–118th Congress (2023–2024) (n 58) at section 7.
62 W Pearson, H Schrieber and G. Zanalda, 'Launch the Orbits Act' *SpaceNews* (6 March 2024) <https://spacenews.com/launch-orbits-act/> accessed 1 November 2024.

states must only fulfil the guidelines 'to the greatest extent possible'[63] but as contended by Viikari, 'the fact that all major spacefaring states take part in the work of the STSC which, moreover, operates by consensus, should facilitate the approval and implementation of the Guidelines on the national level.'[64] For example, the Guidelines have been harnessed by both the UK Space Agency and the New Zealand Space Agency in a bilateral agreement concluded at the International Astronautical Congress in Milan on 17 October 2024 for the removal and servicing of active satellites that are located very close to each other and at risk of colliding.[65] The partnership will seek to facilitate missions such as in-orbit servicing, space debris removal and satellite refueling[66] and has been lauded as a show 'of real leadership . . . and an excellent example of the all-important international collaboration that is vital to the sustainability of space.'[67] In a similar vein, Australia adopted a Space Re-Entry Debris Plan in 2017 which outlines information-sharing procedures and also guidelines for responding to space debris re-entering Earth's atmosphere. Even though the Plan does not specify the measures to be followed to limit the creation of space debris, section 34(2) of the *Space (Launches and Returns) Act 2018 (Cth)* as supplemented by Rule 54 of the *Space (Launches and Returns) (General) Rules 2019* requires that an entity applying for a launch permit must provide a debris mitigation strategy which is based on an 'internationally recognised guideline or standard for debris mitigation.'[68]

A prevalent theme among state legislative approaches to space debris mitigation has been the absence of civil and criminal liability mechanisms. However, recent developments would suggest that this is slowly beginning to change especially among major spacefaring states. For example, in the United States, the Federal Communication Commission imposed the first ever monetary fine on a space company entity for creating space debris.[69] As a result of failing to de-orbit its Echo-Star-7 satellite, the Dish Network was fined $150,000 for placing its satellite 'into a "disposal orbit" at an altitude low enough to pose an orbital risk.'[70] The reputational fallout has been considerable with the company's share price falling 'almost 4 percent that day, chopping $100 million of the company's $4 billion

63 UN Space Debris Mitigation Guidelines of the Committee on the Peaceful Uses of Outer Space, para. 3.

64 Viikari (n 2) 743.

65 UK Space Agency, 'UK and New Zealand Agree Blueprint for Satellite Removal and Servicing Missions' (17 October 2024) <https://www.gov.uk/government/news/uk-and-new-zealand-agree-blueprint-for-satellite-removal-and-servicing-missions> accessed 1 November 2024.

66 UK Space Agency (n 65).

67 UK Space Agency (n 65).

68 Section 34 (2) of the Space (Launches and Returns) Act 2018 (Cth), No. 123, 1998 and Space (Launches and Returns) (General) Rules 2019 (Cth).

69 Abene Clayton, 'US Government Issues First-Ever Space Debris Penalty to Dish Network' *The Guardian* (3 October 2023) <https://www.theguardian.com/science/2023/oct/02/fcc-space-debris-fine-dish-network-satellite#:~:text=The%20US%20Federal%20Communications%20Commission,for%20more%20than%20two%20decades> accessed 1 November 2024.

70 Clayton (n 69).

valuation.'[71] Some researchers believe that this case will prompt some states to re-examine the sufficiency of their laws to mitigate the harm of space debris.[72] There is evidence emerging of this beginning to occur with the European Space Agency publishing its Zero Debris Charter in November 2023, which aims to be a 'major contribution towards space safety and sustainability [by] fostering a community of proactive actors working collectively towards jointly defined ambitious and measurable targets for 2030.' However, the Charter, much like the UN Space Debris Mitigation Guidelines, is non-legally binding. Only 12 European Union member states have become signatory parties, whereas over 100 organizations worldwide have pledged to sign the Charter.[73] With outer space use and exploration exceedingly steered by space companies, a study of the international legal framework is crucial to ensure that they are not operating in a legal void.

Bearing the complexity of domestic legislative approaches to space debris in mind, perhaps it is premature to consider questions of cooperation or compliance mechanisms when the core question is the sufficiency of the UN Space Debris Mitigation Guidelines themselves. Notwithstanding, concerns that the Guidelines are not binding on space companies, what mechanisms will be available at the international level to complain about a space company's conduct? The abundance of space debris issues that arise make it exceptionally difficult to generalize on the state of the literature in the discipline. While most of the current debate is in the detail of the matters discussed in the previous paragraphs, a prevalent theme is that many of the difficulties with interpreting and applying the UN Space Debris Mitigation Guidelines are well known to both states and space companies alike. Nonetheless, the legal solutions to these dilemmas, especially enforcement and liability, continue to be underexplored. This underlines the need for a scholarly approach that perceptively demarcates the issues under consideration and perhaps presumes that a comprehensive all-encompassing approach may not be possible. Bearing this in mind, the next section of this chapter will consider some of the topics that will foreseeability engage legal researchers on space debris over the next decade.

4 Topics for Future Research on Space Debris and Outer Space Law

Research on the regulation of space debris in the context of outer space will continue with regards its conventional topics, specifically the interpretation and enforcement of the outer space treaties and conventions, the UN Space Debris Mitigating Guidelines and domestic law and policies. This section does not purport to have an all-encompassing purpose but instead seeks to determine some of the most pertinent lines of inquiry that will shape the law on space debris in the future. These issues either represent research gaps or warrant further research, so instead

71 Robert Pearson, Harrison Schrieber and Giovanni Zanalda, 'Launch the Orbits Act' *SpaceNews* (6 March 2024) <https://spacenews.com/launch-orbits-act/> accessed 1 November 2024.

72 Pearson and others (n 71).

73 Pearson and others (n 71).

of resolving these issues, this section will briefly analyze each issue, deciphering its key contentions and potential impacts for the management and mitigation of space debris. The selected topics refer to (a) the domestic implementation of the UN Space Debris Mitigation Guidelines and (b) an international legal enforcement mechanism on space debris matters.

(a) Domestic Implementation of the UN Space Debris Mitigation Guidelines

The UN Space Debris Mitigation Guidelines specify that the 'prompt implementation of appropriate debris mitigation measures is . . . considered a prudent and necessary step towards preserving the outer space environment for future generations.'[74] Yet, the Guidelines specify that they are not binding under international law and in any event 'exceptions to the implementation of individual guidelines or elements thereof may be justified, for example, by the provisions of the United Nations treaties and principles on outer space.'[75] An interesting line of research would be to examine how individual states have interpreted the Guidelines and transposed them into their legislative frameworks. Indeed, a comprehensive analysis of justifications by states for making exceptions to the transposition of individual Guidelines into domestic law has not yet been completed. This constitutes the next frontier in space debris research since a comparative analysis of the various approaches adopted by states also does not appear to have been comprehensively examined.

A critical observation is that the existence of a legal duty for both states and space companies to gather and store data about space debris created by launched objects remains unexplored. For example, in the United Kingdom, Section 2 of the *Space Industry Act 2018* requires that the state regulator must take into consideration 'any international obligations of the United Kingdom [and] any space debris mitigation guidelines issued by an international organization.'[76] While the individual or company launching the space object has a duty to outline 'the design and operational procedures that will be used to prevent or mitigate the creation of space debris during proposed spaceflight activities,'[77] there does not appear to be a corresponding duty for operators to monitor and track the impact of their space objects on the outer space environment and collect and store data about any consequential space debris. The UN Space Debris Mitigation Guidelines also do not include a provision encouraging states or space companies to report incidents of space debris creation. An interesting future line of inquiry would be to examine the legislative approach adopted by states with regards this type of reporting, especially when incidents occur that lead to the creation of space debris.

A cursory examination of space debris mitigation measures in several states indicates there is perhaps an emerging practice of active debris removal. For example, in Australia sections 34(2) and 46(G) of the *Space (Launches and*

74 UN Space Debris Mitigation Guidelines, para. 1.
75 UN Space Debris Mitigation Guidelines, para. 3.
76 *Space Industry Act 2018* (c.5) (United Kingdom), Section 2(h).
77 *Space Industry Regulations 2021* (No. 792) (United Kingdom), Schedule 1, Section 14.

Returns) Act 2018 require that in order to be granted a domestic launch permit or an overseas payload permit the operator must supply a debris reduction strategy.[78] New Zealand has a similar requirement with Sections 9, 17 and 25 of the *Outer Space and High-Altitude Activities Act 2017* prescribing that for either a domestic launch license, payload permit or overseas launch permit to be granted an orbital debris plan must be submitted by the operator.[79] During the 60th session of the UNCOPUOS in February 2023, New Zealand announced its memorandum of understanding with Astrocale, proclaiming, 'advances can be made through partnerships between governments and commercial companies with a shared goal of improving the safety and sustainability of space.'[80] Unfortunately, New Zealand did not elaborate its position on whether the scope of outer space law should be expanded to include a duty for space companies to actively remove space debris. Since the use and exploration of outer space will soon be dominated by space companies, future research should clarify what options are best for addressing non-compliance with UN Space Debris Mitigation Guidelines. The search for an efficient compliance mechanism will surely continue to be scrutinized by scholars.

(b) A Legal Enforcement Mechanism for Space Debris at the International and Domestic Levels

The UN Space Debris Mitigation Guidelines do not provide direction on how disputes involving space debris should be resolved.[81] There have been increasing calls for a bespoke international court/tribunal not only to address disputes concerning outer space use and exploration but also to determine questions of liability. Perhaps the emergence of space companies over the last number of decades amplifies this need since the fragmentation of outer space law means that space companies are largely excluded. However, these calls have so far gone unanswered by the international community despite compelling arguments presented by legal scholars.[82] Future research needs to examine whether there would be any objections to the creation of this court and whether it would potentially face

78 *Space (Launches and Returns) Act 2018 (Australia),* Public Act No. 123, date of assent 31 August 2018 Sections 34(2) and 46(G).

79 *Outer Space and High-Altitude Activities Act 2017 (New Zealand),* Public Act No. 29, date of assent 10 July 2017, Sections 9, 17 and 25.

80 New Zealand National Statement, 60th Session of the UNCOPUOS Scientific and Technical Subcommittee, 6–17 February 2023, at page 2.

81 Zannoni (n 7) 297.

82 P.J. Blount, 'Renovating Space: The Future of International Space Law' (2011) 40 Denver Journal of International Law and Policy 515–32; Michael Listner and Joshua Smith, 'A Litigator's Guide to the Galaxy: A Look at the Pragmatic Questions for Adjudicating Future Outer Space Disputes' (2020) 23(1) Vanderbilt Journal of Entertainment and Technology Law 53–98; Arthad Kurlekar, 'Space- The Final Frontier: Analysing Challenges of Dispute Resolution Relating to Outer Space' (2016) 33(4) Journal of International Arbitration 379–415.

political opposition like the International Criminal Court since it is foundation under the Rome Statute in 2002.[83]

While the benefits associated with setting up a separate international space court are undoubtable, future research should examine perceptions that existing dispute resolution mechanisms are unable to resolve disputes efficiently. Current dispute resolution mechanisms, which include the Optional Rules for Arbitration of Disputes Relating to Outer Space (PCA Outer Space Rules),[84] are largely based on the 2010 UN Commission on International Trade Law (UNITRAL) Arbitration Rules. However, it is widely accepted that the PCA Outer Space Rules have not gained a foothold despite being accessible to all space actors including private commercial enterprises.[85] This is despite the fact that the rules are supposed to mirror 'the particular characteristics of disputes having an outer space component involving the use of outer space by States, international organisations and private entities' as well as 'the public international law element that pertains to disputes that may involve States and the use of outer space, and international practice appropriate to such disputes.'[86] An interesting line of scholarly research would be an examination of why both states and non-state actors such as space companies have not frequently endeavored to resolve their disputes using the PCA Outer Space Rules. Surely, an examination of the perceived deficiencies of these rules would enable scholars to more concretely examine not only the case for amending these rules but also the need for a bespoke international space court.

Since the rules became operational on 6 December 2011, the breadth and scope of outer space activity has changed considerably and as noted in Section 1 of this chapter space companies such SpaceX, Maxar Technologies and Rocket Lab increasingly dominate the sector more than states do.[87] A study conducted by Jan Frohloff in 2019 also indicates that a significant portion of disputes involving space companies concern satellites, especially their launch and delivery.[88] As a result, future research needs to scrutinize whether the PCA Outer Space Rules are still fit for purpose or need to be retrofitted for a new generation of space actors and new types of space activity. Unfortunately, the five key outer space law treaties do not deal with dispute resolution in depth and while the Annex to the PCA Outer Space Rules has a sample arbitration clause that can be used in commercial contracts, it is increasingly unclear whether space companies are in fact aware of the dispute resolution mechanism at all.[89] Empirical data on this issue is needed to enable scholars to complete an informed analysis of the efficiency of the rules since disputes

83 *Rome Statute of the International Criminal Court*, adopted by the United Nations Diplomatic Conference of Plenipotentiaries on the Establishment of an International Criminal Court, July 17, 1998, UN Doc. A/CONF.183/9.

84 Permanent Court of Arbitration, Optional Rules for Arbitration of Disputes Relating to Outer Space Activities (2011).

85 United Nations Commission on International Trade Law Arbitration Rules, UN Doc A/31/98, 31st Session Supp No. 17.

86 PCA Outer Space Rules, page 3 at para. (i).

87 See earlier at page 196 of this chapter.

88 Jan Frohloff, 'Arbitration in Space Disputes' (2019) 35(3) Arbitration International 309–29.

89 PCA Outer Space Rules, Annex.

concerning outer space use and exploration create unique challenges, especially for protection of intellectual property, trade secrets and information with national security implications. Moreover, without an effective dispute resolution mechanism, how can operators of space objects be encouraged to comply with their debris mitigation plans as discussed in the previous subsection? Currently, it is unclear whether state regulators must actively monitor the launched object for space debris and take enforcement action against the operator if they fail to comply with their debris mitigation plan.[90] Future research should provide a response to this dilemma especially in view of the non-binding nature of UN Space Debris Mitigation Guidelines.

5 Concluding Thoughts

As discussed in the introduction, outer space law has had very little to do with the protection of the environment, and this chapter has endeavored to analyze an important consequence of this reality with reference to space debris. It has examined the continued impact of the lack of legal research in this area and made suggestions for future research lines of inquiry. While space debris provides many avenues for legal research, only a small portion of this has been considered here. Given the lack of consensus on the need for a binding international legal framework, the argument presented in this chapter may be unsettling. In view of rapidly developing space technologies, the need for a binding international legal framework will become more pressing especially with the emergence of new technologies. Over the course of this chapter, we have queried how compliance with the UN Space Debris Mitigation Guidelines can be realized since there remains no enforcement mechanism at the international level to hold states and space companies accountable for breaches of outer space law. Moreover, can it be argued compellingly that the Guidelines are not about rules at all but a means of pursuing international politics? In a similar way to a lot of outer space law research, this chapter endeavors to ascertain the ambiguities that are problematic and find possible answers to resolve them.

Finally, there continues to be a dearth of empirical and socio-legal research in outer space law, and this is likely to continue to be the state of play. Obviously, the pursuit of doctrinal legal research is still crucial but linkages to other disciplines, especially science and engineering, are imperative to understand how environmental regulations in the outer space realm interrelate with the social, scientific and political perspectives. Notwithstanding the methodical approaches adopted by the present and future generation of outer space law researchers, the ongoing lack of research on space debris regulation will arguably be significant. Uncertainty about the breadth and scope of the duty of space companies to have due regard for the outer space environment and to protect it from harm persists. Legal researchers have considerable heavy lifting to do to fill the void.

90 See generally, Joel Dennerley, 'State Liability for Space Object Collisions: The Proper Interpretation of 'Fault' for the Purposes of International Space Law' (2018) 29(1) European Journal for International Law 281–301, 291.

10 Critical Space Synergies

The European GNSS, Liability, and Sustainable Development Goals

Ioana Bratu

1 Introduction

Space represents an essential element for strategic and economic development among states, offering the grounds for an ecosystem of technological innovation.[1] Space technologies, including global navigation satellite systems (GNSSs), are a key enabler of our modern lives on Earth. GNSSs represent a critical technology for the 21st century and are one of the driving forces for equality, human security, and prosperity. Moreover, GNSSs play an indispensable role in advancing the United Nations Sustainable Development Goals (SDGs) by enhancing the capabilities and efficiencies across diverse sectors, including agriculture, transportation, disaster management, and climate science. These technologies provide precise and reliable location and timing information crucial for various applications, directly supporting sustainable development initiatives worldwide. The contribution of GNSSs to the United Nations SDGs extends beyond specific applications to underpin a broader spectrum of developmental initiatives. By facilitating improved data collection and real-time information access, GNSS technologies enhance decision-making processes across various sectors.[2] This capability is critical for planning and implementing development strategies that are both effective and sustainable. For instance, in urban planning, GNSS data helps optimize traffic flows and reduce congestion, which contributes to reduced greenhouse gas emissions and more liveable cities, aligning with SDG 11 (Sustainable Cities and Communities). Furthermore, the integration of GNSS in healthcare logistics can dramatically improve the delivery of medical supplies, especially in remote areas, thus advancing SDG 3 (Good Health and Well-Being). By ensuring that vaccines and medical aids reach their destinations promptly and safely, GNSS technologies play a vital role in global health security and equity.

1 See Bockel Jean-Marie, 'The Future of Space Industry' (2018) 173 ESC 18 1 <https://www.nato-pa.int/document/2018-future-space-industry-bockel-report-173-esc-18-e-fin> accessed 20 April 2024.

2 See European Union Agency for the Space Programme, 'EUSPA EO and GNSS Market Report' (Publications Office of the European Union 2024) Issue 2 124 <https://data.europa.eu/doi/10.2878/73092> accessed 14 April 2024.

DOI: 10.4324/9781003370499-13

The European GNSS, Galileo, provides a notable example of GNSS's role in sustainable development through its increased accuracy and reliability compared to other systems. Galileo is specifically designed to deliver high-precision services globally, which enhances its utility in critical applications. For example, Galileo supports more efficient natural resource management, such as water conservation and sustainable agricultural practices, thereby contributing to SDG 6 (Clean Water and Sanitation) and SDG 2 (Zero Hunger).[3] Its commitment to providing robust and precise positioning services also enhances search and rescue operations, making it an invaluable asset in emergency response scenarios, directly impacting SDG 11. Notwithstanding its multiple connections with various SDGs, for the purpose of this chapter, it will be analysed how the GNSS, and in particular Galileo, may contribute to SDG 2 (Zero Hunger), SDG 10 (Reduced Inequalities), and SDG 13 (Climate Actions). The purpose of such case studies is to emphasize the critical reliance on GNSS services and to advocate for a future comprehensive legal regime. This is primarily because the increasing dependence on GNSSs does not come without legal implications.[4] Concerns are growing related to GNSS failures caused by electronic, kinetic interferences or other system malfunctions, which may lead to losses in the sectors relying on GNSS services.[5] For example, autonomous vehicles may go out of lane, drones may crash into buildings, aircrafts may crash while landing, the coast guard may no longer be able to search and rescue people on shattered ships, high frequency traders may suffer economic losses because of their inaccurate clocks, and the synchronization of the global Internet might be affected.

This chapter aims to navigate the critical space synergy, 'GNSS—Liability—SDGs', via a holistic approach. First, it is necessary to have a basic understanding on how GNSSs operate. Therefore, Sections 2 and 3 of this chapter present a brief history of their development alongside their technical background. Section 4 demonstrates the unequivocal contributions of GNSSs, including the European GNSS, to future global prosperity, by supporting the fulfilment of the Sustainable Development Goals, and, further, the complexities of GNSS governance and regulation are explained in Section 5. These lay the foundation for framing the concept of 'GNSS liability', in a European tort law context, under Section 6. The key liability elements, fault, damage and causation, are discussed through the lens of Rome II Regulation, applicable to non-contractual obligations,[6] as well as two harmonization

3 See United Nations Office for Outer Space Affairs, *European Global Navigation Satellite System and Copernicus: Supporting the Sustainable Development Goals—Building Blocks Towards the 2030 Agenda* (United Nations 2019) 51, 59 <https://www.un-ilibrary.org/outer-space/european-global-navigation-satellite-system-and-copernicus_bd041258-en> accessed 26 August 2024.

4 See Royal Academy of Engineering, *Global Navigation Space Systems: Reliance and Vulnerabilities* (Royal Academy of Engineering 2011) 27 <https://www.raeng.org.uk/publications/reports/global-navigation-space-systems> accessed 5 June 2021.

5 See Todd Humphreys, 'Interference' in Peter JG Teunissen and Oliver Montenbruck (eds), *Springer Handbook of Global Navigation Satellite Systems* (Springer International Publishing 2017) 469–70 <https://doi.org/10.1007/978-3-319-42928-1_16> accessed 20 April 2024.

6 Regulation (EC) No 864/2007 of the European Parliament and of the Council of 11 July 2007 on the law applicable to non-contractual obligations (Rome II), OJ L 199.

initiatives, the European Group's Principles of European Tort Law (PETL)[7] and the Study Group on a European Civil Code (Proposed European Civil Code).[8] Section 7 concludes the analysis with further recommendations for future governance and regulatory actions concerning GNSS.

2 A Brief History of GNSS

The history of GNSS started back in the 1950s, with what is currently referred to as the 'space race', and involved the major international players, the United States and Russia.[9] The evolution of global navigation satellite systems has seen significant advancements from the early United States' Transit system and the Russian Tsikada system to today's comprehensive arrays like GPS and GLONASS. The Transit system, initiated from detecting Doppler shifts in the signals from the Soviet Union's Sputnik I, marked the beginning of satellite-based global positioning under the sponsorship of the United States Department of Defense (DoD) starting in 1958.[10] This innovation spurred further developments, culminating in the creation of GPS which became fully operational in 1973, intended initially for military use. By the mid-1990s, GPS had launched its first satellite and, influenced by geopolitical events, opened its services to civilian use, which now spans diverse applications across transportation, telecommunications, and emergency services. Similarly, the Soviet Union developed GLONASS, which became fully operational with a complete constellation by 1996. Like GPS, GLONASS transitioned from military to civilian usage in 2007, offering an unencrypted civilian signal globally.[11] China's BeiDou system started as a regional service in 2003 and expanded into a global system by 2020, with a total of 55 satellites providing extensive positioning, navigation, and timing (PNT) services.[12] Japan's Quasi-Zenith Satellite System (QZSS), operational above urban Japan, caters to mobile applications and is designed to deliver enhanced signal accuracy in areas where GPS signals are obstructed.[13] In India, the Regional Navigational Satellite System (IRNSS)

7 Principles of European Tort Law (PETL) (*egtl.org*) <http://www.egtl.org/PETLEnglish.html> accessed 24 April 2024.

8 Christian von Bar and others (eds), *Study Group on a European Civil Code. Principles, Definitions, and Model Rules of European Private Law: Draft Common Frame of Reference (DCFR)* (Interim outline ed, Sellier European Law Publishers 2008).

9 Previously (between 1922 and 1991) known as the Soviet Union.

10 See Ram S Jakhu and Joseph N Pelton, 'Global Navigation Satellite Systems and Services' in Ram S Jakhu and Joseph N Pelton (eds), *Global Space Governance: An International Study* (Springer International Publishing 2017) 186 <https://doi.org/10.1007/978-3-319-54364-2_8> accessed 4 May 2021.

11 See Norman Bonnor, 'A Brief History of Global Navigation Satellite Systems' (2012) 65 The Journal of Navigation 1, 7–8.

12 See, generally, Jun Lu, Xia Guo and Chengeng Su, 'Global Capabilities of BeiDou Navigation Satellite System' (2020) 1 Satellite Navigation 27.

13 See 'Japan Joins the GNSS Table With QZSS | European GNSS Service Centre' <https://www.gsc-europa.eu/news/japan-joins-the-gnss-table-with-qzss-2> accessed 4 May 2021.

comprises seven satellites providing critical navigation services in the Indian Ocean, recognized internationally by the International Maritime Organization in 2020.[14]

Along with the rest of the major spacefaring nations, Europe also demonstrated ambitious plans for developing their own GNSS. The development plans of the European GNSS, Galileo, started in the 1990s and marked the first instance of a civilian-operated system being developed based on the requirements of its users, designed based on users' needs.[15] Galileo was introduced in four phases: (i) the definition phase, from 2000 until 2002; (ii) the development and validation phase, from 2003 until 2005; (iii) the deployment phase, from 2006 until 2007; and (iv) the commercial operation phase, as of 2008. Galileo became operational in December 2016 and has been providing positioning, navigation, and timing services to users worldwide since then.[16] The system is constantly being improved and expanded, with additional satellites being launched to enhance the system's capabilities and improve its coverage.[17] Initially, Galileo was envisaged as a collaboration between the private and the public sector, in the form of a public-private partnership. The idea was abandoned, due to a failure in concession negotiations and, currently, in accordance with Regulation 696/2021,[18] the European Union is the owner of Galileo, while the European Commission, the European Space Agency, and the European Union Agency for the Space Programme share responsibilities from implementation to technical support. Galileo is used for a variety of applications, such as road traffic, including the operation of autonomous vehicles, agriculture, fisheries, civil engineering, emergency services, and the Internet of Things.

3 GNSS Segments and Service Provision

All GNSSs have three segments, namely the space segment, the control segment, and the user segment. The space segment is composed of a constellation of

14 'Explained: What Is the New Regional Navigation Satellite System or IRNSS?' *The Indian Express* (26 November 2020) <https://indianexpress.com/article/explained/explained-what-is-irnss-regional-navigation-satellite-system-7060146/> accessed 23 January 2022.

15 See Joseph Awange, 'Basics of Galileo Satellites' in Joseph Awange (ed), *GNSS Environmental Sensing: Revolutionizing Environmental Monitoring* (Springer International Publishing 2018) 115–16 <https://doi.org/10.1007/978-3-319-58418-8_7> accessed 29 April 2021; for a detailed analysis on the European ambitions in what concerns GNSS, see also Marco Ferrazzani, 'Recent Legal Developments of GNSS in Europe' (2011) 54 Proceedings of the International Institute of Space Law 359.

16 'Galileo' (*defence-industry-space.ec.europa.eu*) <https://defence-industry-space.ec.europa.eu/eu-space-policy/galileo_en> accessed 5 April 2023.

17 European Space Agency, 'Latest Galileo Satellites Join Constellation With Enhanced, Faster Fix' (*https://www.esa.int/*) <https://www.esa.int/Applications/Navigation/Latest_Galileo_satellites_join_constellation_with_enhanced_faster_fix> accessed 5 April 2023.

18 Regulation (EU) 696/2021 of the European Parliament and of the Council of 28 April 2021 establishing the Union Space Programme and the European Union Agency for the Space Programme and repealing Regulations (EU) No 912/2010, (EU) No 1285/2013 and (EU) No 377/2014 and Decision No 541/2014/EU, OJ L 170

satellites orbiting above the Earth, providing signals to the user equipment. GNSSs have their own 'constellation' of satellites, arranged in orbits to provide the desired coverage.[19] Each satellite in a GNSS constellation broadcasts a signal, which enables the identification of the satellite and its time, orbit, and status. In essence, the purpose of satellites is to provide a platform for radio transceivers, computers, and various auxiliary equipment to operate the entire GNSS system.[20] The position of satellites plays an important role in the overall configuration of GNSSs because satellites must be positioned in space to cover a sufficiently large area of the Earth. For example, a global system, as opposed to regional or local systems, requires a minimum of four satellites to be visible at any point on the globe at any time.[21]

The control segment, or the ground segment, is in charge of the proper functioning of satellites, such as maintaining the satellites in their orbital positions, monitoring satellite systems, and activating spare satellites to maintain system availability. This segment is also responsible for the encryption of data and the protection of services against unauthorized users.[22] The user segment consists of GNSS receiving equipment, such as receivers on the ground, at sea, in the air, or in space.[23] The main purpose of the user segment is to process the signals received from GNSS satellites and use them to apply location and time information.[24] All three segments are used for fulfilling the main purpose of GNSSs, that is to provide a signal that allows a receiver to answer the following fundamental question, 'what is a receiver's current location or heading direction?'[25] For doing so, GNSSs, as a generic concept, encompass the following three essential categories of functions.

(a) Basic or Primary Signal Provision

Basic signals carry basic data, and due to this, they could hardly be labelled as 'service-provision'. They are emitted without any 'processing', 'correction', or 'improvement', and therefore are very general in nature. It is unlikely that the

19 Novatel, 'An Introduction to GNSS' (*Novatel.com*) <https://novatel.com/an-introduction-to-gnss/chapter-2-basic-gnss-concepts> accessed 6 May 2021.

20 See Bernhard Hofmann-Wellenhof, Herbert Lichtenegger and Elmar Wasle (eds), 'Introduction' in *GNSS—Global Navigation Satellite Systems: GPS, GLONASS, Galileo, and More* (Springer 2008) 6 <https://doi.org/10.1007/978-3-211-73017-1_1> accessed 2 May 2021.

21 See John-Olof Nilsson, Dave Zachariah and Isaac Skog, 'Global Navigation Satellite Systems: An Enabler for In-Vehicle Navigation' in Azim Eskandarian (ed), *Handbook of Intelligent Vehicles* (Springer 2012) 321 <https://doi.org/10.1007/978-0-85729-085-4_13> accessed 8 April 2021.

22 See Hofmann-Wellenhof, Lichtenegger and Wasle (n 20) 7.

23 See Richard B Langley, Peter JG Teunissen and Oliver Montenbruck, 'Introduction to GNSS' in Peter JG Teunissen and Oliver Montenbruck (eds), *Springer Handbook of Global Navigation Satellite Systems* (Springer International Publishing 2017) 16 <https://doi.org/10.1007/978-3-319-42928-1_1> accessed 7 February 2021.

24 European Space Agency, 'GPS User Segment' (*gssc.esa.int*) <https://gssc.esa.int/navipedia/index.php/GPS_User_Segment> accessed 7 May 2021.

25 See Jay A Farrell, *The Global Positioning System & Inertial Navigation* (McGraw Hill Professional 1999) 14.

recipient would take any action depending on it alone.[26] Usually, the end-user matches this basic signal with information provided by other sources.

(b) Augmented or Secondary Signal Provision

For offering PNT services, the GNSS signals need to observe four performance indicators: (i) accuracy, meaning the difference or error between actual PNT information and computed PNT information; (ii) availability, referring to the percentage of time that the services are available to the user within a certain coverage area; (ii) integrity, meaning the ability of the system to warn users when the signal is not adequate for navigation; and (iv) continuity, meaning the ability to provide the required performances during an operation without interruption once the operation has started.[27] Due to a variety of factors, including electronic and kinetic interferences, the GNSS signal performance indicators are not always reached.[28] GNSS augmentation systems, either ground- or space-based, rely on technical means to enable precise positioning through fixed ground stations that transmit a corrected GNSS signal to the receiver. If a GNSS signal is augmented, the original signal will be considered the 'core signal' or 'basic signal', while the improved signal processed by the augmentation process will be defined as the 'augmented signal'.[29] Since these augmented signals carry more than basic data, they can be categorized as service provision.[30] Examples of existing augmentation systems include the Wide Area Augmentation Service, which is used for improving GPS signals and was developed for aviation purposes by the United States Federal Aviation Administration; the European Geostationary Navigation Overlay Service (EGNOS), which is currently augmenting the signals of Galileo and GPS; MTSAT Satellite Augmentation System, a Japanese space-based augmentation system, designed to supplement GNSSs by reporting and improving the reliability and accuracy of the signals; and the GPS Aided GEO Augmented Navigation system (GAGAN), an implementation of a regional space-based augmentation system implemented by the Government of India.

(c) Value-Added Service Provision

Value-added services are provided based on basic signals or augmented signals. These services can be categorized according to the industries in which they are offered, including but not limited to the aviation, rail, and maritime industries.

26 See Souichirou Kozuka, 'Third Party Liability Arising From GNSS-Related Services 52nd Colloquium on the Law of Outer Space: 3. Third Party Liability Issues in Commercial Space Activities' (2009) 52 Proceedings of the International Institute of Space Law 232, 237.

27 'GNSS Performances—Navipedia' (*gssc.esa.int*) <https://gssc.esa.int/navipedia/index.php/GNSS_Performances> accessed 24 April 2024.

28 See Section 5 later.

29 Frans von der Dunk, 'Liability for Global Navigation Satellite Services: A Comparative Analysis of GPS and Galileo' (2004) 30 Journal of Space Law 129, 136.

30 Von der Dunk (n 29).

Common examples of value-added services include the navigation services provided by Google Maps and other similar service providers. The sophisticated architecture and functionality of GNSS demonstrate its essential role in contemporary navigation and positioning, highlighting the complex interplay of technology and coordination necessary for its operation. This intricate system not only provides critical support across various sectors but also lays the groundwork for significant contributions to the Sustainable Development Goals, as will be further demonstrated in the present chapter.

4 Navigating the Future: GNSS Contributions to the United Nations Sustainable Development Goals

The United Nations Sustainable Development Goals are a collection of 17 global objectives established in 2015 to address some of the world's most pressing issues by 2030. These goals focus on a wide range of social, economic, and environmental challenges aiming to promote prosperity while protecting the planet. The SDGs include goals like no poverty, zero hunger, good health and well-being, quality education, gender equality, clean water and sanitation, affordable and clean energy, decent work and economic growth, reduced inequalities, sustainable cities and communities, responsible consumption and production, climate action, life below water, life on land, peace, justice, and strong institutions, and partnerships for the goals. Each goal is underpinned by specific targets, totalling 169, with over 200 measurable indicators that vary by region, enabling tailored approaches to development.[31] The SDGs call for universal action, moving beyond a focus solely on developing countries to include developed nations as well, highlighting a global responsibility towards sustainable development.[32]

The 2030 Agenda also has its 'space' equivalent. Via the resolution adopted by the General Assembly on 25 October 2021, space is being acknowledged as the driver for sustainable global development.[33] Moreover, the peaceful exploration of outer space has vastly expanded knowledge and transformed life on Earth. Space science and technology have become integral to everyday activities, offering a myriad of unique and essential benefits. As the space community advances its exploratory efforts, space will persist as a beacon of inspiration and innovation, continuing to develop applications that benefit humanity.[34] Out of the multiple

31 See Jyri Mustajoki and others, 'Ambitiousness of Sustainable Development Goal (SDG) Targets: Classification and Implications for Policy Making' (2022) 3 Discover Sustainability 36, 2.

32 United Nations and others, 'The 17 Goals | Sustainable Development' (*sdgs.un*) <https://sdgs.un.org/goals> accessed 14 April 2024.

33 United Nations, 'United Nations Resolution. Space as a Driver of Sustainable Development' (2021) Resolution adopted by the General Assembly A/RES/76/3 <https://www.unoosa.org/res/oosadoc/data/resolutions/2021/general_assembly_76th_session/ares763_html/A_RES_76_3_E.pdf>.

34 Overarching objective 3 from the Resolution is the following: 'Improve access to space for all and ensure that all countries can benefit socioeconomically from space science and technology applications and space-based data, information and products, thereby supporting the achievement of the Sustainable Development Goals.'

space infrastructures that can benefit the fulfilment of the sustainable goals, GNSSs, and in particular the European GNSS, play a distinctive role in achieving the following goals: SDG 2 (Zero Hunger), SDG 11 (Sustainable Cities and Communities), and SDG 13 (Climate Action).

5 The European GNSS and the Sustainable Development Goals

(a) SDG 2 (Zero Hunger)

SDG 2, 'Zero Hunger', aims to end hunger, achieve food security and improved nutrition, and promote sustainable agriculture. This goal emphasizes the importance of ensuring access to sufficient and nutritious food all year round for all people, particularly the poor and people in vulnerable situations, including infants. It also focuses on sustainable food production systems and resilient agricultural practices that increase productivity and production, help maintain ecosystems, and strengthen capacity for adaptation to climate change, extreme weather, drought, flooding, and other disasters. The targets of the goal include ensuring access to safe, nutritious, and sufficient food, ending all forms of malnutrition, doubling the agricultural productivity and incomes of small-scale food producers, ensuring sustainable food production systems, and maintaining the genetic diversity of seeds, cultivated plants, and farmed animals.[35]

As of 2023, the global situation regarding hunger and famine continues to be alarming. According to recent data, the number of people facing acute food insecurity has significantly increased from 135 million before the Covid-19 pandemic to now 276 million, largely due to disruptions connected with the Russian-Ukrainian conflict which affected global food supply chains and caused food prices to surge.[36] It is currently believed that the primary solution to diminishing hunger and food insecurity and ensuring adequate nutrition lies in promoting sustainable agriculture by 2030.[37]

The European GNSS has the potential to address food security by improving the efficient use of existing resources—such as land, seeds, fertilizers, pesticides, and water—through applications that include precision guidance for farm machinery, targeted irrigation, and variable rate applications. Galileo is already instrumental in precision farming, enhancing seed spacing and fertilizer usage to increase productivity. Complementing this with Earth observation techniques facilitated by the European Copernicus[38] significantly boosts agricultural output. Insights into soil

35 United Nations, 'Goal 2 | Department of Economic and Social Affairs' (*sdgs.un.org*) <https://sdgs.un.org/goals/goal2#targets_and_indicators> accessed 14 April 2024.

36 '47 Million People in the World Are on the Edge of Famine. What Can Be Done?' (*World Economic Forum*, 29 April 2022) <https://www.weforum.org/agenda/2022/04/world-hunger-war-ukraine-world-food-programme/> accessed 14 April 2024.

37 See Gheorghe Hurduzeu and others, 'The Development of Sustainable Agriculture in EU Countries and the Potential Achievement of Sustainable Development Goals Specific Targets (SDG 2)' (2022) 14(3) Sustainability 15798.

38 'About Copernicus | Copernicus' (*Copernicus.eu*) <https://www.copernicus.eu/en/about-copernicus> accessed 9 November 2022.

moisture aid in optimizing water resource use, particularly crucial during times or in regions where water is scarce. The integration of Galileo and Copernicus is also beneficial for livestock management: Galileo-enabled collars monitor livestock, assisting breeders, while data from Copernicus help pinpoint optimal grazing areas.[39] In aquaculture, GNSS technology is used for site selection, monitoring of environmental conditions, and logistics management. By providing precise and reliable location data, GNSS helps aquaculture operators to optimize the placement of cages and equipment in marine environments, enhancing productivity while minimizing environmental impact.[40] Moreover, in the fisheries sector, the European GNSS helps in the accurate tracking of fishing vessels, which aids in managing fishing efforts and in enforcing fishing quotas and areas, thereby promoting sustainable fishing practices. The systems also support critical maritime applications such as search and rescue operations, maritime traffic monitoring, and environmental protection initiatives.[41]

(b) SDG 10 (Reduced Inequalities)

SDG 10, 'Reduced Inequalities', is committed to addressing disparities both within and among countries to foster a fairer and more equitable world. This goal not only targets reducing income inequality but also aims to eliminate disparities based on age, sex, disability, race, ethnicity, origin, religion, economic, or other statuses within a country. The overarching objective is to ensure social, economic, and political inclusion for all individuals.[42] SDG 10 sets forth a comprehensive array of targets designed to support this mission. These include, among others, achieving and sustaining income growth for the bottom 40% of the population at a rate higher than the national average, thus enhancing their economic stability and well-being;[43] it also aims to empower and promote the inclusion of all people, ensuring equal opportunities.[44] Thus, SDG 10 relates to eliminating discriminatory laws, policies, and practices that hinder fairness and equality as well facilitating orderly, safe, and responsible migration and mobility of people through the implementation of well-managed migration policies.[45]

39 See United Nations Office for Outer Space Affairs, *Contribution to the 'Space 2030' Agenda: EU Space -Supporting a World of 8 Billion People* (United Nations 2023) 38–39 <https://www.un-ilibrary.org/content/books/9789213587560> accessed 22 March 2024.

40 See European Union Agency for the Space Programme, 'Report on Maritime, Inland Waterways, Fisheries and Aquaculture. User Needs and Requirements' (2023) 12 <https://www.gsc-europa.eu/sites/default/files/sites/all/files/report_on_maritime_user_needs_and_requirements.pdf>.

41 See European Union Agency for the Space Programme. (n 2) 20, 107–10.

42 United Nations, 'Goal 10 | Department of Economic and Social Affairs' (*sdgs.un.org*) <https://sdgs.un.org/goals/goal10> accessed 15 April 2024.

43 United Nations (n 42).

44 See Medani P Bhandari, 'What Is Next for the Sustainable Development Goals, What Are the Challenges Concerning SDG 10—Reduced Inequalities?' (2024) 7(23) Sustainable Earth Reviews 3–4.

45 For a comprehensive analysis, see Sinan Küfeoğlu, 'SDG-10: Reduced Inequalities' in Sinan Küfeoğlu (ed), *Emerging Technologies : Value Creation for Sustainable Development* (Springer International Publishing 2022) <https://doi.org/10.1007/978-3-031-07127-0_12> accessed 15 April 2024.

In the 21st century, migration has transformed into a global phenomenon. This transformation is not just due to the vast numbers involved—284 million international migrants, constituting 3% of the global population—but more so due to its universal presence: there is no region or country worldwide that remains untouched by migratory flows.[46] Every nation is implicated in some manner, whether as a point of departure, a destination, or a transit hub, with many countries participating in all three roles to varying degrees.[47]

Space technology's role in monitoring migration patterns and supplying data to early warning systems is pivotal. For example, in relation to migrant smuggling, data from Galileo can track locations and device histories to reveal consistent pathways. Additionally, optical and radar satellite technologies can be employed to identify vessels likely involved in human smuggling, activities that frequently jeopardize the safety of migrants.[48] Other space technologies, such as satellite-based Internet services, can provide remote or rural areas with better access to quality education resources and e-learning platforms.[49] This democratizes education, allowing students from economically disadvantaged backgrounds to access the same quality of education as those in more affluent areas.

(c) SDG 13 (Climate Action)

SDG 13, 'Climate Action', recognizes the need to strengthen resilience and adaptive capacity to climate-related hazards and natural disasters in all countries. It emphasizes the importance of integrating climate change measures into national policies, strategies, and planning to reduce the release of greenhouse gases. Additionally, SDG 13 seeks to improve education, awareness-raising, and human and institutional capacity on climate change mitigation, adaptation, impact reduction, and early warning.[50] Its targets include enhancing the resilience and adaptive capabilities of all countries to climate-related hazards and natural disasters, ensuring that these strategies are well integrated into national policies, strategies, and planning. Furthermore, the goal advocates for improving educational outreach, raising awareness, and building both human and institutional capacities on climate change mitigation, adaptation, and early warning systems.

Climate change is a major challenge that humanity is now confronting, posing a range of environmental, social, and economic risks. The scientific consensus is clear that human activities, such as burning fossil fuels, deforestation, and

46 See Catherine Wihtol de Wenden, 'International Migration as a World Issue' in Catherine Wihtol de Wenden (ed), *Migration and International Relations: IMISCOE Short Reader* (Springer International Publishing 2023) 2–4 <https://doi.org/10.1007/978-3-031-31716-3_1> accessed 15 April 2024.

47 For a comprehensive analysis, see *World Migration Report 2022* (2020) 21–28 <https://publications.iom.int/books/world-migration-report-2022> accessed 26 August 2024.

48 See United Nations Office for Outer Space Affairs (n 39) 65.

49 For more details, see Mathy Vanbuel, *Improving Access to Further and Higher Education via Satellites* (JISC 2004).

50 United Nations, 'Goal 13 | Department of Economic and Social Affairs' (*sdgs.un.org*) <https://sdgs.un.org/goals/goal13> accessed 15 April 2024.

industrial agriculture, are driving unprecedented changes to the Earth's climate system, leading to rising temperatures, sea level rise, extreme weather events, and other impacts. Human activities have already caused 1.1°C of warming above pre-industrial levels, and without rapid and significant reductions in greenhouse gas emissions, global temperatures are projected to exceed 1.5°C above pre-industrial levels by as early as 2030.[51]

Satellite-based navigation can significantly contribute to combating climate change through various applications. GNSSs support environmental monitoring by providing data essential for tracking changes in the Earth's environment and global warming.[52] This includes monitoring sea levels, ice melt, and deforestation, all of which are crucial for assessing and understanding climate change dynamics. In addition, GNSS-enabled precision agriculture supports reducing the overuse of water, fertilizers, and pesticides, which in turn decreases the agricultural carbon footprint. This method enhances crop yield and reduces waste, contributing to more sustainable farming practices.[53] GNSSs are also instrumental in disaster response and management by facilitating accurate and timely data for evacuation plans, disaster tracking, and post-disaster management.[54] This helps in minimizing the impacts of climate-induced disasters such as floods, hurricanes, and wildfires.

Overall, as already presented, the GNSSs, including the European GNSS, are instrumental across various SDGs, providing technologies that enhance productivity, support sustainable practices, and ensure safety and inclusivity, thereby making significant contributions to global efforts aimed at achieving a more equitable, safe, and resilient future. Through its diverse applications, GNSS technologies are central to tackling some of the most pressing challenges outlined in the United Nations' Sustainable Development Goals.

6 GNSS Threats and the Complexities of Governance and Regulation

While the advantages of GNSSs are indisputable, it is equally important to acknowledge the persistent threats that accompany their usage. The service provision enabled by GNSS is threatened by a series of risks. GNSS signals are weak and may be easily interfered with via a series of harmful interferences. These can

51 See Intergovernmental Panel on Climate Change, *Global Warming of 1.5°C: IPCC Special Report on Impacts of Global Warming of 1.5°C Above Pre-Industrial Levels in Context of Strengthening Response to Climate Change, Sustainable Development, and Efforts to Eradicate Poverty* (1st edn, CUP 2022) 4.

52 See, generally, Hans Gleisner, Mark A Ringer and Sean B Healy, 'Monitoring Global Climate Change Using GNSS Radio Occultation' (2022) 5 NPJ Climate and Atmospheric Science 1.

53 See Manuel Perez-Ruiz and others, 'GNSS in Precision Agricultural Operations' in *New Approach of Indoor and Outdoor Localization Systems* (IntechOpen 2012) 11–12 <https://www.intechopen.com/chapters/39780> accessed 15 April 2024.

54 For a detailed analysis, see Yusuf S Hascicek, Serdar Kose and Enes Koytak, 'An Overview of the Use of Satellite Navigation for Disaster Management and Emergency Response' (2014) 10 International Journal of Emergency Management 1.

be caused intentionally or unintentionally. Jamming or spoofing devices are utilized by a range of entities, such as private individuals seeking to safeguard their personal privacy, government officials, and terrorists, and their intentional purpose is to interfere with the proper functioning of GNSS-based applications.[55]

Unintentional harmful interferences can arise due to various factors such as debris, out-of-band emissions from other radio frequency systems, and urban landscape obstructions that may impede the signals.[56] The conditions of troposphere, such as temperature, pressure, humidity, and the ionosphere, can also affect the GNSS signal quality.[57] Natural phenomena, such as a solar flare or coronal mass ejection from the sun, can also impact satellite operations, leading to a total loss of GNSS capabilities.[58] A GNSS signal may also be lost when moving through various obstacles, such as tunnels or urban areas, causing error and noise in the location signal and leading to an inaccurate location.[59]

Such interferences may lead to global catastrophes or disturbances: for instance, an aircraft might crash into a densely populated area or a fully booked ocean cruiser might sink, causing loss of lives or significant destruction of properties. Similar effects may occur when GNSSs are utilized in rescue operations, where a GNSS malfunction could prevent timely assistance from being rendered, resulting in injuries or, once again, fatalities. From an economic perspective, comparable observations apply. For example, in a report commissioned by the UK Space Agency, the economic impact to the UK of a five-day disruption to GNSSs has been estimated at £5.2 billion.[60] Building on the understanding of GNSS history, its foundational technical components, and its pivotal role in advancing sustainable societies, it becomes evident that recognizing the potential threats to GNSS operations underscores the critical need for a robust legal framework. Such a framework is essential to ensure fair and equitable remedies in instances where damages arise from GNSS malfunctions. This acknowledgment acts as a crucial bridge to forthcoming discussions on governance and regulation, highlighting the necessity of comprehensive policies to safeguard the integrity and effectiveness of GNSS applications in diverse contexts.

55 See, generally, Manuel Cuntz and others, 'Jamming and Spoofing in GPS/GNSS Based Applications and Services—Threats and Countermeasures' in Nils Aschenbruck and others (eds), *Future Security* (Springer 2012).

56 SeeDejian Kong, 'Shaping a Uniform Governance Structure Over Global Navigation Satellite System (GNSS): The Way of Risk Management' (2016) 21 Uniform Law Review 393, 397.

57 See Nader Al Bitar, Alexander Gavrilov, and Wassim Khalaf, 'Artificial Intelligence Based Methods for Accuracy Improvement of Integrated Navigation Systems During GNSS Signal Outages: An Analytical Overview' (1 January 2020) 11(1) Gyroscopy and Navigation 41.

58 For a detailed discussion on space weather and its economic consequences, see JP Eastwood and others, 'The Economic Impact of Space Weather: Where Do We Stand?' (2017) 37 Risk Analysis 206.

59 See Jianfeng Zhao, Bodong Liang and Qiuxia Chen, 'The Key Technology Toward the Self-Driving Car' (1 January 2018) 6(1) International Journal of Intelligent Unmanned Systems 5.

60 Cf. London Economics, 'Economic Impact to the UK of a Disruption to GNSS' (2017) Showcase Report 4 <https://assets.publishing.service.gov.uk/government/uploads/system/uploads/attachment_data/file/619545/17.3254_Economic_impact_to_UK_of_a_disruption_to_GNSS_-_Showcase_Report.pdf>.

The GNSS governance structure is inevitably impacted by its global coverage and global deployment. In reaching their global functions GNSSs usually require international collaboration for signal augmentation, system interoperability, and GNSS ground facilities. Such international components lead to a series of difficulties related to, for example, identifying the applicable laws for GNSS, managing the multiple actors involved and contractual relationships, applying international conventions, and most importantly, assigning liability in case of damage caused by GNSS malfunction. In international law, generally, GNSS liability could arise following a breach laid down by treaty law.[61] Given that GNSSs are space assets, liability would fall under international space law, specifically, the Liability Convention[62] and the Outer Space Treaty.[63] The plethora of GNSS applications also renders applicable specific international conventions, such as those concerning air,[64] maritime,[65] road and rail transportation,[66] and oil[67] and nuclear damage.[68] In some cases, the provisions of these international conventions may cover compensation for damage caused by GNSS malfunctions, but only coincidentally and not because they include specific GNSS-related compensation mechanisms.

National law would be applicable for any claims which would arise following an obligation under law or a breach of contract, governed by a specific national law. However, due to the transnational characteristics of GNSS, there is a high probability that damage would involve more than one jurisdiction. In such cases, it may happen that the applicable law for the case is different from the law of the forum, *lex fori*, leading to a conflict of laws. For identifying which law must be applied by the court, a qualification of the legal obligation is required.[69] Usually,

61 See Lesley Jane Smith, 'Legal Aspects of Satellite Navigation' in Frans von der Dunk and Fabio Tronchetti (eds), *Handbook of Space Law* (Edward Elgar Publishing 2015) 580.

62 Convention on International Liability for Damage Caused by Space Objects (1971) 961 UNTS 187.

63 Treaty on the Principles Governing the Activities of States in the Exploration and Use of Outer Space (1967) 610 UNTS 205.

64 For example, the Chicago Convention; Convention on Damage Caused by Foreign Aircraft to Third Parties on the Surface, Rome, 7 October 1952; Protocol to Amend the Convention on Damage Caused by Foreign Aircraft to Third Parties on the Surface signed at Rome on 7 October 1952, Montreal, 23 September 1978.

65 For example, Athens Convention relating to the Carriage of Passengers and their Luggage by Sea, 1974, 13 December 1974, 1463 UNTS 20.

66 For example, the Convention on Civil Liability for Damage Caused during Carriage of Dangerous Goods by Road, Rail and Inland Navigation Vessels, Geneva, 10 October 1989; Convention on the Contract for the International Carriage of Goods by Road (CMR), 19 May 1956, Protocol to the Convention on the Contract for the International Carriage of Goods by Road (CMR), 5 July 1978 and Additional Protocol to the CMR, Geneva, 20 February 2008.

67 International Convention on Civil Liability for Oil Pollution Damage, 29 November 1969, 973 UNTS 3, as amended by Protocol of 1992 to amend the International Convention on Civil Liability for Oil Pollution Damage, 1969, 27 November 1992, 1956 UNTS 285).

68 For example, Vienna Convention on Civil Liability for Nuclear Damage, 21 May 1963, 1063 UNTS 266.

69 For details on conflict of laws and how to choose the applicable law in case on cross-border cases, see, e.g., K Lipstein, *Principles of the Conflict of Laws National and International* (Springer

national rules determine this qualification and, consequently, the substantive law to be applied to the specific cross-border case. In Europe, conflict of laws is regulated via two pieces of legislation, Rome I Regulation, applicable to contractual obligations,[70] and Rome II Regulation. Related to non-contractual obligations, two European harmonization initiatives are noteworthy: PETL and the Proposed European Civil Code. Both initiatives are structured around the classical components of liability: damage, fault, and causation. The purpose of the European Civil Code is to provide principles, definitions, and model rules for assisting in the improvement of legislation at the European level, the *acquis Communautaire*, while the purpose of PETL is related to the enhancement and harmonization of the law of torts in Europe. Although they do not have legal force, both instruments have been taken into consideration in European legislative reforms,[71] while an increasing number of national courts are relying on PETL provisions in cases of domestic law.[72] As expected, the two initiatives do not contain any GNSS-specific provisions. However, they will be analysed in the forthcoming sections, as potential guidelines for formulating legal solutions in GNSS liability scenarios.

Harmonizing European tort law raises a series of challenges considering the national legal traditions and divergences in judicial systems across member states, each possessing unique procedural norms and doctrinal foundations that reflect deeply rooted cultural and historical perspectives. Nevertheless, considering the evolution of technologies characterized by global coverage, such as GNSS, but also artificial intelligence, the future of European tort law might lie in (partial) harmonization.[73] Determining the applicable legal framework for GNSS governance and liability is critically important, as the absence of a clear legal foundation can result in liability voids—circumstances where liability for damage cannot be attributed.

7 GNSS and European Tort Law: An Unsolved Legal Matter

Historically, the concept of GNSS liability was not particularly relevant, especially because the United States and the Soviet Union did not accept any international

Science & Business Media 2013); Gilles Cuniberti, *Conflict of Laws: A Comparative Approach: Text and Cases* (Edward Elgar Publishing 2017).

70 Regulation (EC) No 593/2008 of the European Parliament and of the Council of 17 June 2008 on the law applicable to contractual obligations (Rome I), OJ L 6.

71 See, e.g., Anton Dulak, 'Slovakia' in Helmut Koziol and Barbara C Steininger (eds), *European Tort Law 2007* (Springer 2008) 523–24 <https://doi.org/10.1007/978-3-211-77992-7_27> accessed 20 April 2024.

72 See Jordi Ribot and Albert Ruda, 'Spain' in Helmut Koziol and Barbara C Steininger (eds), *European Tort Law 2007* (Springer 2008) 553–54 <https://doi.org/10.1007/978-3-211-77992-7_29> accessed 20 April 2021.

73 For an example for a partial harmonization initiative in the field of European tort law, see Proposal for a Directive of the European Parliament and of the Council on adapting non-contractual civil liability rules to artificial intelligence (AI Liability Directive), COM(2022) 496 final, 28 September 2022.

liability arising out of signal failure caused by their navigation satellites.[74] On the other hand, the European Union, as the owner of Galileo, considered accepting liability, given that Galileo was initially designed for offering commercial services subject to payment. This laid the grounds for the assumption that the problem of GNSS liability is in fact a 'European problem'.[75] In the absence of a special legal framework focused on GNSS liability, it is necessary to analyse each key liability component from a potential tort law claim: fault, damage, and causation. References to liability in the absence of fault (strict liability, or, more specifically, product liability) are also included.[76]

(a) GNSS and Fault-Based Liability

The notion of 'fault' represents an essential element in a tort law claim. This evidence will not be required in a strict liability regime, such as product liability, where fault is presumed by law. The Proposed European Civil Code, in Book VI on non-contractual liabilities, refers to 'contributory fault' under defences (Section 1 VI.—5:102); however, it fails to provide additional insights, such as a definition of 'fault' or other corresponding elements. PETL is more useful in this respect. Liability based on fault is analysed under Chapter 4 and includes the classical dichotomy, intentional versus negligent conduct. The latter may be divided into two other sub-categories: gross and slight negligence (*culpa lata* versus *culpa levis* or *levissima*). Intentional conduct refers to the state of mind of a person who knowingly engages in an action or omits to act, knowing full well the consequences that will follow such actions or inactions. Negligence refers to the situation in which an individual causes damage by engaging in an action or omitting to act due to an absence of care, which would have been exercised by a reasonably prudent person under a similar circumstance.[77] The majority of tort law claims arise from acts of negligence as opposed to deliberate misconduct. In instances of deliberate actions, fault is primarily assessed using objective measures, such as the reasonable person standard and the standard (or duties) of care, which are commonly known as the 'negligence tests'.[78] The applicability of the aforementioned criteria is contingent upon several factors, including but not limited to the type of rights being

74 See Ram S Jakhu, *National Regulation of Space Activities* (Springer Science & Business Media 2010) 118.

75 Cf. Ingo Baumann, 'Liability for GNSS Signals and Services' (*Inside GNSS—Global Navigation Satellite Systems Engineering, Policy, and Design*, December 2015) 39 <https://www.insidegnss.com/auto/novdec15-LAW.pdf>.

76 The present chapter does not include an analysis of 'public tort law'. It will not assess Art. 340 of the Consolidated version of the Treaty on the Functioning of the European Union, Official Journal 115, 09/05/2008 P. 0193–0193, dealing with the liability of the European Union for 'damage caused by its institutions or by its servants in the performance of their duties'.

77 See generally Garrath Williams, 'Taking Responsibility for Negligence and Non-Negligence' (1 April 2020) 14(1) Criminal Law and Philosophy 113–34.

78 See, generally, Guido Calabresi and Alvin K Klevorick, 'Four Tests for Liability in Torts' (1985) 14 The Journal of Legal Studies 585.

safeguarded, the degree of danger associated with the undertaking, the proficiencies, aptitude, and knowledge that can be reasonably anticipated of an individual participating in a given activity, the interrelationship between the parties involved, the expenses incurred by the activity, and the potential availability of alternative or precautionary measures.[79] For instance, life and physical integrity are considered fundamental rights that hold significant value. Consequently, it is generally expected that a considerable degree of care be exercised in their protection. Conversely, when considering economic interests, which are deemed less significant than physical well-being, a commensurately reduced standard of care is necessary.[80]

In the realm of GNSS, the attribution of fault for damage ensuing from system malfunctions necessitates a nuanced legal analysis. Intentional misconduct within GNSS contexts, while rare, would involve scenarios where an entity or individual knowingly undertakes harmful actions or neglects to take necessary actions despite understanding the likely adverse outcomes. Such instances might include deliberately transmitting incorrect signals or unjustifiably disabling system functionalities. Conversely, negligence might be a more prevalent concern in a GNSS context, and may include, for example, improper implementation of established safety standards in the system's design, maintenance, or operational protocols, such as neglecting software updates essential for satellite functionality. The evaluation of negligence in instances of GNSS malfunctions is intricately linked to the standard negligence tests. As such, the expected level of expertise and competencies of GNSS operators, who are presumed to possess substantial technical knowledge, elevates the standard of care. The duty of care is further nuanced by the relational dynamics between the GNSS provider and its users, potentially varying based on contractual or statutory frameworks.

(b) GNSS and Product Liability

In legal doctrine, product liability is defined as an indirect form of liability. That is because applying it involves imposing liability due to damage caused using a product manufactured or placed on the market and not directly upon someone for damage caused as a consequence of certain activities performed.[81] Product liability is also a strict form of liability, based on which producers are liable irrespective of fault (negligence) for the damage caused by a defective product.[82]

Legal scholars analysed GNSS in the context of product liability laws, by focusing on the possibility of assigning liability to the GNSS signal provider, subject to

79 Parts of these criteria have been mentioned ever since the last century, in the well-known work of Holmes. See Oliver Wendell Holmes, *The Common Law* (Macmillan 1960) 86–87.

80 See Cees Van Dam, 'Intention and Negligence' in *European Tort Law* (OUP 2013) 225–26 <http://oxford.universitypressscholarship.com/view/10.1093/acprof:oso/9780199672264.001.0001/acprof-9780199672264-chapter-8> accessed 18 April 2022.

81 Cf. von der Dunk (n 29) 135.

82 See Helmut Koziol and others, *Product Liability: Fundamental Questions in a Comparative Perspective* (De Gruyter 2017) 3 <https://doi.org/10.1515/9783110547559>.

qualifying the GNSS signal as a product.[83] The existing European Product Liability Directive[84] defines products as movable objects, even when incorporated into another movable or into an immovable object. According to this definition, an item will be considered a 'product' only if it is tangible.[85] Exceptions to this rule are limited. Electricity, as an intangible item, was included under the provisions of the Product Liability Directive, but such exception was formulated in a narrow way. This inclusion was directly connected with a ruling of the Court of Justice of the European Union (CJEU), Case C-158/94, Commission versus Italy, dated 23 October 1997, according to which damage from defective products was associated with the qualification of electricity as a 'good'.[86] Given that an extension of the provisions of the Product Liability Directive followed a CJEU case, it is difficult to imagine how another deviation would be possible in the absence of relevant case law. Therefore, it appears that including GNSS services under the provisions of the Product Liability Directive would require either a formal amendment of the Directive, a repeal of the Directive followed by the enactment of a new legislative instrument, or a CJEU ruling. Under the existing European Product Liability Directive, claims would need to be based on defective GNSS 'hardware', such as the satellite components and receivers,[87] and not on intangibles, GNSS signals, or services.

However, under a new product liability regime proposed by the European Commission in September 2022,[88] GNSS services are qualified as 'digital services'. The new product liability rules, though not specifically targeting services, have been expanded to include intangible assets. They will now also apply to digital services that are integrated into or connected with a product, such that the absence of these services would hinder the product's ability to perform one of its functions. The 'continuous supply of traffic data in a navigation system' is used as a specific example of such a digital service.[89] If the proposal is approved in its current version, it will allow victims to pursue compensation claims against specific categories of GNSS services, such as value-added service providers.[90]

83 See Andreas Loukakis, 'Product Liability Ramifications for Erroneous GNSS Signals: Is an Alternative Approach Possible?' (2013) 56 305, 308; see also Smith (n 61) 589–90; Caroline Videlier, 'Legal Qualification of Signal in Space and Relevant Liability Regimes Emerging Legal Issues in Satellite Telecommunications' (2001) 44 Proceedings on the Law of Outer Space 212.

84 Council Directive 85/374/EEC of 25 July 1985 on the approximation of the laws, regulations and administrative provisions of the Member States concerning liability for defective products 1985 (210).

85 Art. 2, Council Directive 85/374/EEC of 25 July 1985 (n 84) 385.

86 C-158/94, Commission v Italy, 1997, ECR 1997 I–05789.

87 See Smith (n 61) 591.

88 European Commission, 'Proposal of the European Commission for a Directive of the European Parliament and of the Council on Liability for Defective Products' (European Commission 2022) COM(2022) 495 final <https://eur-lex.europa.eu/resource.html?uri=cellar:b9a6a6fe-3ff4-11ed-92ed-01aa75ed71a1.0001.02/DOC_1&format=PDF> (New Product Liability Directive).

89 Recital 15 New Product Liability Directive.

90 For a detailed analysis, see Ioana Bratu, 'A First Critical Analysis of the European Approach to Damage Caused by Artificial Intelligence Enabled by Global Navigation Satellite Systems. A Bridge

(c) GNSS Damage

Damage is one of the key elements of liability, either contractual or tort and irrespective of being based on fault (negligence) or on strict rules. Rome II Regulation and PETL do not provide for a definition of the term. The Proposed European Civil Code, in Chapter 2 of Book 6, only refers to 'legally relevant damage', which is defined as 'loss, whether economic or non-economic, or injury'.[91] Both loss and economic or non-economic injury are 'legally relevant' if they result from a violation of a right otherwise conferred by the law[92] or from a violation of an interest worthy of legal protection.[93] Additional details on the notion of 'damage' were not included since it would have been impossible to define which kinds of detrimental effects generate a right to legal redress and under which conditions.[94] The positive aspect in not having a clear definition of 'damage' in the European tort law landscape is that liability might cover any kind of damage, without limitations.

Damage serves as a remedy for both material and non-material harm (such as mental suffering, damage to reputation or prestige, and loss of a chance) to a legally protected right, and the conditions under which compensation is granted are usually included in national laws.[95] In general, damage can be categorized as compensatory or punitive. Compensatory damages are intended to provide reimbursement for actual harm suffered, while punitive damages are intended to deter harmful behaviour.[96] The concept of compensatory damage covers both direct damage, a loss *stricto senso*, an actual reduction in a person's assets (*damnum emergens*), and indirect damage, a loss of an increase in those assets that would have occurred in the absence of the harmful act (*lucrum cessans*).[97] In practice, in some jurisdictions, courts seem reluctant to compensate indirect damage, especially when a specific provision is not included in the applicable legislation. Sporadically, some pieces of legislation provide that both direct and indirect damage are compensable, such as Directive 2004/35/EC on environmental damage.[98]

---

to Nowhere or a Cloud With a Silver Lining?' (2023) International Review of Law, Computers & Technology 1.

91 Art. 2:101 Book VI (1) Proposed European Civil Code.

92 Art. 2:101 Book VI (1) (b) Proposed European Civil Code.

93 Art. 2:101 Book VI (1) (c) Proposed European Civil Code.

94 See Christian von Bar, 'Non-Contractual Liability Arising out of Damage Caused to Another Under the DCFR' (2008) 9 ERA Forum 33, 36.

95 See Stefano Troiano, 'Tort Law and the Romanic Legal Family' in Helmut Koziol and Reiner Schulze (eds), *Tort Law of the European Community*, Tort and Insurance Law (Springer 2008) 427.

96 See Keith N Hylton, *Tort Law: A Modern Perspective* (CUP 2016) 407.

97 See Dam, 'Damage and Damages' (n 416) 348; but see Benedict Winiger and others, *Essential Cases on Damage* (Walter de Gruyter 2011) 326 for an opinion mentioning that the classification of damage in direct and indirect has no practical consequences since both of them need to be compensated.

98 Art. 2(2) 'Directive 2004/35/CE of the European Parliament and of the Council of 21 April 2004 on environmental liability with regard to the prevention and remedying of environmental damage', Pub. L. No. 32004L0035, OJ L 143 (2004).

As detailed under Section 5, a series of events may lead to GNSS malfunctions. Irrespective of their source, such disturbances may result in (i) direct physical damage, such as injury, death, loss of property, economic loss, and environmental damage, or (ii) indirect non-physical damage, such as moral damage and mental injury. Catastrophic losses are not necessarily the rule in case of GNSS signal failures. For example, in case of navigation used in road traffic, a system's failure causing a car's navigation system not to work may lead to accidents involving victims but also only to traffic congestions or delays.[99] In the latter case, the loss would be one of economic nature, but it would not involve other harms. More serious harms, however, may occur when GNSSs are used in rescue operations. A GNSS malfunction in such a case would hinder providing assistance in good time and might lead to injuries or even loss of life.

(d) GNSS and Causation

In tort law, causation refers to the connection deemed necessary, on the one hand, a defendant's misconduct, and on the other, compensable damage. Rome II Regulation emphasizes that the damage must be caused by the event giving rise to damage.[100] The event should be the present or future act, omission, or any other event based on which the claimant's claim is founded.[101] The location of the damage caused by the event is of particular importance because it will enable the applicable law. Rome II Regulation opted for *lex loci delicti*, the place where the damage occurs, as the solution for the applicable law in case of multiple jurisdictions involved. One of the reasons for this choice was to limit the number of potentially applicable laws in a conflict case and to ensure predictability in case of litigation. In the Proposed European Civil Code, the provisions on causation were kept short and are only meant to provide a general formula for causation. Art. 4:101(1) from Book VI, Chapter 4, provides that a person causes damage to another if the damage is to be regarded as a consequence of either that person's conduct or a source of danger for which that person is accountable. Under PETL, Chapter 3 contains a two-staged approach for determining a direct causal link: (i) the *conditio sine qua non* test and (ii) the scope of liability. Art. 3:101 (Conditio sine qua non) provides that an activity is a cause of the victim's damage if, in the absence of the activity, the damage would not have occurred. In other words, applying the *conditio sine qua non* test helps deciding whether there is a causal link between an activity and an alleged damage, thus leading to attribution of liability.[102] If an activity is a *conditio sine qua non* of a

99 See Ulrich Magnus, 'Civil Liability for Satellite-Based Services' (2008) 13 Uniform Law Review 935, 935.

100 Art. 2(1) and Art 4(1).

101 Art 2(3)(a). See Andrew Dickinson, *The Rome II Regulation: The Law Applicable to Non-Contractual Obligations* (OUP) 313 <http://olrl.ouplaw.com/view/10.1093/law/9780199289684.001.0001/law-9780199289684> accessed 15 July 2021.

102 See Francesco D Busnelli and others, 'Causation' in Francesco D Busnelli and others (eds), *Principles of European Tort Law: Text and Commentary* (Springer 2005) 44 <https://doi.org/10.1007/3-211-27751-X_4> accessed 8 July 2021.

loss, the next step would be to identify the losses attributable to the activity, that is the extent of liability. The purpose of this attribution rule is to limit the scope of liability described under Art. 3:201, which provides that the scope of liability depends on a number of factors. These include foreseeability, the nature and the value of the protected interest, the basis of liability, the extent of the ordinary risks of life, and the protective purpose of the rule that has been violated. The two-staged approach to causation may be used to exclude damage, which is considered, for example, too remote, or in more complex cases involving multiple causes, where it is not easy to identify the unlawful activity or conduct leading to damage.[103]

In the context of GNSS, proving causation may prove challenging, considering the technological complexities.[104] In the absence of any legal requirements imposed on GNSS signal providers to offer explanations regarding the technology, victims might be hindered in obtaining compensation, due to the so-called black-box phenomenon. This is especially encountered in similar advanced technologies, such as artificial intelligence,[105] and it refers to an opaque, impenetrable system, where inputs and operations are not visible for their users or other interested parties.[106] For example, in machine learning, a sub-type of artificial intelligence, black-box models are created directly by algorithms from supplied data. This means that even those who design the models would not be able to understand how variables were combined to make predictions. With the level of GNSS technology advancing, it would be difficult for a claimant to prove the exact cause of an incident. Moreover, since GNSSs start to be integrated as essential components in the operation of other complex technologies,[107] it might become almost impossible to demonstrate that the GNSS signal was the factor contributing to an incident. Access to understanding GNSS technology might also be hindered by confidentiality requirements, especially in cases where such technologies have a dual purpose, military and civil, such as the case of GPS. In light of these difficulties and in the absence of a *lex specialis* referring to GNSS, each GNSS claim would have to be treated separately, taking into consideration the particularities of each case.

8 Conclusions and Policy Recommendations for a Future European GNSS Framework

The purpose of this chapter was to introduce the innovative synergy 'GNSS—Liability—SDGs'. For addressing the potential impact of GNSS-related damage,

103 See Mark Wissink, 'Overview' in Helmut Koziol and Reiner Schulze (eds), *Tort Law of the European Community* (Springer 2008) 354 <https://doi.org/10.1007/978-3-211-77586-8_15> accessed 23 July 2021.

104 See International Civil Aviation Organization, 'Global Navigation Satellite System (GNSS) Manual' (2005) 9849 AN/457 6–3.

105 See, generally, Davide Castelvecchi, 'Can We Open the Black Box of AI?' (2016) 538 Nature 20.

106 See Yavar Bathaee, 'The Artificial Intelligence Black Box and the Failure of Intent and Causation' (2018) 31 Harvard Journal of Law & Technology 894.

107 See, e.g., Stefan Muckenhuber and others, 'Sensors for Automated Driving' in Steven Van Uytsel and Danilo Vasconcellos Vargas (eds), *Autonomous Vehicles: Business, Technology and Law* (Springer 2021) 116 <https://doi.org/10.1007/978-981-15-9255-3_6> accessed 1 April 2021.

it is crucial to understand how the technologies operate as well as their critical role in supporting and advancing global prosperity on Earth, as defined via the United Nations SDGs. It was demonstrated that GNSS, and, in particular, the European Galileo, may actively contribute to the fulfilment of SDGs 2 (Zero Hunger), 10 (Reduced Inequalities), and 13 (Climate Action).

Such critical importance is not properly reflected in the legal environment. GNSS governance and regulation are characterized by fragmentation and unclarity. Various legal regimes may become applicable in a GNSS-related damage, including international space law, air law, environmental law, technology law, national laws, and so on, making it difficult for the affected parties to obtain compensation in cases involving various types of damage. European law is also limited in this respect. In Europe, tort law is not harmonized. The Rome II Regulation and the initiatives PETL and the Proposed European Civil Code may provide the foundations for a GNSS-related claim; however, any interpretation of their provisions remains uncertain, on one hand due to absence of case law (in what concerns Rome II Regulation), and on the other hand due to their lack of a legally binding character (for PETL and the Proposed European Civil Code).

Thus, it is stringently necessary to reassess the topic of GNSS liability in a coherent and comprehensive manner. The European legislator should consider initiating a legislative proposal for a GNSS legal framework, which, even though possibly limited in its applicability to the European landscape, it might set a positive example and lead to similar regional and, ideally, global initiatives. Alternatively, the European legislator should consider specifically addressing the 'European GNSS Governance and Liability' in the upcoming European space law, announced in September 2023,[108] which aims to, among others, provide a framework for ensuring the safety of critical space infrastructures.[109] The main legislative principles on a European GNSS Governance and Liability framework should include the following key aspects:

1. *Technological Transparency*: Require open reporting of GNSS operational policies and practices, including more transparent public dissemination of information related to system status. Such a requirement will allow users to receive reliable access to information in case of incidents resulting in damage. This is particularly important where a fault-based liability regime must be used by victims, requiring proof of fault and causation, which may prove challenging without proper access to information. Properly address limitations caused by national security interests, while balancing the need of user protection.
2. *Security and Protection Against Threats*: Provide for transparent obligations connected to implementing comprehensive security measures to protect GNSS infrastructure from physical and cyber threats. A thorough assessment is required

108 Cf. European Commission, 'State of the Union 2023. Letter of Intent' (2023) 4 <https://state-of-the-union.ec.europa.eu/state-union-2023_en> accessed 26 April 2024.

109 See European Commission, 'European Union Space Strategy for Security and Defence' (2023) Joint Communication to the European Parliament and the Council JOIN(2023) 9 final <https://opil.ouplaw.com/view/10.1093/law-oeeul/law-oeeul-e66> accessed 26 March 2024.

for properly identifying all actors involved in the GNSS ecosystem for attributing relevant security obligations, depending on their roles and contributions.

3. *Sustainability and Environmental Consideration*: Integrate sustainability considerations into the development and expansion of GNSS infrastructure, ensuring that GNSS operations actively contribute to SDGs and to efforts concerning the mitigation of climate change.
4. *Innovation and Advancement*: Encourage continuous innovation and technological advancement in GNSS applications. Support research and development initiatives that enhance GNSS technology and expand its applications across different sectors.
5. *Regulatory Compliance and Enforcement*: Define specific regulatory requirements for GNSS providers and users, with clear guidelines on compliance. Set up an enforcement mechanism to ensure adherence to such regulations, with penalties for non-compliance.
6. *Liability and Compensation Framework*: Establish a clear and fair liability regime for damage or losses resulting from GNSS malfunctions or failures, beyond sector-specific rules. This includes defining the conditions under which GNSS owners, operators, manufacturers, and value-added service providers are liable and the mechanisms for compensating affected parties. Reconsider the suitability of liability disclaimers attached to open signals and correlate the framework with existing initiatives.[110]
7. *International Collaboration for a Future Global Regulation*: Foster international collaboration for knowledge sharing and to promote the need for a future international framework for GNSS, using the European legislative instrument as the foundation. Such principles would ensure that the European GNSS framework is robust, adaptive, and well protected against both current and future challenges, thereby supporting its sustainable operation and reliability, while at the same time aiming to promote a global standard. A future European GNSS framework is still uncertain. Nevertheless, it is stringently important that matters concerning the legal rules applicable to GNSS, with a focus on liability matters addressed through the lens of sustainable global development, remain part of the international agenda of policy makers.

Bibliography

'47 Million People in the World Are on the Edge of Famine. What Can Be Done?' (*World Economic Forum*, 29 April 2022) <https://www.weforum.org/agenda/2022/04/world-hunger-war-ukraine-world-food-programme/> accessed 14 April 2024.

'About Copernicus | Copernicus' (*Copernicus.eu*) <https://www.copernicus.eu/en/about-copernicus> accessed 9 November 2022.

110 See the disclaimers of liability related to Galileo Open Signal, in European Union Agency for the Space Programme, 'Galileo Open Service: Service Definition Document (OS SDD): Issue 1.3' (Publications Office of the European Union 2023) <https://data.europa.eu/doi/10.2878/08361> accessed 24 April 2024.

Nader Al Bitar, Alexander Gavrilov and Wassim Khalaf, 'Artificial Intelligence Based Methods for Accuracy Improvement of Integrated Navigation Systems During GNSS Signal Outages: An Analytical Overview' (1 January 2020) 11(1) Gyroscopy and Navigation 41.

Athens Convention relating to the Carriage of Passengers and their Luggage by Sea, 1974, 13 December 1974, 1463 UNTS 20.

Joseph Awange, 'Basics of Galileo Satellites' in Joseph Awange (ed), *GNSS Environmental Sensing: Revolutionizing Environmental Monitoring* (Springer International Publishing 2018) 115–16 <https://doi.org/10.1007/978-3-319-58418-8_7> accessed 29 April 2021; For a detailed analysis on the European ambitions in what concerns GNSS, see also Marco Ferrazzani, 'Recent Legal Developments of GNSS in Europe' (2011) 54 Proceedings of the International Institute of Space Law 359.

Yavar Bathaee, 'The Artificial Intelligence Black Box and the Failure of Intent and Causation' (2018) 31 Harvard Journal of Law & Technology 894.

Ingo Baumann, 'Liability for GNSS Signals and Services' (*Inside GNSS—Global Navigation Satellite Systems Engineering, Policy, and Design*, December 2015) 39 <https://www.insidegnss.com/auto/novdec15-LAW.pdf>.

Medani P Bhandari, 'What Is Next for the Sustainable Development Goals, What Are the Challenges Concerning SDG 10—Reduced Inequalities?' (2024) 7(23) Sustainable Earth Reviews.

Norman Bonnor, 'A Brief History of Global Navigation Satellite Systems' (2012) 65 The Journal of Navigation 1.

Ioana Bratu, 'A First Critical Analysis of the European Approach to Damage Caused by Artificial Intelligence Enabled by Global Navigation Satellite Systems. A Bridge to Nowhere or a Cloud With a Silver Lining?' (2023) International Review of Law, Computers & Technology 1.

Francesco D Busnelli and others, 'Causation' in Francesco D Busnelli and others (eds), *Principles of European Tort Law: Text and Commentary* (Springer 2005) 44 <https://doi.org/10.1007/3-211-27751-X_4> accessed 8 July 2021.

C-158/94, Commission v Italy, 1997, ECR 1997 I–05789.

Guido Calabresi and Alvin K Klevorick, 'Four Tests for Liability in Torts' (1985) 14 The Journal of Legal Studies 585.

Davide Castelvecchi, 'Can We Open the Black Box of AI?' (2016) 538 Nature 20.

Convention on Civil Liability for Damage Caused during Carriage of Dangerous Goods by Road, Rail and Inland Navigation Vessels, Geneva, 10 October 1989; Convention on the Contract for the International Carriage of Goods by Road (CMR), 19 May 1956, Protocol to the Convention on the Contract for the International Carriage of Goods by Road (CMR), 5 July 1978 and Additional Protocol to the CMR, Geneva, 20 February 2008.

Convention on International Liability for Damage Caused by Space Objects (1971) 961 UNTS 187.

Council Directive 85/374/EEC of 25 July 1985 on the approximation of the laws, regulations and administrative provisions of the Member States concerning liability for defective products 1985 (210).

Gilles Cuniberti, *Conflict of Laws: A Comparative Approach: Text and Cases* (Edward Elgar Publishing 2017).

Manuel Cuntz and others, 'Jamming and Spoofing in GPS/GNSS Based Applications and Services—Threats and Countermeasures' in Nils Aschenbruck and others (eds), *Future Security* (Springer 2012).

Catherine Wihtol de Wenden, 'International Migration as a World Issue' in Catherine Wihtol de Wenden (ed), *Migration and International Relations: IMISCOE Short Reader* (Springer International Publishing 2023) 2–4 <https://doi.org/10.1007/978-3-031-31716-3_1> accessed 15 April 2024.

Andrew Dickinson, *The Rome II Regulation: The Law Applicable to Non-Contractual Obligations* (OUP) 313 <http://olrl.ouplaw.com/view/10.1093/law/9780199289684.001.0001/law-9780199289684> accessed 15 July 2021.

Anton Dulak, 'Slovakia' in Helmut Koziol and Barbara C Steininger (eds), *European Tort Law 2007* (Springer 2008) 523–24 <https://doi.org/10.1007/978-3-211-77992-7_27> accessed 20 April 2024.

JP Eastwood and others, 'The Economic Impact of Space Weather: Where Do We Stand?' (2017) 37 Risk Analysis 206.

European Commission, 'European Union Space Strategy for Security and Defence' (2023) Joint Communication to the European Parliament and the Council JOIN(2023) 9 final <https://opil.ouplaw.com/view/10.1093/law-oeeul/law-oeeul-e66> accessed 26 March 2024.

European Commission, 'Proposal of the European Commission for a Directive of the European Parliament and of the Council on Liability for Defective Products' (European Commission 2022) COM(2022) 495 final <https://eur-lex.europa.eu/resource.html?uri=cellar:b9a6a6fe-3ff4-11ed-92ed-01aa75ed71a1.0001.02/DOC_1&format=PDF> (New Product Liability Directive).

European Commission, 'State of the Union 2023. Letter of Intent' (2023) 4 <https://state-of-the-union.ec.europa.eu/state-union-2023_en> accessed 26 April 2024.

European Space Agency, 'GPS User Segment' (*gssc.esa.int*) <https://gssc.esa.int/navipedia/index.php/GPS_User_Segment> accessed 7 May 2021.

European Space Agency, 'Latest Galileo Satellites Join Constellation With Enhanced, Faster Fix' (*https://www.esa.int/*) <https://www.esa.int/Applications/Navigation/Latest_Galileo_satellites_join_constellation_with_enhanced_faster_fix> accessed 5 April 2023.

European Union Agency for the Space Programme, 'EUSPA EO and GNSS Market Report' (Publications Office of the European Union 2024) Issue 2 124 <https://data.europa.eu/doi/10.2878/73092> accessed 14 April 2024.

European Union Agency for the Space Programme, 'Report on Maritime, Inland Waterways, Fisheries and Aquaculture. User Needs and Requirements' (2023) 12 <https://www.gsc-europa.eu/sites/default/files/sites/all/files/report_on_maritime_user_needs_and_requirements.pdf>.

'Explained: What Is the New Regional Navigation Satellite System or IRNSS?' *The Indian Express* (26 November 2020) <https://indianexpress.com/article/explained/explained-what-is-irnss-regional-navigation-satellite-system-7060146/> accessed 23 January 2022.

Jay A Farrell, *The Global Positioning System & Inertial Navigation* (McGraw Hill Professional 1999) 14.

'Galileo' (*defence-industry-space.ec.europa.eu*) <https://defence-industry-space.ec.europa.eu/eu-space-policy/galileo_en> accessed 5 April 2023.

'GNSS Performances—Navipedia' (*gssc.esa.int*) <https://gssc.esa.int/navipedia/index.php/GNSS_Performances> accessed 24 April 2024.

Yusuf S Hascicek, Serdar Kose and Enes Koytak, 'An Overview of the Use of Satellite Navigation for Disaster Management and Emergency Response' (2014) 10 International Journal of Emergency Management 1.

Bernhard Hofmann-Wellenhof, Herbert Lichtenegger and Elmar Wasle (eds), 'Introduction' in *GNSS—Global Navigation Satellite Systems: GPS, GLONASS, Galileo, and More* (Springer 2008) 6 <https://doi.org/10.1007/978-3-211-73017-1_1> accessed 2 May 2021.

Oliver Wendell Holmes, *The Common Law* (Macmillan 1960).

Todd Humphreys, 'Interference' in Peter JG Teunissen and Oliver Montenbruck (eds), *Springer Handbook of Global Navigation Satellite Systems* (Springer International Publishing 2017) 469–70 <https://doi.org/10.1007/978-3-319-42928-1_16> accessed 20 April 2024.

Gheorghe Hurduzeu and others, 'The Development of Sustainable Agriculture in EU Countries and the Potential Achievement of Sustainable Development Goals Specific Targets (SDG 2)' (2022) 14(3) Sustainability 15798.

Keith N Hylton, *Tort Law: A Modern Perspective* (CUP 2016) 407.

Intergovernmental Panel on Climate Change, *Global Warming of 1.5°C: IPCC Special Report on Impacts of Global Warming of 1.5°C Above Pre-Industrial Levels in Context of Strengthening Response to Climate Change, Sustainable Development, and Efforts to Eradicate Poverty* (1st edn, CUP 2022) 4.

International Civil Aviation Organization, 'Global Navigation Satellite System (GNSS) Manual' (2005) 9849 AN/457 6–3.

International Convention on Civil Liability for Oil Pollution Damage, 29 November 1969, 973 UNTS 3, as amended by Protocol of 1992 to amend the International Convention on Civil Liability for Oil Pollution Damage, 1969, 27 November 1992, 1956 UNTS 285).

'Japan Joins the GNSS Table With QZSS | European GNSS Service Centre' <https://www.gsc-europa.eu/news/japan-joins-the-gnss-table-with-qzss-2> accessed 4 May 2021.

Ram S Jakhu, *National Regulation of Space Activities* (Springer Science & Business Media 2010) 118.

Ram S Jakhu and Joseph N Pelton, 'Global Navigation Satellite Systems and Services' in Ram S Jakhu and Joseph N Pelton (eds), *Global Space Governance: An International Study* (Springer International Publishing 2017) 186 <https://doi.org/10.1007/978-3-319-54364-2_8> accessed 4 May 2021.

Bockel Jean-Marie, 'The Future of Space Industry' (2018) 173 ESC 18 1 <https://www.nato-pa.int/document/2018-future-space-industry-bockel-report-173-esc-18-e-fin> accessed 20 April 2024.

Dejian Kong, 'Shaping a Uniform Governance Structure Over Global Navigation Satellite System (GNSS): The Way of Risk Management' (2016) 21 Uniform Law Review 393.

Helmut Koziol and others, *Product Liability: Fundamental Questions in a Comparative Perspective* (De Gruyter 2017) 3 <https://doi.org/10.1515/9783110547559>.

Souichirou Kozuka, 'Third Party Liability Arising From GNSS-Related Services 52nd Colloquium on the Law of Outer Space: 3. Third Party Liability Issues in Commercial Space Activities' (2009) 52 Proceedings of the International Institute of Space Law 232.

Sinan Küfeoğlu, 'SDG-10: Reduced Inequalities' in Sinan Küfeoğlu (ed), *Emerging Technologies : Value Creation for Sustainable Development* (Springer International Publishing 2022) <https://doi.org/10.1007/978-3-031-07127-0_12> accessed 15 April 2024.

Richard B Langley, Peter JG Teunissen and Oliver Montenbruck, 'Introduction to GNSS' in Peter JG Teunissen and Oliver Montenbruck (eds), *Springer Handbook of Global Navigation Satellite Systems* (Springer International Publishing 2017) 16 <https://doi.org/10.1007/978-3-319-42928-1_1> accessed 7 February 2021.

K Lipstein, *Principles of the Conflict of Laws National and International* (Springer Science & Business Media 2013).

London Economics, 'Economic Impact to the UK of a Disruption to GNSS' (2017) Showcase Report 4 <https://assets.publishing.service.gov.uk/government/uploads/system/uploads/attachment_data/file/619545/17.3254_Economic_impact_to_UK_of_a_disruption_to_GNSS_-_Showcase_Report.pdf>.

Andreas Loukakis, 'Product Liability Ramifications for Erroneous GNSS Signals: Is an Alternative Approach Possible?' (56th IISL Colloquium on the Law of Outer Space, 2013) 56, 305.

Jun Lu, Xia Guo and Chengeng Su, 'Global Capabilities of BeiDou Navigation Satellite System' (2020) 1 Satellite Navigation 27.

Ulrich Magnus, 'Civil Liability for Satellite-Based Services' (2008) 13 Uniform Law Review 935.

Stefan Muckenhuber and others, 'Sensors for Automated Driving' in Steven Van Uytsel and Danilo Vasconcellos Vargas (eds), *Autonomous Vehicles: Business, Technology and Law* (Springer 2021) 116 <https://doi.org/10.1007/978-981-15-9255-3_6> accessed 1 April 2021.

Jyri Mustajoki and others, 'Ambitiousness of Sustainable Development Goal (SDG) Targets: Classification and Implications for Policy Making' (2022) 3(36) Discover Sustainability 2.

John-Olof Nilsson, Dave Zachariah and Isaac Skog, 'Global Navigation Satellite Systems: An Enabler for In-Vehicle Navigation' in Azim Eskandarian (ed), *Handbook of Intelligent Vehicles* (Springer 2012) 321 <https://doi.org/10.1007/978-0-85729-085-4_13> accessed 8 April 2021.

Novatel, 'An Introduction to GNSS' (*Novatel.com*) <https://novatel.com/an-introduction-to-gnss/chapter-2-basic-gnss-concepts> accessed 6 May 2021.

Manuel Perez-Ruiz and others, 'GNSS in Precision Agricultural Operations' in *New Approach of Indoor and Outdoor Localization Systems* (IntechOpen 2012) 11–12 <https://www.intechopen.com/chapters/39780> accessed 15 April 2024.

Principles of European Tort Law (PETL) (*egtl.org*) <http://www.egtl.org/PETLEnglish.html> accessed 24 April 2024.

Regulation (EC) No 593/2008 of the European Parliament and of the Council of 17 June 2008 on the law applicable to contractual obligations (Rome I), OJ L 6.

Regulation (EU) No 696/2021 of the European Parliament and of the Council of 28 April 2021 establishing the Union Space Programme and the European Union Agency for the Space Programme and repealing Regulations (EU) No 912/2010, (EU) No 1285/2013 and (EU) No 377/2014 and Decision No 541/2014/EU, OJ L 170

Regulation (EC) No 864/2007 of the European Parliament and of the Council of 11 July 2007 on the law applicable to non-contractual obligations (Rome II), OJ L 199.

Jordi Ribot and Albert Ruda, 'Spain' in Helmut Koziol and Barbara C Steininger (eds), *European Tort Law 2007* (Springer 2008) 553–54 <https://doi.org/10.1007/978-3-211-77992-7_29> accessed 20 April 2021.

Royal Academy of Engineering, 'Global Navigation Space Systems: Reliance and Vulnerabilities' (Royal Academy of Engineering 2011) 27 <https://www.raeng.org.uk/publications/reports/global-navigation-space-systems> accessed 5 June 2021.

Lesley Jane Smith, 'Legal Aspects of Satellite Navigation' in Frans von der Dunk and Fabio Tronchetti (eds), *Handbook of Space Law* (Edward Elgar Publishing 2015) 580.

Treaty on the Principles Governing the Activities of States in the Exploration and Use of Outer Space (1967) 610 UNTS 205.

Stefano Troiano, 'Tort Law and the Romanic Legal Family' in Helmut Koziol and Reiner Schulze (eds), *Tort Law of the European Community*, Tort and Insurance Law (Springer 2008) 427.

United Nations, 'Goal 2 | Department of Economic and Social Affairs' (*sdgs.un.org*) <https://sdgs.un.org/goals/goal2#targets_and_indicators> accessed 14 April 2024.

United Nations, 'United Nations Resolution. Space as a Driver of Sustainable Development' (2021) Resolution adopted by the General Assembly A/RES/76/3 <https://www.unoosa.org/res/oosadoc/data/resolutions/2021/general_assembly_76th_session/ares763_html/A_RES_76_3_E.pdf>. and space-based data, information and products, thereby supporting the achievement of the Sustainable Development Goals.'

United Nations and others, 'THE 17 Goals | Sustainable Development' (*sdgs.un*) <https://sdgs.un.org/goals> accessed 14 April 2024.

United Nations Office for Outer Space Affairs, *Contribution to the "Space2030" Agenda: EU Space -Supporting a World of 8 Billion People* (United Nations 2023) 38–39 <https://www.un-ilibrary.org/content/books/9789213587560> accessed 22 March 2024.

United Nations Office for Outer Space Affairs, *European Global Navigation Satellite System and Copernicus: Supporting the Sustainable Development Goals—Building Blocks Towards the 2030 Agenda* (United Nations 2019) 51, 59 <https://www.un-ilibrary.org/outer-space/european-global-navigation-satellite-system-and-copernicus_bd041258-en> accessed 26 August 2024.

Cees Van Dam, 'Intention and Negligence' in *European Tort Law* (OUP 2013) 225–26 <http://oxford.universitypressscholarship.com/view/10.1093/acprof:oso/9780199672264.001.0001/acprof-9780199672264-chapter-8> accessed 18 April 2022.

Mathy Vanbuel, *Improving Access to Further and Higher Education via Satellites* (JISC 2004).

Caroline Videlier, 'Legal Qualification of Signal in Space and Relevant Liability Regimes Emerging Legal Issues in Satellite Telecommunications' (2001) 44 Proceedings on the Law of Outer Space 212.

Vienna Convention on Civil Liability for Nuclear Damage, 21 May 1963, 1063 UNTS 266.

Christian von Bar, 'Non-Contractual Liability Arising out of Damage Caused to Another Under the DCFR' (2008) 9 ERA Forum 33.

Christian von Bar and others (eds), *Study Group on a European Civil Code. Principles, Definitions, and Model Rules of European Private Law: Draft Common Frame of Reference (DCFR)* (Interim outline ed, Sellier European Law Publishers 2008).

Frans von der Dunk, 'Liability for Global Navigation Satellite Services: A Comparative Analysis of GPS and Galileo' (2004) 30 Journal of Space Law 129.

Garrath Williams, 'Taking Responsibility for Negligence and Non-Negligence' (1 April 2020) 14(1) Criminal Law and Philosophy 113–34.

Benedict Winiger and others, *Essential Cases on Damage* (Walter de Gruyter 2011) 326.

Mark Wissink, 'Overview' in Helmut Koziol and Reiner Schulze (eds), *Tort Law of the European Community* (Springer 2008) 354 <https://doi.org/10.1007/978-3-211-77586-8_15> accessed 23 July 2021.

World Migration Report 2022 (2020) 21–28 <https://publications.iom.int/books/world-migration-report-2022> accessed 26 August 2024.

Jianfeng Zhao, Bodong Liang and Qiuxia Chen, 'The Key Technology Toward the Self-Driving Car' (1 January 2018) 6(1) International Journal of Intelligent Unmanned Systems 5.

11 Conclusion

Hypothesising the Future of Outer Space Law

Anna Marie Brennan

1 The Future of Asymmetrical Challenges

As we enter 2025, outer space law scholars are increasingly disillusioned with the Outer Space Treaty 1967 due to the emergence of several asymmetrical challenges. While the Treaty has endeavoured to protect space and its resources for 'the province of all [hu]mankind,' the proliferation of private space actors as well as smaller nations such as Luxemburg, the United Arab Emirates, and Japan was not anticipated at the height of Cold War tensions when the Treaty was drafted and adopted. In the collection *A Research Agenda for Space Policy* edited by Kai-Uwe Schrogl, Christina Giannopapa, and Ntorina Antoni and published in 2021, the authors acknowledged, '"societies" increasing dependence on space technologies and approaches to protect critical infrastructures by making space systems resilient presents governance challenges.'[1] Such challenges include China's and India's unilateral rise which has led to concerns about a myriad of actual, potential, and attempted non-compliance with outer space law in both civil and military space realms.[2] The de-regulation of the space industry especially in the United States with the passing of the Spurring Private Aerospace Competitiveness and Entrepreneurship Act of 2015 (SPACE Act) and the Artemis Accords 2020 has amplified concerns about the sustainable use and development of outer space.[3] Nevertheless, commercial operators increasingly advocate for the private ownership of space resources, and as a result, the SPACE Act and the Artemis Accords, in tandem, permit citizens of the United States to use and possess materials extracted

1 Kai-Uwe Schrogl, Christina Giannopapa and Ntorina Antoni, 'Introduction: A Research Agenda for Space Policy in the 2020s' in Kai-Uwe Schrogl, Christina Giannopapa and Ntorina Antoni (eds), *A Research Agenda for Space Policy* (Edward Elgar Publishing 2021) xxxiv.

2 Dimitrios Stroikos, 'Still Lost in Space? Understanding China and India's Anti-Satellite Tests Through an Eclectic Approach' (2023) 21(2–3) Astropolitics 179–205; Fikri Haikal Akbar, 'Competition Among Spacefaring States in the Exploration of "Terra Nulius" in Outer Space: A Neorealist Approach' (2023) 21(2–3) Astropolitics 206–13; Most Sharmin, 'China's Increasing Space Power and India-China Orbital Competitions: Implications in the Indo-Pacific With a Focus on South Asia' (2023) Journal of Indo-Pacific Affairs 53.

3 Kurt Taylor, 'Fictions of the Final Frontier: Why the United States SPACE Act of 2015 is Illegal' (2019) 33(4) Emory International Law Review 653–78.

DOI: 10.4324/9781003370499-14

from celestial bodies.[4] All citizens of signatory parties to the Artemis Accords such as the United Kingdom, New Zealand, and Australia can exercise the privilege. States will continue to play a key part in operating, regulating, and investing in critical space infrastructure well into the future but 'the international dimension needs to be taken into consideration when developing and realizing governance mechanisms.'[5] Even though efforts to 'promote exchanges of information, reciprocal confidence-building measures, and potentially adapt public financial planning concerning investments in critical infrastructures' will be pivotal, it is increasingly acknowledged that the setting up of an international civil space organisation is needed to facilitate this.[6]

Unquestionably, outer space affairs will continue to be macerated in politics, but can outer space lawyers also be described as idealist? Steeped in a final frontier belief system, is there a danger that the privatisation of outer space use and exploration is framed as 'entrepreneurship' by scholars, thereby reinforcing 'the capitalist ideology of growth through expansionist, mercantilist and colonial means'?[7] With an increasing number of states and corporations embarking on the use and exploration of outer space, is it no longer realistic to view it as *terra nullius*? Governments worldwide are grappling with the previous unfettered prerogative of states, with the aim of distilling the new values emerging in outer space affairs, especially those related to human rights and the protection of the environment.[8] Thus, the space race is rapidly evolving, and a new ethos is slowly being realised, if not already taking shape. Outer space law researchers examining the future of the discipline have traditionally sought to restrain militarisation, foster international cooperation and diplomacy, and make modest proposals for future reform. While there is serious and justified critique of the corpus of outer space law, there is no sense that the flaws in the project of outer space law are so great as to justify disengagement, even from the scholars who are most sceptical of the corpus of outer space law.

This edited collection of essays has moved away from seeking agreement about accomplishing Utopia and consensus about legal reform to instead consider the possible 'future' of outer space law. Our contributors have highlighted how outer space law deals with friction involving colonialism, universalism, and technological and environmental change. Moreover, this collection has also sought to offer a starting point for critical engagement and acknowledgement of the governance challenges prevalent in the outer space realm. Is it surprising that in 2024 the United Nations Security Council failed to adopt the first-ever resolution on outer

4 Melissa de Zwart, Stacey Henderson and Michelle Neumann, 'Space Resource Activities and the Evolution of International Space Law' (2023) 211 Acta Astronautica 155–62.

5 Schrogl, Giannopapa and Antoni (n 1) xxxiv.

6 Schrogl, Giannopapa and Antoni (n 1).

7 Matjaz Vidmar and Saskia Vermeylen, 'Utopia(s), Outer Space Law and Ecology' (2022) 41(1) EASST Review <https://easst.net/easst-review/411/utopias-outer-space-law-and-ecology/> accessed 1 November 2024.

8 Vidmar and Vermeylen (n 7).

space which would have affirmed that member states have a duty to comply with the Outer Space Treaty and not place any objects carrying nuclear weapons in orbit around Earth? It is hoped that the diversity of interdisciplinary approaches showcased in this book, including politics, human rights, engineering, international relations, and colonialism studies can enrich academic scholarship on the future of outer space law. Contributors did not utilise a reformist or critical approach but have instead addressed their individual fields in a spirit of inquiry to propose insights into the potential future of outer space law. Thus, to conclude this collection I aim to reflect on the state of outer space affairs in late 2024 and note how these events respond to our authors' ideas about the future of the law in this sphere.

2 The Quest for Reform

The outer space realm faced significant challenges in 2024, from a general lack of state and non-state actor compliance with its main international treaties to a debate over the concepts of 'province of all [hu]mankind' and 'national appropriation.'[9] While historically the key spacefaring leaders include the United States, Russia, China, and the European Space Agency, a cache of middle space powers which consists of India, New Zealand, Australia, Japan, and South Korea is swiftly emerging. General apathy towards the regulation of non-state actors in outer space use and exploration has led to a lack of controls on the number of satellites an actor, regardless of whether they are public or private, can launch into outer space. For example, SpaceX seeks to launch approximately 42,000 satellites by the end of the decade, raising concerns amongst astronomers about the impact of light pollution in the night sky as well as the potential for collisions and near misses.[10] SpaceX has swiftly responded to these concerns stating that the reliability of its satellite network is greater than 99% and that it has also effected an 'advanced collision avoidance system' that mandates avoidance manoeuvres if there is a 'greater than 1/100,000 probability of collision.'[11] Debate remains strong about Ukraine's Starlink usage for operating drones during its armed conflict with Russia.[12] SpaceX decided to limit its usage since the service was 'never meant to be weaponised,' but it has since developed Starshield which is a militarised version

9 Articles I and II of the Outer Space Treaty.

10 Tereza Pultarova and Elizabeth Howell, 'Starlink Satellites: Facts, Tracking and Impact on Astronomy' (*Space.com*, 28 September 2024) <https://www.space.com/spacex-starlink-satellites.html> accessed 1 November 2024.

11 Tereza Pultarova, 'SpaceX Starlink Satellites Had to Make 25,000 Collision-Avoidance Maneuvers in Just 6 Months—And It will Only Get Worse' (*Space.com*, 7 July 2023) <https://www.space.com/starlink-satellite-conjunction-increase-threatens-space-sustainability> accessed 1 November 2024.

12 Nicky Paton Walsh and others, 'Ukraine Relies on Starlink for Its Drone War: Russia Appears to Be Bypassing Sanctions to Use the Devices Too' *CNN* (26 March 2024) <https://edition.cnn.com/2024/03/25/europe/ukraine-starlink-drones-russia-intl-cmd/index.html> accessed 1 November 2024.

of Starlink internet satellites with security features such as enhanced encryption.[13] In October 2024, it was announced that the United States had awarded SpaceX a $733.5 million contract to launch nine satellites into low-Earth orbit to enhance its military capabilities.[14]

Nevertheless, debate has remained strong about the future of outer space law in domestic legal systems, the potential for domestic courts to resolve disputes concerning outer space activity, and the questions of when and where the foundation of specialised judicial mechanisms may be preferable. However, there is also clearly a need for a new international legal framework that is not merely state-centric in scope but is broad enough to reflect modern-day technological endeavours. With predictions that space mining will commence as early as 2030, a legal framework is urgently needed to determine how resources extracted from celestial bodies can be used by both state actors and commercial entities in such a way that is not detrimental to the principle of equal access as enshrined in Article 1 of the Outer Space Treaty.[15] How do we ensure accountability for non-state actors who play a significant role in outer space use and exploration despite the parameters of the international legal framework being restricted to state actors? Scholars are increasingly concerned that without a clear basis to attribute liability to commercial entities and protect their investment in the development of space technology, the risk of political tensions and disputes is heightened.[16] Indeed, there is no international consensus on the right to extract and appropriate resources from celestial bodies. Could this present the risk of disputes leading to armed conflict?

Any negotiations for a new international treaty or convention to govern outer space activity will no doubt increase militarisation, especially in relation to dual-use technologies. While Article IV of the Outer Space Treaty does not permit 'objects carrying nuclear weapons or any kinds of weapons of mass destruction' in

---

13 Joey Roulette, 'SpaceX Curbed Ukraine's Use of Starlink Internet for Drones—Company President' *Reuters* (10 February 2023) <https://www.reuters.com/business/aerospace-defense/spacex-curbed-ukraines-use-starlink-internet-drones-company-president-2023-02-09/> accessed 1 November 2024; Joey Roulette and Marisa Taylor, 'Exclusive: Musk's SpaceX Is Building Spy Satellite Network for US Intelligence Agency, Sources Say' *Reuters* (17 March 2024) <https://www.reuters.com/technology/space/musks-spacex-is-building-spy-satellite-network-us-intelligence-agency-sources-2024-03-16/> accessed 1 November 2024.

14 Giulia Bernacchi, 'SpaceX to Launch Nine Satellites for US Military Under $733M Contract' *The Defense Post* (22 October 2024) <https://thedefensepost.com/2024/10/22/spacex-us-military-satellites/> accessed 1 November 2024.

15 Christian Davenport, 'This Company Intends to Be the First to Mine the Moon' *The Washington Post* (13 March 2024) <https://www.washingtonpost.com/technology/2024/03/13/moon-mining-plans-interlune/> accessed 1 November 2024.

16 Bartosz Ziemblicki and Yevgeniya Oralova, 'Private Entities in Outer Space Activities: Liability Regime Reconsidered' (2021) 56 Space Policy 101427; Elina Morozova and Alena Laurenava, 'International Liability for Commercial Space Activities and Related Issues of Debris' (2021) Oxford Research Encyclopedia of Planetary Science <https://oxfordre.com/planetaryscience/view/10.1093/acrefore/9780190647926.001.0001/acrefore-9780190647926-e-63> accessed 1 November 2024.

orbit, outer space is widely regarded as the final frontier for armed conflict.[17] In a major development, the United States has made its stance clear by establishing a new wing of its military, the United States Space Force.[18] While this development amplifies concerns about balancing security interests with transparency and peace, other nations are nevertheless considering the possibility of establishing military branches for space operations. With the emergence of commercial entities, the role of the state in outer space use and exploration is beginning to evolve from exploration to militarisation. The United States and Japan concurrently sought a UN Security Resolution calling upon member states to reaffirm their commitment to the Outer Space Treaty and not develop or use nuclear weapons in outer space.[19] In a meeting of the UN Security Council, the United States proclaimed, 'any placement of nuclear weapons into orbit around the Earth would be unprecedented, dangerous, and unacceptable.'[20] Some commentators believe that the United States statement was not non-specific, given reports that Russia has developed weapons with anti-satellite capabilities.[21] Even though Russia argues that the United States has already developed similar capabilities, its reply to the proposed resolution was not surprisingly labelled as propaganda. The Russian ambassador to the UN, Dmitry Polansky, expressed later in a press conference that the proposed resolution was 'yet another propaganda stunt by Washington' and 'divorced from reality.'[22] Essentially, the ambassador linked international opposition to Russia's invasion into Ukraine to negotiations on the regulation of weapons deployment in outer space.[23] While the militarisation of outer space brings with it many risks and concerns, it is difficult to comprehend how both the United States and NATO could appease what many view as ultimatums. Consequently, negotiations on nuclear proliferation in outer space will not be on the horizon any time soon. As explored by Tronchetti in this edited collection of essays, the dearth of restrictions on

17 Article IV of the Outer Space Treaty. See generally Cassandra Steer and Matthew Hersch (eds), *War in Peace in Outer Space* (OUP 2021).

18 Mike Wall, 'Trump Signs Directive to Create a Military Space Force' (*Space.com*, 21 February 2019) <https://www.space.com/president-trump-space-force-directive.html> accessed 1 November 2024.

19 United States Mission to the United Nations, 'Press Release: U.S. and Japan-Drafted UN Security Council Resolution on Preventing Nuclear Weapons in Space Receives More Than 60 Cosponsors' (24 April 2024) https://usun.usmission.gov/press-release-u-s-and-japan-drafted-un-security-council-resolution-on-preventing-nuclear-weapons-in-space-receives-more-than-60-cosponsors/ accessed 1 November 2024.

20 Edith Lederer, 'U.S. and Japan Seek UN Resolution Calling on All Nations to Ban Nuclear Weapons in Outer Space' (*Associated Press*, 28 September 2024) <https://apnews.com/article/un-nuclear-weapons-space-us-japan-russia-37daa4642da601e641500299061fd9d8> accessed 1 November 2024.

21 Jo Joyce, 'The Militarisation of Space: Navigating the Legal Void' (*Taylor Wessing*, 2 May 2024) <https://www.taylorwessing.com/en/interface/2024/the-space-race/the-militarisation-of-space-navigating-the-legal-void> accessed 1 November 2024.

22 The Guardian, 'U.S. and Japan Push for Ban on Nuclear Weapons in Space With UN Security Council Resolution' (19 March 2024) <https://www.theguardian.com/world/2024/mar/19/us-japan-nuclear-weapons-ban-space-un-war> accessed 1 November 2024.

23 Joyce (n 21).

weapons in outer space and the lack of a legal enforcement mechanism is likely to lead to further militarisation. Given the current political climate there is also potential that hostilities on Earth could escalate and impact the operations of commercial entities in outer space.

As we quickly advance into an era where the semi-permanent and even permanent residence of celestial bodies is becoming a rapid realisation, there is a clear need not only for international cooperation and diplomacy on outer space militarisation but also a legal enforcement mechanism to resolve disputes. While an independent court at the international level resolving disputes on outer space matters would be welcome if established, it is likely to have limited resources as we have seen with other international courts and tribunals, most notably the International Criminal Court and the International Tribunal on the Law of the Sea. If multiple situations and disputes are referred to the mechanism for adjudication, will there be a need to prioritise the resolution of some disputes over others in the interests of international peace and security, especially if resources are limited? Crucially, what factors could potentially be taken into consideration when measuring the success and efficiency of the mechanism? Clearly, sufficient links would be needed between key performance indicators and the mechanism's budget to make conclusions on its performance to assess efficiency and effectiveness. An evaluation of these indicators could be harnessed to improve the Court's performance by assisting with budget preparations, forecasting the timing of hearings, and ascertaining areas in need of improvement as well as determining the needs of the Court. In determining the effectiveness of the Court, its impact would also need to be measured such as its potential deterrent effect and outcomes for individuals and entities affected by breaches of outer space law. I would recommend that the proposed Court harness academics and civil society organisations to accomplish this goal since they already have existing partnerships with stakeholders such as commercial entities, regional and national space agencies, and international organisations.

3 Emerging Issues

(a) Sustainability and Outer Space

UN General Assembly Resolution 77/121, passed on 12 December 2022, considered it 'essential that Member Sates pay more attention to the problem of the gradually increasing probability of collisions of space objects, especially those with nuclear power sources' and called for 'the development of improved technology for the monitoring of space debris and for the compilation and dissemination of data on space debris.'[24] However, this request lacks quantifiable details and creates a legal vacuum where no party (state, international organisation, or commercial entity) assumes responsibility for fostering sustainability in their outer

24 UN General Assembly Resolution 77/121 (12 December 2022).

space operations. To overcome this challenge, we note that leadership through international cooperation and diplomacy is crucial as well as a resilient regulatory approach in individual member states to encourage all parties involved in the space sector, especially private commercial entities, to comply. Unfortunately, some states have merely announced seed funding for feasibility studies on outer space sustainability, and thus, more coherent efforts are imperative to streamline regulation. Despite robust and accelerated growth in the space sector, clarity on non-state actors' obligations to conduct their space business responsibly and sustainably has been severely lacking at the state level. Several states note sustainability as a core value in their national space strategies and policies, but most do not define the concept or include a description of specific approaches or initiatives to nurture it. As the sector grows amid ambiguity caused by climate change, the Ukraine-Russo War, and expeditious scientific and technological developments, guidelines on the relationship between state and non-state actors are pivotal. Likewise, clarity is needed on who precisely is responsible for striking a balance between regulation and the environmental and social impacts of outer space activities. Approaching sustainability in this way could address concerns in a more balanced way, instead of the profit-led approach that views sustainable development as a mere afterthought.

(b) The Second Term of Donald Trump as the United States President

In the aftermath of Donald Trump's election for a second term as United States president, it remains to be seen how his administration will approach outer space use and exploration. With his decision to appoint Elon Musk, CEO of SpaceX, to lead the newly created Department of Government Efficiency, a different approach is perhaps on the horizon for industrial and human spaceflight.[25] Aside from the increased commercialisation of NASA's operations which was initiated during the Obama Administration, the foundation of the US Space Force in 2018 was 'mostly bureaucratic and organisational' and did not significantly change the space capabilities of the United States.[26] With the announcement that Vice President J.D. Vance will chair the National Space Council, it remains to be seen whether it will become a casualty of Elon Musk's aim to 'dismantle government bureaucracy' and 'slash regulations.'[27] As Bleddyn Bowen and P.J. Blunt posit, '[i]f the council becomes purely industry driven and shaped by personal rule, it could destroy a balance struck during the first Trump administration between enhancing U.S.

25 Aleks Phillips, 'Why Is Elon Musk Becoming Donald Trump's Efficiency Tsar?' *BBC News* (14 November 2024) <https://www.bbc.com/news/articles/cpqd4vw0ejeo> accessed 14 November 2024.

26 Bleddyn Bowen and P.J. Blount, 'Donald Trump's Approach to U.S. Space Policy Could Throw Up Some Surprises, Especially With Elon Musk on Board' *The Conversation* (14 November 2024) <https://theconversation.com/donald-trumps-approach-to-us-space-policy-could-throw-up-some-surprises-especially-with-elon-musk-on-board-243435> accessed 14 November 2024.

27 Bowen and Blount (n 26).

Space industry and performing a collaborative leader within the international community.'[28] Thus, there is potential that Donald Trump's second term in office could herald a reduction in red tape for the commercial space sector. Concerns have also emerged about the implications of his second term for international relations. In 2022, outgoing Vice President Kamala Harris declared a U.S. ban on destructive direct-ascent anti-satellite missile testing and called 'on other nations to make similar commitments and to work together in establishing this as a norm, making the case that such efforts benefit all nations.'[29] Apart from Russia and China, several states have agreed to the ban, and it is has also spurred on dialogue at the UN General Assembly and the Open-Ended Working Group on Reducing Space Threats Through Norms, Rules and Principles of Responsible Behaviours. If Trump backtracks on the ban, several experts are concerned not only about peace and security in outer space but also the momentum that has been fostered at the UN over the last few years.

(c) Artificial Intelligence

Despite the enormous potential of artificial intelligence (AI), there are considerable gaps in the regulatory frameworks. While the AI Act (Regulation (EU) 23024/1689) adopted by the European Union is widely regarded as a comprehensive framework, it does not address the regulation of AI in outer space. Major spacefaring nations such as the United States, Russia, and China have also not yet adopted laws regulating the use of this technology in outer space. With the space industry expected to grow exponentially over the next 30 years, the lack of regulation leads to considerable ambiguity. While the data extracted from AI has the potential to revolutionise the maintenance of satellite constellations and offer greater energy efficiency, it is unclear where responsibility should lie for damage caused by AI. Article VI of the Outer Space Treaty provides that states must 'bear international responsibility for national activities in outer space, including the Moon and other celestial bodies.'[30] Consequently, state parties to the Treaty are directly responsible for the activities of commercial entities and individuals conducting space operations from their territory and an inquiry into attribution of the action is not warranted.[31] In view of the predicted use of AI in space applications, future lines of research inquiry need to consider whether the state where the software was developed can be held liable under Article VI of the Outer Space Treaty in the event of a malfunction.

28 Bowen and Blount (n 26).

29 The White House, 'Fact Sheet: Vice President Harris Advances National Security Norms in Space' (*Briefing Room*, 18 April 2022) <https://www.whitehouse.gov/briefing-room/statements-releases/2022/04/18/fact-sheet-vice-president-harris-advances-national-security-norms-in-space/> accessed 1 November 2024.

30 Article VI of the Outer Space Treaty.

31 Ram Jakhu and Steven Freeland, *The Relationship Between the Outer Space Treaty and Customary International Law* (International Astronautical Federation 2016) <https://iafastro.directory/iac/archive/browse/IAC-16/E7/2/32294/> accessed 1 November 2024.

4 Concluding Thoughts

This review of emerging issues and current events does not provide a clear vision for the future of outer space use and exploration, but perhaps it does enable us to consider the concept of 'future' in relation to outer space law. Questions about how space corporations are regulated and the relationship between space corporations and states and how this should be measured respond to the concerns raised by Melissa de Zwart, Jennifer Brobst, and Danny Johannsen. These dilemmas are embedded in the 'viscousness' of the Outer Space Treaty and the reports and guidelines of UNCOPUOS as well as debates about the nature and purpose of outer space use and exploration. Bearing in mind emerging debates about how to institutionalise outer space law, P.J. Blount has critiqued the instillation of 'narratives' into discussion of outer space norm development—in relation to established and emerging modes of outer space use and exploration. Concerns about possible violence in outer space perhaps stem from the colonial histories of the major spacefaring nations, and outer space law has also not really contemplated a model of justice for compliance failures. Past efforts to resolve this dilemma have been further hampered by current intersecting political, technological, and environmental tensions. Fabio Tronchetti's exploration of the right to self-defence in the context of outer space highlights how the potential for violence continues to persist in the shifting context of outer space, where friction between peace, justice, and technological development continue to emerge but have yet to be solved. Amidst all this tension and complexity, the contributors to this collection have sought to address persistent outer space law problems—linking together both past and recent events to hypothesise on the future direction of outer space governance. However, these proposals are likely to be challenged by their 'viscousness' to old international law institutions and practices.

In any event, as science and technology develop, Matthew Stubbs, Lachlan Blake, and Danny Johansen drew inspiration from current international laws to present new ideas for extraterrestrial exploration. Meanwhile, William P. Schonberg and Anna Marie Brennan argued that the continuing and even growing complexity of the space debris dilemma necessitates a new framework of liability. That said, outer space law continues to struggle to respond to tensions involving compliance and enforcement and, in particular, technological development and environmental change. The contributors to this volume have showcased the importance of decisive engagement and recognised the possibility of future change in the outer space law realm, including reversion. Further, ascertaining resulting challenges and solutions, including legal enforcement and human rights protection, to address the future of outer space may present additional complications. Nevertheless, an analytical examination of the possible future of outer space law continues to be a crucial endeavour.

Bibliography

Fikri Haikal Akbar, 'Competition Among Spacefaring States in the Exploration of "Terra Nulius" in Outer Space: A Neorealist Approach' (2023) 21(2–3) Astropolitics 206.

Giulia Bernacchi, 'SpaceX to Launch Nine Satellites for US Military Under $733M Contract' *The Defense Post* (22 October 2024) <https://thedefensepost.com/2024/10/22/spacex-us-military-satellites/> accessed 1 November 2024.

Bleddyn Bowen and P.J. Blount, 'Donald Trump's Approach to U.S. Space Policy Could Throw Up Some Surprises, Especially With Elon Musk on Board' *The Conversation* (14 November 2024) <https://theconversation.com/donald-trumps-approach-to-us-space-policy-could-throw-up-some-surprises-especially-with-elon-musk-on-board-243435> accessed 14 November 2024.

Christian Davenport, 'This Company Intends to Be the First to Mine the Moon' *The Washington Post* (13 March 2024) <https://www.washingtonpost.com/technology/2024/03/13/moon-mining-plans-interlune/> accessed 1 November 2024.

Melissa de Zwart, Stacey Henderson and Michelle Neumann, 'Space Resource Activities and the Evolution of International Space Law' (2023) 211 Acta Astronautica 155–62.

Ram Jakhu and Steven Freeland, *The Relationship Between the Outer Space Treaty and Customary International Law* (International Astronautical Federation 2016) <https://iafastro.directory/iac/archive/browse/IAC-16/E7/2/32294/> accessed 1 November 2024.

Jo Joyce, 'The Militarisation of Space: Navigating the Legal Void' (*Taylor Wessing*, 2 May 2024) <https://www.taylorwessing.com/en/interface/2024/the-space-race/the-militarisation-of-space-navigating-the-legal-void> accessed 1 November 2024.

Edith Lederer, 'U.S. and Japan Seek UN Resolution Calling on All Nations to Ban Nuclear Weapons in Outer Space' (*Associated Press*, 28 September 2024) <https://apnews.com/article/un-nuclear-weapons-space-us-japan-russia-37daa4642da601e641500299061fd9d8> accessed 1 November 2024.

Elina Morozova and Alena Laurenava, 'International Liability for Commercial Space Activities and Related Issues of Debris' (2021) Oxford Research Encyclopedia of Planetary Science <https://oxfordre.com/planetaryscience/view/10.1093/acrefore/9780190647926.001.0001/acrefore-9780190647926-e-63> accessed 1 November 2024.

Aleks Phillips, 'Why Is Elon Musk Becoming Donald Trump's Efficiency Tsar?' *BBC News* (14 November 2024) <https://www.bbc.com/news/articles/cpqd4vw0ejeo> accessed 14 November 2024.

Tereza Pultarova, 'SpaceX Starlink Satellites Had to Make 25,000 Collision-Avoidance Maneuvers in Just 6 Months—And It Will Only Get Worse' (*Space.com*, 7 July 2023) <https://www.space.com/starlink-satellite-conjunction-increase-threatens-space-sustainability> accessed 1 November 2024.

Tereza Pultarova and Elizabeth Howell, 'Starlink Satellites: Facts, Tracking and Impact on Astronomy' (*Space.com*, 28 September 2024) <https://www.space.com/spacex-starlink-satellites.html> accessed 1 November 2024.

Joey Roulette, 'SpaceX Curbed Ukraine's Use of Starlink Internet for Drones—Company President' *Reuters* (10 February 2023) <https://www.reuters.com/business/aerospace-defense/spacex-curbed-ukraines-use-starlink-internet-drones-company-president-2023-02-09/> accessed 1 November 2024.

Joey Roulette and Marisa Taylor, 'Exclusive: Musk's SpaceX is Building Spy Satellite Network for US Intelligence Agency, Sources Say' *Reuters* (17 March 2024) <https://www.reuters.com/technology/space/musks-spacex-is-building-spy-satellite-network-us-intelligence-agency-sources-2024-03-16/> accessed 1 November 2024.

Kai-Uwe Schrogl, Christina Giannopapa and Ntorina Antoni, 'Introduction: A Research Agenda for Space Policy in the 2020s' in Kai-Uwe Schrogl, Christina Giannopapa and Ntorina Antoni (eds), *A Research Agenda for Space Policy* (Edward Elgar Publishing 2021) xxxiv.

Most Sharmin, 'China's Increasing Space Power and India-China Orbital Competitions: Implications in the Indo-Pacific With a Focus on South Asia' (2023) Journal of Indo-Pacific Affairs 53.

Cassandra Steer and Matthew Hersch (eds), *War in Peace in Outer Space* (OUP 2021).

Dimitrios Stroikos, 'Still Lost in Space? Understanding China and India's Anti-Satellite Tests Through an Eclectic Approach' (2023) 21(2–3) Astropolitics 179–205.

Kurt Taylor, 'Fictions of the Final Frontier: Why the United States SPACE Act of 2015 Is Illegal' (2019) 33(4) Emory International Law Review 653.

The Guardian, 'U.S. and Japan Push for Ban on Nuclear Weapons in Space With UN Security Council Resolution' (19 March 2024) <https://www.theguardian.com/world/2024/mar/19/us-japan-nuclear-weapons-ban-space-un-war> accessed 1 November 2024.

The White House, 'Fact Sheet: Vice President Harris Advances National Security Norms in Space' *Briefing Room* (18 April 2022) <https://www.whitehouse.gov/briefing-room/statements-releases/2022/04/18/fact-sheet-vice-president-harris-advances-national-security-norms-in-space/> accessed 1 November 2024.

UN General Assembly Resolution 77/121 (12 December 2022).

United States Mission to the United Nations, 'Press Release: U.S. and Japan-Drafted UN Security Council Resolution on Preventing Nuclear Weapons in Space Receives More Than 60 Cosponsors' (24 April 2024) <https://usun.usmission.gov/press-release-u-s-and-japan-drafted-un-security-council-resolution-on-preventing-nuclear-weapons-in-space-receives-more-than-60-cosponsors/> accessed 1 November 2024.

Matjaz Vidmar and Saskia Vermeylen, 'Utopia(s), Outer Space Law and Ecology' (2022) 41(1) EASST Review <https://easst.net/easst-review/411/utopias-outer-space-law-and-ecology/> accessed 1 November 2024.

Mike Wall, 'Trump Signs Directive to Create a Military Space Force' (*Space.com*, 21 February 2019) <https://www.space.com/president-trump-space-force-directive.html> accessed 1 November 2024.

Nicky Paton Walsh and others, 'Ukraine Relies on Starlink for its Drone War: Russia Appears to be Bypassing Sanctions to Use the Devices Too' *CNN* (26 March 2024) <https://edition.cnn.com/2024/03/25/europe/ukraine-starlink-drones-russia-intl-cmd/index.html> accessed 1 November 2024.

Bartosz Ziemblicki and Yevgeniya Oralova, 'Private Entities in Outer Space Activities: Liability Regime Reconsidered' (2021) 56 Space Policy 101427.

Index

FSC
www.fsc.org
MIX
Papier | Fördert
gute Waldnutzung
FSC® C083411

Kolibri 360 GmbH
Ferdinand-Jühlke-Straße 7
99095 Erfurt, Deutschland
produktsicherheit@kolibri360.de